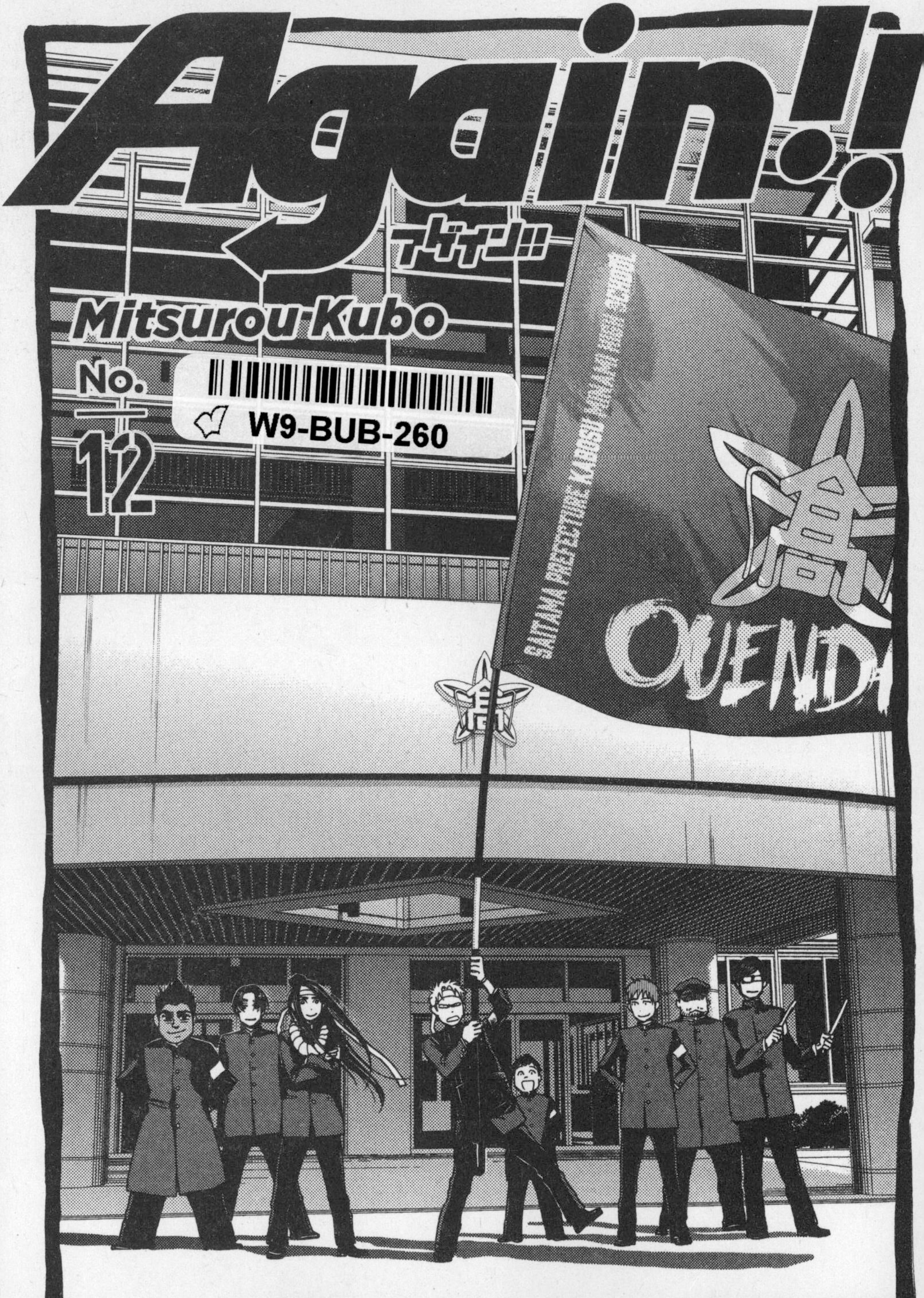
Again!!
アゲイン!!
Mitsurou Kubo
No. 12
SAITAMA PREFECTURE KABUSU MINAMI HIGH SCHOOL
OUENDA

contents

125. ON YOUR MARK

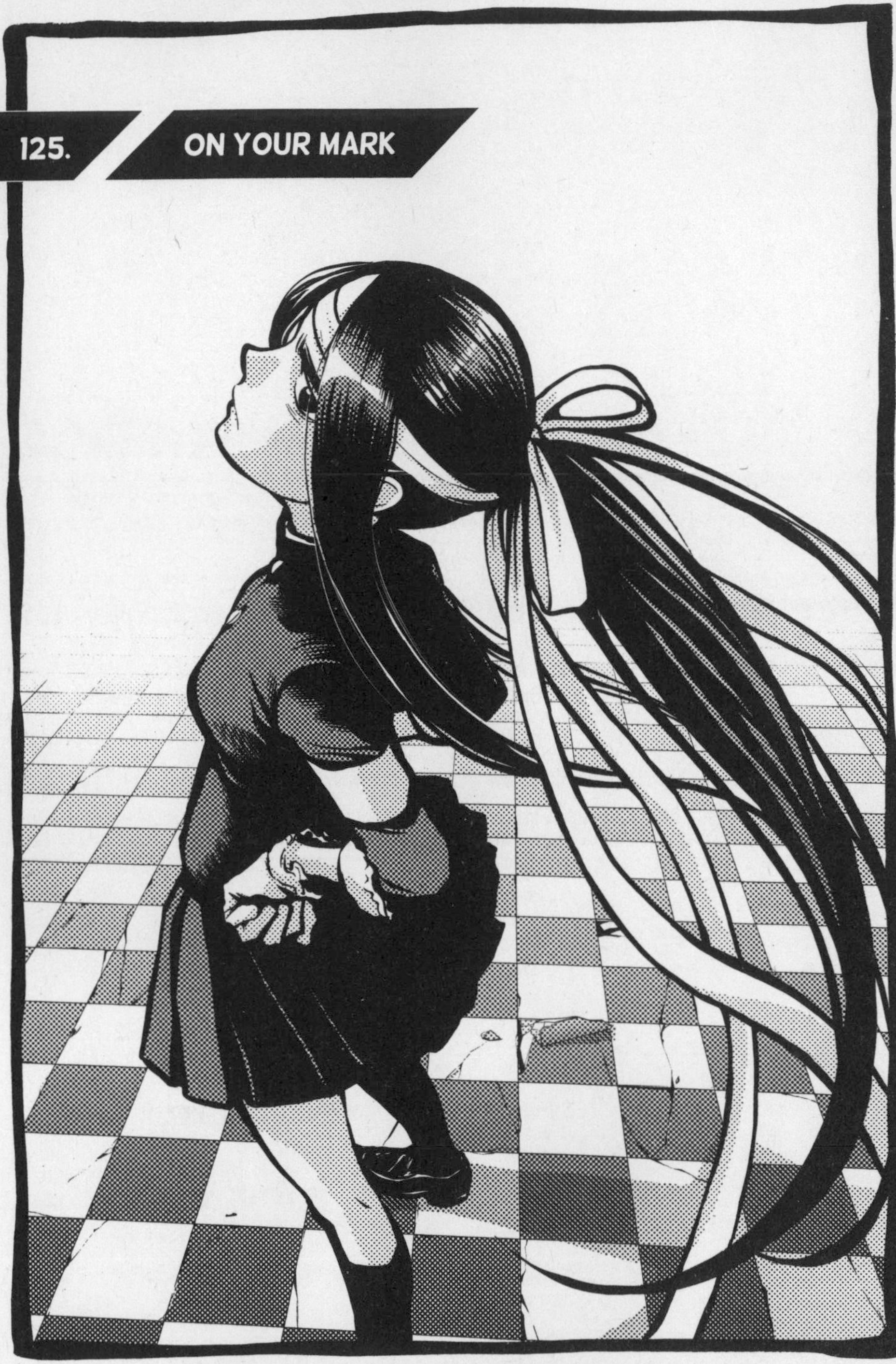

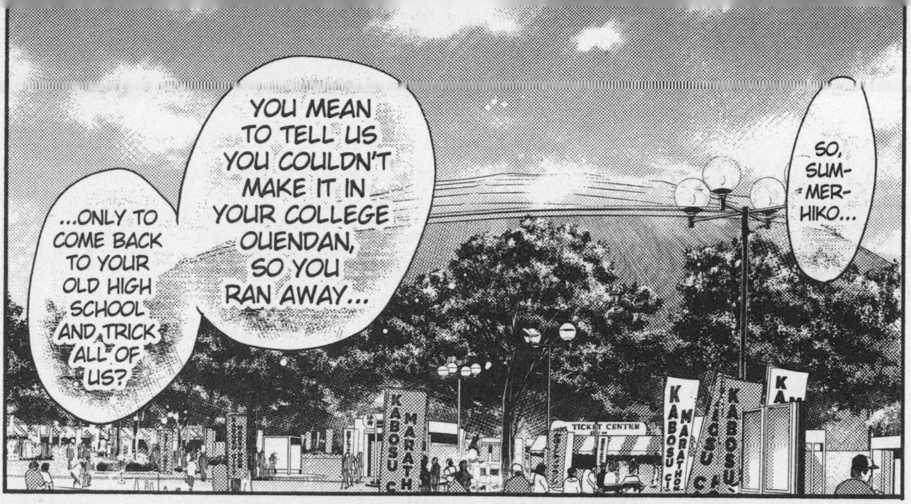
SO, SUMMER-HIKO...
YOU MEAN TO TELL US YOU COULDN'T MAKE IT IN YOUR COLLEGE OUENDAN, SO YOU RAN AWAY...
...ONLY TO COME BACK TO YOUR OLD HIGH SCHOOL AND TRICK ALL OF US?
TICKET CENTER

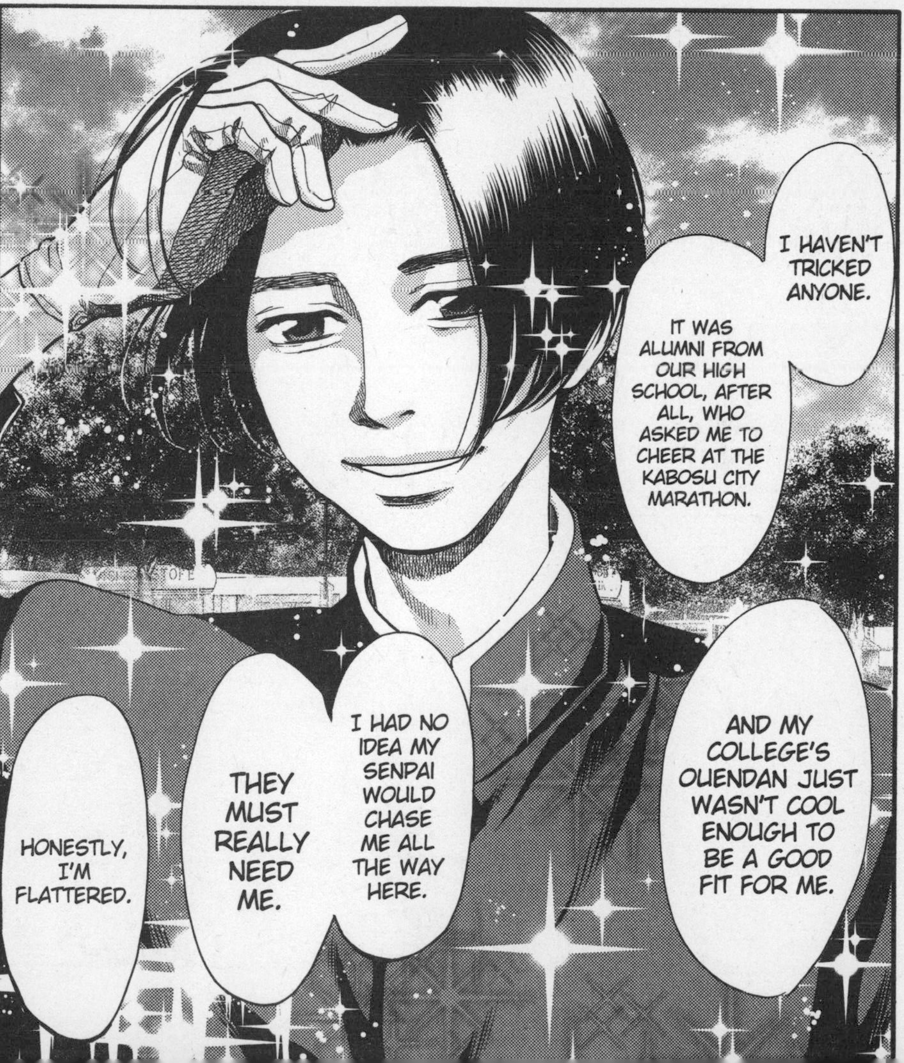
I HAVEN'T TRICKED ANYONE.
IT WAS ALUMNI FROM OUR HIGH SCHOOL, AFTER ALL, WHO ASKED ME TO CHEER AT THE KABOSU CITY MARATHON.
AND MY COLLEGE'S OUENDAN JUST WASN'T COOL ENOUGH TO BE A GOOD FIT FOR ME.
I HAD NO IDEA MY SENPAI WOULD CHASE ME ALL THE WAY HERE.
THEY MUST REALLY NEED ME.
HONESTLY, I'M FLATTERED.

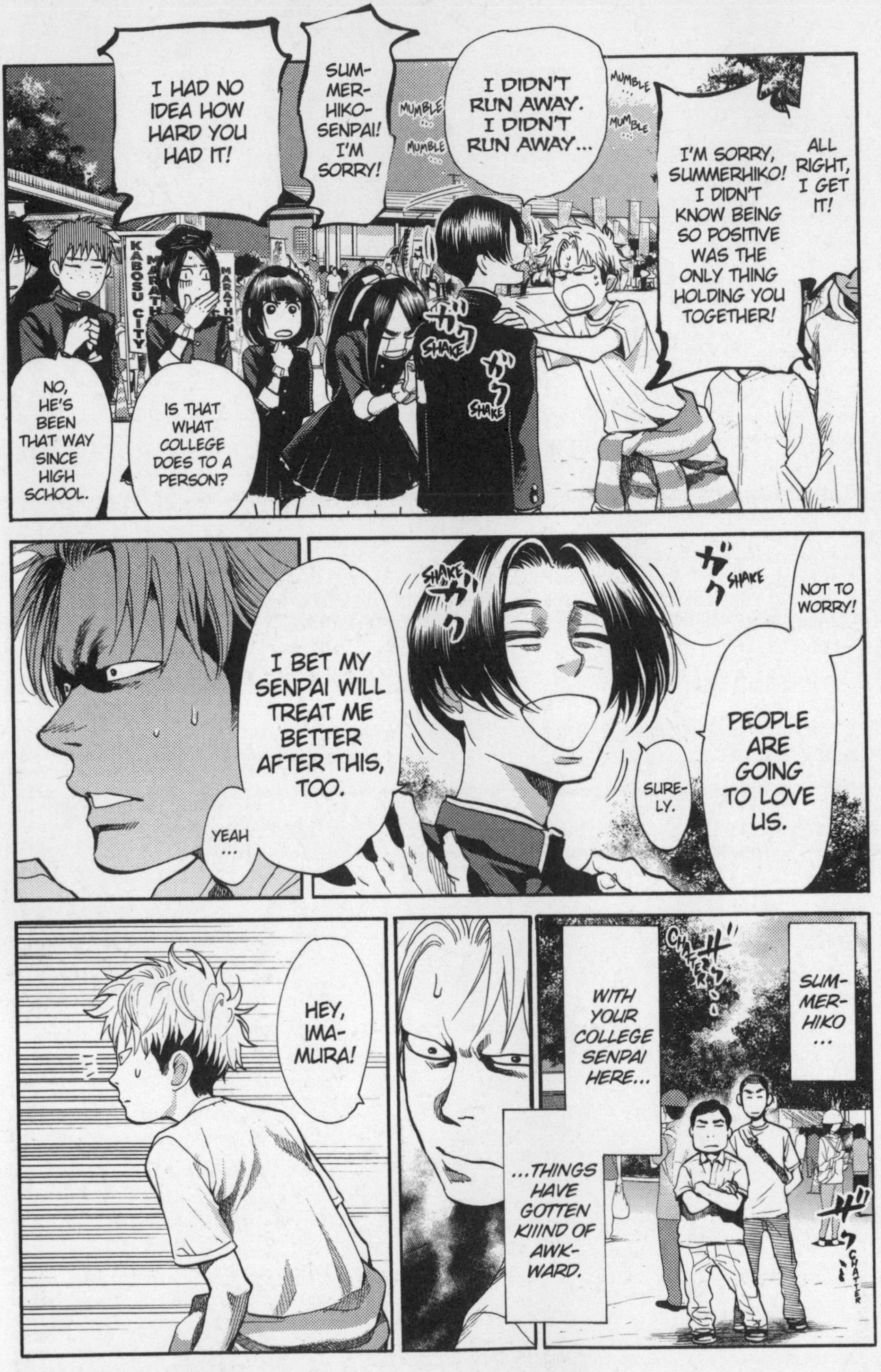
ALL RIGHT, I GET IT!
I'M SORRY, SUMMERHIKO! I DIDN'T KNOW BEING SO POSITIVE WAS THE ONLY THING HOLDING YOU TOGETHER!
MUMBLE... MUMBLE...
I DIDN'T RUN AWAY. I DIDN'T RUN AWAY...
MUMBLE... MUMBLE...
SUMMERHIKO-SENPAI! I'M SORRY!
I HAD NO IDEA HOW HARD YOU HAD IT!
SHAKE SHAKE
KABOSU CITY MARATHON
IS THAT WHAT COLLEGE DOES TO A PERSON?
NO, HE'S BEEN THAT WAY SINCE HIGH SCHOOL.
SHAKE
NOT TO WORRY!
PEOPLE ARE GOING TO LOVE US.
SURELY.
SHAKE
I BET MY SENPAI WILL TREAT ME BETTER AFTER THIS, TOO.
YEAH...
SUMMERHIKO...
CHATTER
CHATTER
WITH YOUR COLLEGE SENPAI HERE...
...THINGS HAVE GOTTEN KIIIND OF AWKWARD.
HEY, IMAMURA!

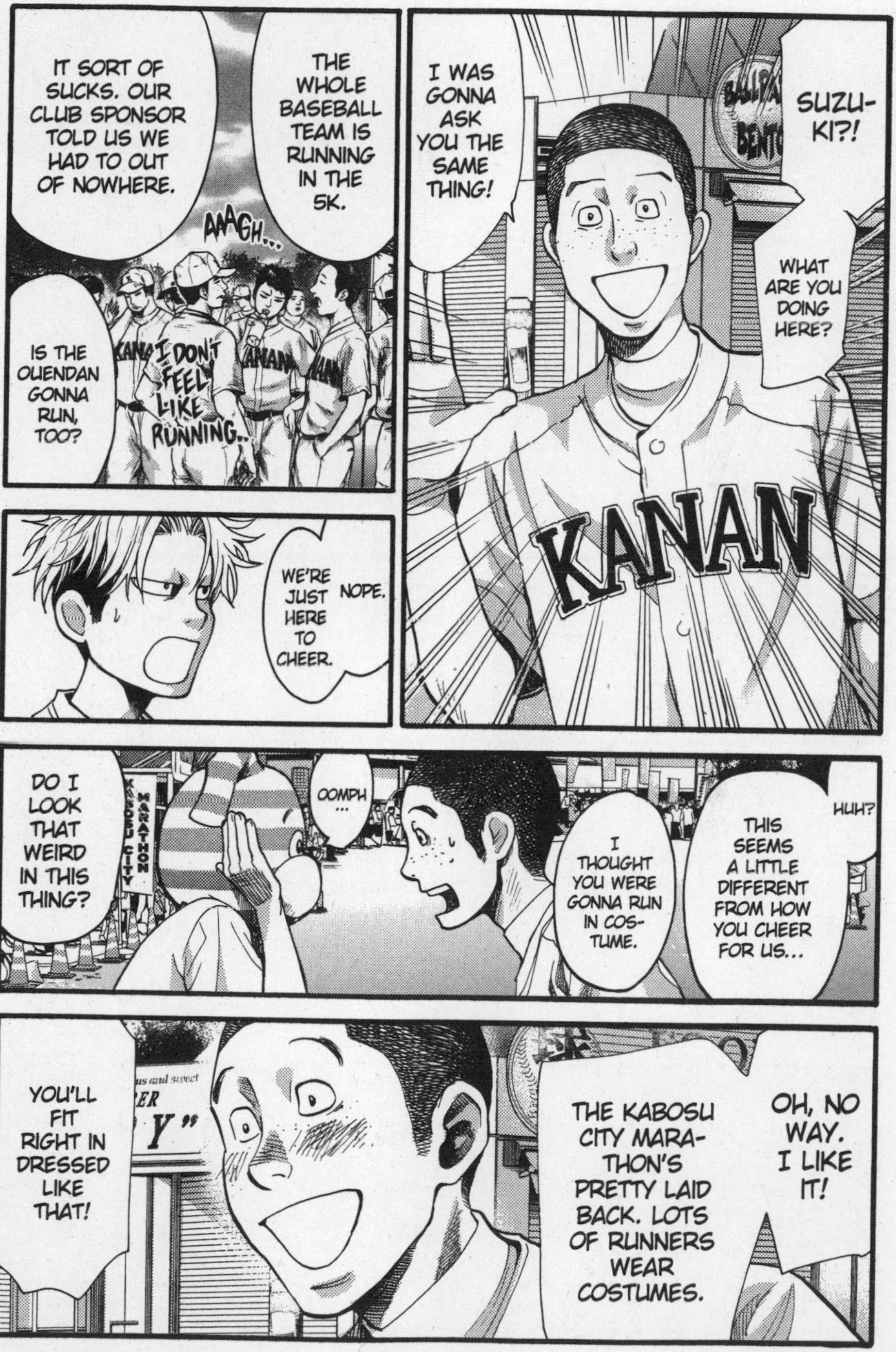
SUZU-KI?!
WHAT ARE YOU DOING HERE?
I WAS GONNA ASK YOU THE SAME THING!
THE WHOLE BASEBALL TEAM IS RUNNING IN THE 5K.
IT SORT OF SUCKS. OUR CLUB SPONSOR TOLD US WE HAD TO OUT OF NOWHERE.
AAAGH...
KANAN
I DON'T FEEL LIKE RUNNING...
IS THE OUENDAN GONNA RUN, TOO?
NOPE.
WE'RE JUST HERE TO CHEER.
KANAN
HUH?
THIS SEEMS A LITTLE DIFFERENT FROM HOW YOU CHEER FOR US...
I THOUGHT YOU WERE GONNA RUN IN COS-TUME.
OOMPH...
KABOSU CITY MARATHON
DO I LOOK THAT WEIRD IN THIS THING?
OH, NO WAY. I LIKE IT!
THE KABOSU CITY MARA-THON'S PRETTY LAID BACK. LOTS OF RUNNERS WEAR COSTUMES.
YOU'LL FIT RIGHT IN DRESSED LIKE THAT!

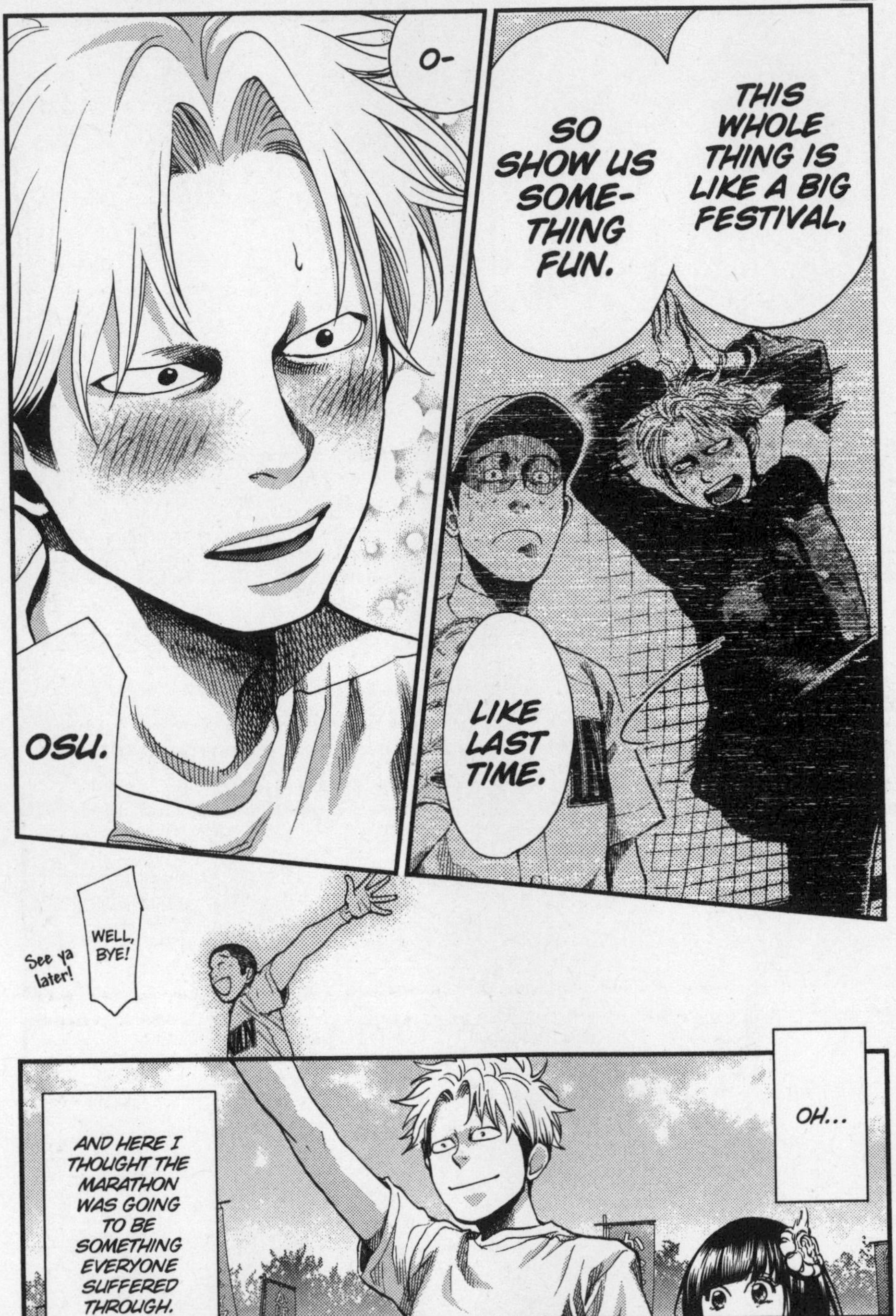

THIS WHOLE THING IS LIKE A BIG FESTIVAL,
SO SHOW US SOMETHING FUN.
LIKE LAST TIME.
O-
OSU.
WELL, BYE!
See ya later!
OH...
AND HERE I THOUGHT THE MARATHON WAS GOING TO BE SOMETHING EVERYONE SUFFERED THROUGH.

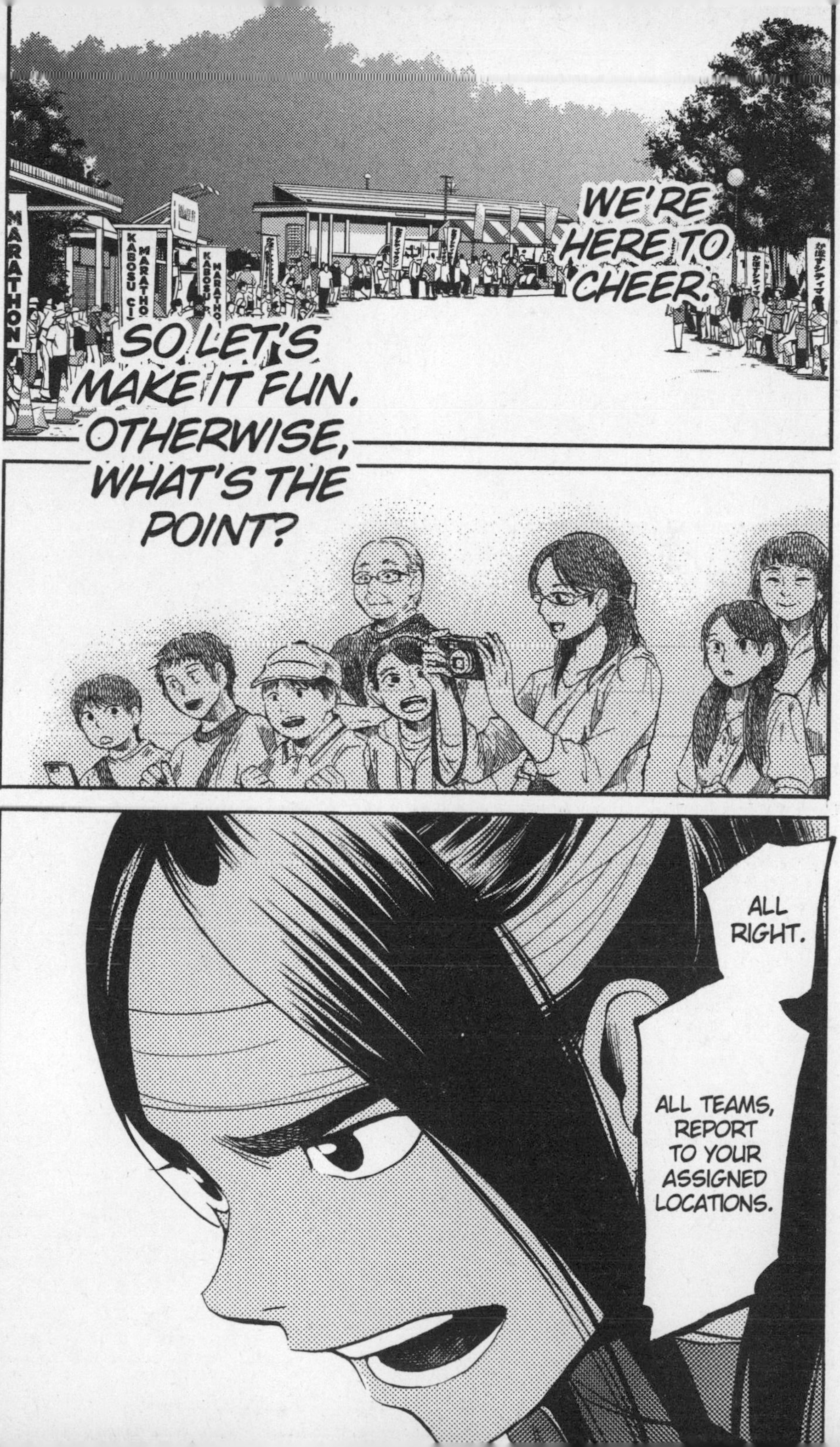
MARATHON
WE'RE HERE TO CHEER.
SO LET'S MAKE IT FUN. OTHERWISE, WHAT'S THE POINT?
ALL RIGHT.
ALL TEAMS, REPORT TO YOUR ASSIGNED LOCATIONS.

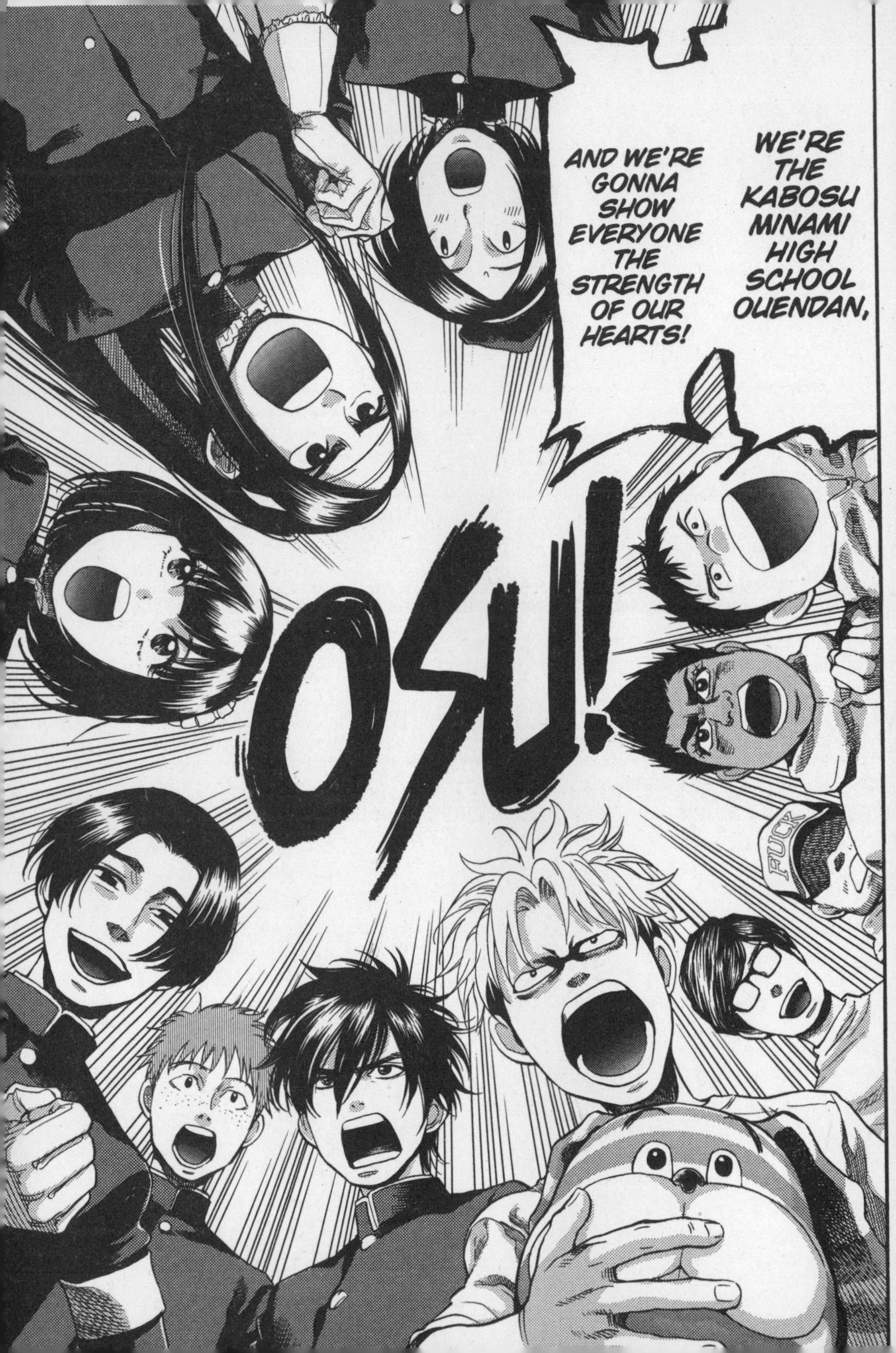
WE'RE THE KABOSU MINAMI HIGH SCHOOL OUENDAN,
AND WE'RE GONNA SHOW EVERYONE THE STRENGTH OF OUR HEARTS!
OSU!
FUCK

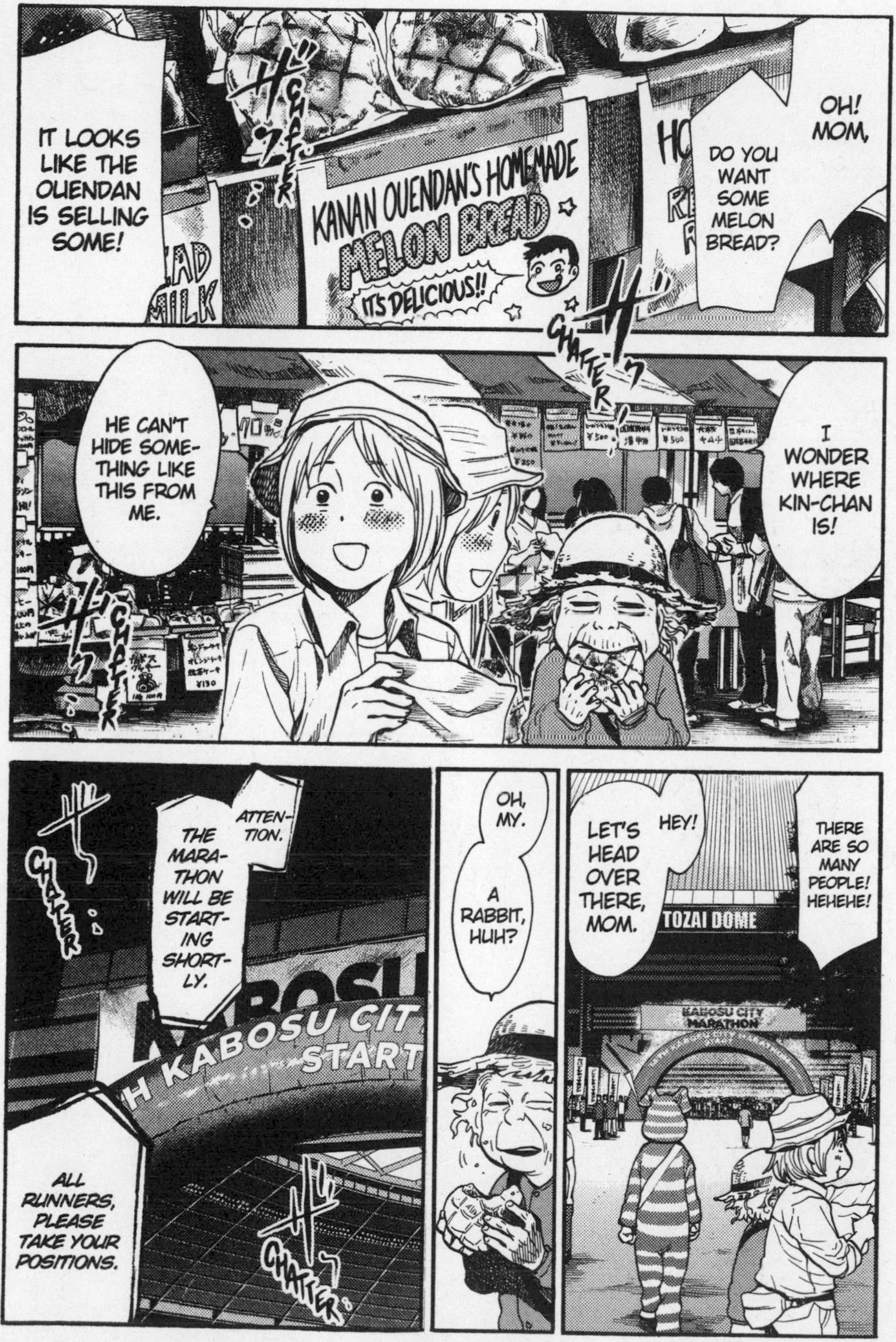
OH! MOM,
DO YOU WANT SOME MELON BREAD?
KANAN OUENDAN'S HOMEMADE MELON BREAD
IT'S DELICIOUS!!
CHATTER
IT LOOKS LIKE THE OUENDAN IS SELLING SOME!
CHATTER
I WONDER WHERE KIN-CHAN IS!
HE CAN'T HIDE SOMETHING LIKE THIS FROM ME.
CHATTER
THERE ARE SO MANY PEOPLE! HEHEHE!
HEY!
LET'S HEAD OVER THERE, MOM.
TOZAI DOME
KABOSU CITY MARATHON
OH, MY.
A RABBIT, HUH?
ATTENTION.
THE MARATHON WILL BE STARTING SHORTLY.
START
CHATTER
ALL RUNNERS, PLEASE TAKE YOUR POSITIONS.
CHATTER

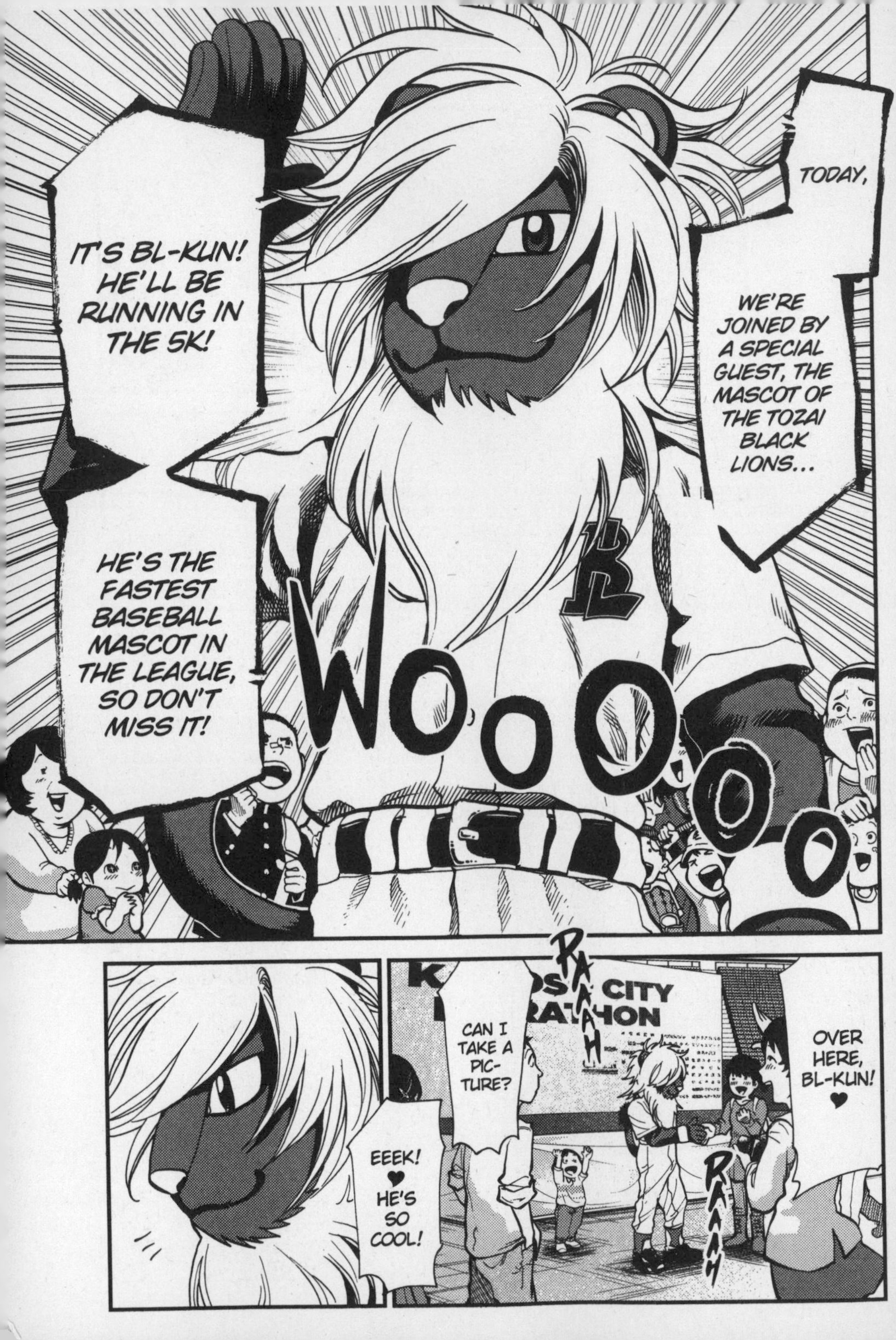
TODAY,
WE'RE JOINED BY A SPECIAL GUEST, THE MASCOT OF THE TOZAI BLACK LIONS...
IT'S BL-KUN! HE'LL BE RUNNING IN THE 5K!
HE'S THE FASTEST BASEBALL MASCOT IN THE LEAGUE, SO DON'T MISS IT!
WOOOOOOO
RAAAAH
OVER HERE, BL-KUN! ♥
CAN I TAKE A PIC-TURE?
RAAAH
EEEK! ♥ HE'S SO COOL!

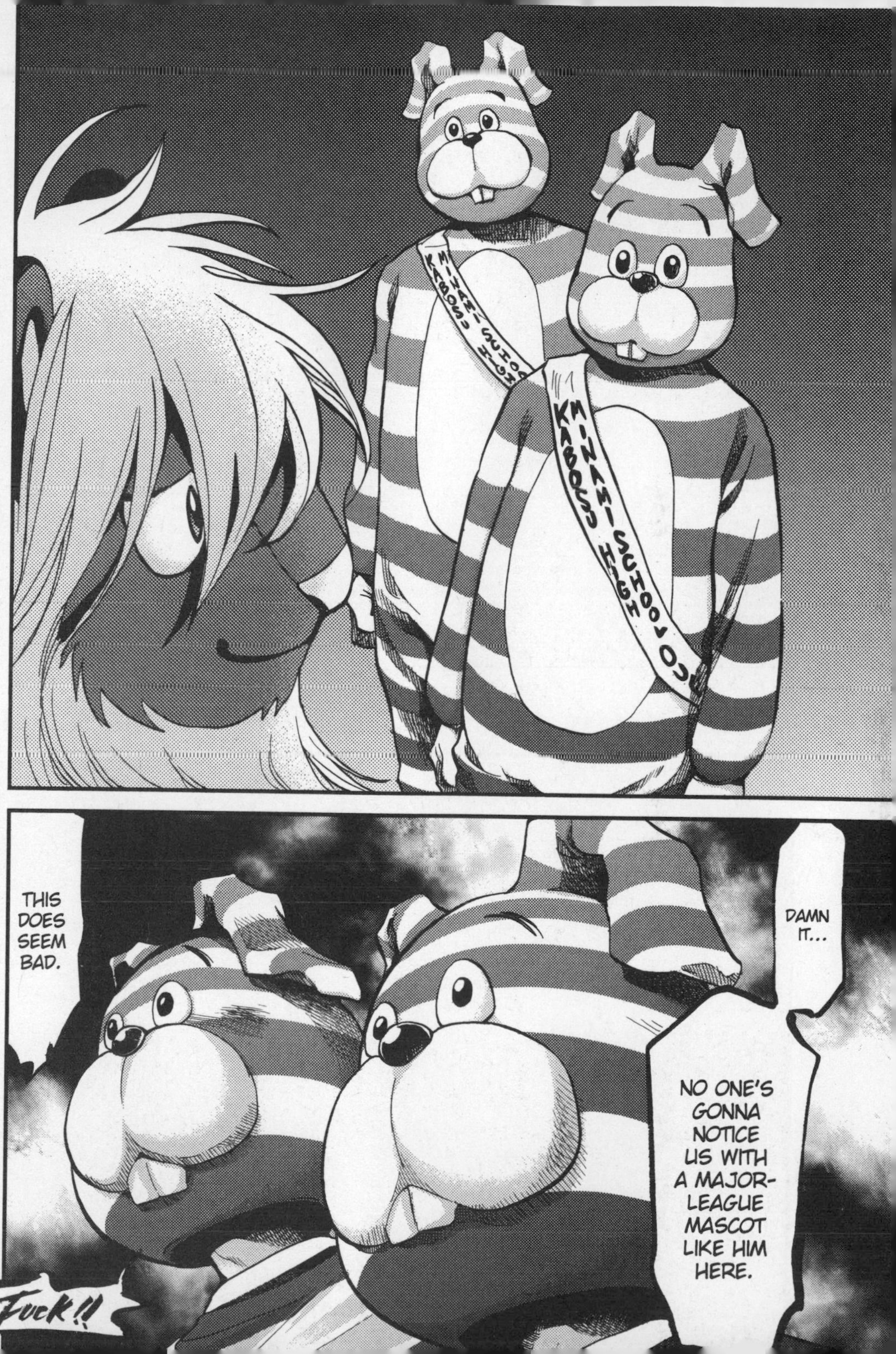
MINAMI SCHOOL
KABOSU HIGH
DAMN IT...
NO ONE'S GONNA NOTICE US WITH A MAJOR-LEAGUE MASCOT LIKE HIM HERE.
THIS DOES SEEM BAD.
FUCK!!

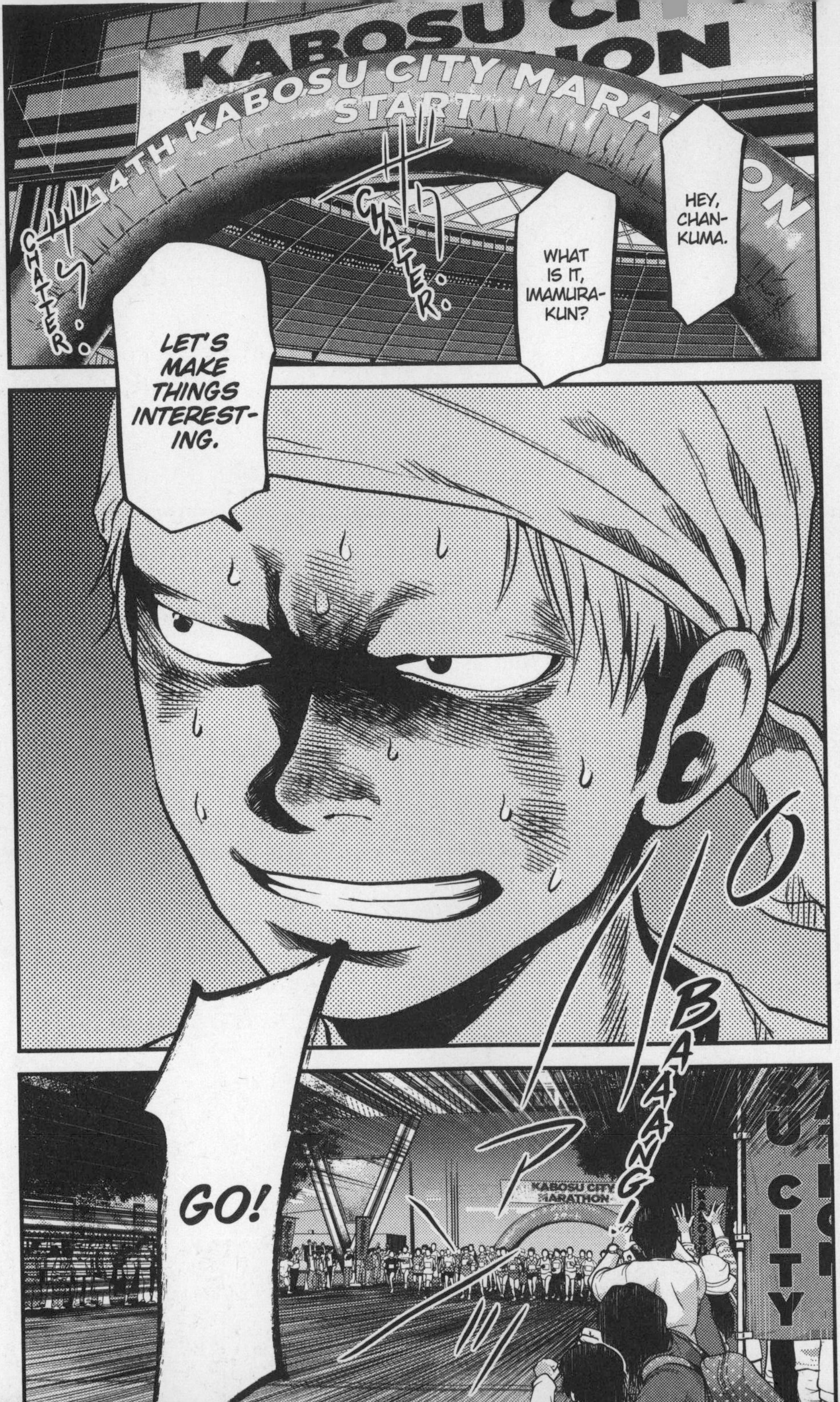
START
HEY, CHAN-KUMA.
WHAT IS IT, IMAMURA-KUN?
CHATTER...
CHATTER...
LET'S MAKE THINGS INTERESTING.
BAAANG!!
GO!
KABOSU CITY MARATHON
CITY

Again!!
アゲイン!!

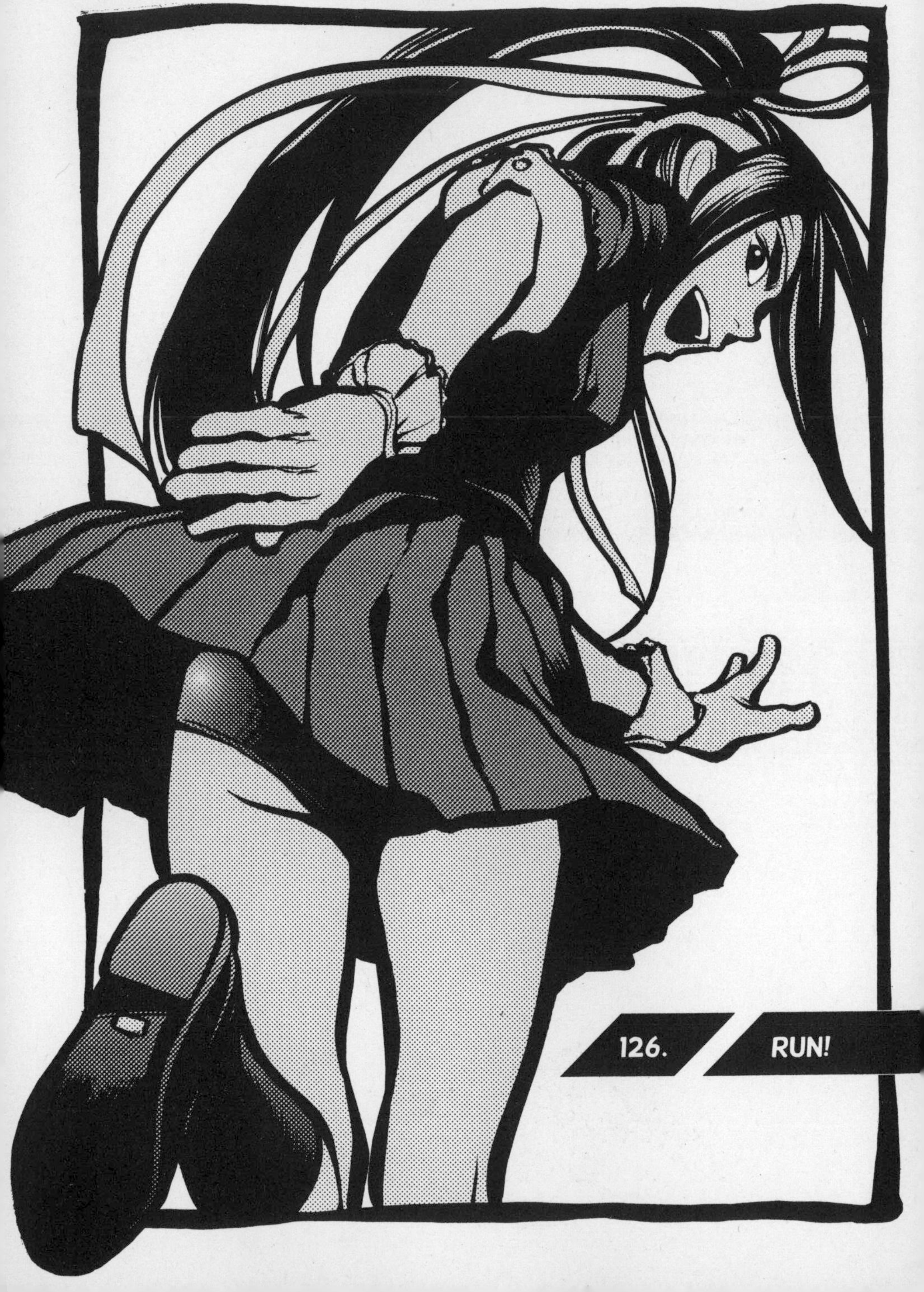
126.
RUN!

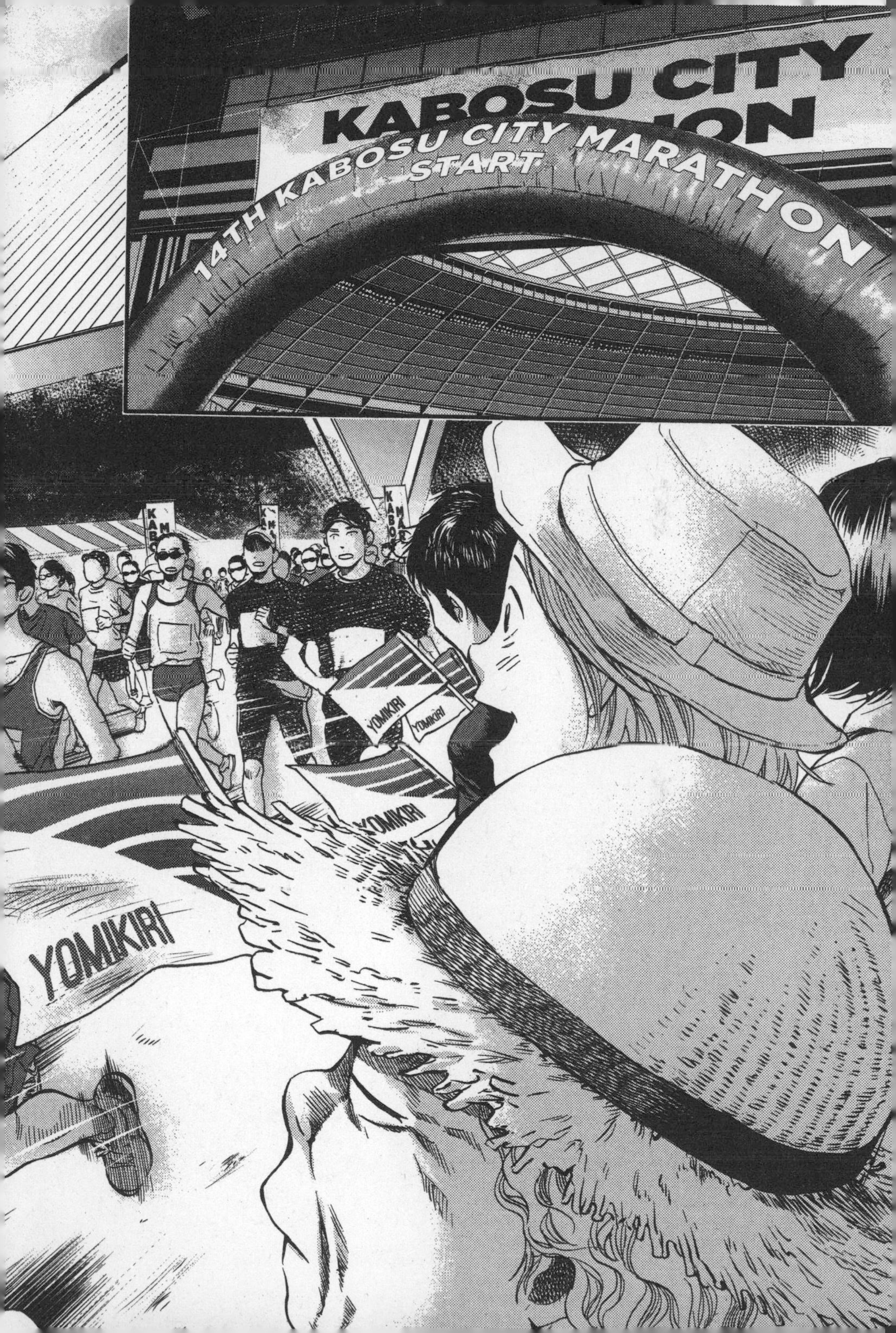
KABOSU CITY
14TH KABOSU CITY MARATHON
START
YOMIKIRI
YOMIKIRI
YOMIKIRI
YOMIKIRI

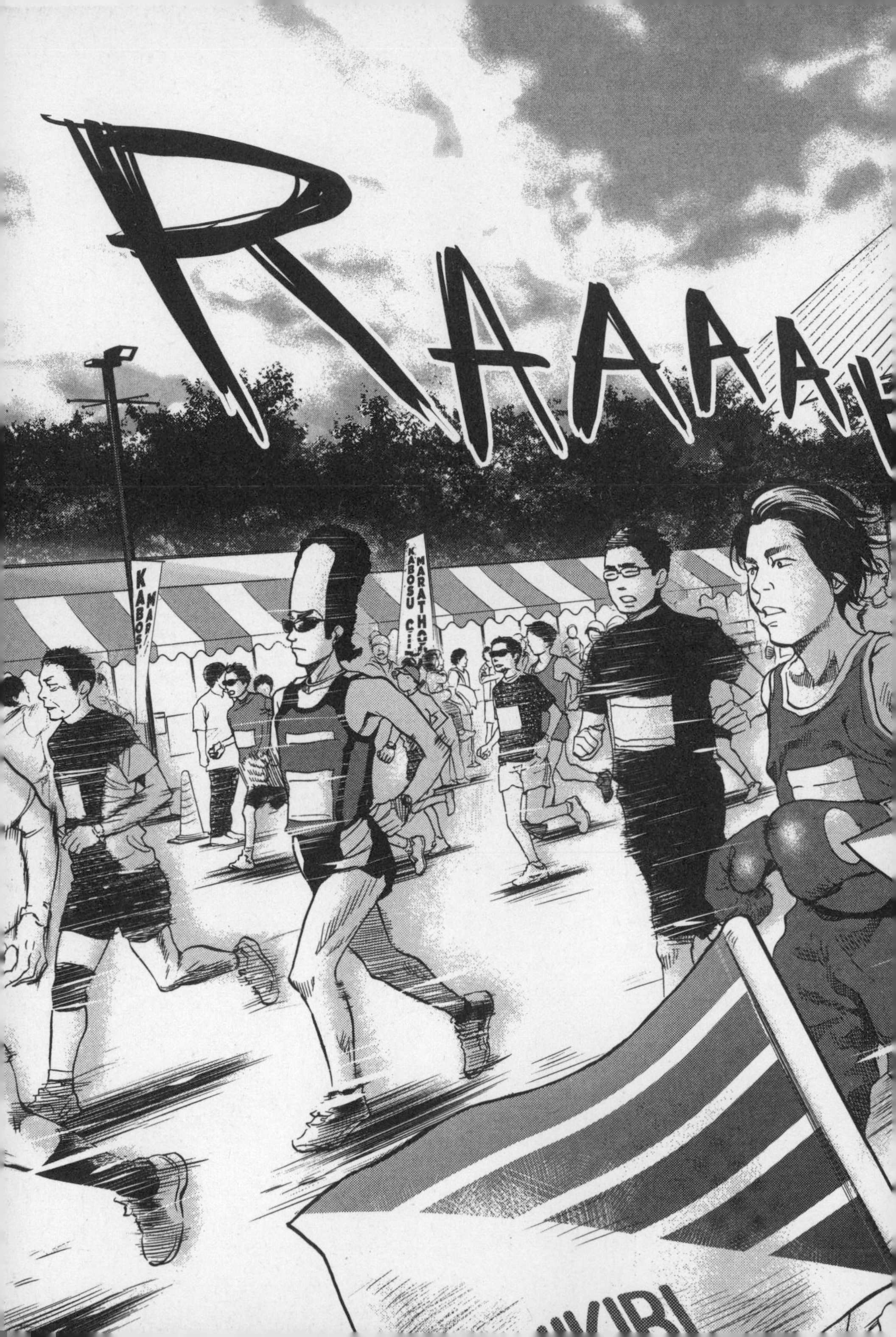
RAAAA
KABOSU MARA
KABOSU CITY MARATHON
KIBI

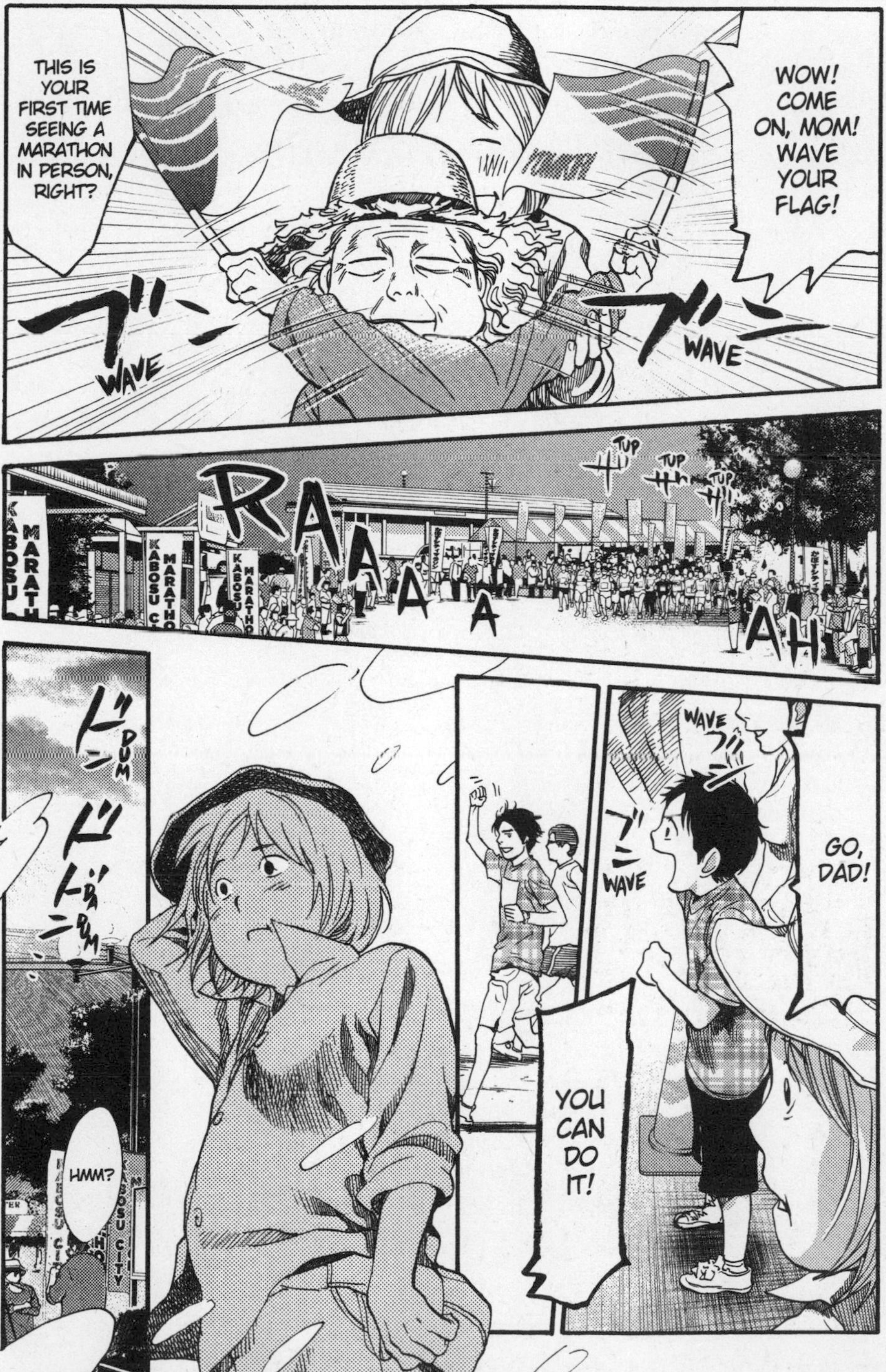
WOW! COME ON, MOM! WAVE YOUR FLAG!
WAVE
THIS IS YOUR FIRST TIME SEEING A MARATHON IN PERSON, RIGHT?
WAVE
TUP
TUP
TUP
AH
RAAAAA
KABOSU MARATHON
KABOSU CITY MARATHON
WAVE
GO, DAD!
WAVE
YOU CAN DO IT!
DUM
BA-DUM
HMM?
KABOSU CITY

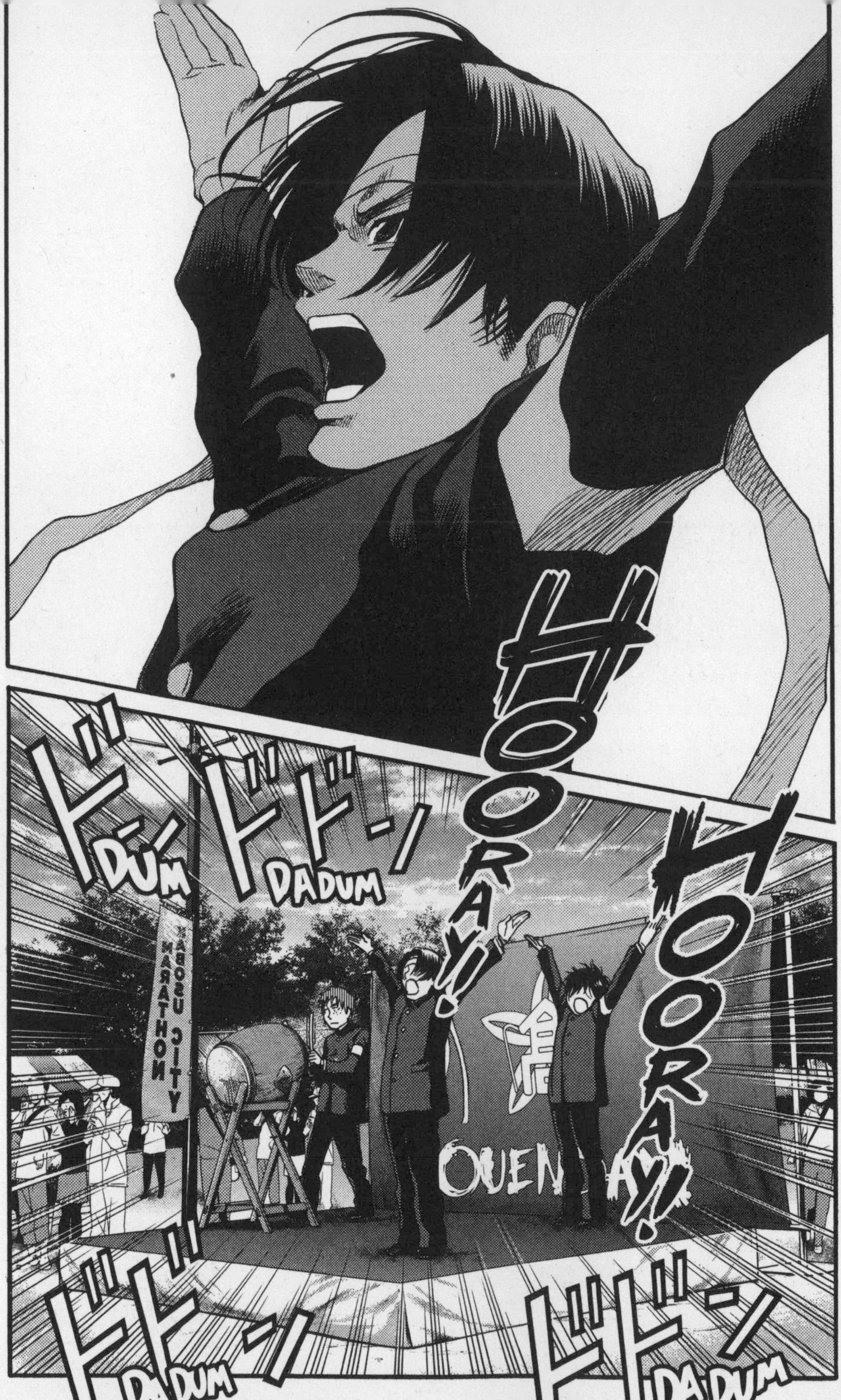
HOORAY!
HOORAY!
ドドーン
DADUM
ドーン
DUM
YABOSU CITY MARATHON
OUEN
ドドーン
DADUM
ドドーン
DADUM

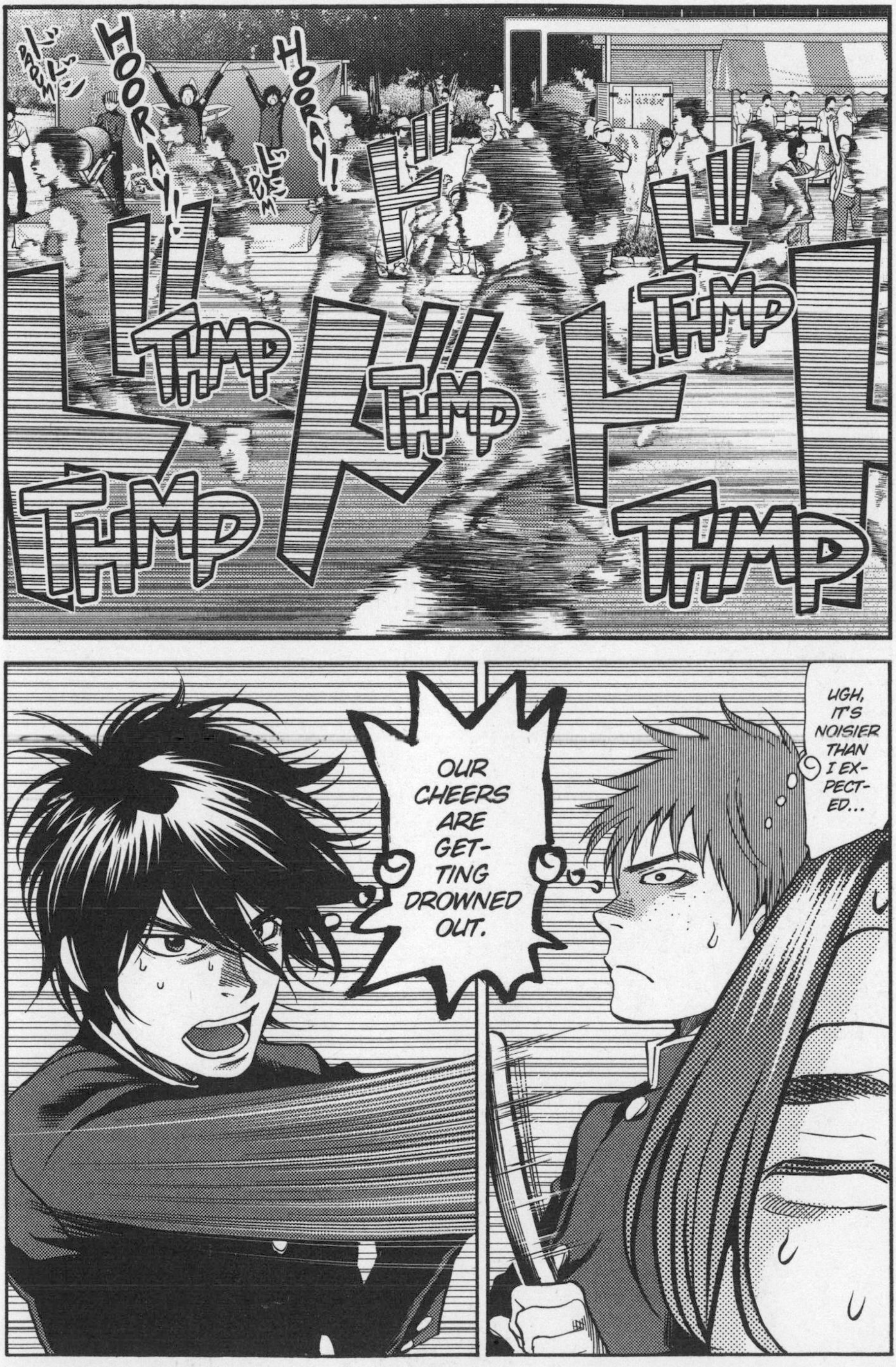
THMP
THMP
HOORAY!
THMP
THMP
HOORAY!
THMP
UGH, IT'S NOISIER THAN I EXPECTED...
OUR CHEERS ARE GETTING DROWNED OUT.

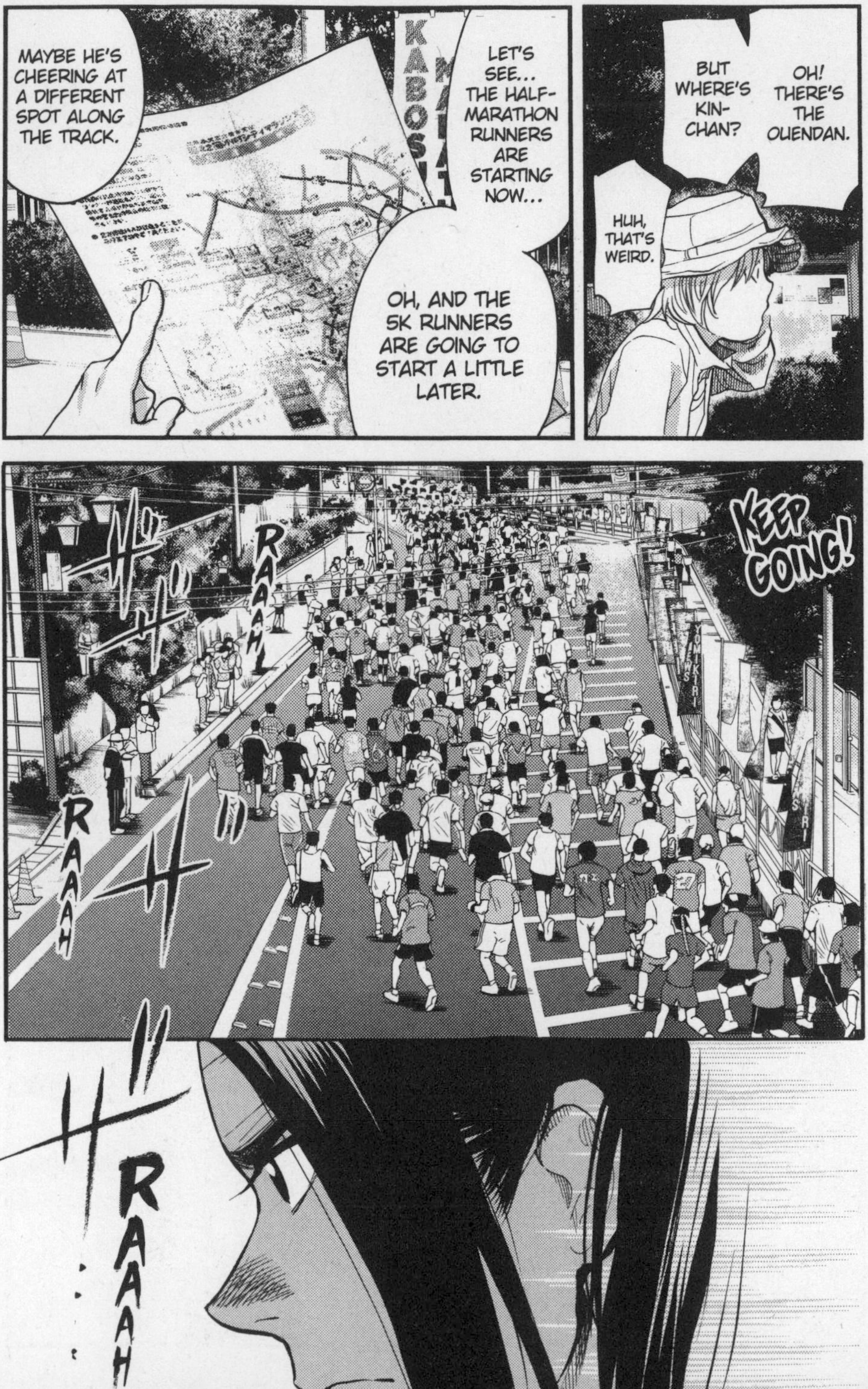
OH! THERE'S THE OUENDAN.
BUT WHERE'S KIN-CHAN?
HUH, THAT'S WEIRD.
LET'S SEE... THE HALF-MARATHON RUNNERS ARE STARTING NOW...
OH, AND THE 5K RUNNERS ARE GOING TO START A LITTLE LATER.
MAYBE HE'S CHEERING AT A DIFFERENT SPOT ALONG THE TRACK.
KEEP GOING!
RAAAH!
RAAAH
RAAAH

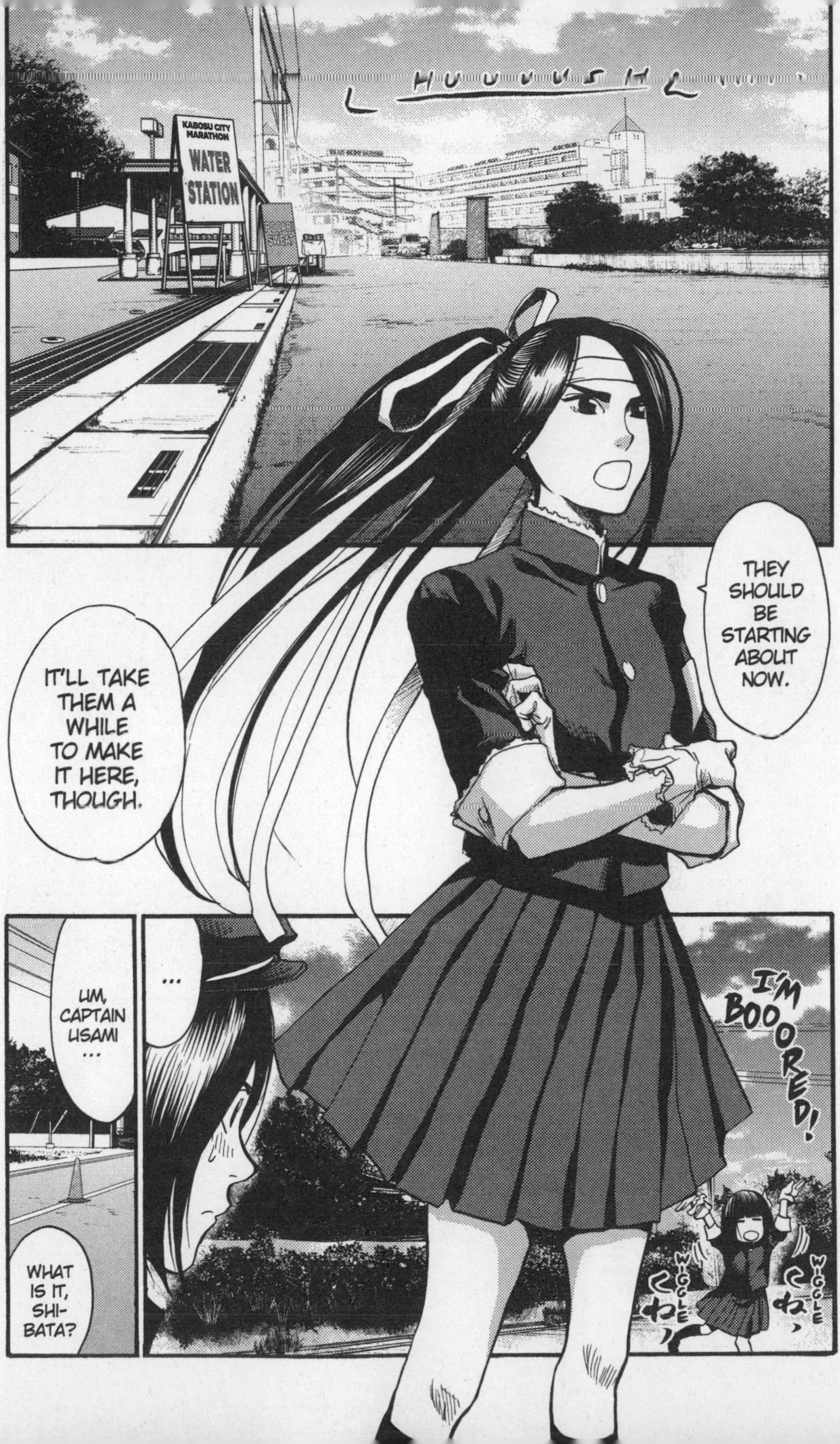
HUUUUSH
KABOSU CITY MARATHON
WATER STATION
POCARI SWEAT
THEY SHOULD BE STARTING ABOUT NOW.
IT'LL TAKE THEM A WHILE TO MAKE IT HERE, THOUGH.
I'M BOOOORED!
WIGGLE
WIGGLE
...
UM, CAPTAIN USAMI ...
WHAT IS IT, SHI-BATA?

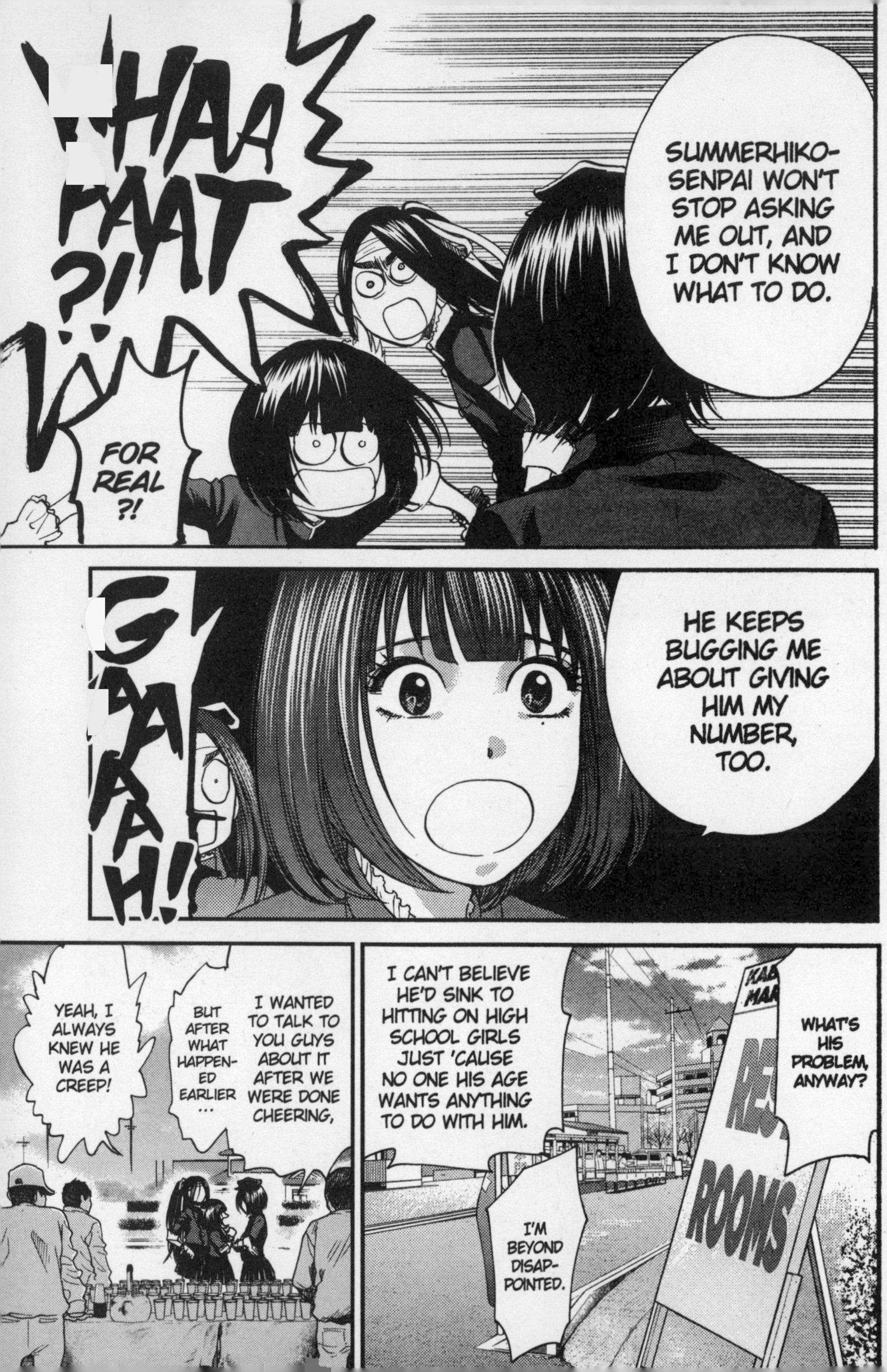
SUMMERHIKO-SENPAI WON'T STOP ASKING ME OUT, AND I DON'T KNOW WHAT TO DO.
FOR REAL ?!
HE KEEPS BUGGING ME ABOUT GIVING HIM MY NUMBER, TOO.
WHAT'S HIS PROBLEM, ANYWAY?
I CAN'T BELIEVE HE'D SINK TO HITTING ON HIGH SCHOOL GIRLS JUST 'CAUSE NO ONE HIS AGE WANTS ANYTHING TO DO WITH HIM.
ROOMS
I'M BEYOND DISAP-POINTED.
I WANTED TO TALK TO YOU GUYS ABOUT IT AFTER WE WERE DONE CHEERING,
BUT AFTER WHAT HAPPEN-ED EARLIER ...
YEAH, I ALWAYS KNEW HE WAS A CREEP!

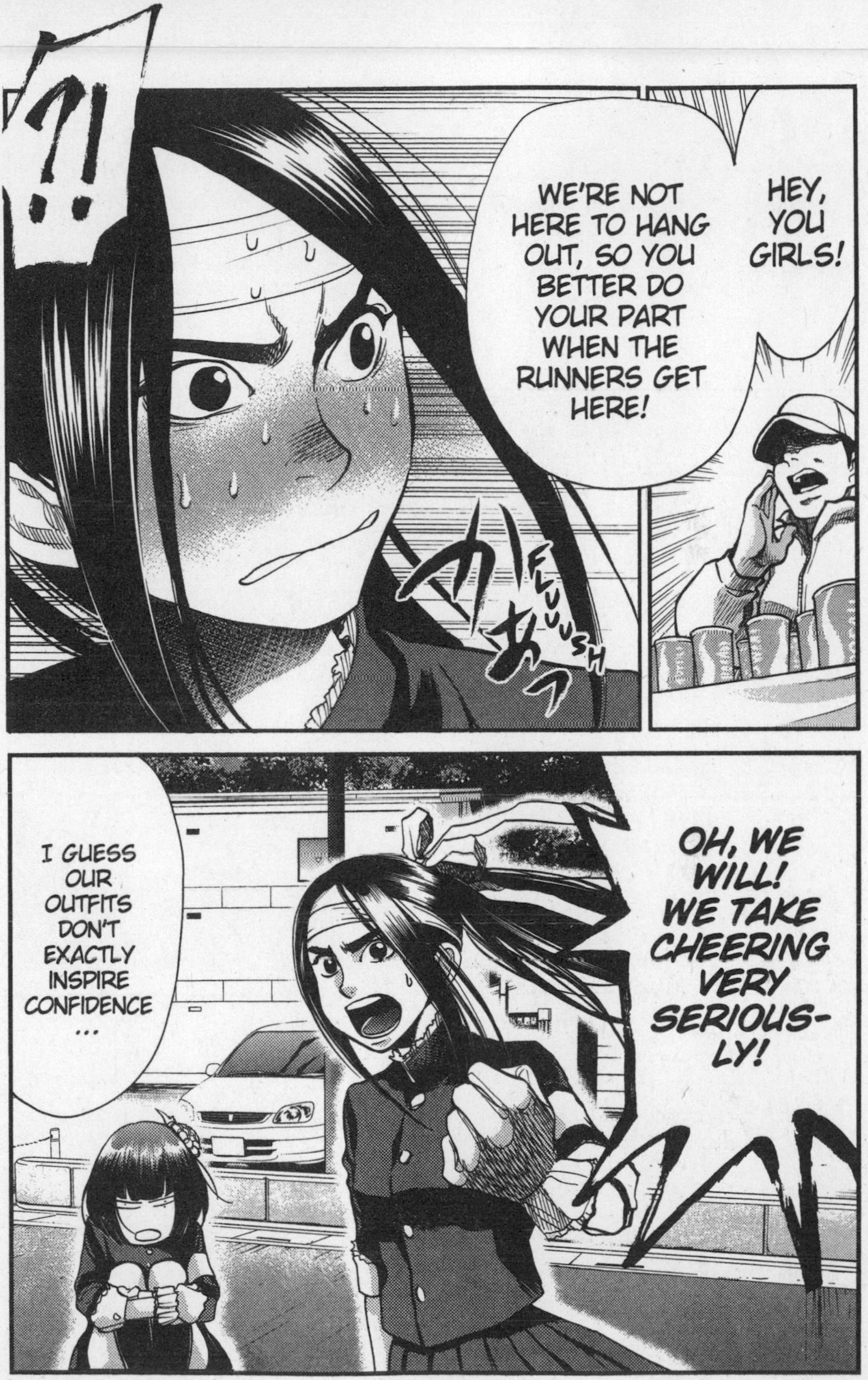
HEY, YOU GIRLS!
WE'RE NOT HERE TO HANG OUT, SO YOU BETTER DO YOUR PART WHEN THE RUNNERS GET HERE!
?!
FLUUUSH
OH, WE WILL! WE TAKE CHEERING VERY SERIOUS-LY!
I GUESS OUR OUTFITS DON'T EXACTLY INSPIRE CONFIDENCE ...

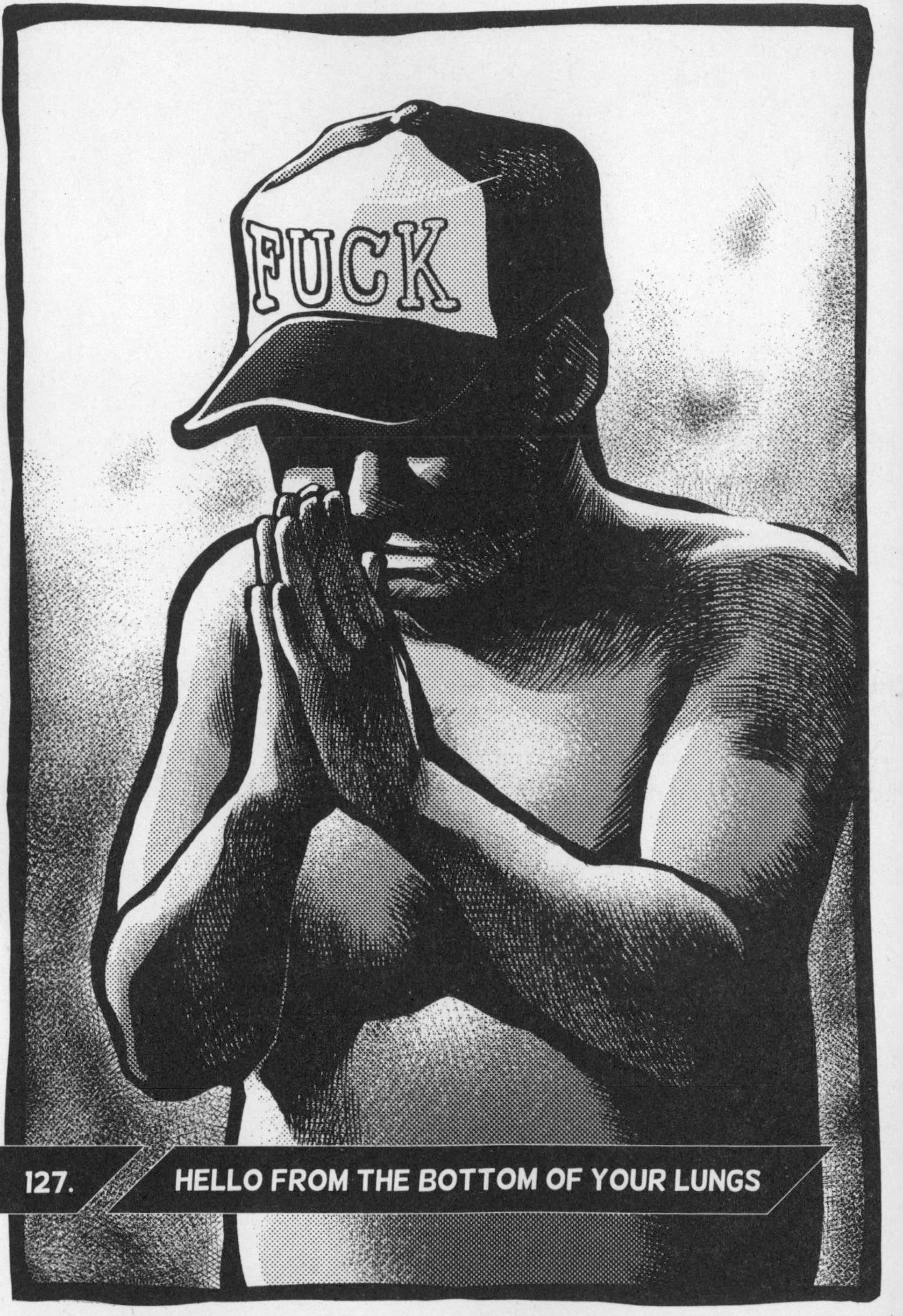
FUCK

127. HELLO FROM THE BOTTOM OF YOUR LUNGS

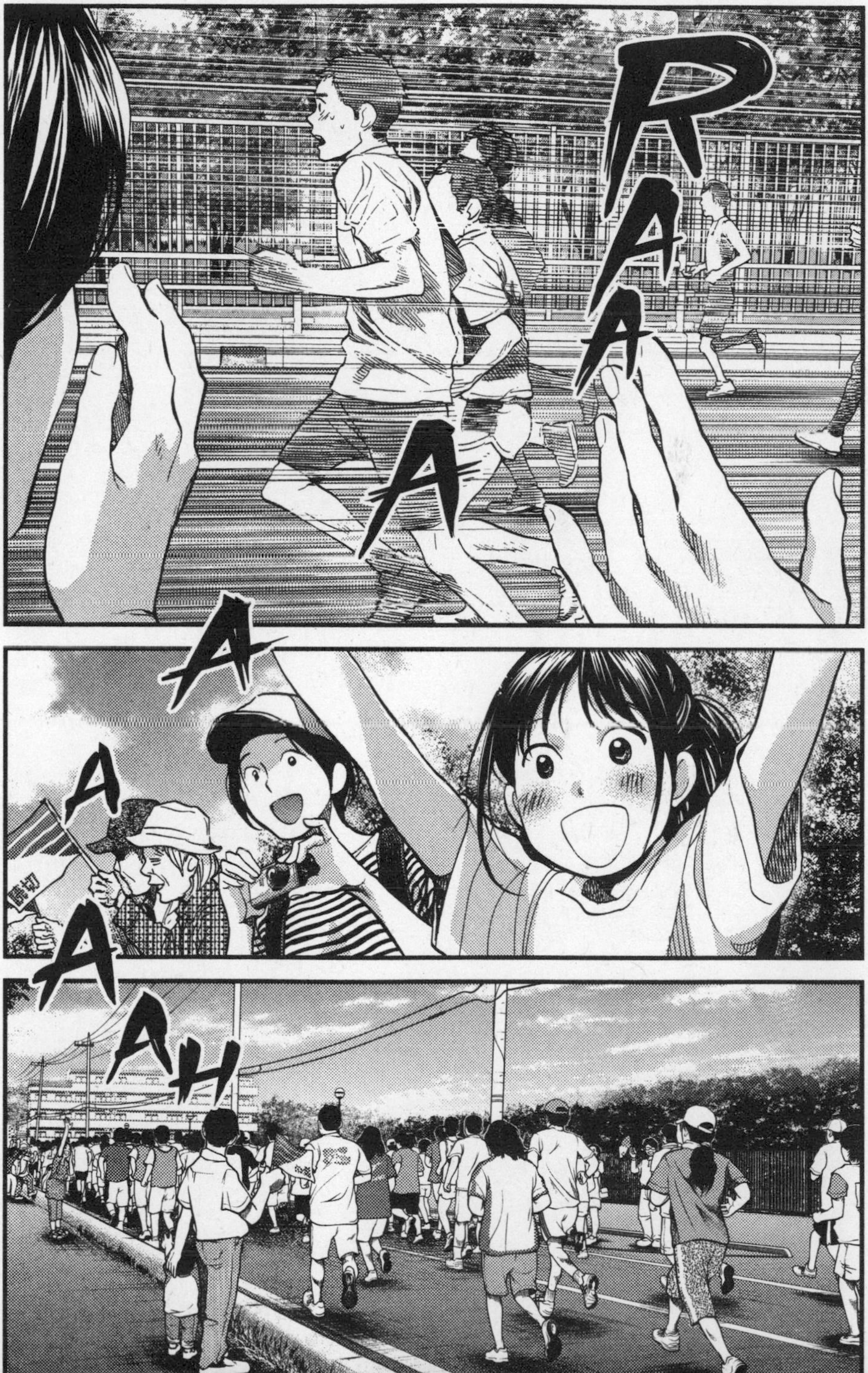
RAAAAAAAH

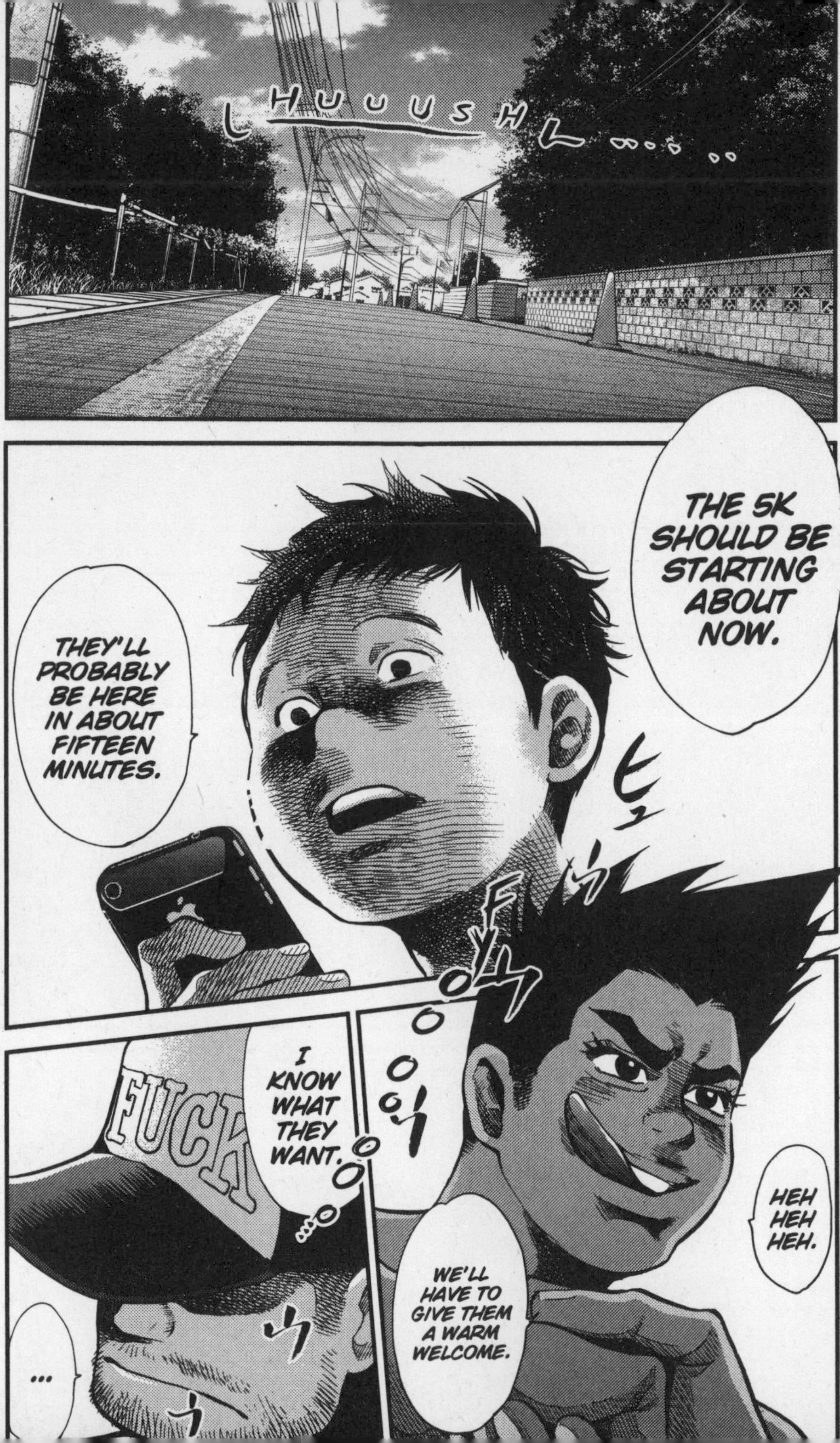
HUUUSH
THE 5K SHOULD BE STARTING ABOUT NOW.
THEY'LL PROBABLY BE HERE IN ABOUT FIFTEEN MINUTES.
HEH HEH HEH.
WE'LL HAVE TO GIVE THEM A WARM WELCOME.
I KNOW WHAT THEY WANT.
...
FUCK

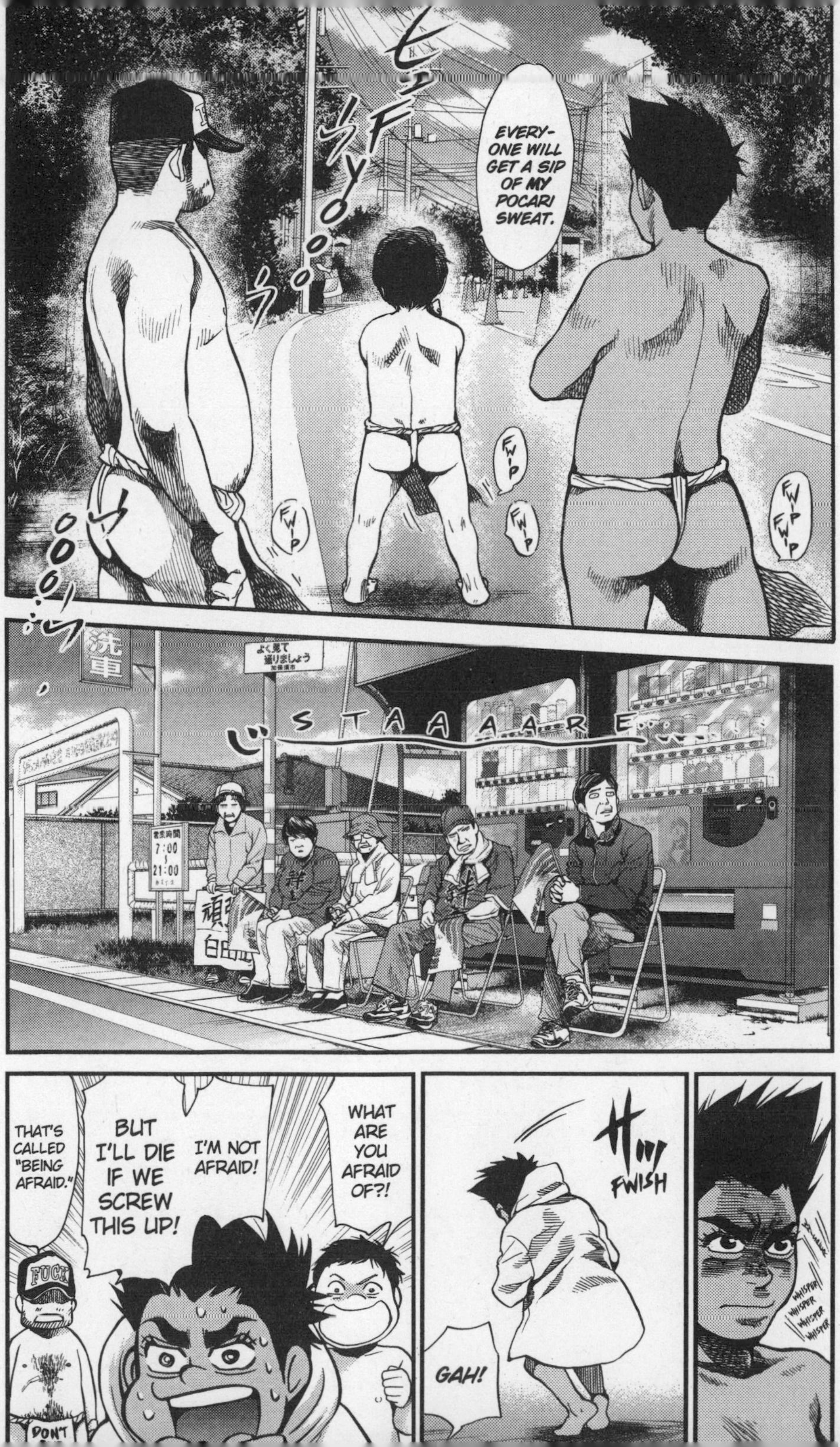
EVERY-ONE WILL GET A SIP OF MY POCARI SWEAT.
FWIP FWIP
FWIP
FWIP
FWIP
洗車
よく見て 渡りましょう
7:00 ~ 21:00
STAAAAARE
WHISPER WHISPER WHISPER WHISPER
FWISH
GAH!
WHAT ARE YOU AFRAID OF?!
I'M NOT AFRAID!
BUT I'LL DIE IF WE SCREW THIS UP!
THAT'S CALLED "BEING AFRAID."
FUCK
DON'T

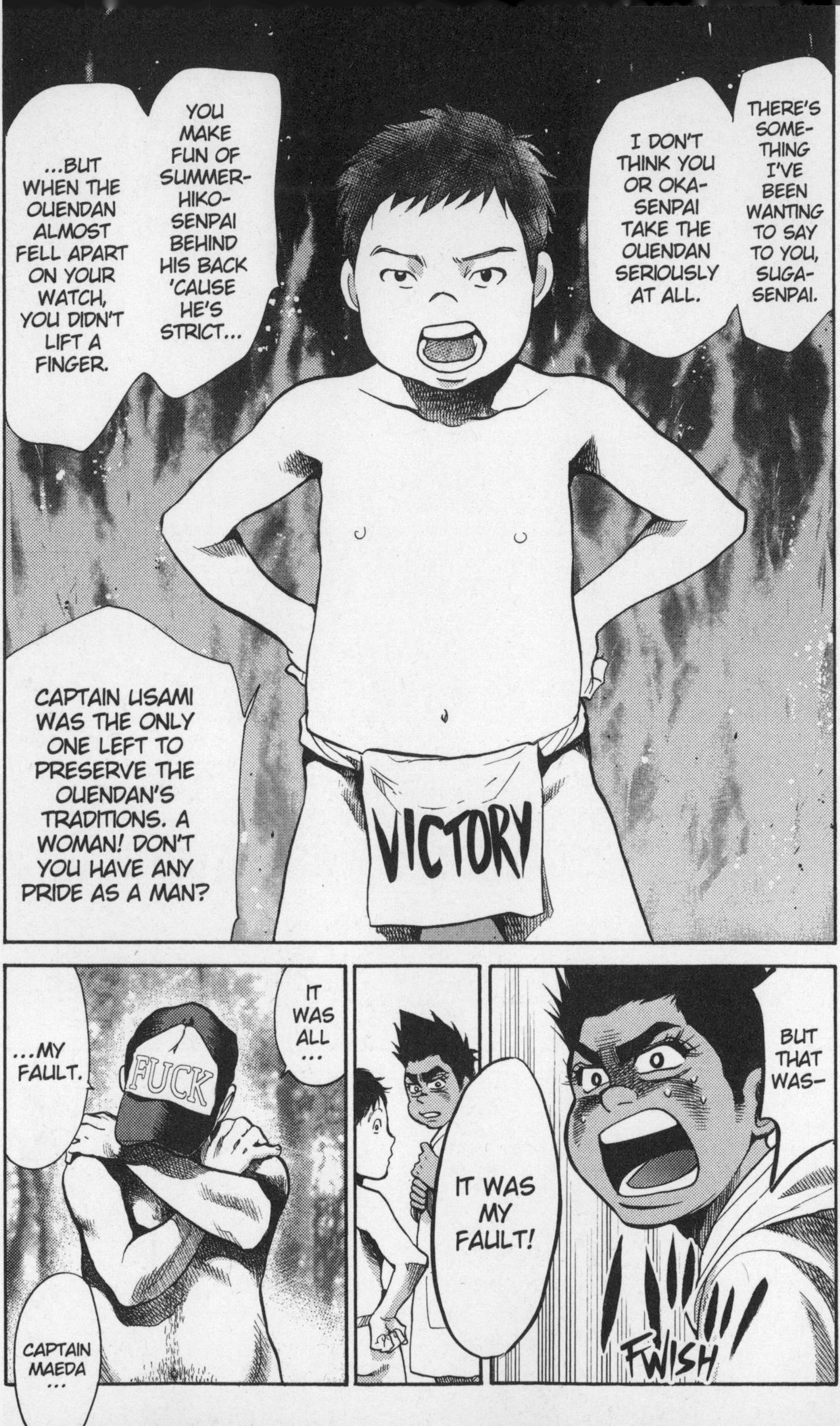
THERE'S SOME-THING I'VE BEEN WANTING TO SAY TO YOU, SUGA-SENPAI.
I DON'T THINK YOU OR OKA-SENPAI TAKE THE OUENDAN SERIOUSLY AT ALL.
YOU MAKE FUN OF SUMMER-HIKO-SENPAI BEHIND HIS BACK 'CAUSE HE'S STRICT...
...BUT WHEN THE OUENDAN ALMOST FELL APART ON YOUR WATCH, YOU DIDN'T LIFT A FINGER.
VICTORY
CAPTAIN USAMI WAS THE ONLY ONE LEFT TO PRESERVE THE OUENDAN'S TRADITIONS. A WOMAN! DON'T YOU HAVE ANY PRIDE AS A MAN?
BUT THAT WAS-
IT WAS MY FAULT!
FWISH
IT WAS ALL ...
...MY FAULT.
FUCK
CAPTAIN MAEDA ...

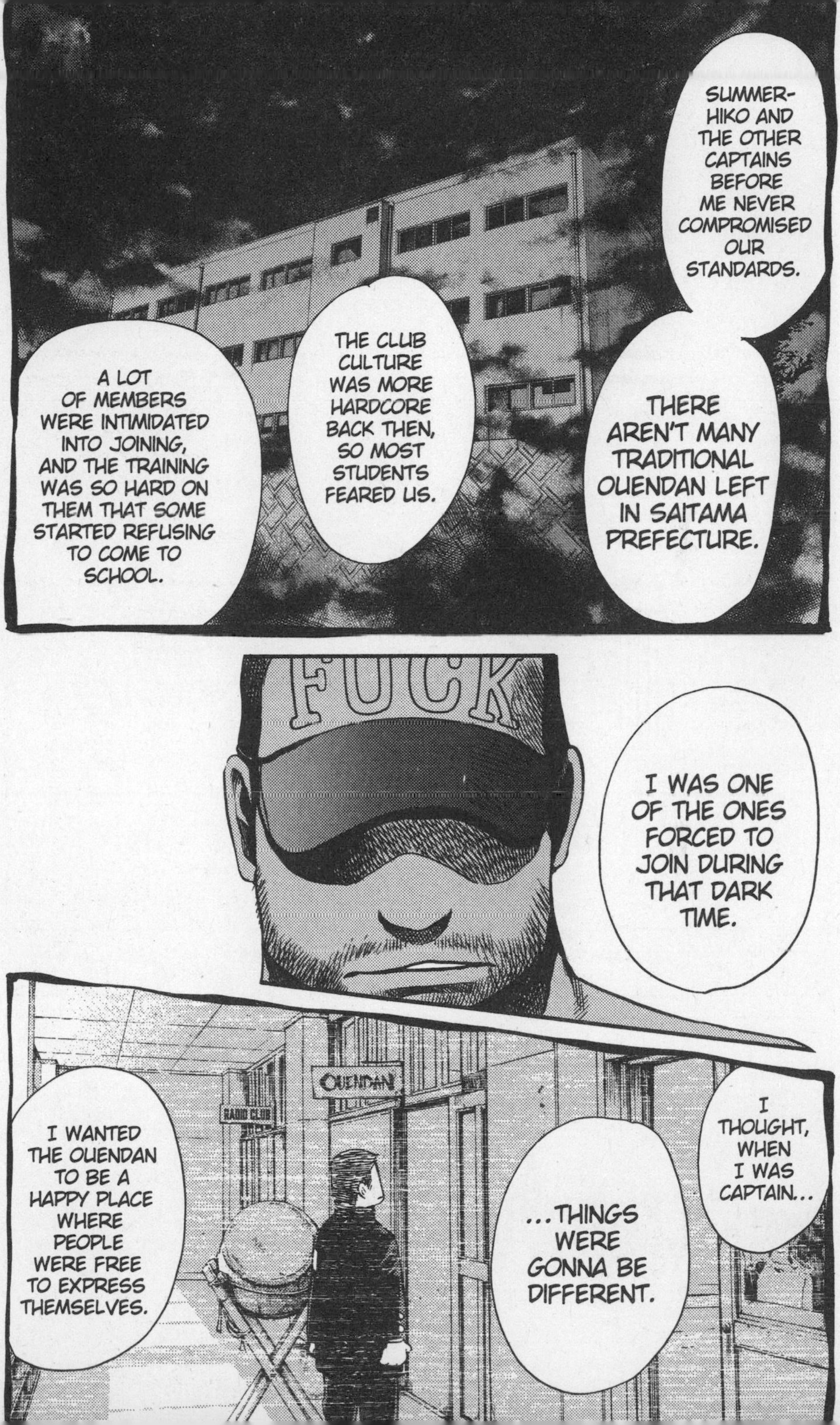
SUMMER-HIKO AND THE OTHER CAPTAINS BEFORE ME NEVER COMPROMISED OUR STANDARDS.
THERE AREN'T MANY TRADITIONAL OUENDAN LEFT IN SAITAMA PREFECTURE.
THE CLUB CULTURE WAS MORE HARDCORE BACK THEN, SO MOST STUDENTS FEARED US.
A LOT OF MEMBERS WERE INTIMIDATED INTO JOINING, AND THE TRAINING WAS SO HARD ON THEM THAT SOME STARTED REFUSING TO COME TO SCHOOL.
FUCK
I WAS ONE OF THE ONES FORCED TO JOIN DURING THAT DARK TIME.
I THOUGHT, WHEN I WAS CAPTAIN...
...THINGS WERE GONNA BE DIFFERENT.
OUENDAN
RADIO CLUB
I WANTED THE OUENDAN TO BE A HAPPY PLACE WHERE PEOPLE WERE FREE TO EXPRESS THEMSELVES.

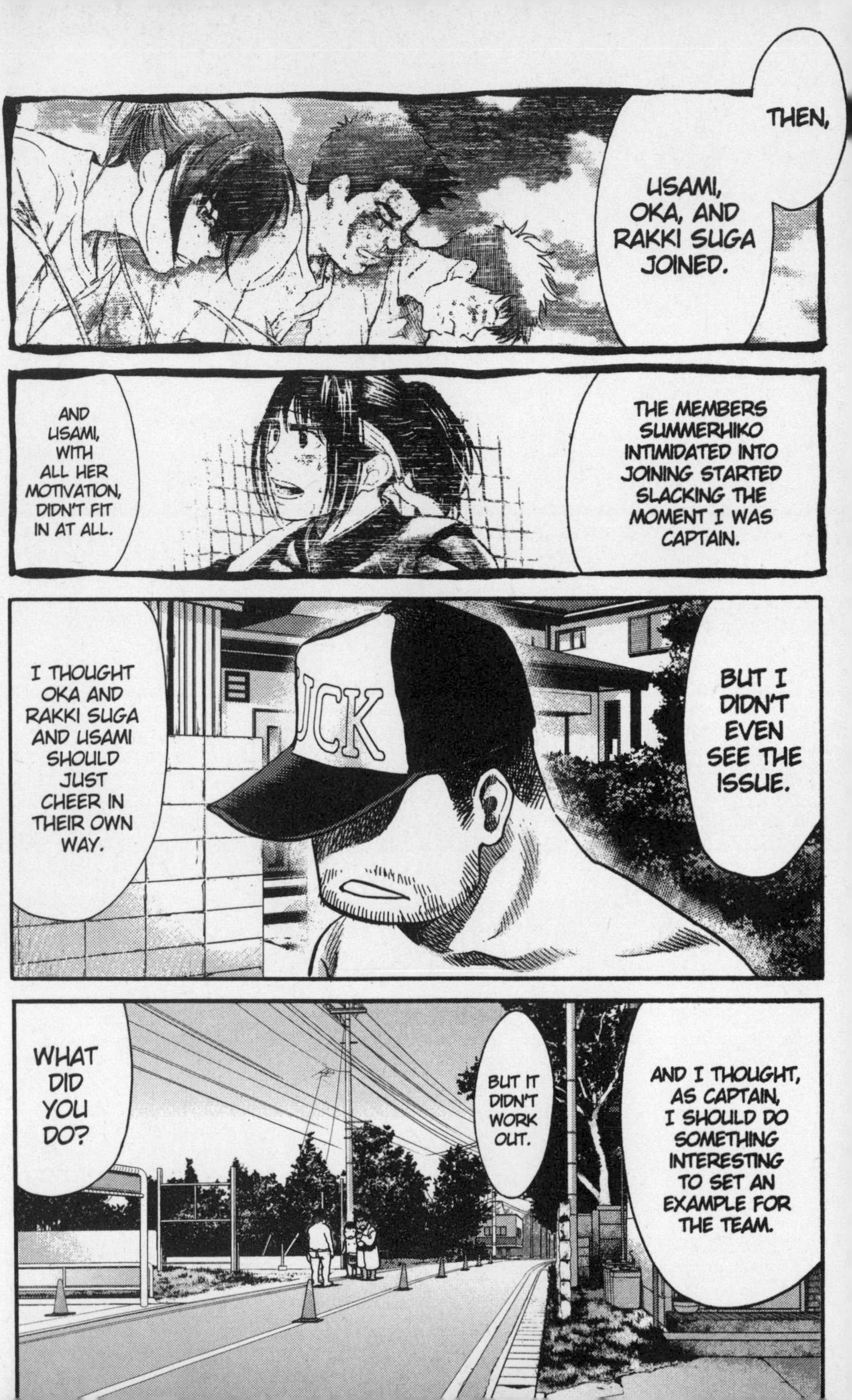
THEN,
USAMI, OKA, AND RAKKI SUGA JOINED.
THE MEMBERS SUMMERHIKO INTIMIDATED INTO JOINING STARTED SLACKING THE MOMENT I WAS CAPTAIN.
AND USAMI, WITH ALL HER MOTIVATION, DIDN'T FIT IN AT ALL.
BUT I DIDN'T EVEN SEE THE ISSUE.
I THOUGHT OKA AND RAKKI SUGA AND USAMI SHOULD JUST CHEER IN THEIR OWN WAY.
AND I THOUGHT, AS CAPTAIN, I SHOULD DO SOMETHING INTERESTING TO SET AN EXAMPLE FOR THE TEAM.
BUT IT DIDN'T WORK OUT.
WHAT DID YOU DO?

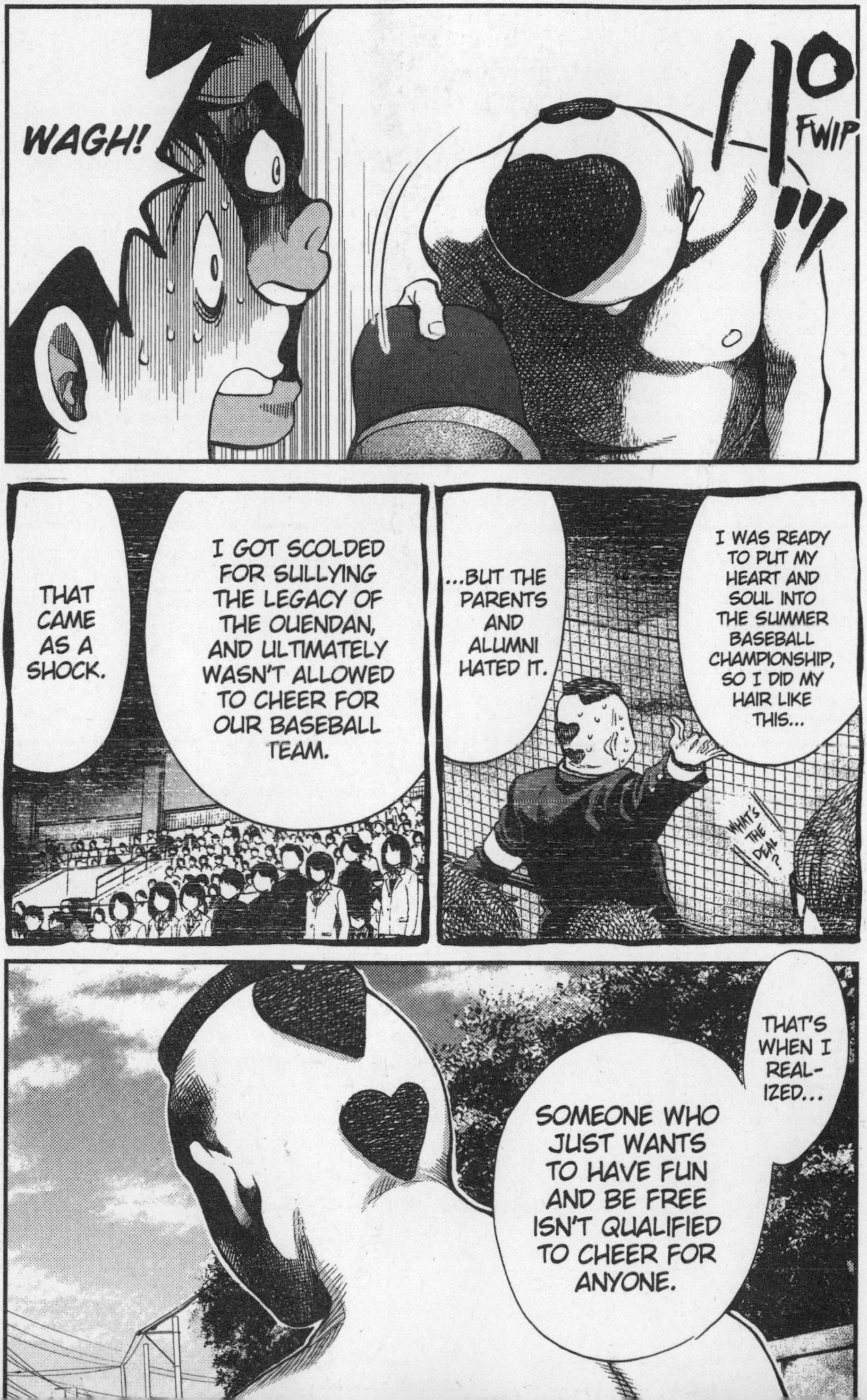
FWIP
WAGH!
I WAS READY TO PUT MY HEART AND SOUL INTO THE SUMMER BASEBALL CHAMPIONSHIP, SO I DID MY HAIR LIKE THIS...
...BUT THE PARENTS AND ALUMNI HATED IT.
WHAT'S THE DEAL?
I GOT SCOLDED FOR SULLYING THE LEGACY OF THE OUENDAN, AND ULTIMATELY WASN'T ALLOWED TO CHEER FOR OUR BASEBALL TEAM.
THAT CAME AS A SHOCK.
THAT'S WHEN I REALIZED...
SOMEONE WHO JUST WANTS TO HAVE FUN AND BE FREE ISN'T QUALIFIED TO CHEER FOR ANYONE.

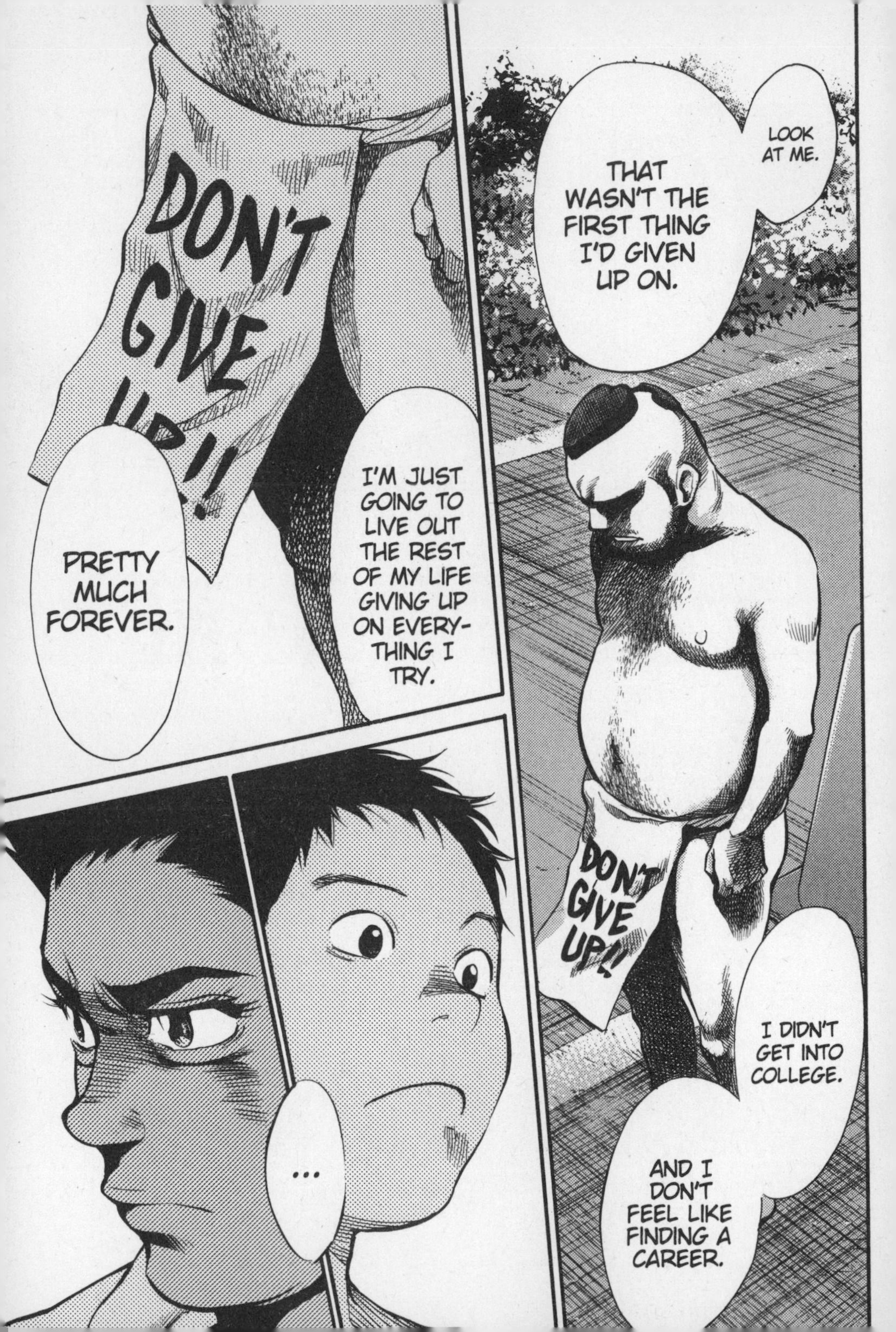
LOOK AT ME.
THAT WASN'T THE FIRST THING I'D GIVEN UP ON.
DON'T GIVE UP!!
I DIDN'T GET INTO COLLEGE.
AND I DON'T FEEL LIKE FINDING A CAREER.
DON'T GIVE UP!!
I'M JUST GOING TO LIVE OUT THE REST OF MY LIFE GIVING UP ON EVERY-THING I TRY.
PRETTY MUCH FOREVER.
...

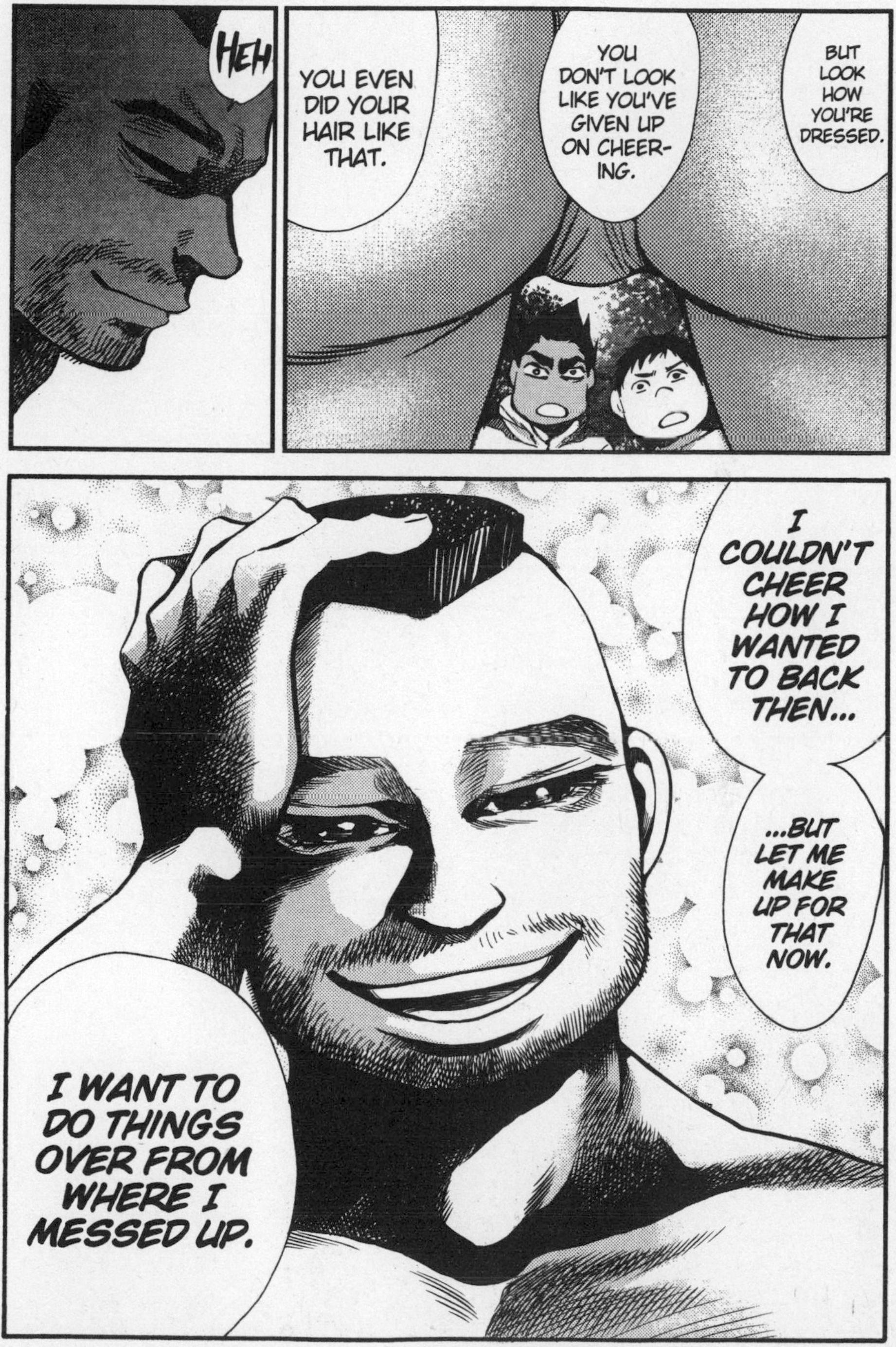
BUT LOOK HOW YOU'RE DRESSED.
YOU DON'T LOOK LIKE YOU'VE GIVEN UP ON CHEER-ING.
YOU EVEN DID YOUR HAIR LIKE THAT.
HEH
I COULDN'T CHEER HOW I WANTED TO BACK THEN...
...BUT LET ME MAKE UP FOR THAT NOW.
I WANT TO DO THINGS OVER FROM WHERE I MESSED UP.

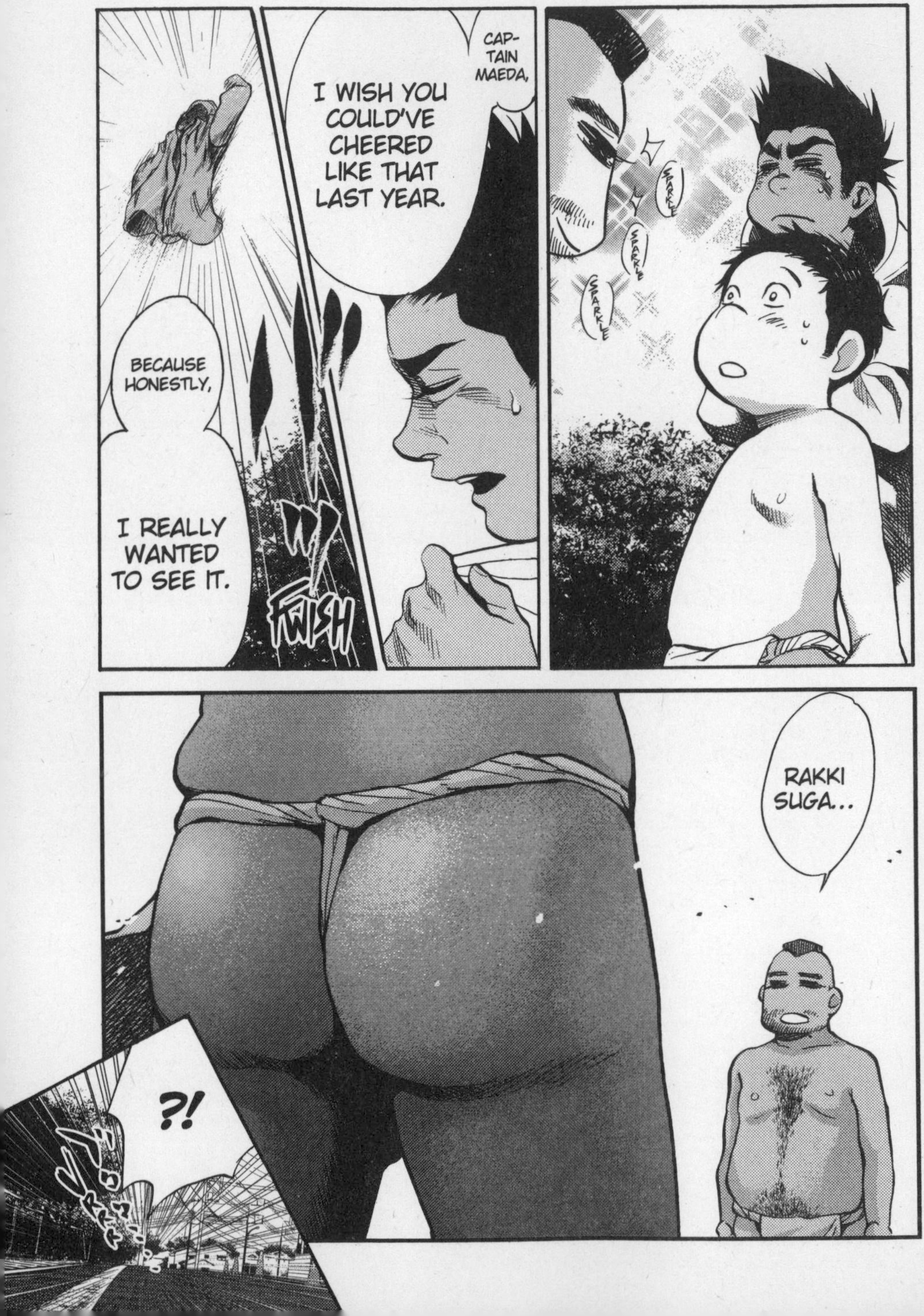
SPARKLE
SPARKLE
SPARKLE
CAPTAIN MAEDA,
I WISH YOU COULD'VE CHEERED LIKE THAT LAST YEAR.
BECAUSE HONESTLY,
I REALLY WANTED TO SEE IT.
FWISH
RAKKI SUGA...
?!

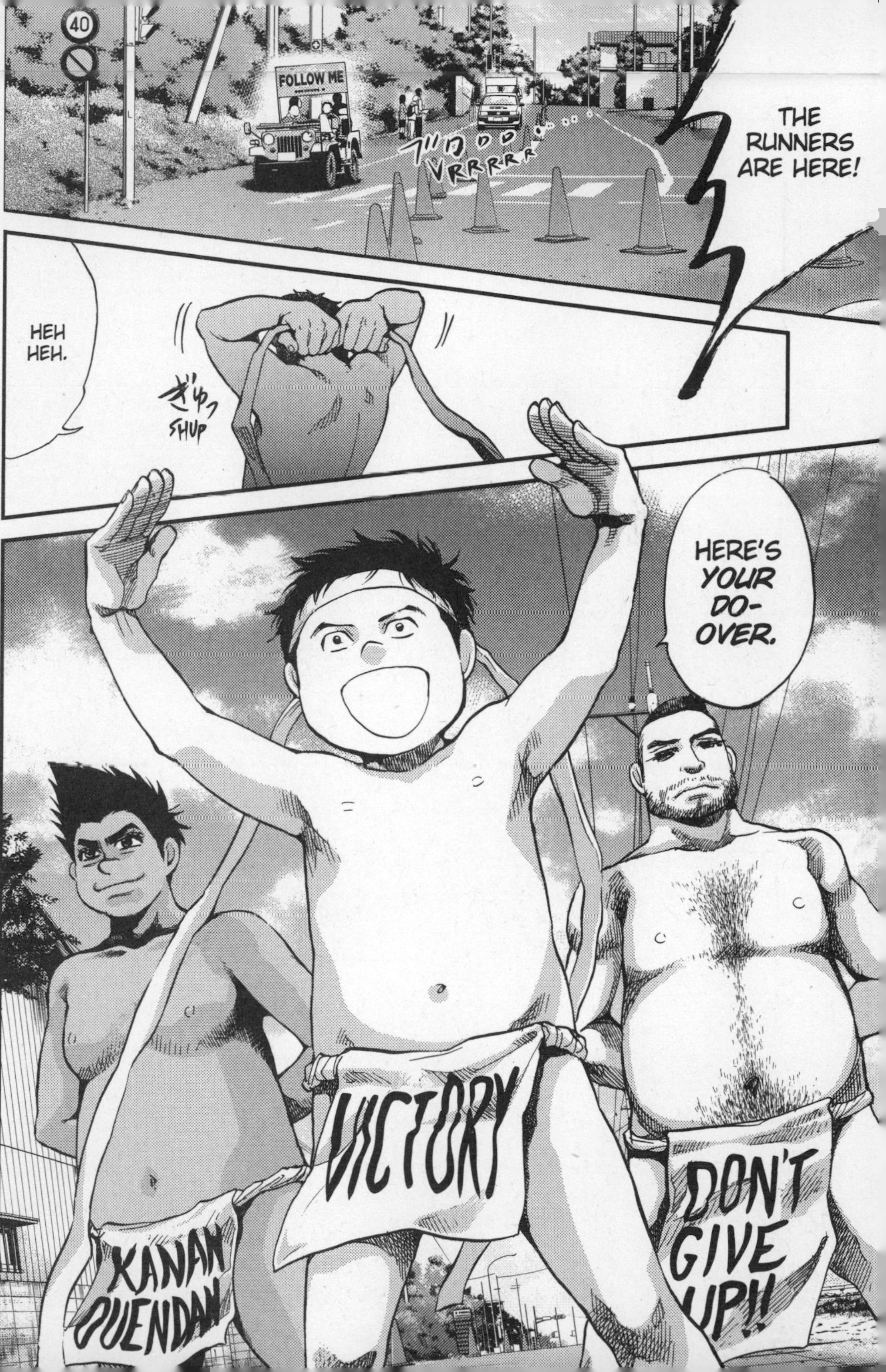
THE RUNNERS ARE HERE!
40
FOLLOW ME
ブロロロロ
VRRRRR
HEH HEH.
ぎゅっ
SHUP
HERE'S YOUR DO-OVER.
DON'T GIVE UP!!
VICTORY
KANAN OUENDAN

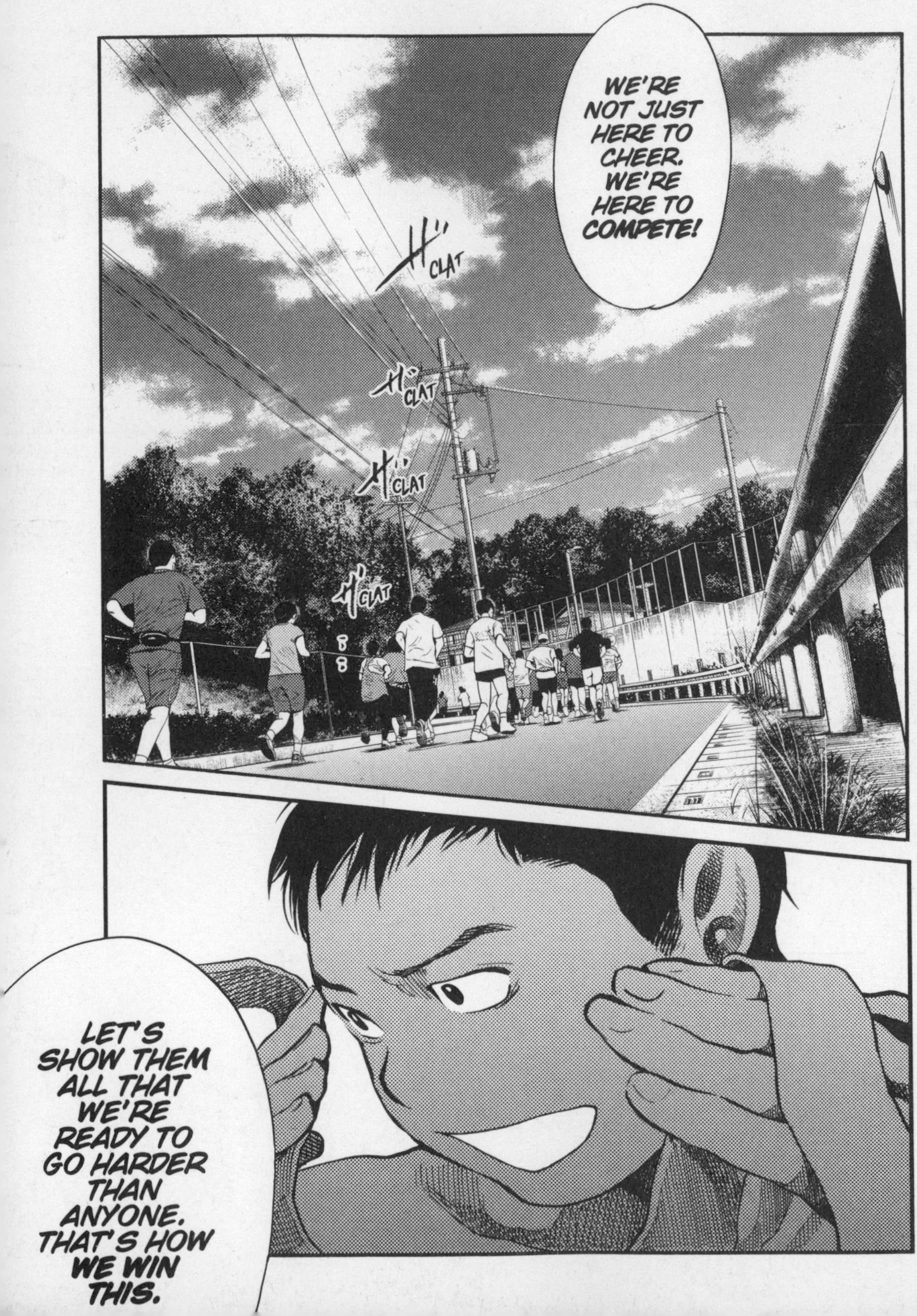
WE'RE NOT JUST HERE TO CHEER. WE'RE HERE TO COMPETE!
CLAT
CLAT
CLAT
CLAT
LET'S SHOW THEM ALL THAT WE'RE READY TO GO HARDER THAN ANYONE. THAT'S HOW WE WIN THIS.

Again!!
アゲイン!!

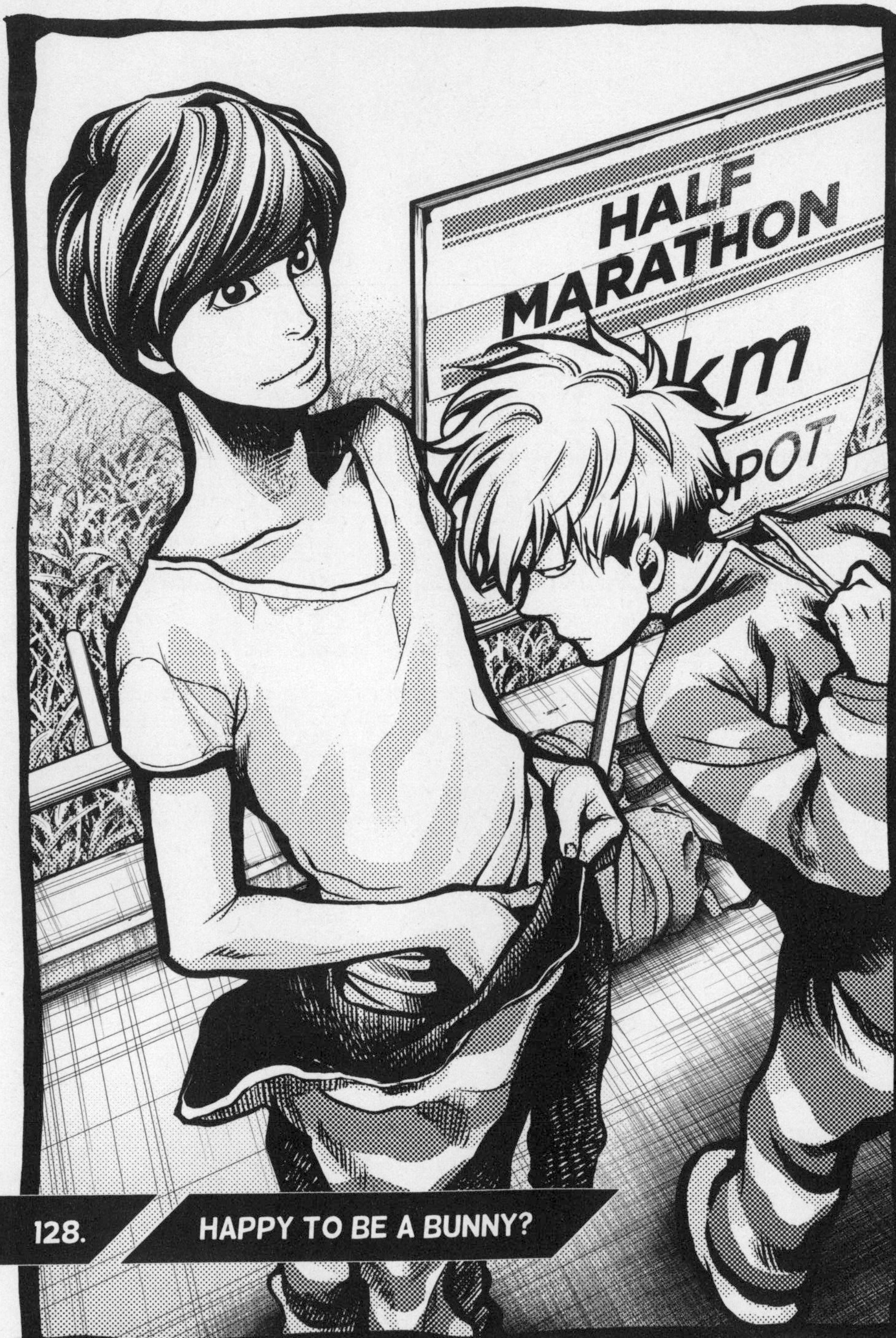
HALF MARATHON

128. HAPPY TO BE A BUNNY?

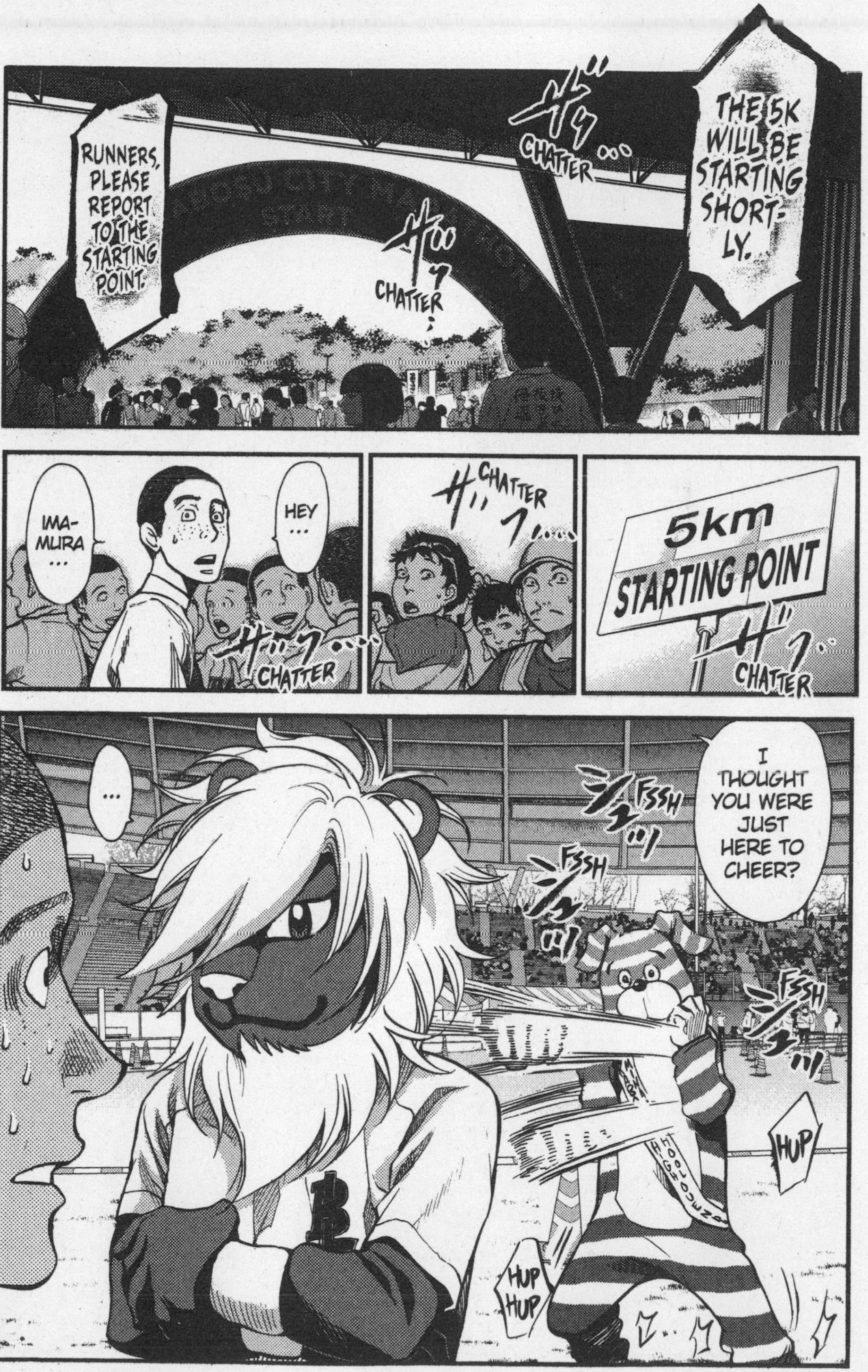
THE 5K WILL BE STARTING SHORT-LY.
CHATTER
CHATTER
RUNNERS, PLEASE REPORT TO THE STARTING POINT.
5km
STARTING POINT
CHATTER
CHATTER
HEY ...
IMA-MURA ...
CHATTER
I THOUGHT YOU WERE JUST HERE TO CHEER?
FSSH
FSSH
FSSH
...
HUP
HUP HUP

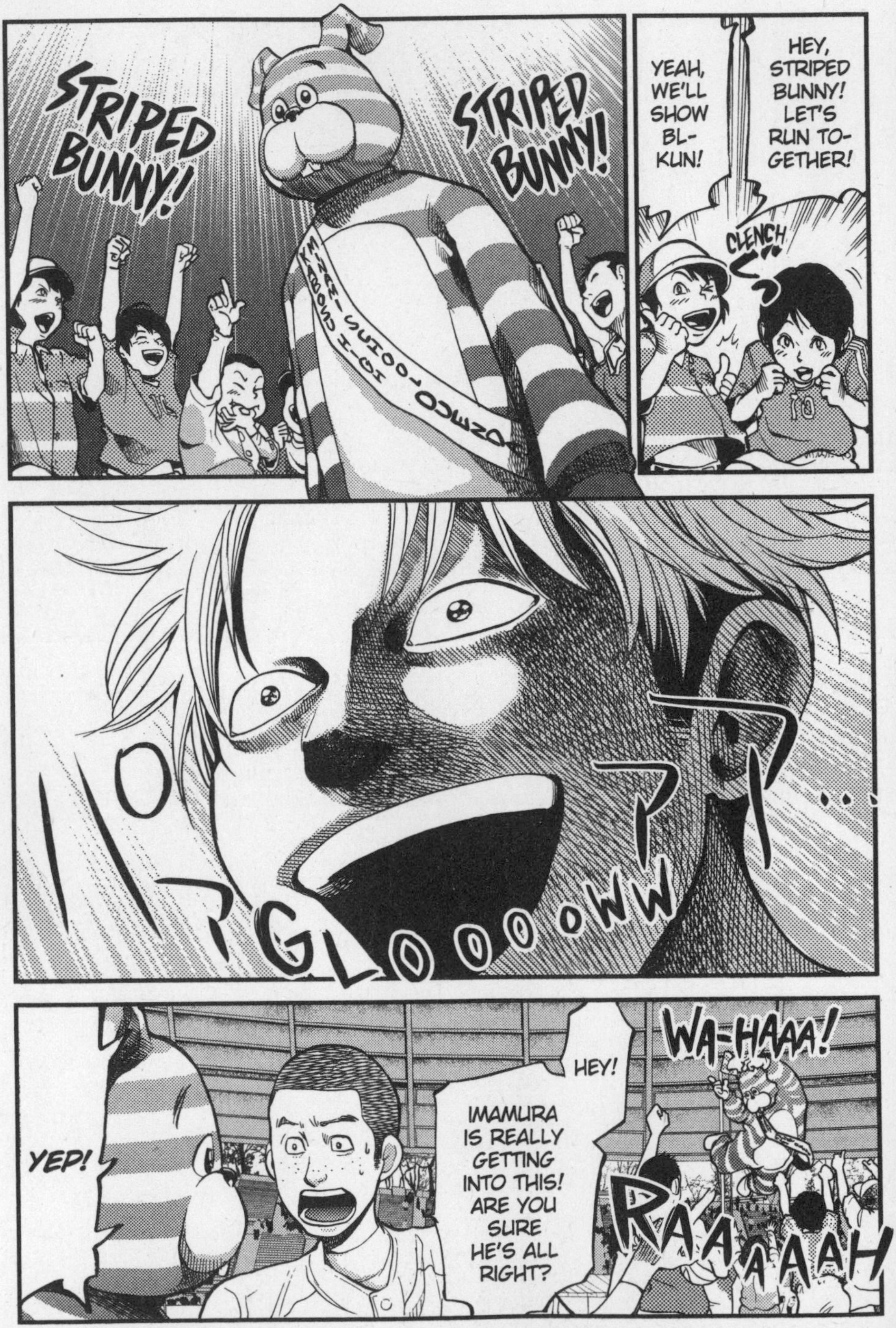
HEY, STRIPED BUNNY! LET'S RUN TO-GETHER!
YEAH, WE'LL SHOW BL-KUN!
CLENCH
STRIPED BUNNY!
STRIPED BUNNY!
GLOOOOOWW
WA-HAAA!
RAAAAAAH
HEY!
IMAMURA IS REALLY GETTING INTO THIS! ARE YOU SURE HE'S ALL RIGHT?
YEP!

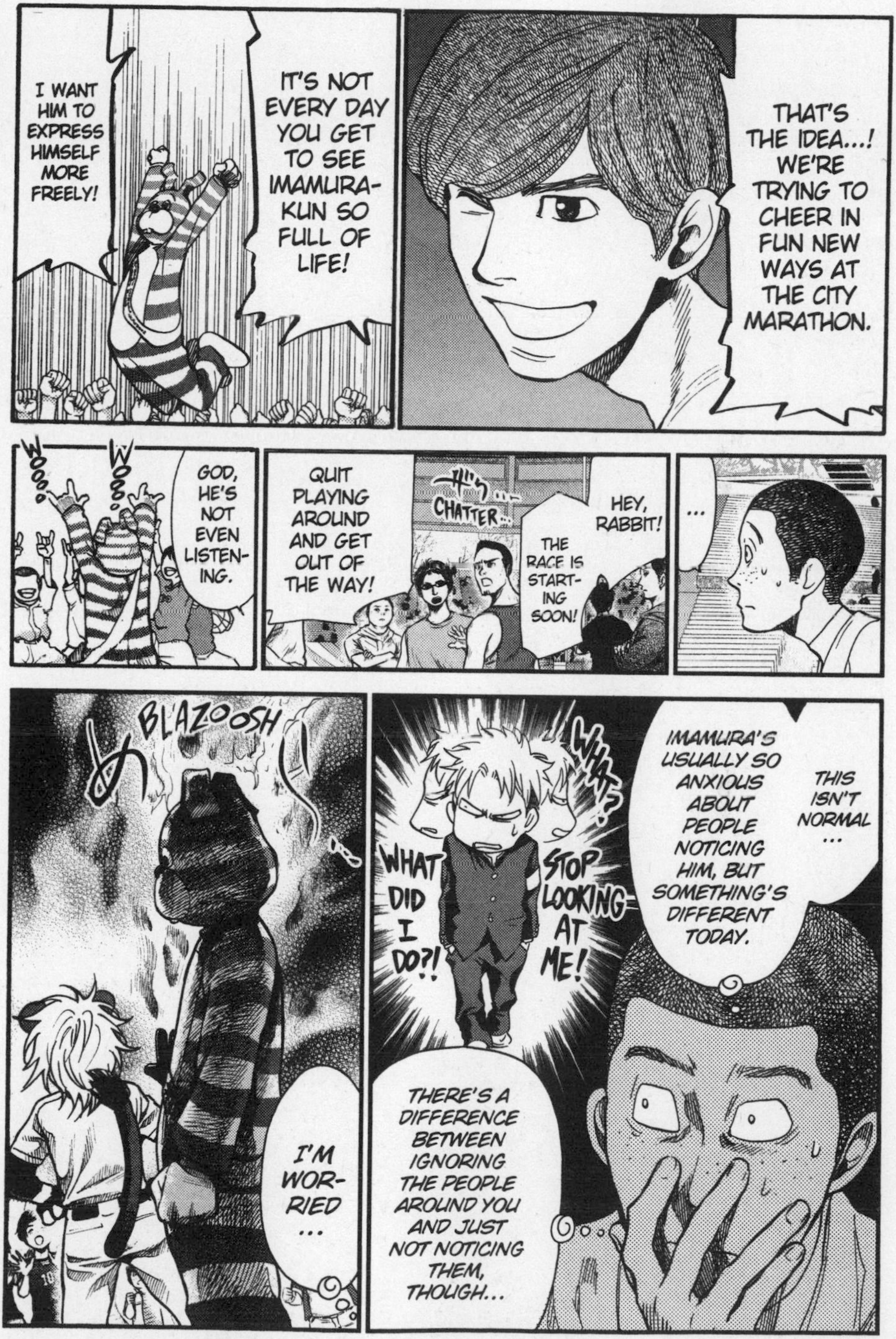
THAT'S THE IDEA...! WE'RE TRYING TO CHEER IN FUN NEW WAYS AT THE CITY MARATHON.
IT'S NOT EVERY DAY YOU GET TO SEE IMAMURA-KUN SO FULL OF LIFE!
I WANT HIM TO EXPRESS HIMSELF MORE FREELY!
...
HEY, RABBIT!
THE RACE IS STARTING SOON!
CHATTER...
QUIT PLAYING AROUND AND GET OUT OF THE WAY!
GOD, HE'S NOT EVEN LISTENING.
WOOOO
WOOOO
THIS ISN'T NORMAL...
IMAMURA'S USUALLY SO ANXIOUS ABOUT PEOPLE NOTICING HIM, BUT SOMETHING'S DIFFERENT TODAY.
WHAT?
STOP LOOKING AT ME!
WHAT DID I DO?!
THERE'S A DIFFERENCE BETWEEN IGNORING THE PEOPLE AROUND YOU AND JUST NOT NOTICING THEM, THOUGH...
BLAZOOSH
I'M WORRIED...

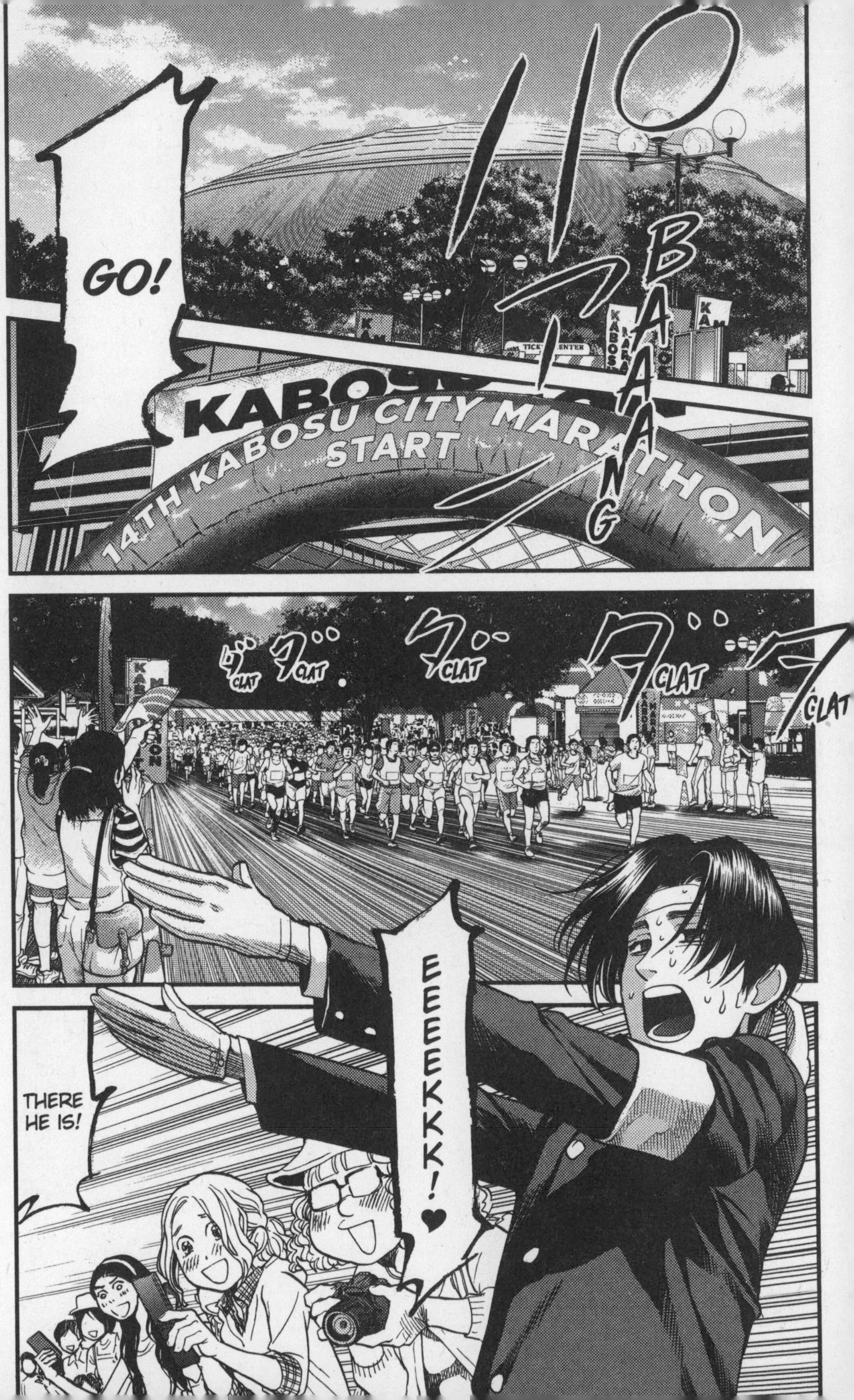
BABAANG
GO!
KABOSU CITY MARATHON
14TH KABOSU CITY MARATHON START
TICKET CENTER
CLAT CLAT CLAT CLAT CLAT CLAT
EEEEEKKK!♥
THERE HE IS!

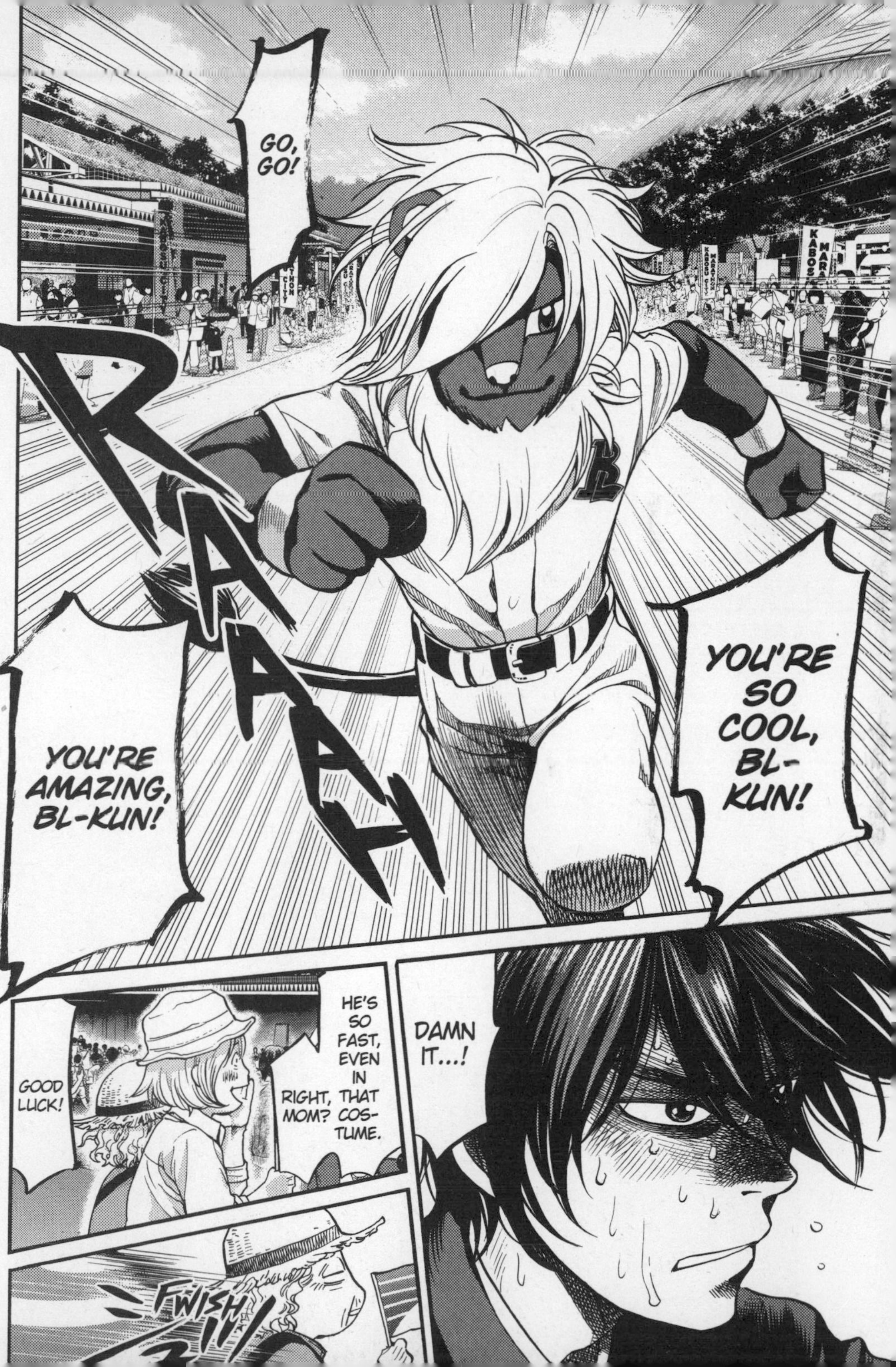
GO, GO!
YOU'RE SO COOL, BL-KUN!
RAAAH
YOU'RE AMAZING, BL-KUN!
DAMN IT...!
HE'S SO FAST, EVEN IN THAT COSTUME.
RIGHT, MOM?
GOOD LUCK!
FWISH

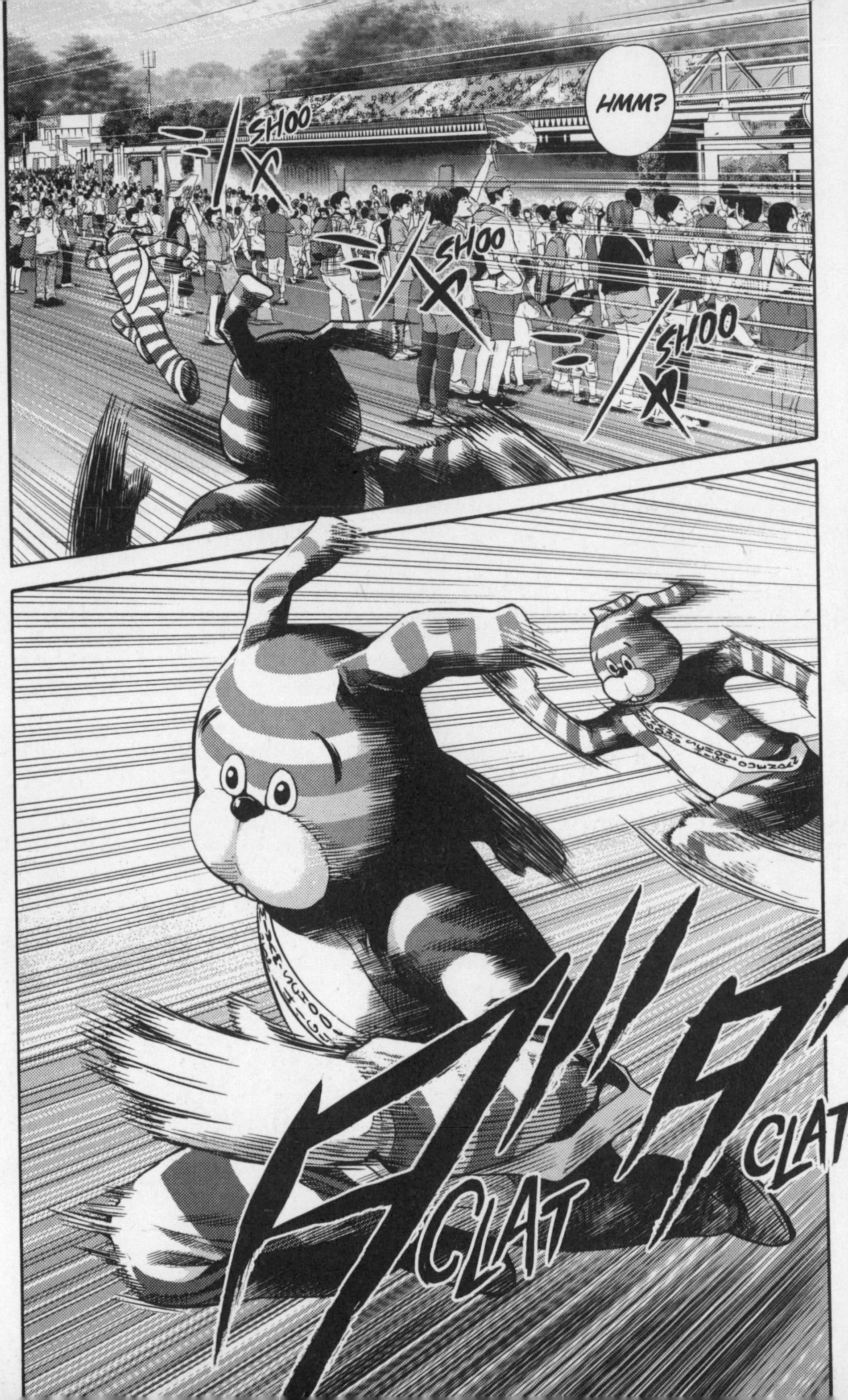

HMM?
SHOO
SHOO
SHOO
CLAT
CLAT

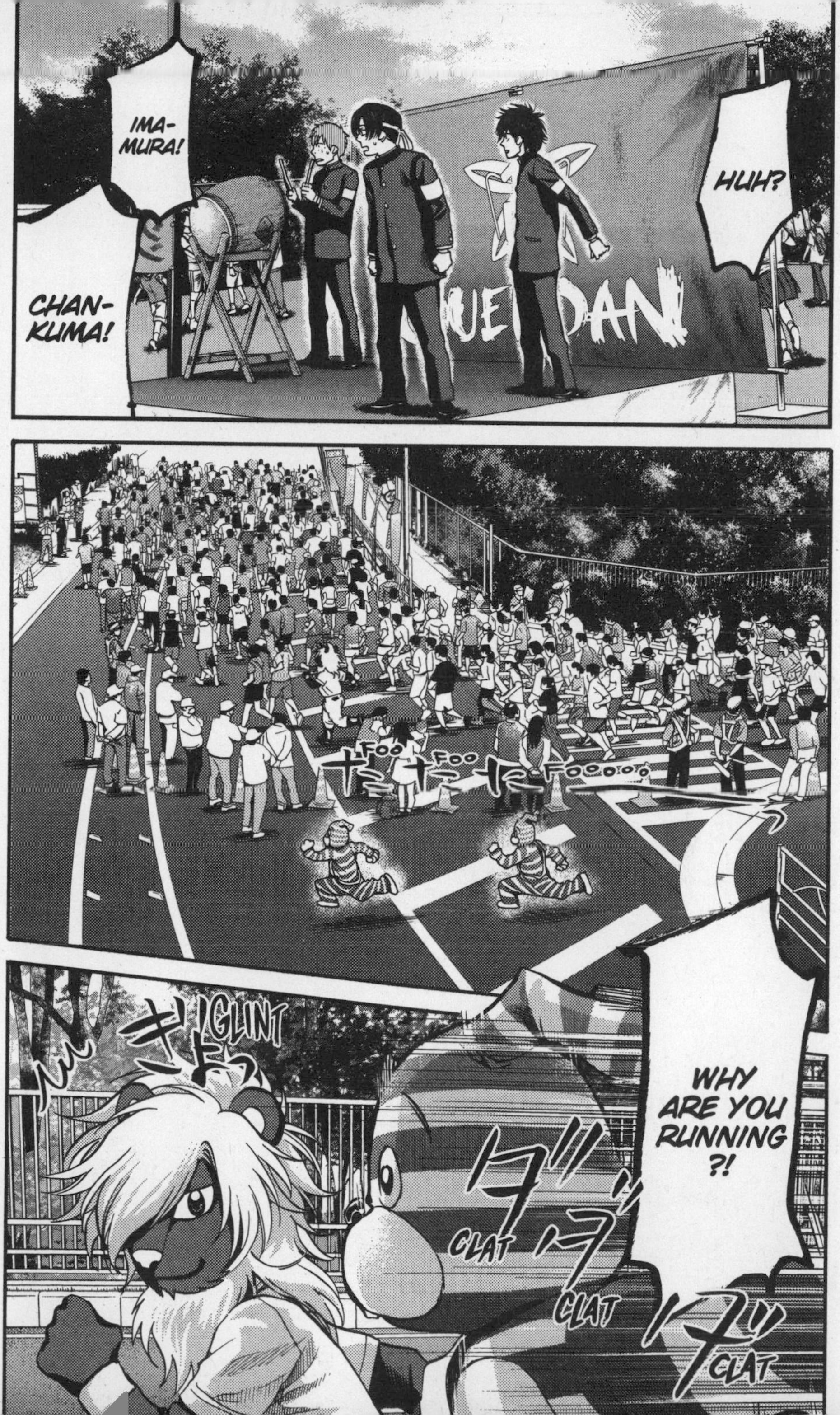
HUH?
IMA-MURA!
CHAN-KUMA!
FOO FOO FOOOOOO
WHY ARE YOU RUNNING?!
CLAT
CLAT
CLAT
CLAT
GLINT

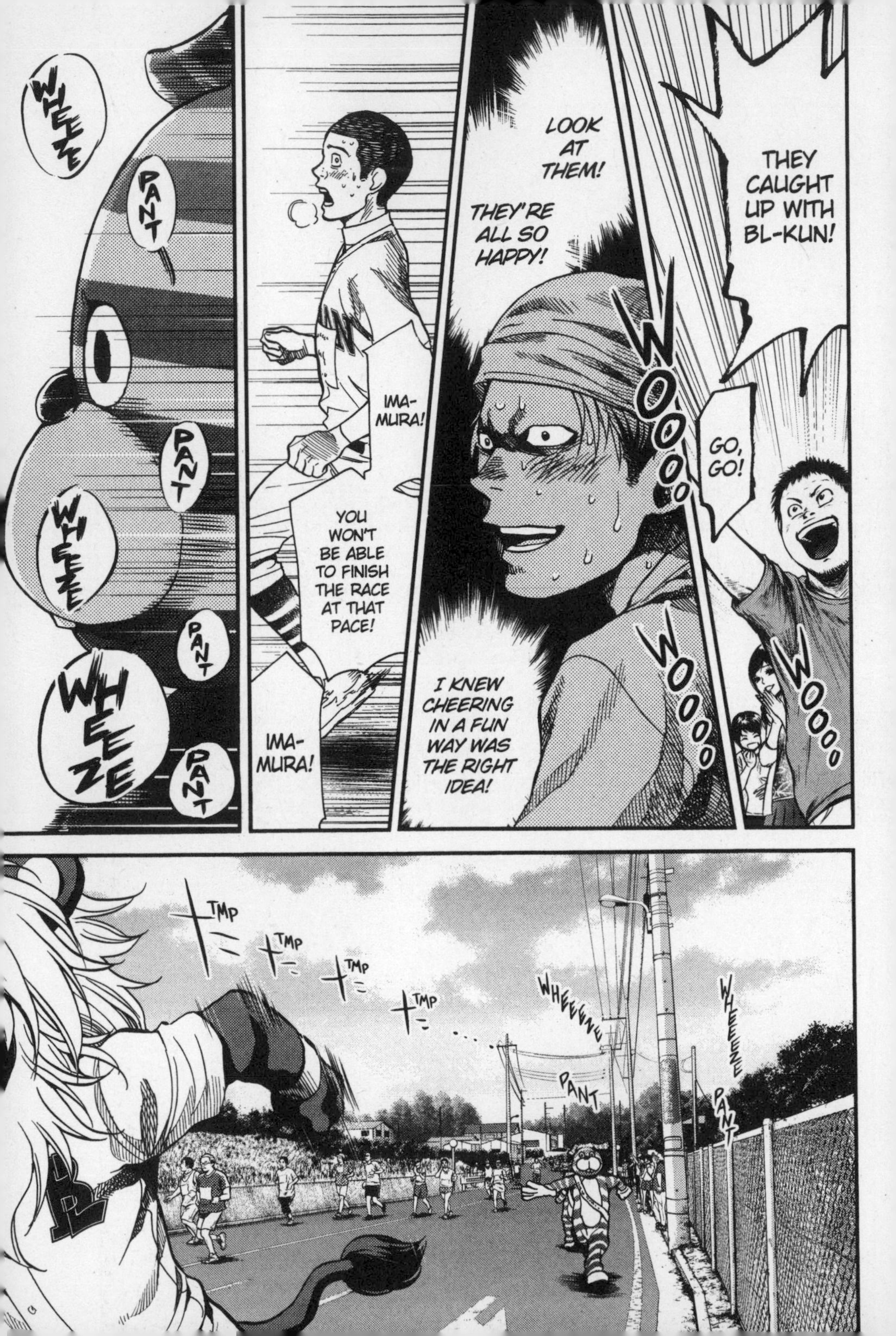

THEY CAUGHT UP WITH BL-KUN!
GO, GO!
WOOOO
LOOK AT THEM!
THEY'RE ALL SO HAPPY!
WOOOO
WOOOO
I KNEW CHEERING IN A FUN WAY WAS THE RIGHT IDEA!
IMA-MURA!
YOU WON'T BE ABLE TO FINISH THE RACE AT THAT PACE!
IMA-MURA!
WHEEZE
PANT
PANT
WHEEZE
PANT
WHEEZE
PANT
WHEEZE
PANT
TMP
TMP
TMP
TMP
PANT

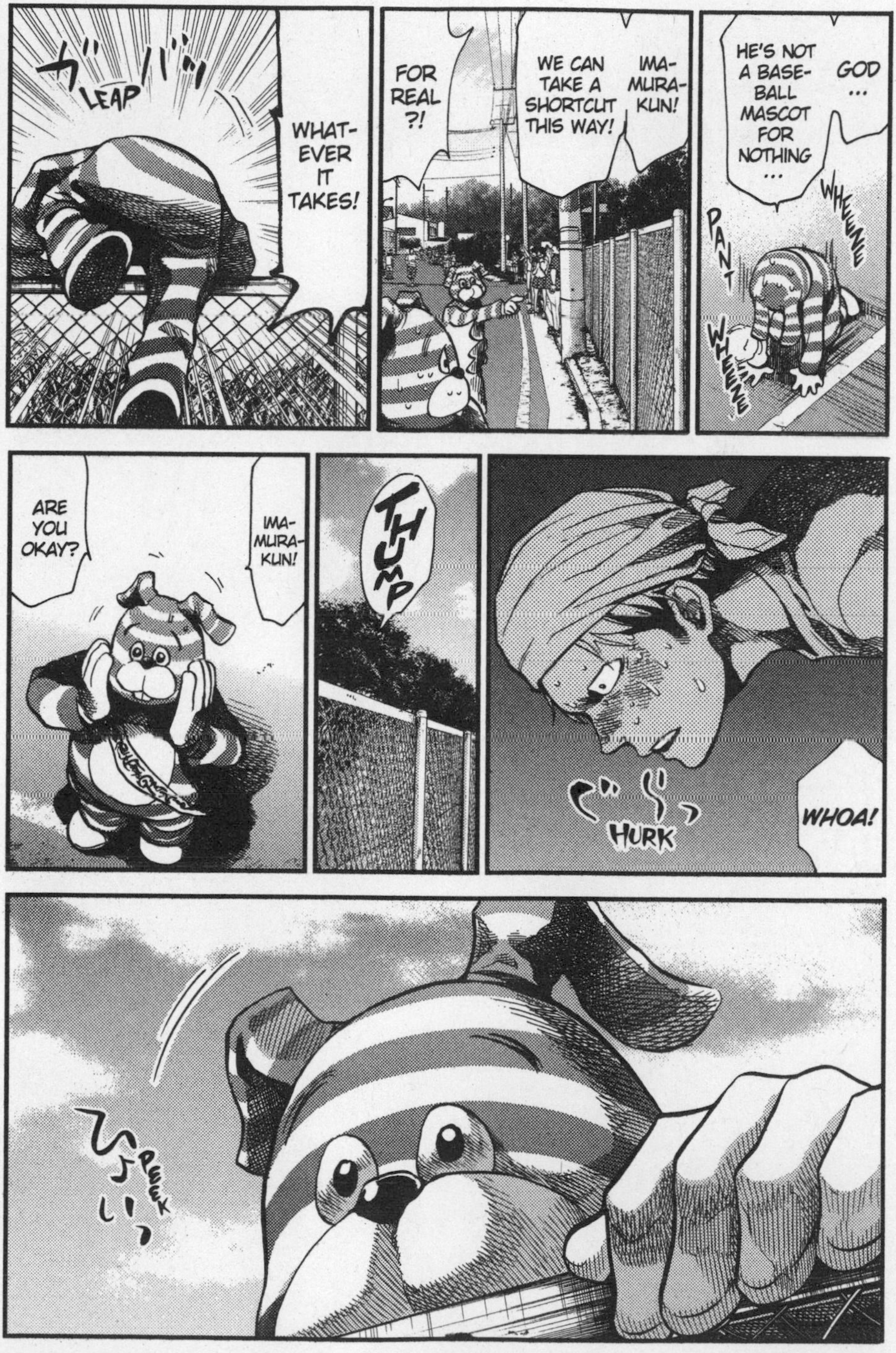
GOD ...
HE'S NOT A BASE-BALL MASCOT FOR NOTHING ...
WHEEZE
PANT
WHEEZE
IMA-MURA-KUN!
WE CAN TAKE A SHORTCUT THIS WAY!
FOR REAL?!
WHAT-EVER IT TAKES!
LEAP
WHOA!
HURK
THUMP
IMA-MURA-KUN!
ARE YOU OKAY?
PEEK

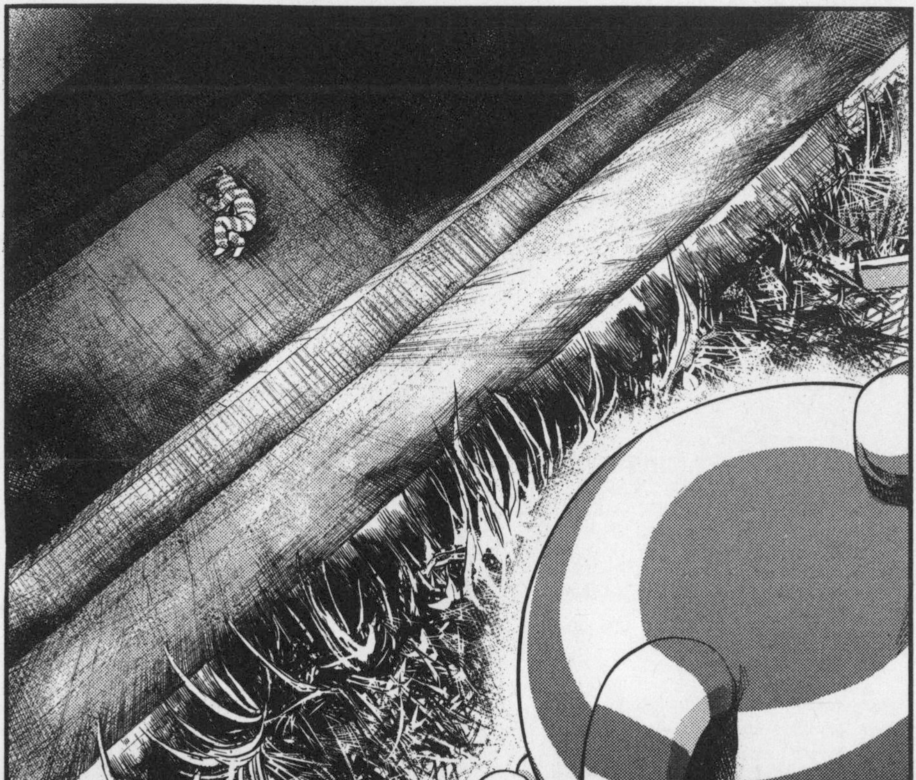
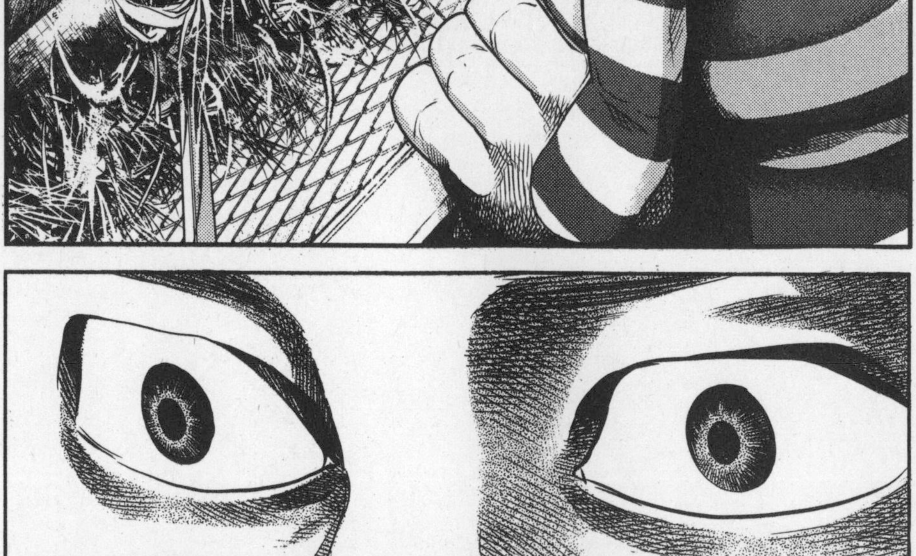

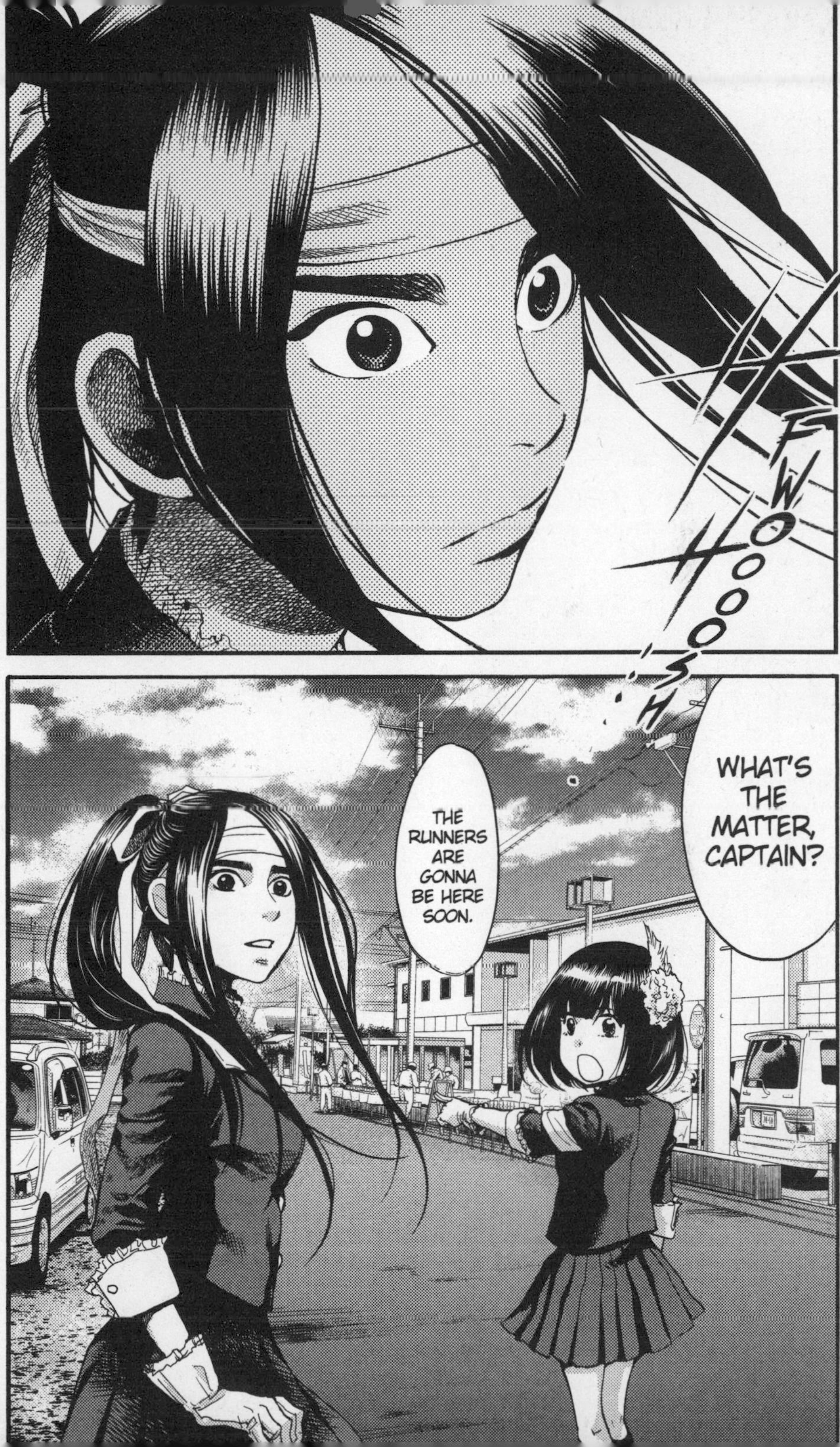
FWOOOOSH
WHAT'S THE MATTER, CAPTAIN?
THE RUNNERS ARE GONNA BE HERE SOON.

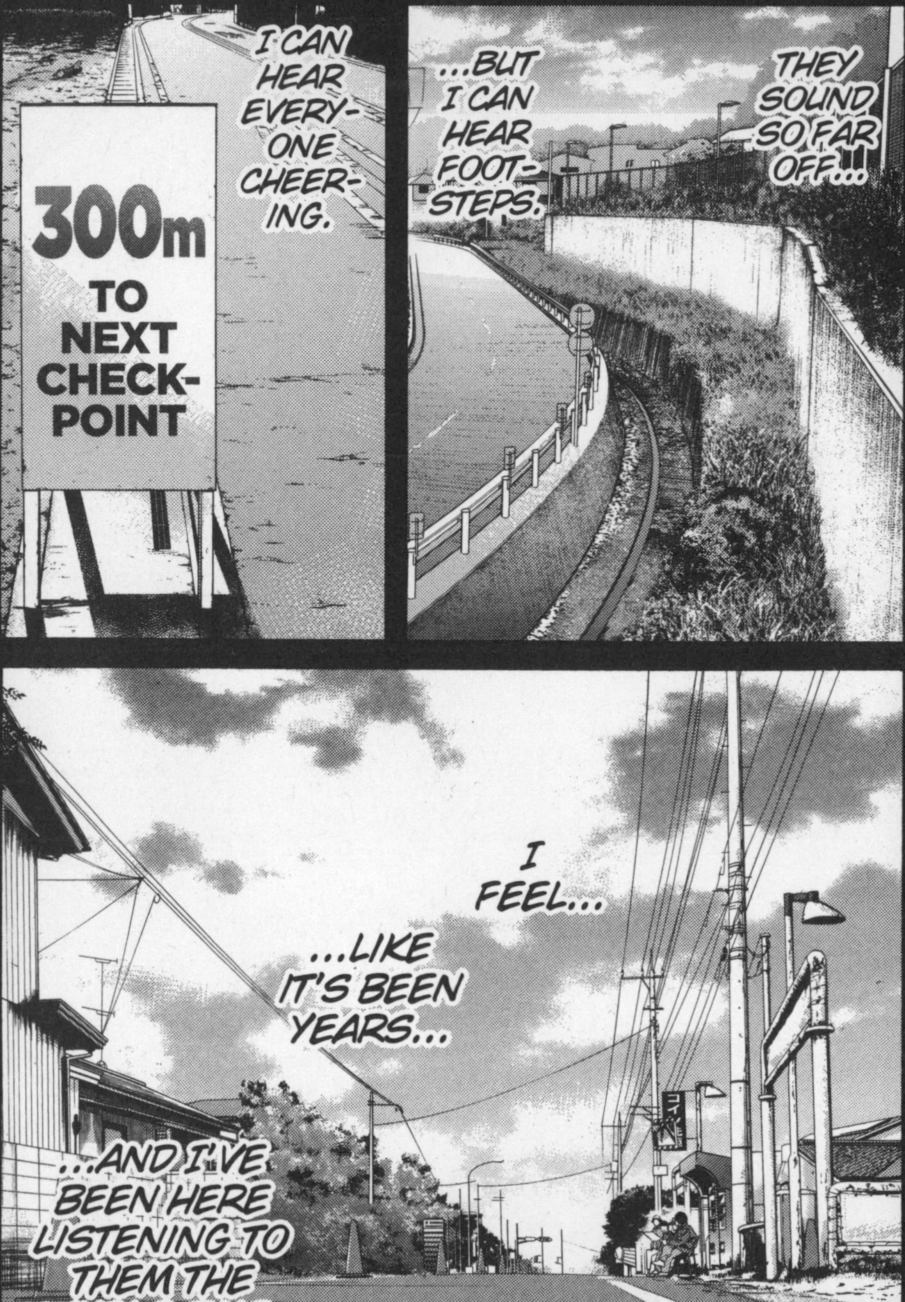
THEY SOUND SO FAR OFF...
...BUT I CAN HEAR FOOT-STEPS.
I CAN HEAR EVERY-ONE CHEER-ING.
300m TO NEXT CHECK-POINT
I FEEL...
...LIKE IT'S BEEN YEARS...
...AND I'VE BEEN HERE LISTENING TO THEM THE WHOLE TIME...

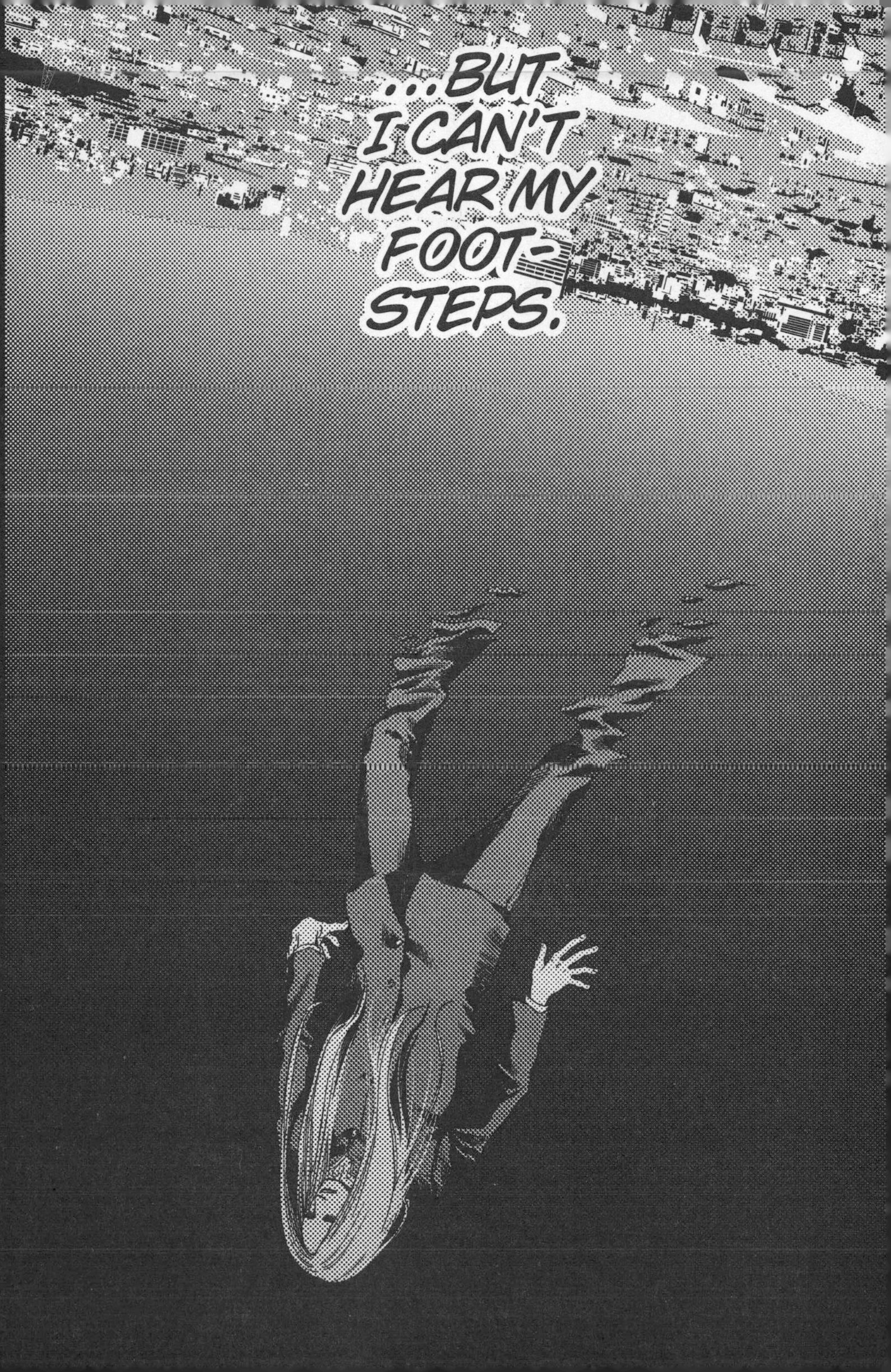
...BUT I CAN'T HEAR MY FOOT-STEPS.

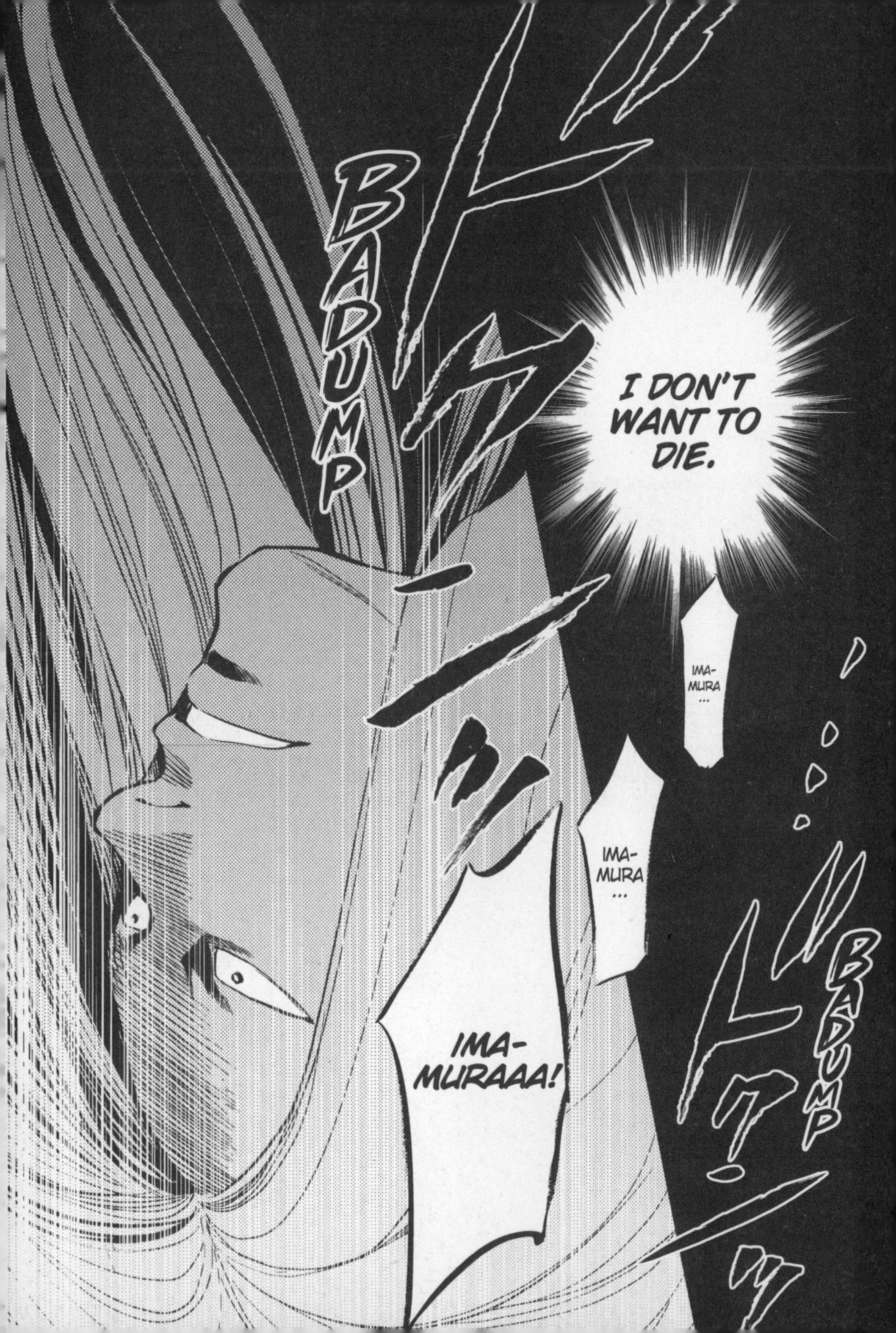
I DON'T WANT TO DIE.
BADUMP
BADUMP
IMA-MURA...
IMA-MURA...
IMA-MURAAA!

Again!!

アゲイン!!

129. CAME A LONG WAY?!

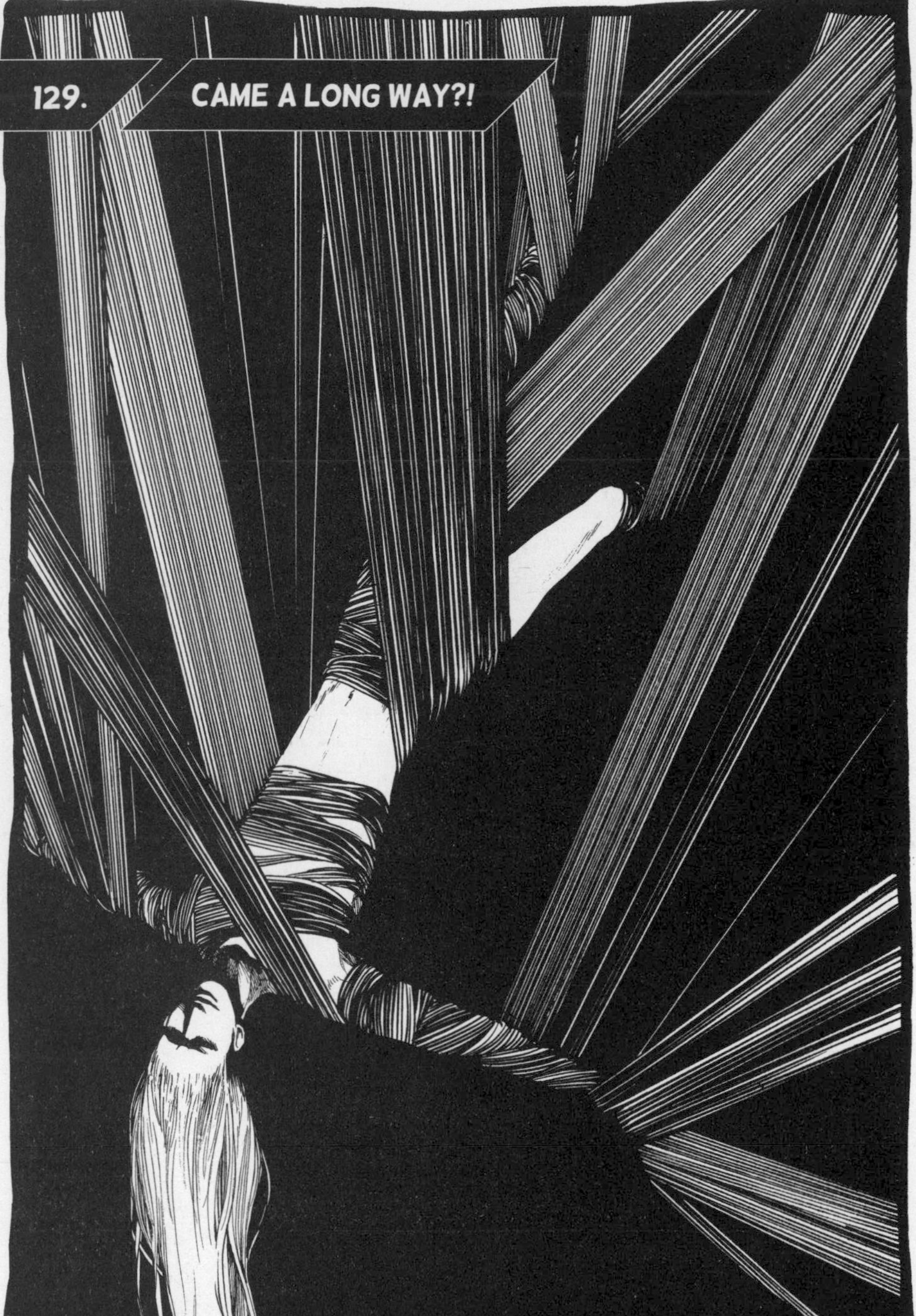

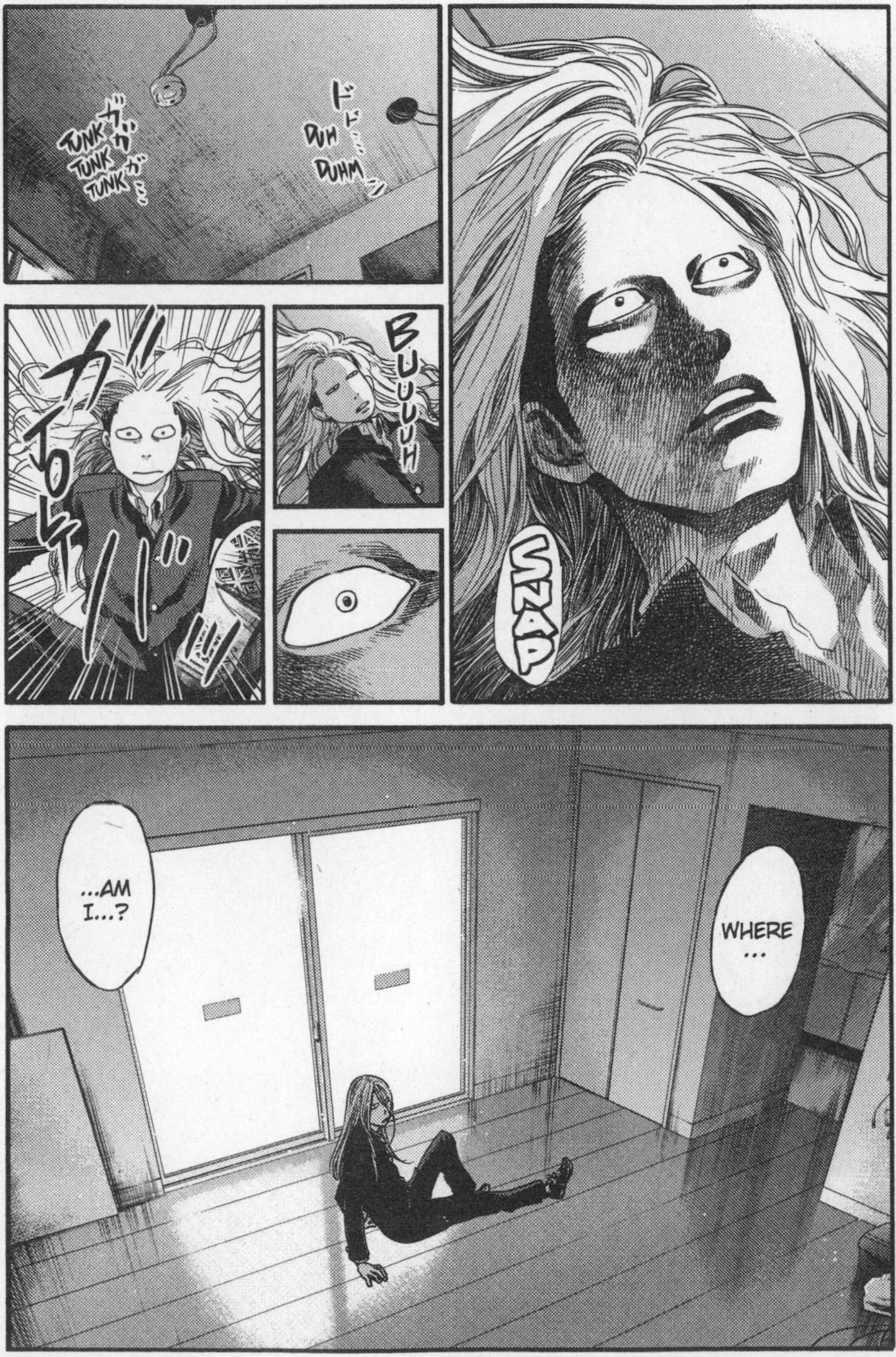
SNAP
DUH DUHM
TUNK TUNK TUNK
BUUUUH
WHERE ...
...AM I...?

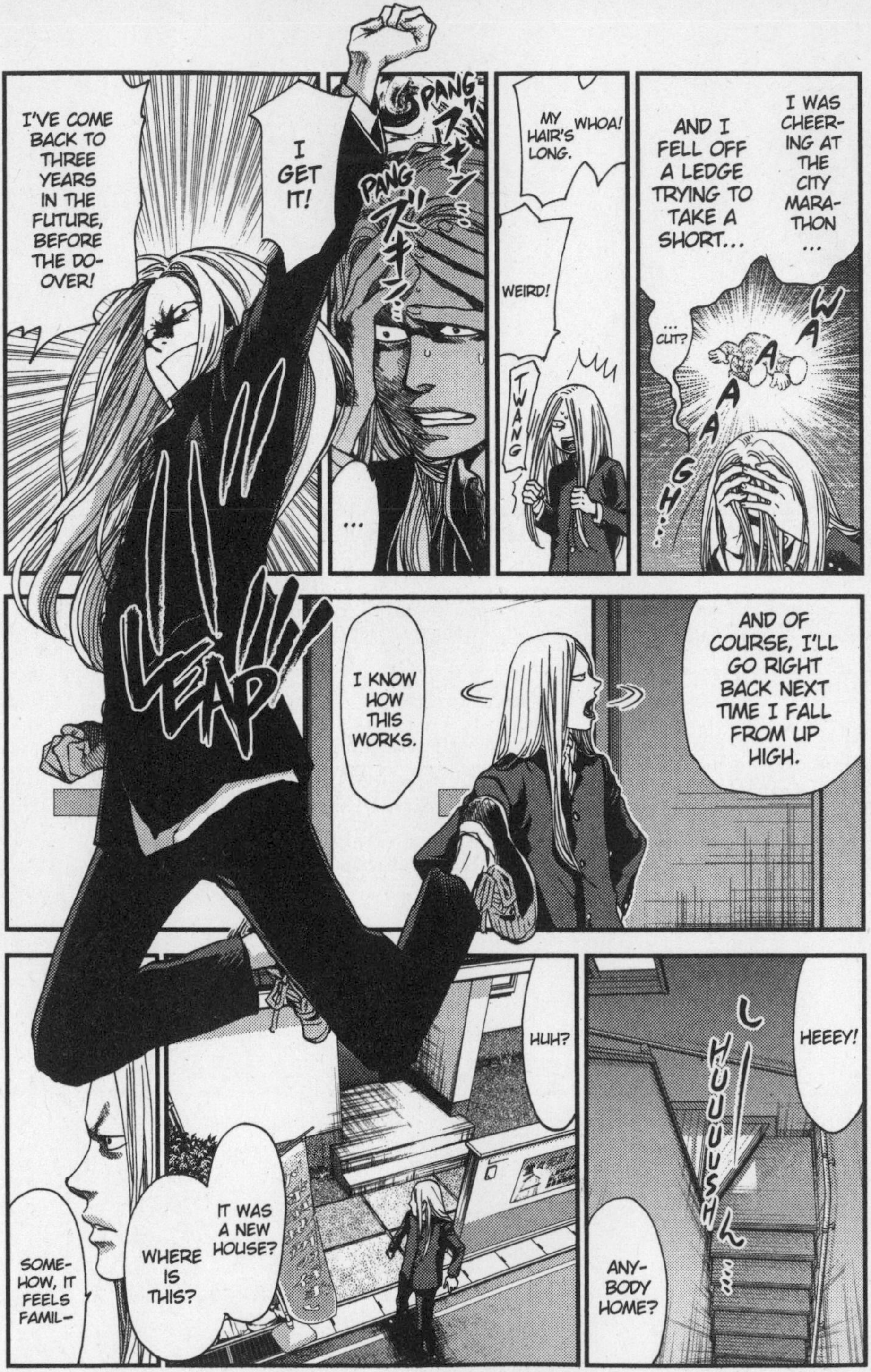
I WAS CHEERING AT THE CITY MARATHON...
AND I FELL OFF A LEDGE TRYING TO TAKE A SHORT...
...CUT?
WAAAAGH...
WHOA!
MY HAIR'S LONG.
WEIRD!
TWANG
SPANG
PANG
...
I GET IT!
I'VE COME BACK TO THREE YEARS IN THE FUTURE, BEFORE THE DO-OVER!
LEAP
AND OF COURSE, I'LL GO RIGHT BACK NEXT TIME I FALL FROM UP HIGH.
I KNOW HOW THIS WORKS.
HEEEY!
HUUUUSH...
ANYBODY HOME?
HUH?
IT WAS A NEW HOUSE?
WHERE IS THIS?
SOMEHOW, IT FEELS FAMIL-

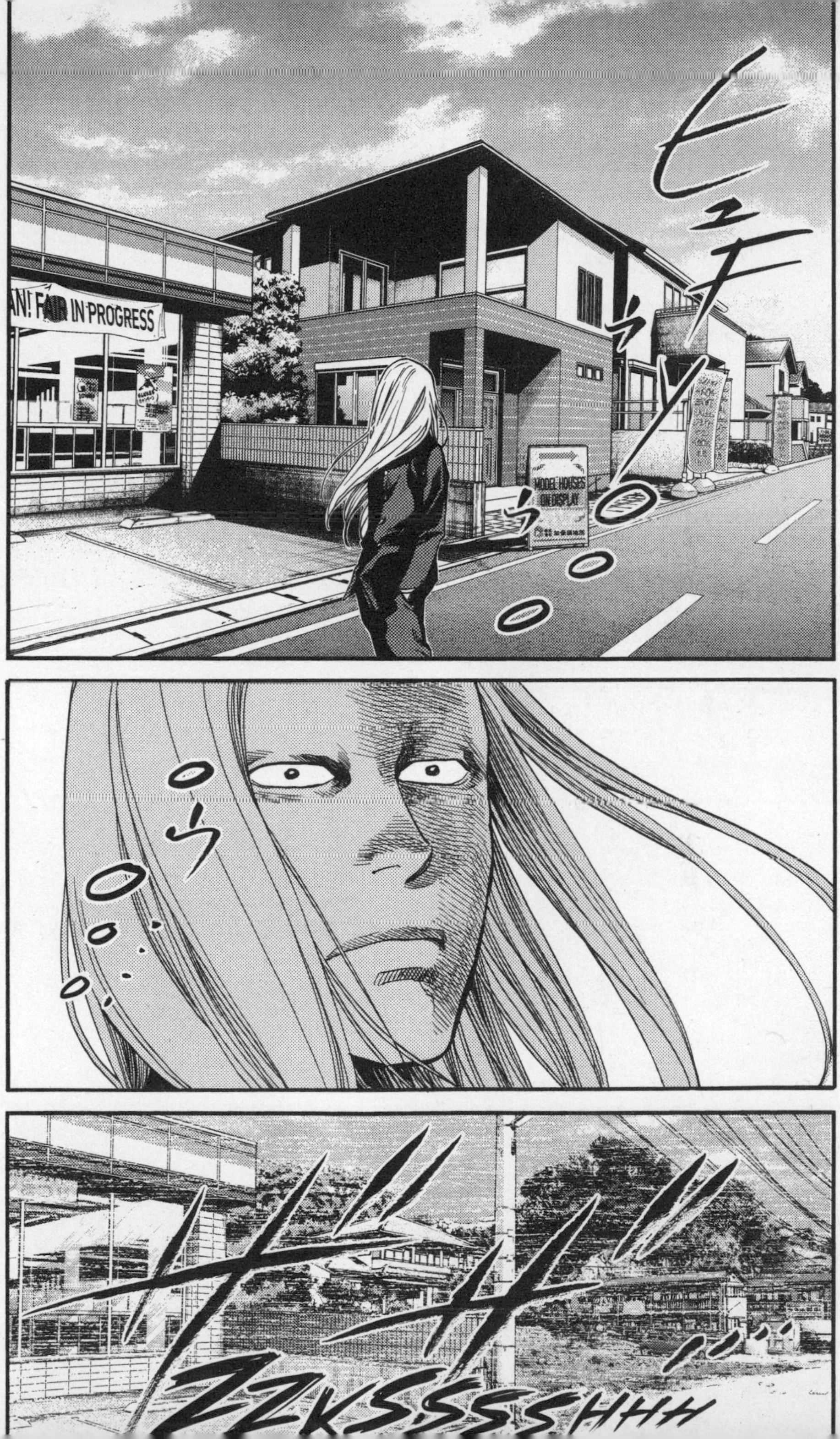
IN PROGRESS
MODEL HOUSES ON DISPLAY
ZZKSSSSSHHH

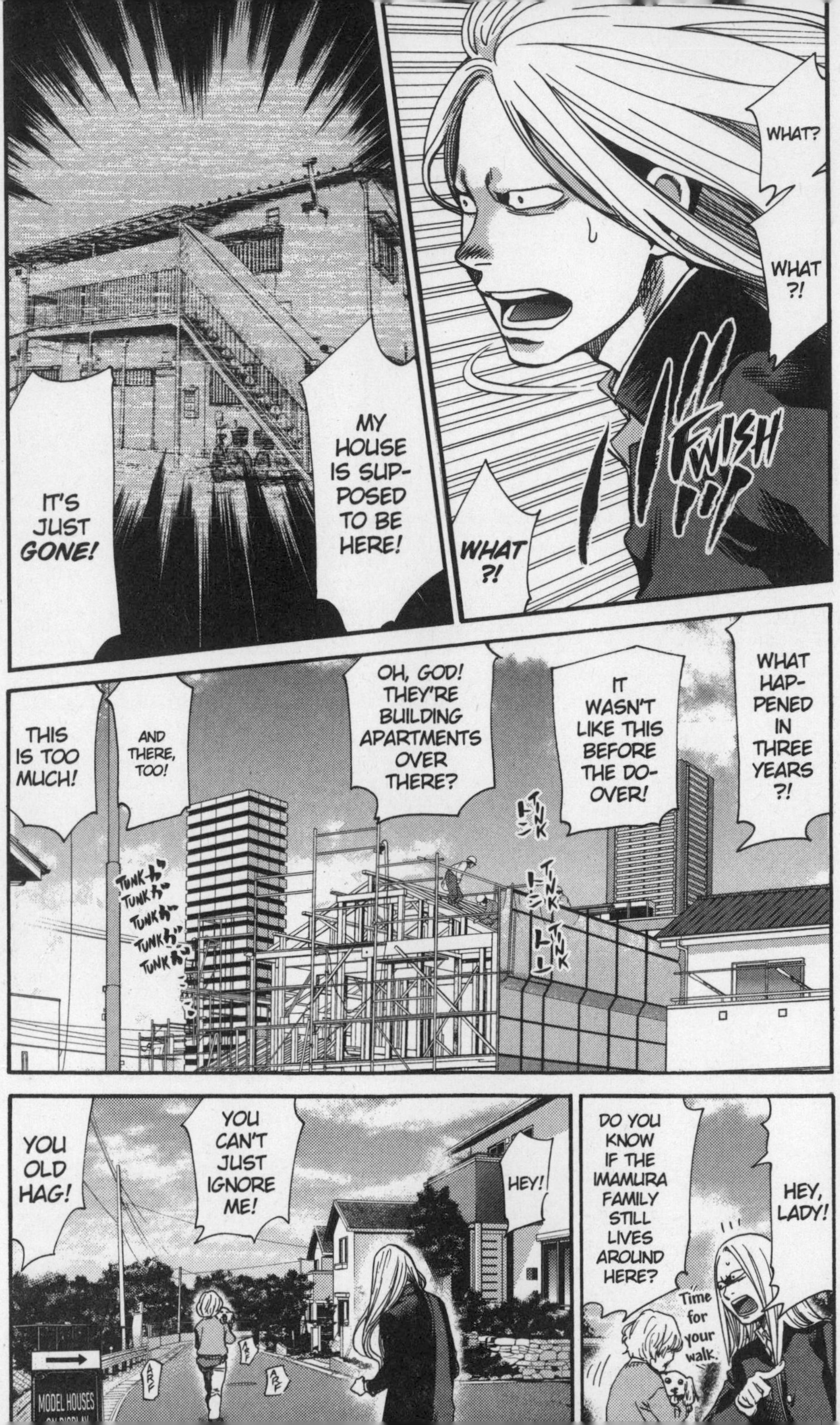
WHAT?
WHAT ?!
FWISH
WHAT ?!
MY HOUSE IS SUP-POSED TO BE HERE!
IT'S JUST GONE!
WHAT HAP-PENED IN THREE YEARS ?!
IT WASN'T LIKE THIS BEFORE THE DO-OVER!
TINK
TINK
TINK
OH, GOD! THEY'RE BUILDING APARTMENTS OVER THERE?
AND THERE, TOO!
THIS IS TOO MUCH!
TUNK TUNK TUNK TUNK TUNK
HEY, LADY!
DO YOU KNOW IF THE IMAMURA FAMILY STILL LIVES AROUND HERE?
Time for your walk.
HEY!
YOU CAN'T JUST IGNORE ME!
YOU OLD HAG!
ARF
ARF
ARF
MODEL HOUSES

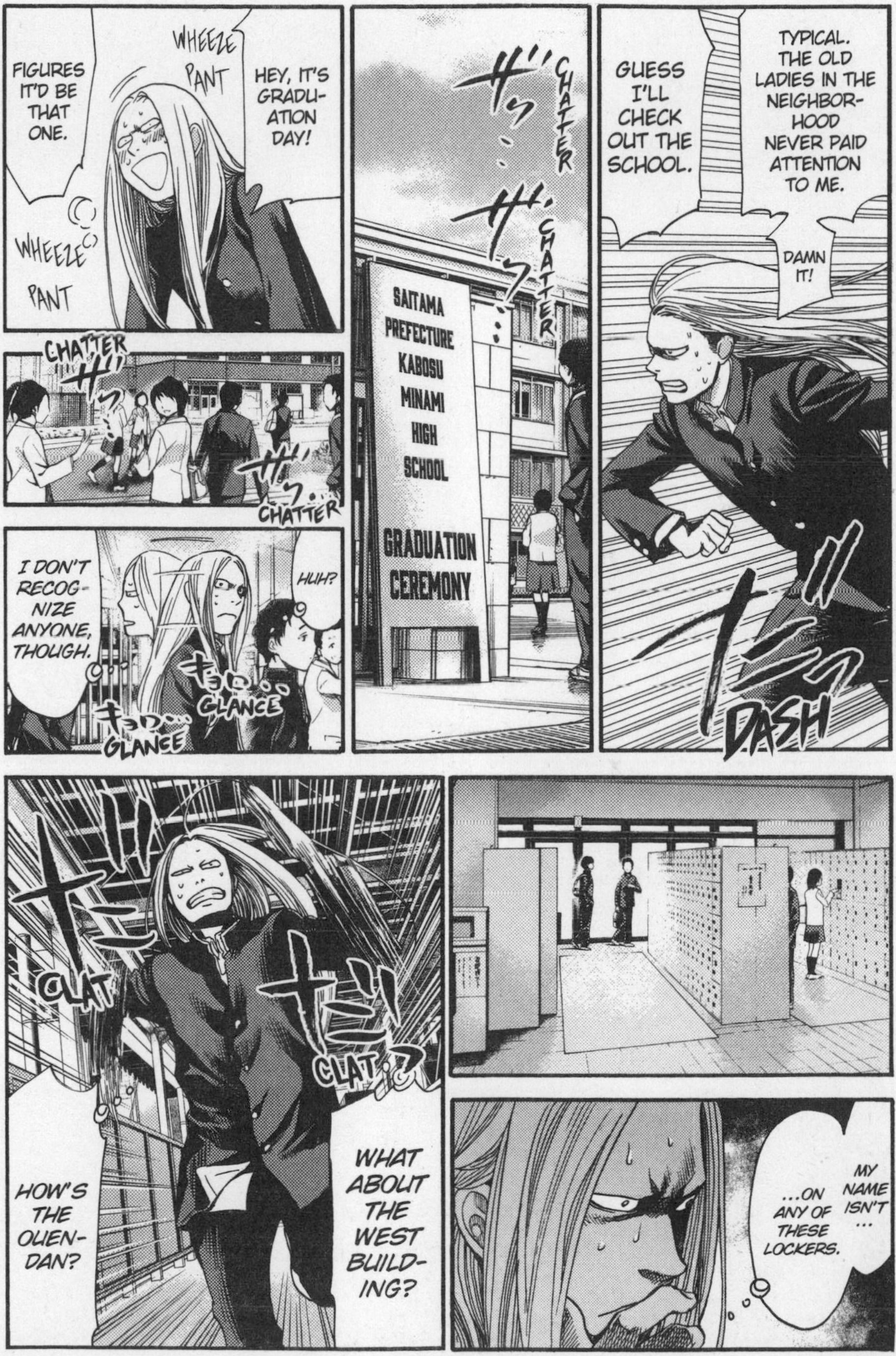
TYPICAL. THE OLD LADIES IN THE NEIGHBORHOOD NEVER PAID ATTENTION TO ME.
GUESS I'LL CHECK OUT THE SCHOOL.
DAMN IT!
DASH
CHATTER
CHATTER
CHATTER
SAITAMA PREFECTURE KABOSU MINAMI HIGH SCHOOL
GRADUATION CEREMONY
HEY, IT'S GRADUATION DAY!
WHEEZE
PANT
FIGURES IT'D BE THAT ONE.
WHEEZE
PANT
CHATTER
CHATTER
HUH?
I DON'T RECOGNIZE ANYONE, THOUGH.
GLANCE
GLANCE
MY NAME ISN'T...
...ON ANY OF THESE LOCKERS.
WHAT ABOUT THE WEST BUILDING?
HOW'S THE OUEN-DAN?
CLAT
CLAT

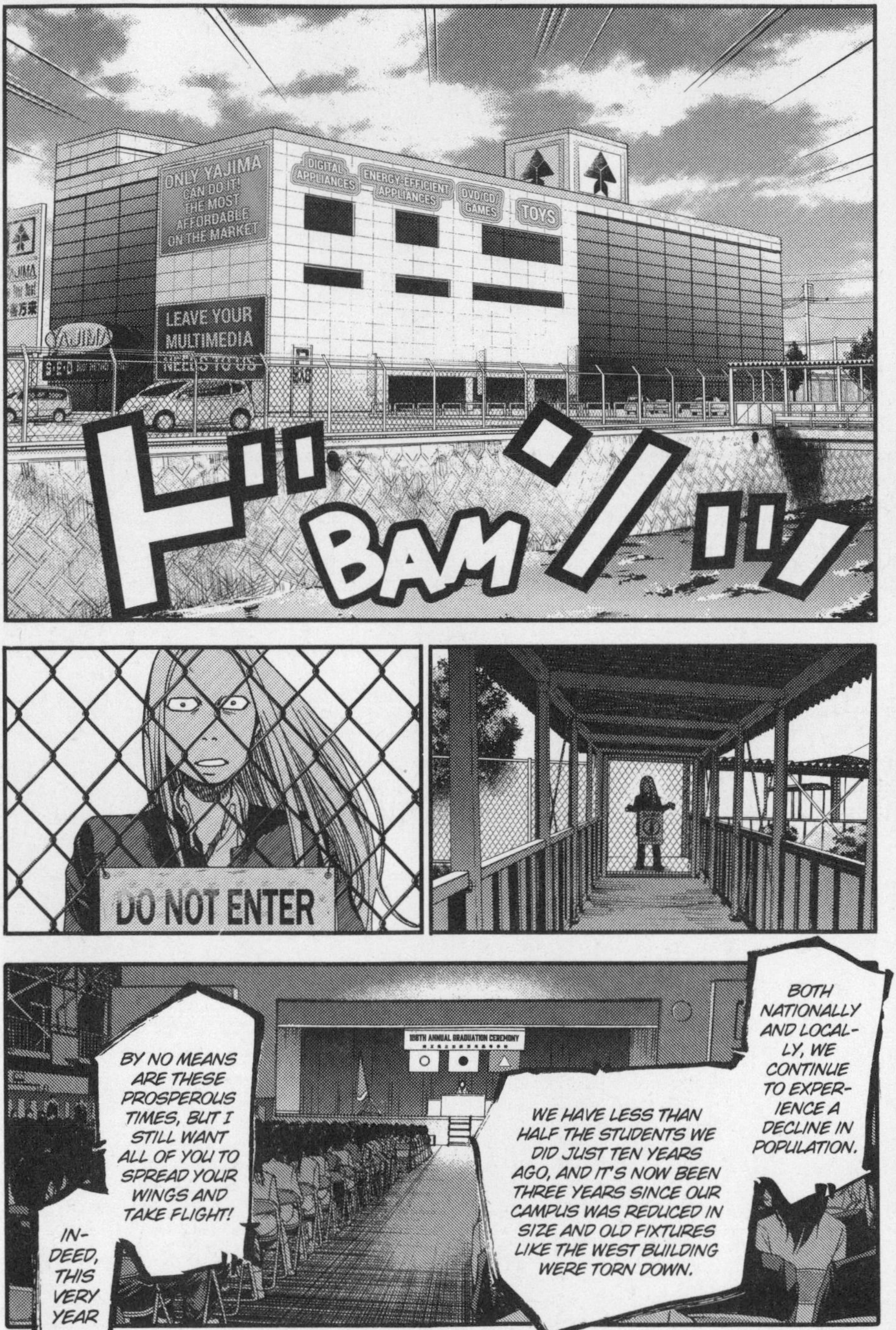
ONLY YAJIMA CAN DO IT! THE MOST AFFORDABLE ON THE MARKET
DIGITAL APPLIANCES
ENERGY-EFFICIENT APPLIANCES
DVD/CD/GAMES
TOYS
LEAVE YOUR MULTIMEDIA NEEDS TO US
YAJIMA
BAM
DO NOT ENTER
BOTH NATIONALLY AND LOCAL-LY, WE CONTINUE TO EXPER-IENCE A DECLINE IN POPULATION.
WE HAVE LESS THAN HALF THE STUDENTS WE DID JUST TEN YEARS AGO, AND IT'S NOW BEEN THREE YEARS SINCE OUR CAMPUS WAS REDUCED IN SIZE AND OLD FIXTURES LIKE THE WEST BUILDING WERE TORN DOWN.
BY NO MEANS ARE THESE PROSPEROUS TIMES, BUT I STILL WANT ALL OF YOU TO SPREAD YOUR WINGS AND TAKE FLIGHT!
IN-DEED, THIS VERY YEAR ...

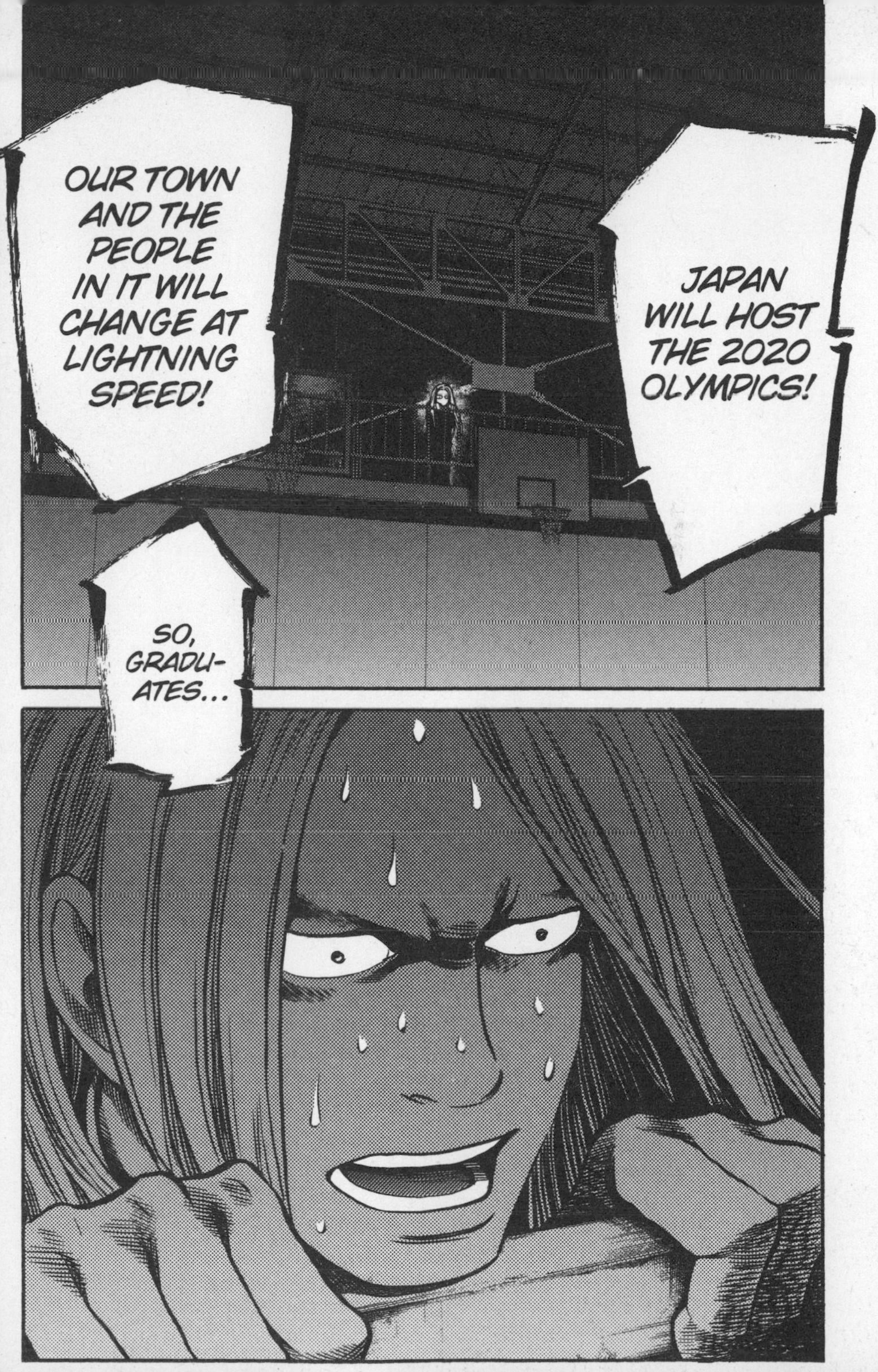
JAPAN WILL HOST THE 2020 OLYMPICS!
OUR TOWN AND THE PEOPLE IN IT WILL CHANGE AT LIGHTNING SPEED!
SO, GRADUATES...

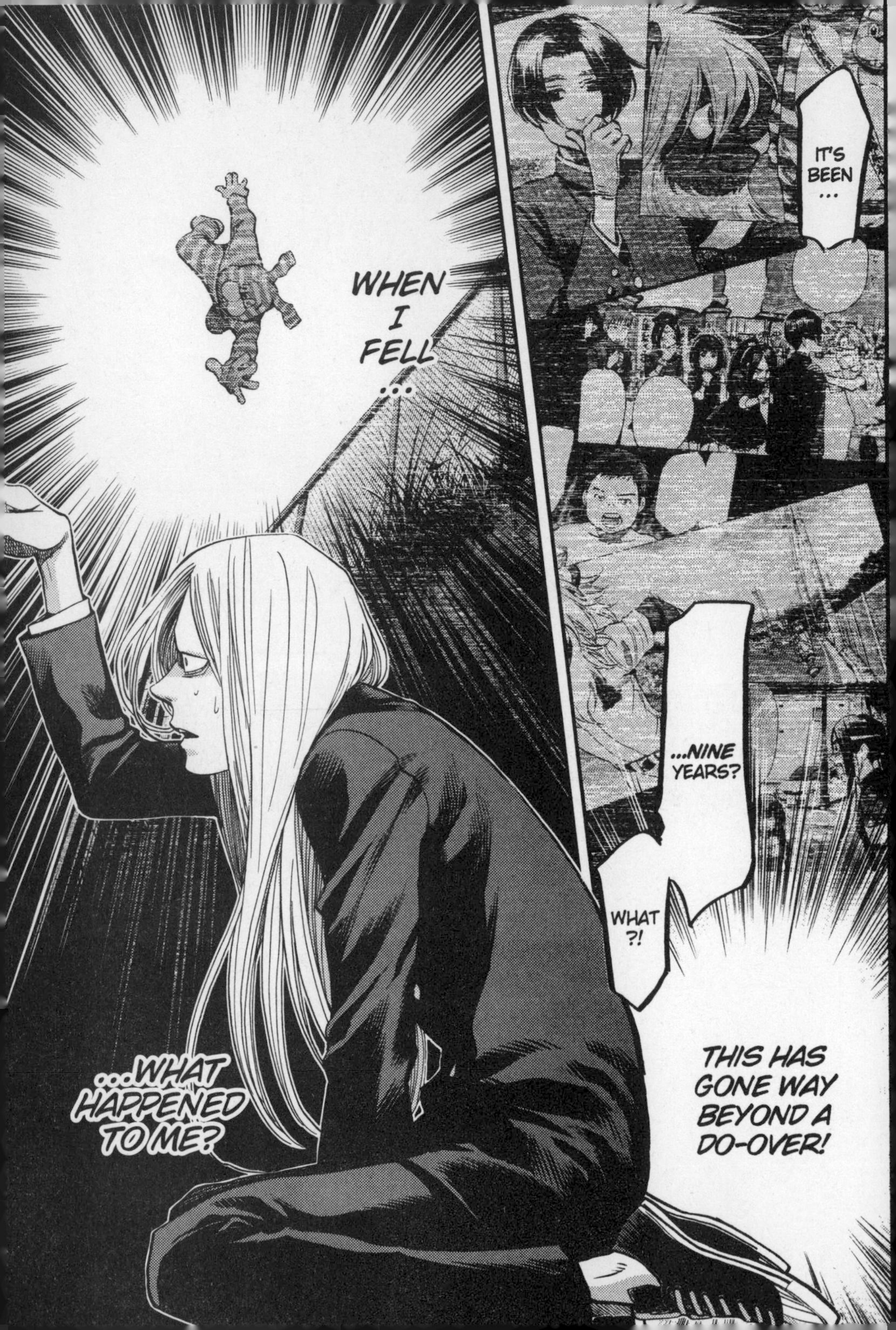
IT'S BEEN ...
...NINE YEARS?
WHAT ?!
WHEN I FELL ...
THIS HAS GONE WAY BEYOND A DO-OVER!
...WHAT HAPPENED TO ME?

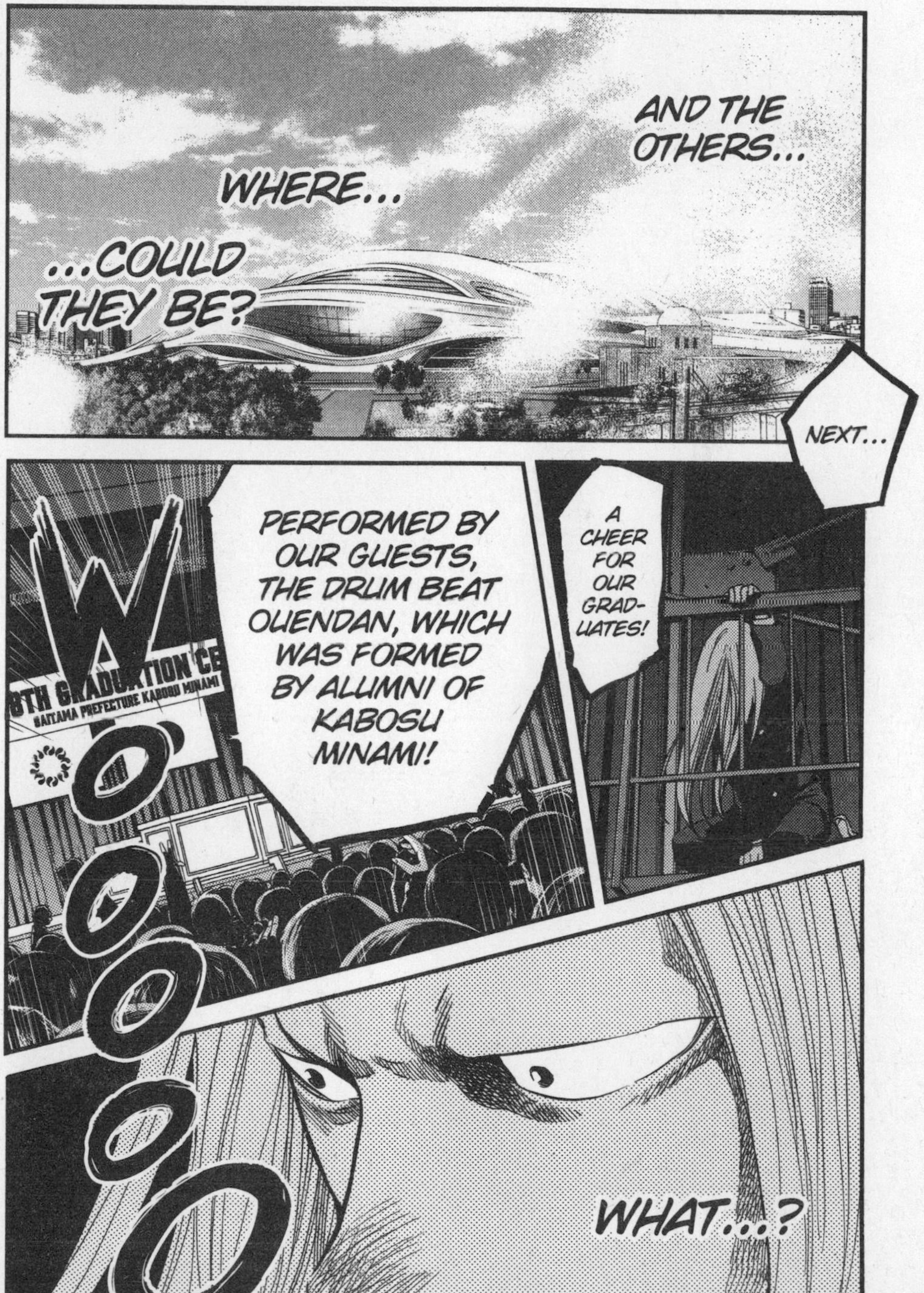
AND THE OTHERS...
WHERE...
...COULD THEY BE?
NEXT...
A CHEER FOR OUR GRAD-UATES!
PERFORMED BY OUR GUESTS, THE DRUM BEAT OUENDAN, WHICH WAS FORMED BY ALUMNI OF KABOSU MINAMI!
WOOOOOO
WHAT...?

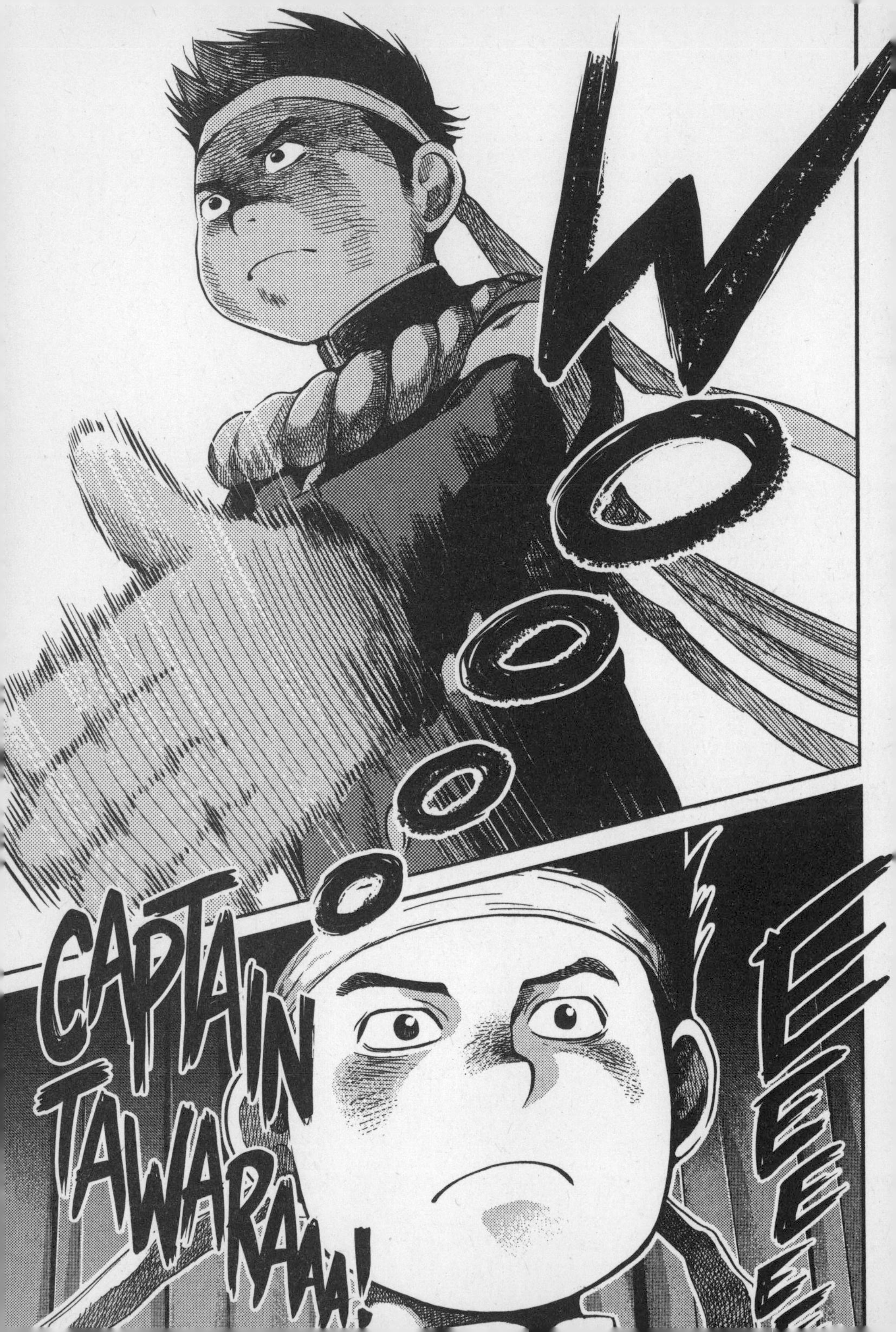

WOOOO
EEEE
CAPTAIN TAWARAAAA!

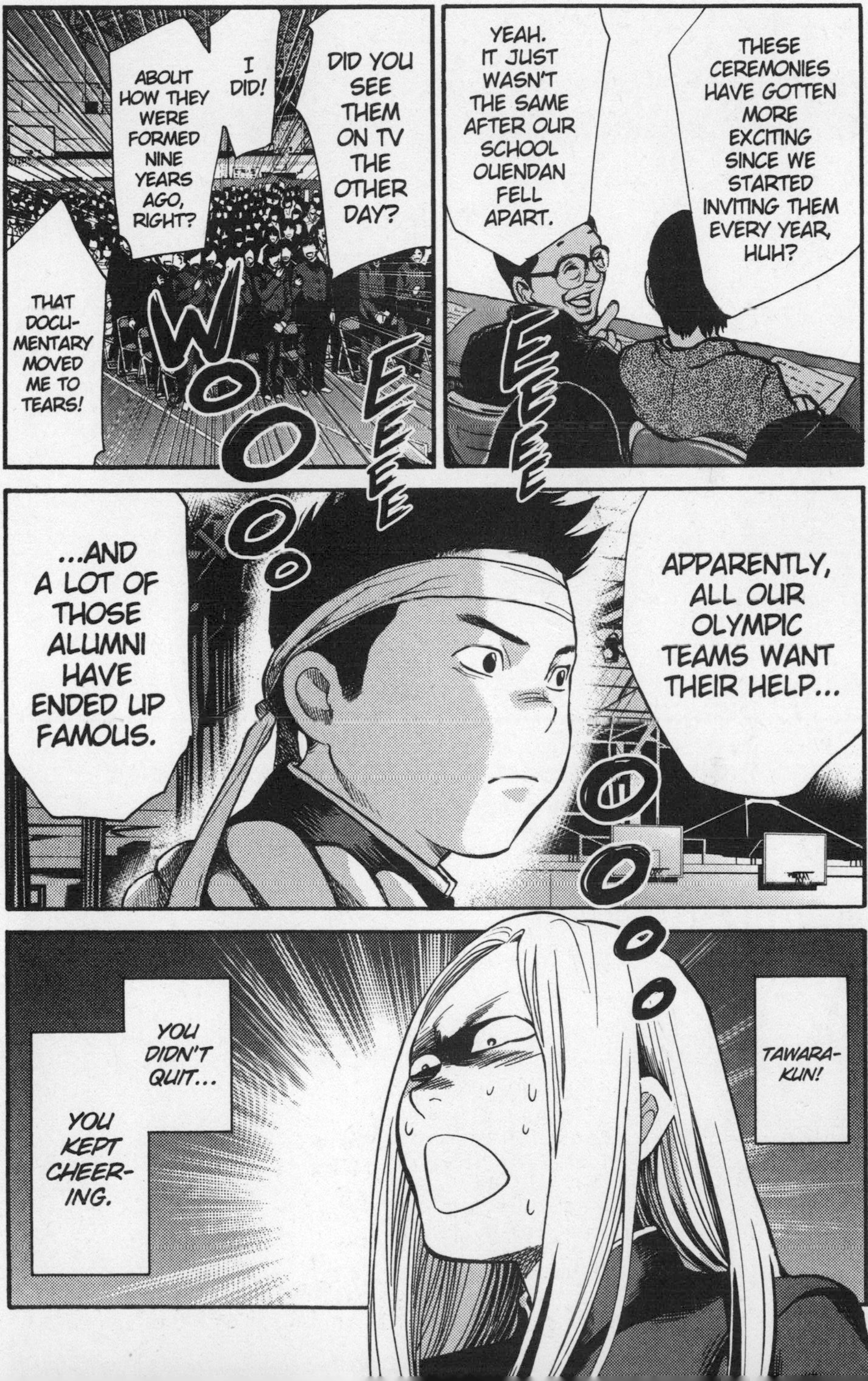
THESE CEREMONIES HAVE GOTTEN MORE EXCITING SINCE WE STARTED INVITING THEM EVERY YEAR, HUH?
YEAH. IT JUST WASN'T THE SAME AFTER OUR SCHOOL OUENDAN FELL APART.
DID YOU SEE THEM ON TV THE OTHER DAY?
I DID!
ABOUT HOW THEY WERE FORMED NINE YEARS AGO, RIGHT?
THAT DOCUMENTARY MOVED ME TO TEARS!
APPARENTLY, ALL OUR OLYMPIC TEAMS WANT THEIR HELP...
...AND A LOT OF THOSE ALUMNI HAVE ENDED UP FAMOUS.
TAWARA-KUN!
YOU DIDN'T QUIT...
YOU KEPT CHEERING.

130. NINE YEARS LATER

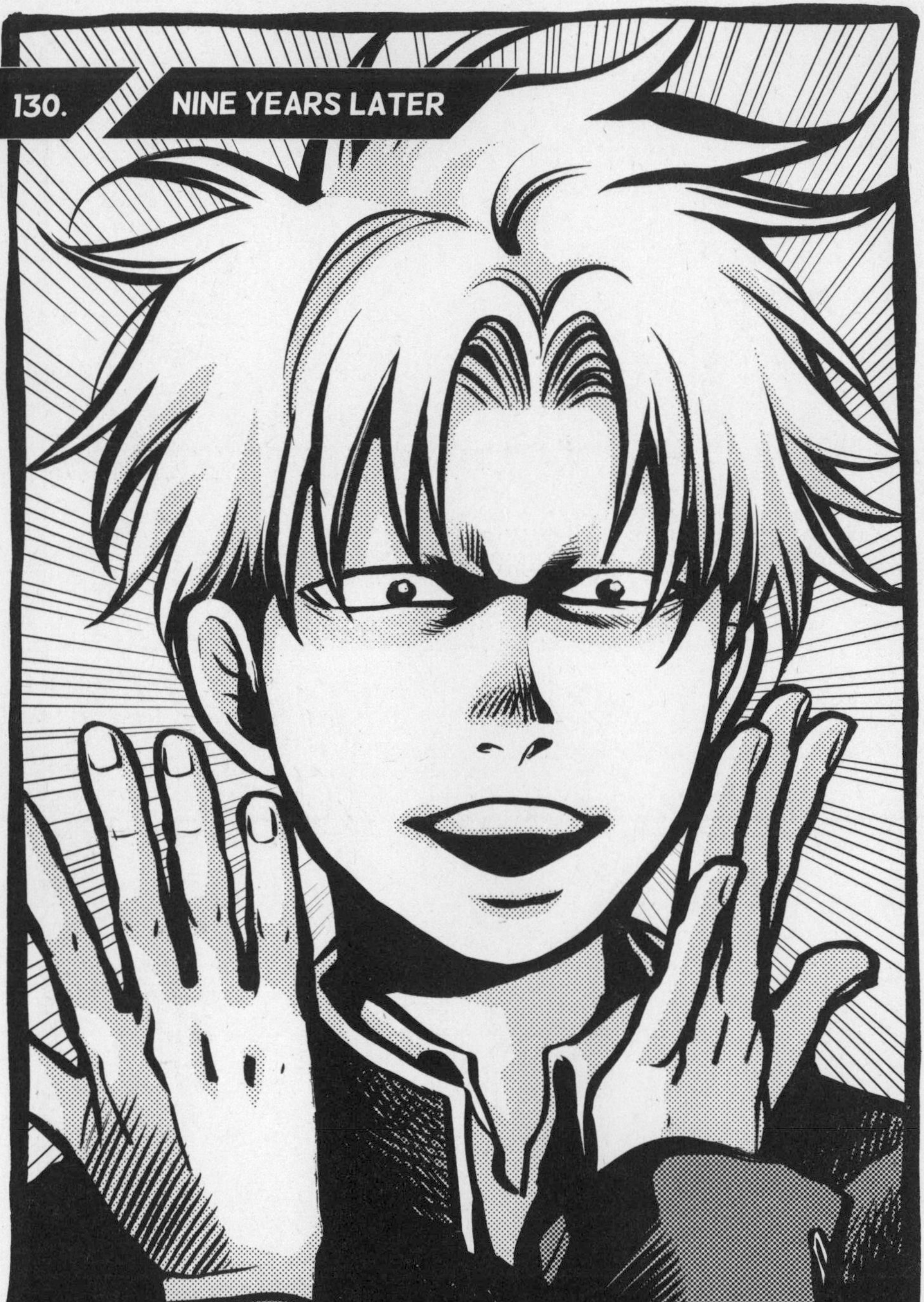

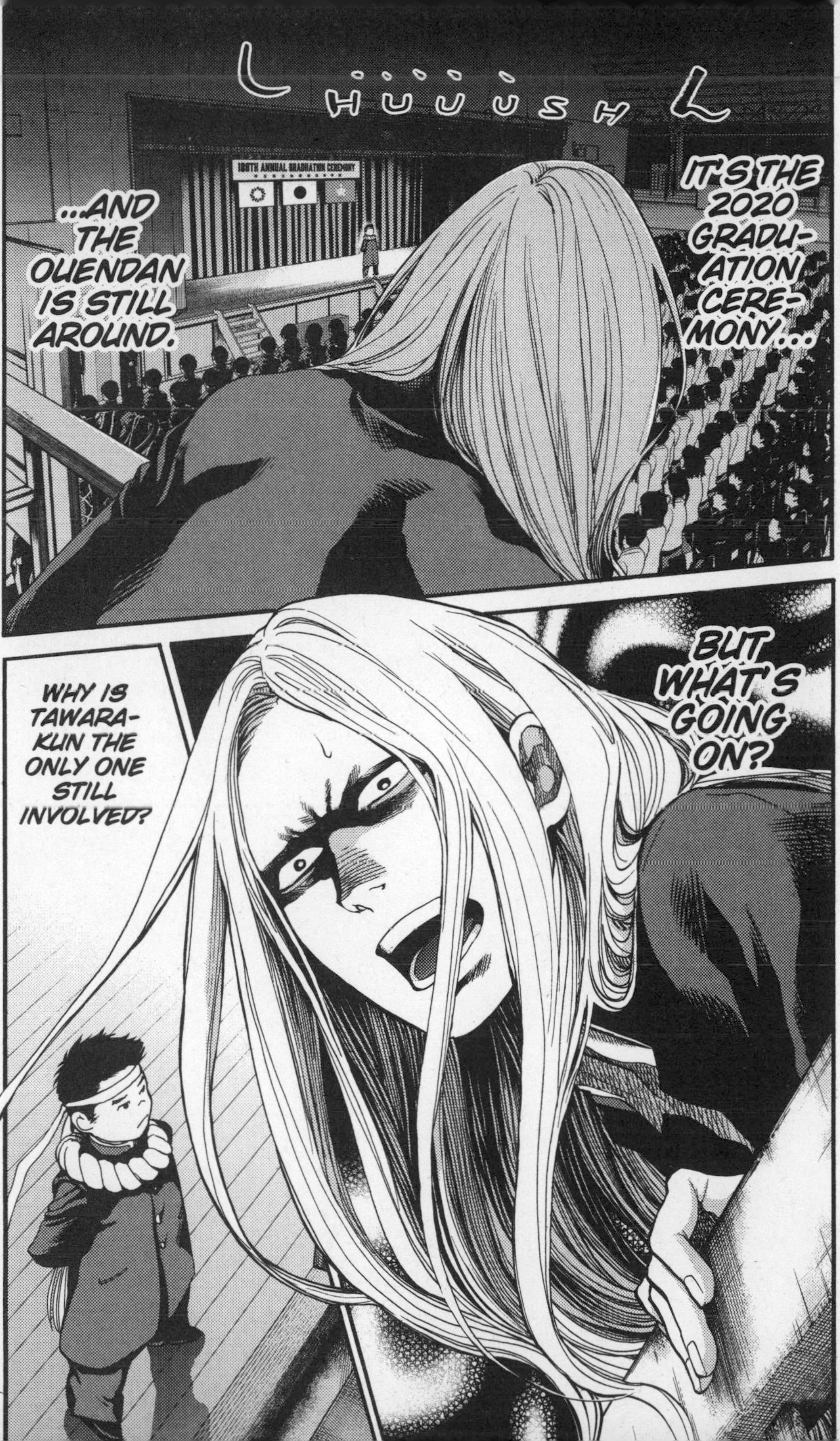
HUUUSH
IT'S THE 2020 GRADUATION CEREMONY...
...AND THE OUENDAN IS STILL AROUND.
BUT WHAT'S GOING ON?
WHY IS TAWARA-KUN THE ONLY ONE STILL INVOLVED?

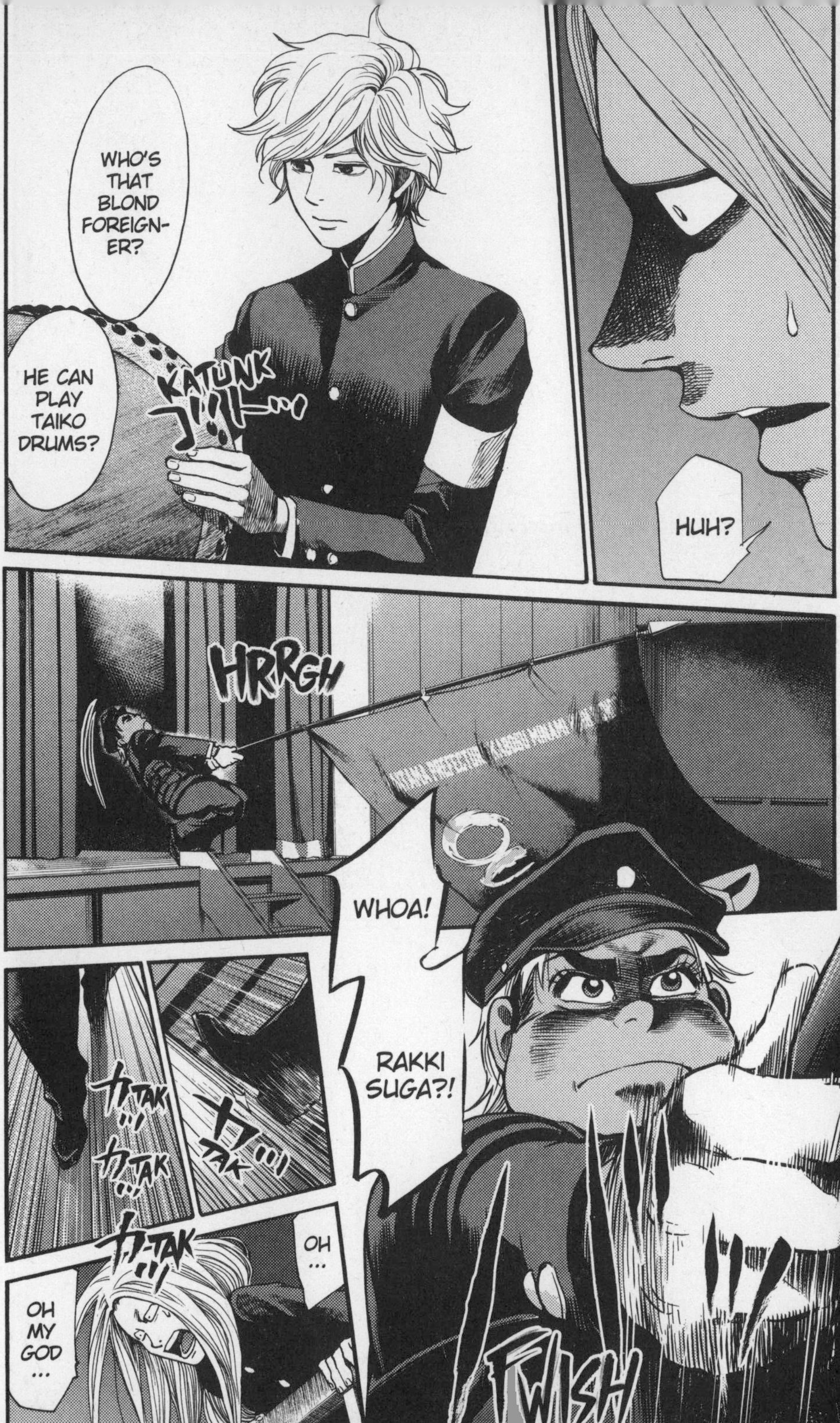
HUH?
WHO'S THAT BLOND FOREIGNER?
HE CAN PLAY TAIKO DRUMS?
KATUNK
HRRGH
WHOA!
RAKKI SUGA?!
FWISH
TAK
TAK
TAK
TAK
OH ...
OH MY GOD ...

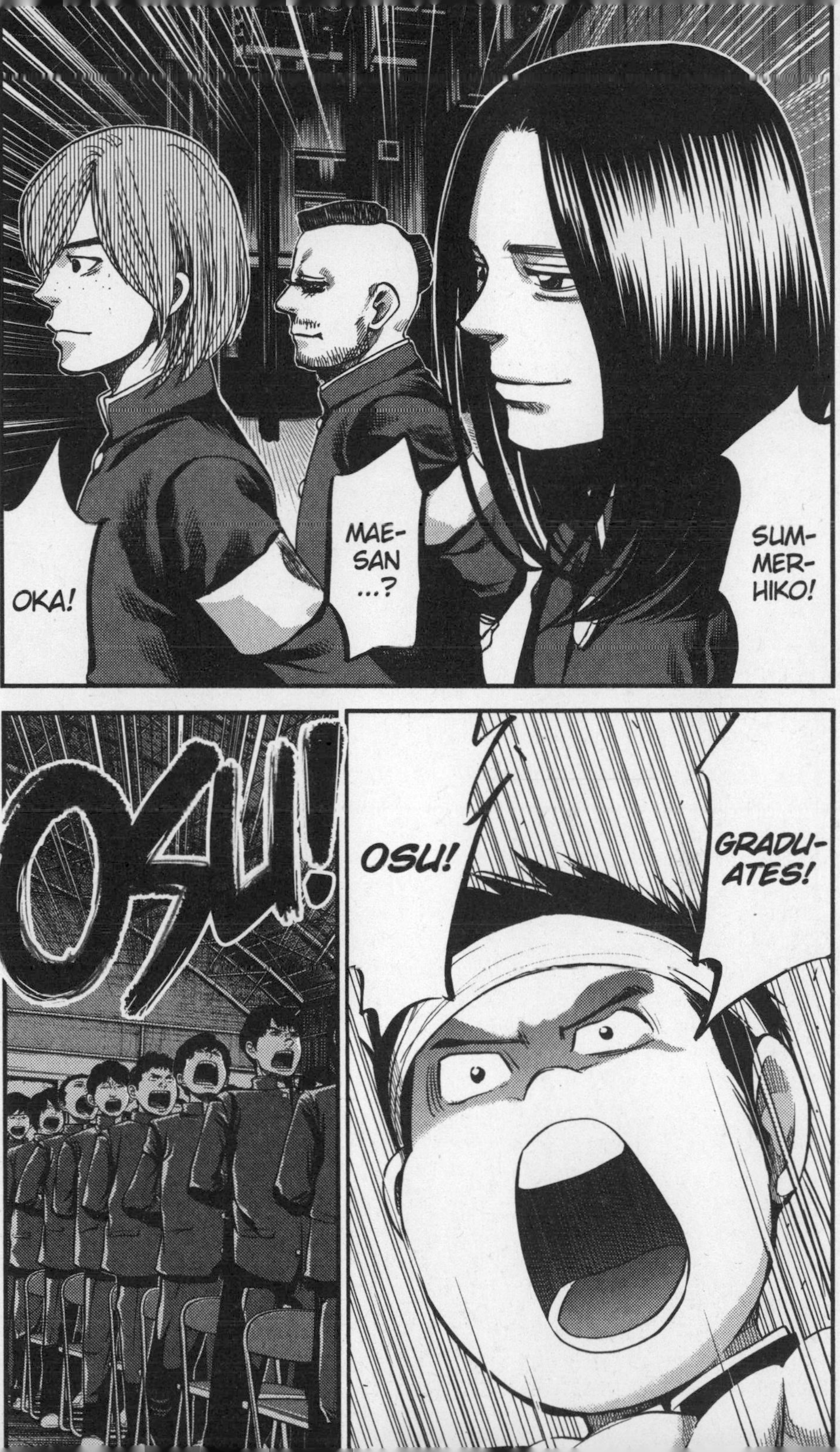
SUM-
MER-
HIKO!
MAE-
SAN
...?
OKA!
GRADU-
ATES!
OSU!
OSU!

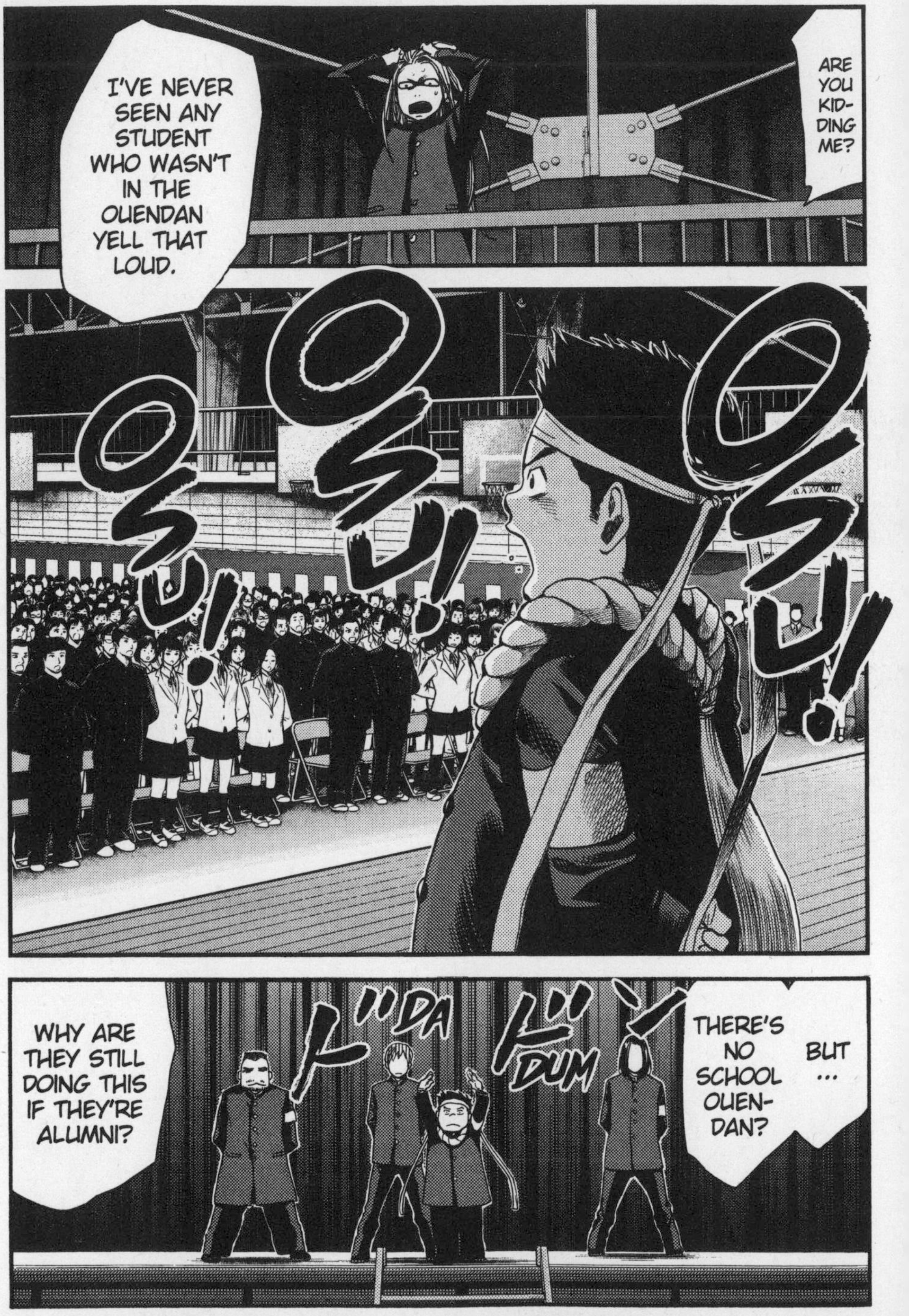
ARE YOU KID-DING ME?
I'VE NEVER SEEN ANY STUDENT WHO WASN'T IN THE OUENDAN YELL THAT LOUD.
BUT ...
THERE'S NO SCHOOL OUEN-DAN?
DUM
DA
WHY ARE THEY STILL DOING THIS IF THEY'RE ALUMNI?

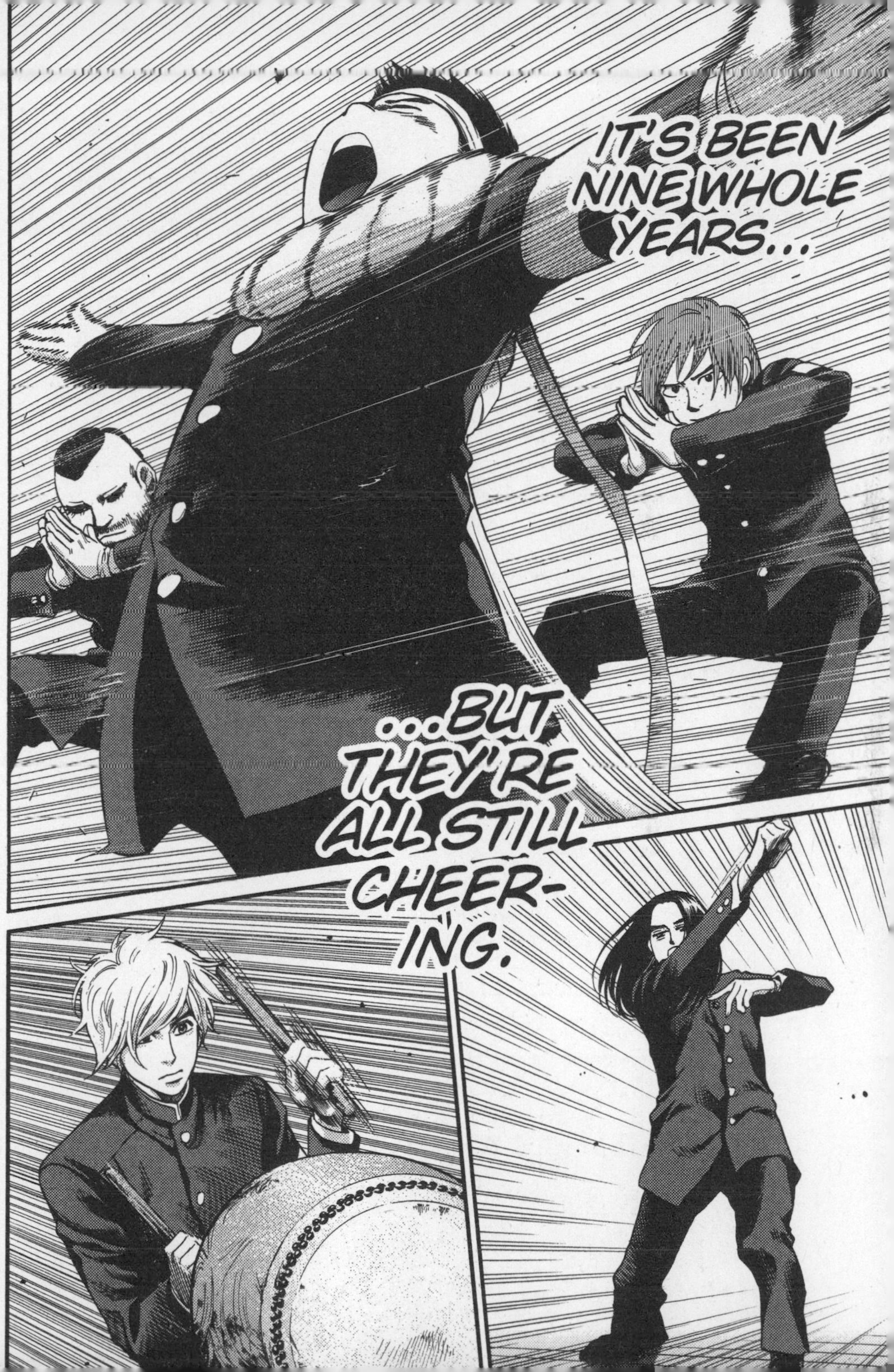
IT'S BEEN NINE WHOLE YEARS...
...BUT THEY'RE ALL STILL CHEER-ING.

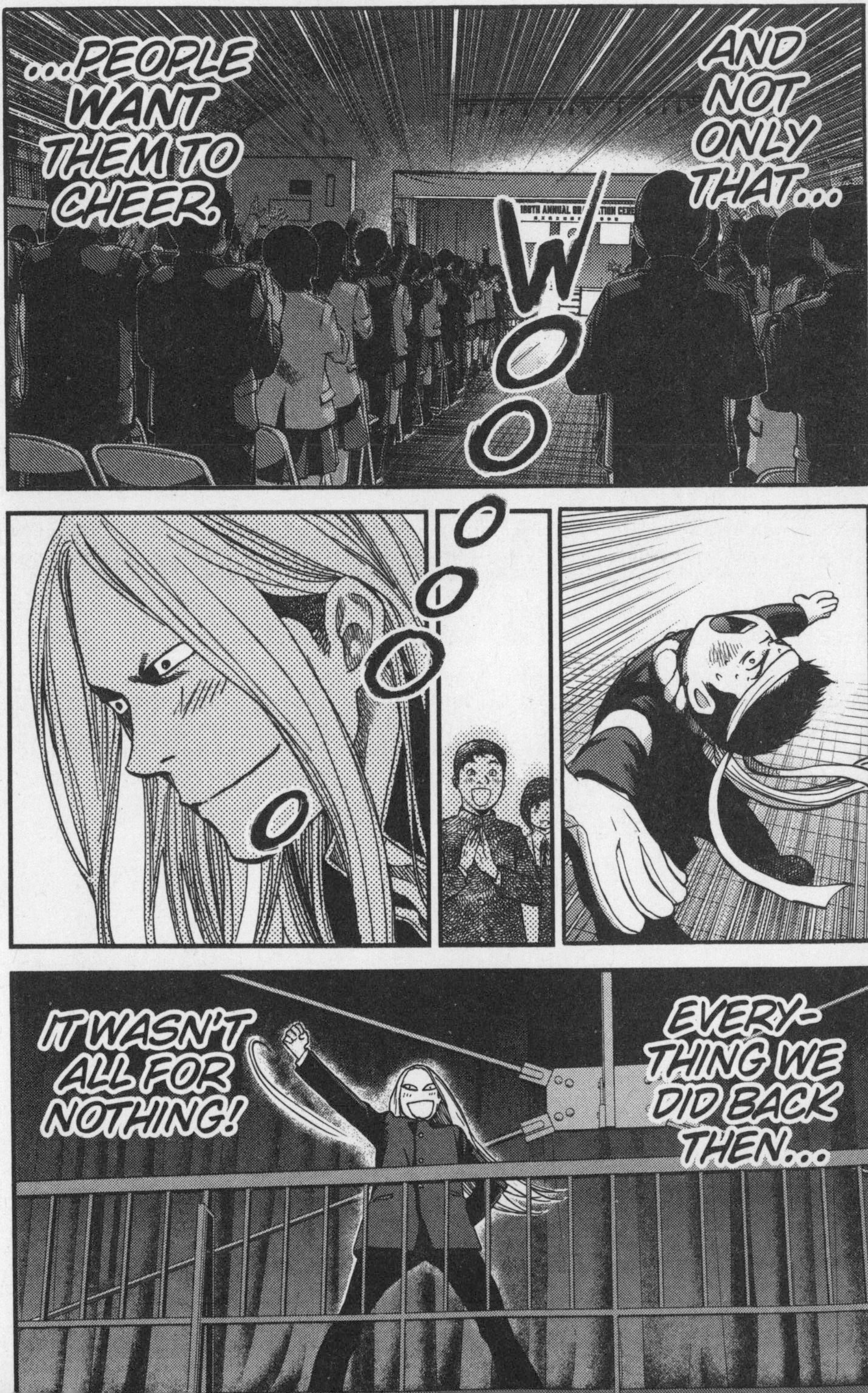
AND NOT ONLY THAT...
...PEOPLE WANT THEM TO CHEER.
WOOOOOOO
EVERY-THING WE DID BACK THEN...
IT WASN'T ALL FOR NOTHING!

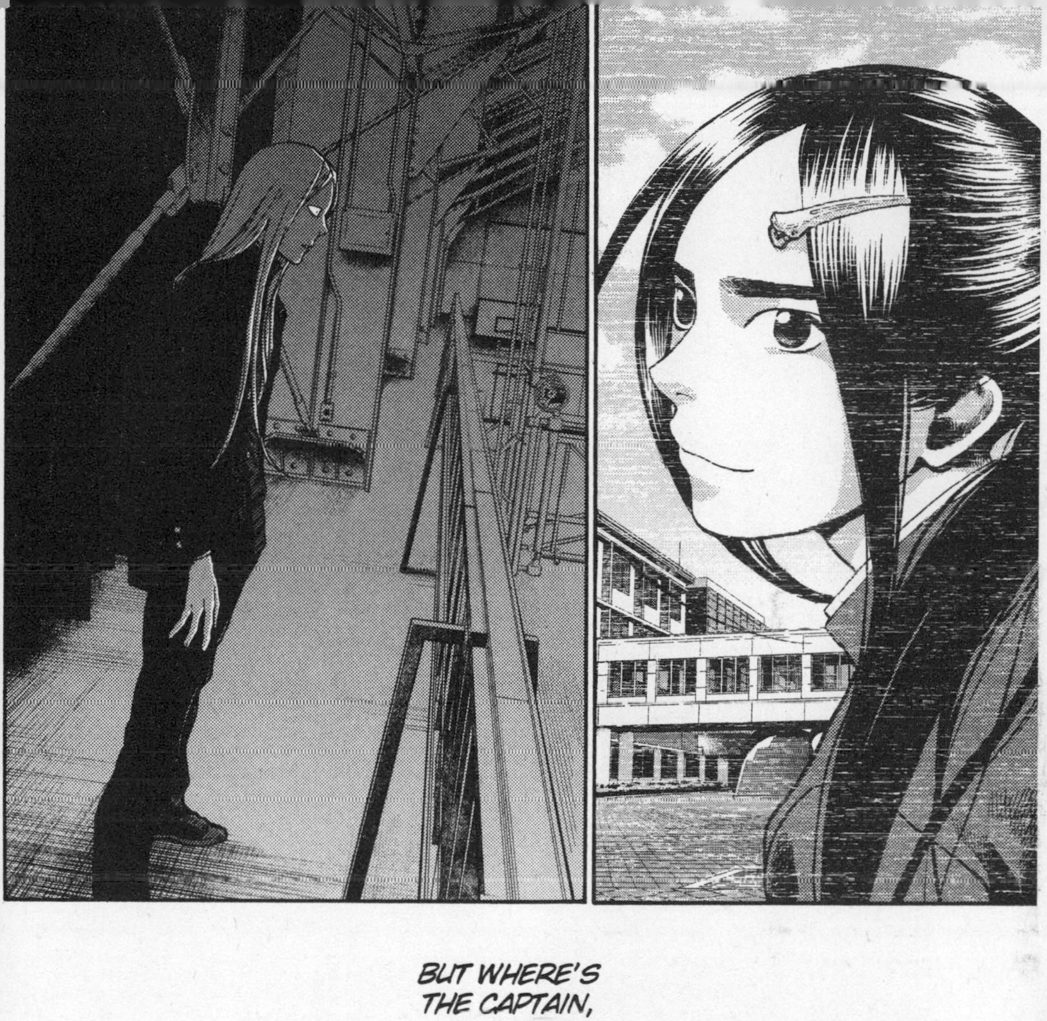
BUT WHERE'S THE CAPTAIN, THOUGH?
NOT TO MENTION FUJIEDA AND SHIBATA...
HMMM...
DID THEY GET MAR-RIED OR SOME-THING?
GOOD JOB OUT THERE!
THANK YOU VERY MUCH!
YOUR CHEERING WAS SPLENDID, AS ALWAYS.

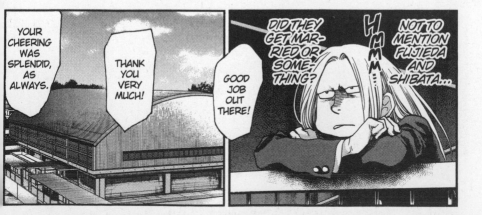

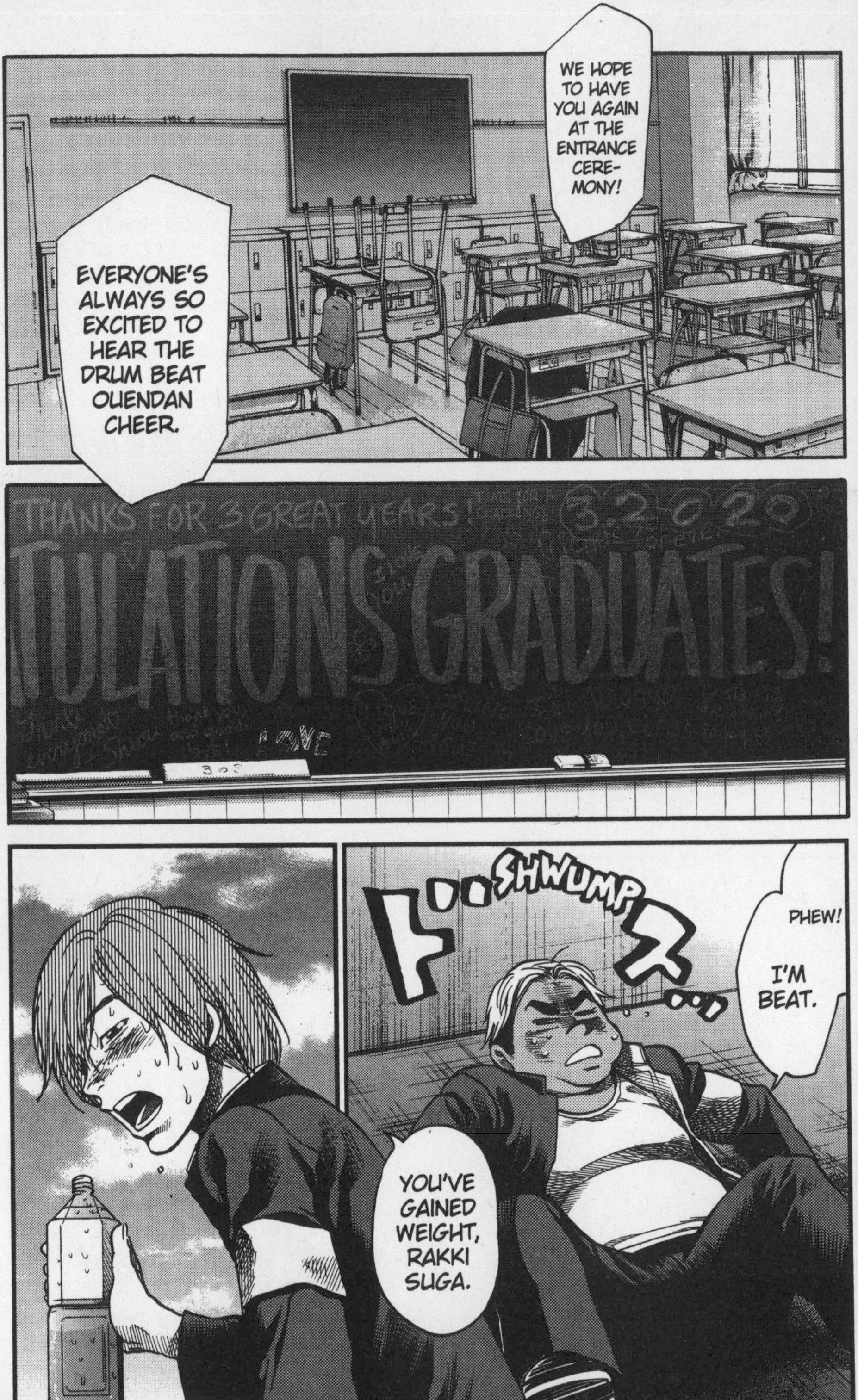
WE HOPE TO HAVE YOU AGAIN AT THE ENTRANCE CEREMONY!
EVERYONE'S ALWAYS SO EXCITED TO HEAR THE DRUM BEAT OUENDAN CHEER.
THANKS FOR 3 GREAT YEARS!
TULATIONS GRADUATES!
PHEW!
I'M BEAT.
SHWUMP
YOU'VE GAINED WEIGHT, RAKKI SUGA.

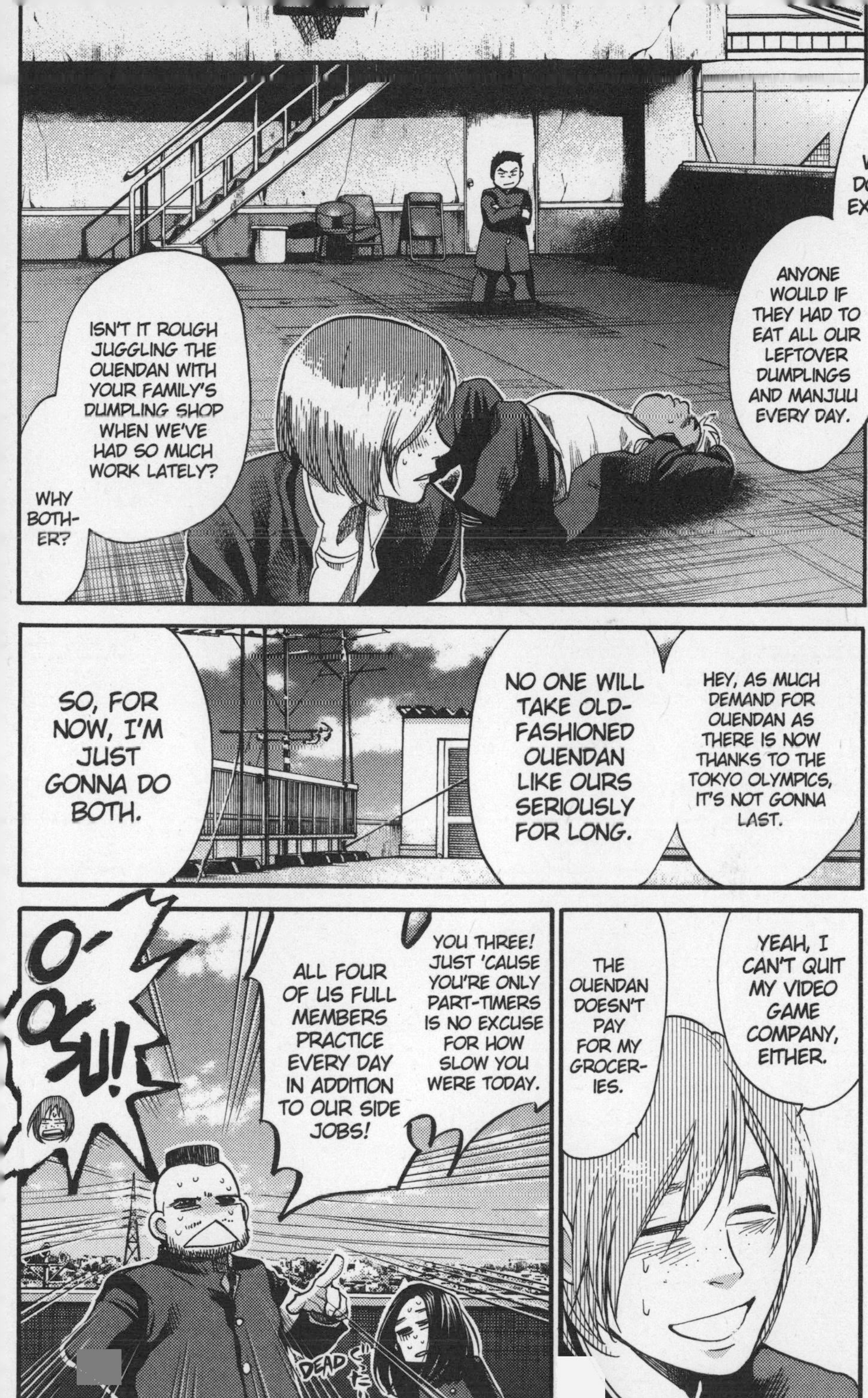
WHAT DO YOU EXPECT?
ANYONE WOULD IF THEY HAD TO EAT ALL OUR LEFTOVER DUMPLINGS AND MANJUU EVERY DAY.
ISN'T IT ROUGH JUGGLING THE OUENDAN WITH YOUR FAMILY'S DUMPLING SHOP WHEN WE'VE HAD SO MUCH WORK LATELY?
WHY BOTHER?
HEY, AS MUCH DEMAND FOR OUENDAN AS THERE IS NOW THANKS TO THE TOKYO OLYMPICS, IT'S NOT GONNA LAST.
NO ONE WILL TAKE OLD-FASHIONED OUENDAN LIKE OURS SERIOUSLY FOR LONG.
SO, FOR NOW, I'M JUST GONNA DO BOTH.
YEAH, I CAN'T QUIT MY VIDEO GAME COMPANY, EITHER.
THE OUENDAN DOESN'T PAY FOR MY GROCERIES.
YOU THREE! JUST 'CAUSE YOU'RE ONLY PART-TIMERS IS NO EXCUSE FOR HOW SLOW YOU WERE TODAY.
ALL FOUR OF US FULL MEMBERS PRACTICE EVERY DAY IN ADDITION TO OUR SIDE JOBS!
O-OSU!
DEAD

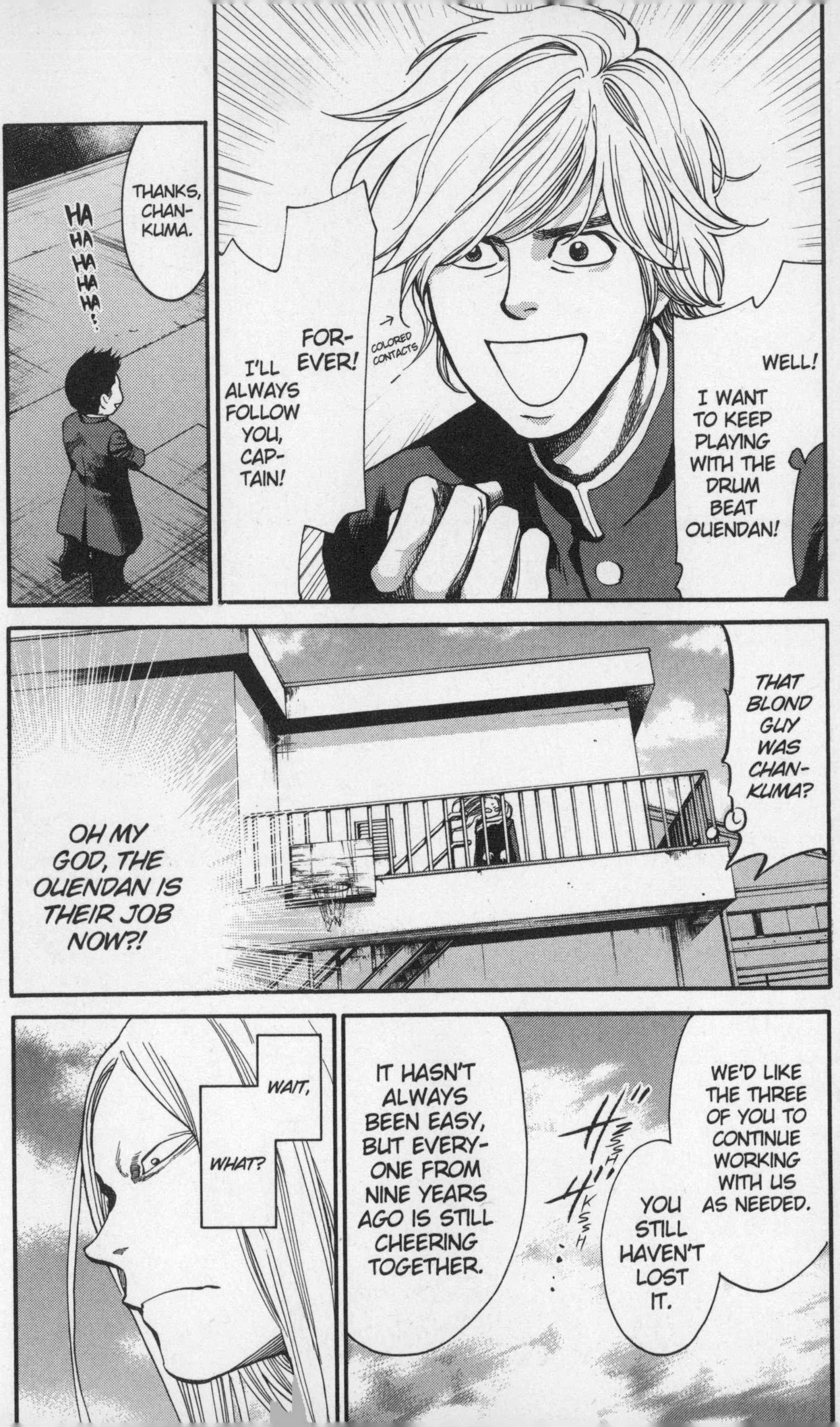
WELL!
I WANT TO KEEP PLAYING WITH THE DRUM BEAT OUENDAN!
COLORED CONTACTS
I'LL ALWAYS FOLLOW YOU, CAP-TAIN!
FOR-EVER!
THANKS, CHAN-KUMA.
HA HA HA HA HA!
THAT BLOND GUY WAS CHAN-KUMA?
OH MY GOD, THE OUENDAN IS THEIR JOB NOW?!
WE'D LIKE THE THREE OF YOU TO CONTINUE WORKING WITH US AS NEEDED.
YOU STILL HAVEN'T LOST IT.
HSSH
KSSH
IT HASN'T ALWAYS BEEN EASY, BUT EVERY-ONE FROM NINE YEARS AGO IS STILL CHEERING TOGETHER.
WAIT,
WHAT?

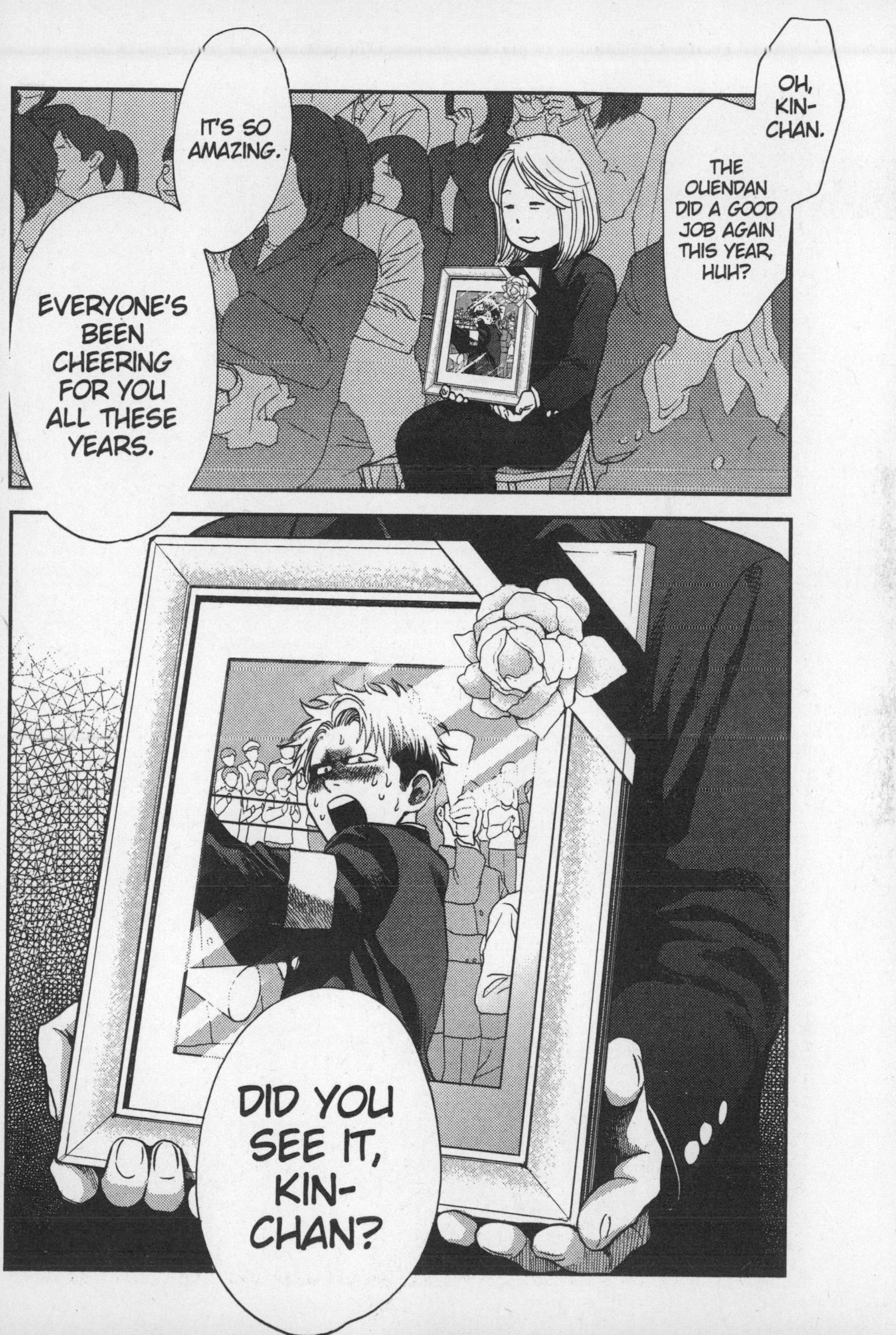
OH, KIN-CHAN.
THE OUENDAN DID A GOOD JOB AGAIN THIS YEAR, HUH?
IT'S SO AMAZING.
EVERYONE'S BEEN CHEERING FOR YOU ALL THESE YEARS.
DID YOU SEE IT, KIN-CHAN?

131. ALONE AGAIN

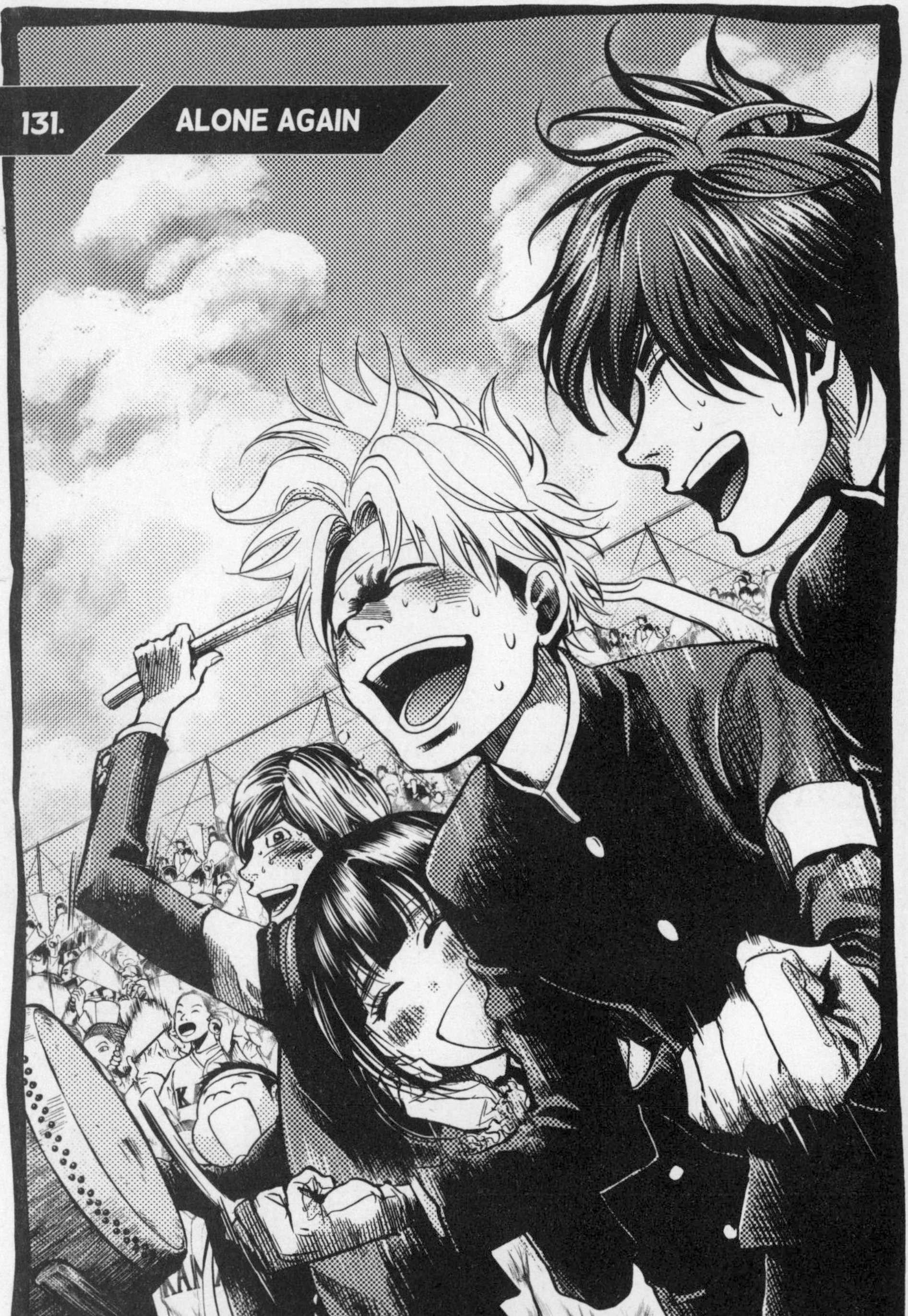

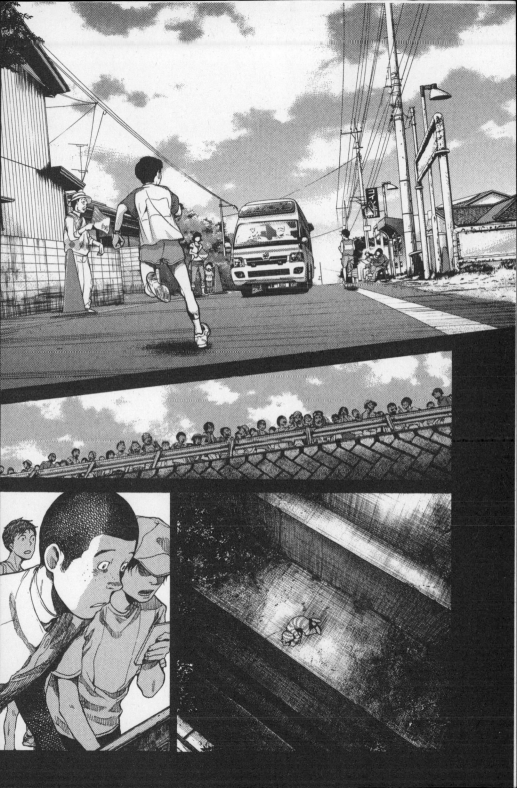

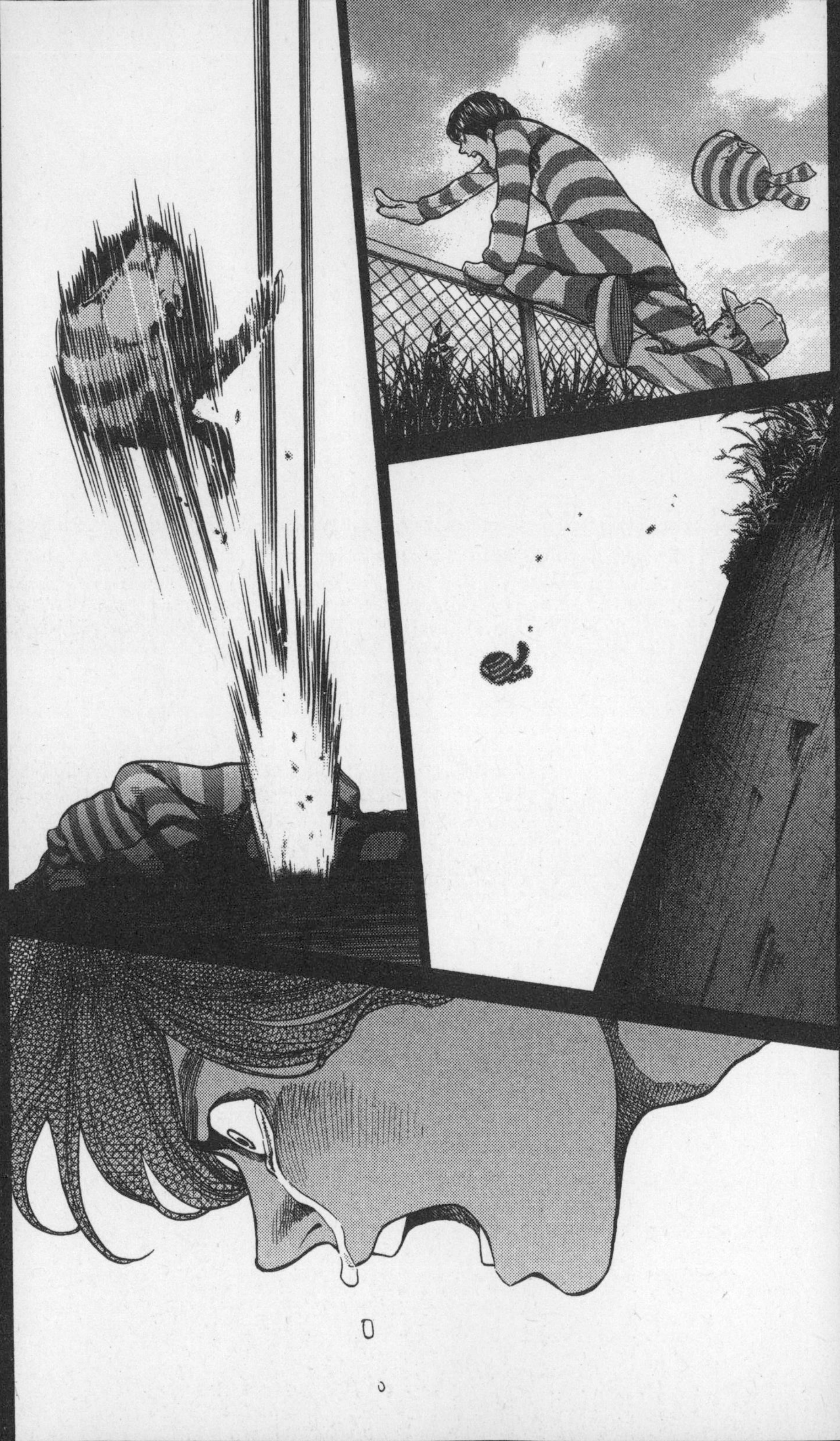

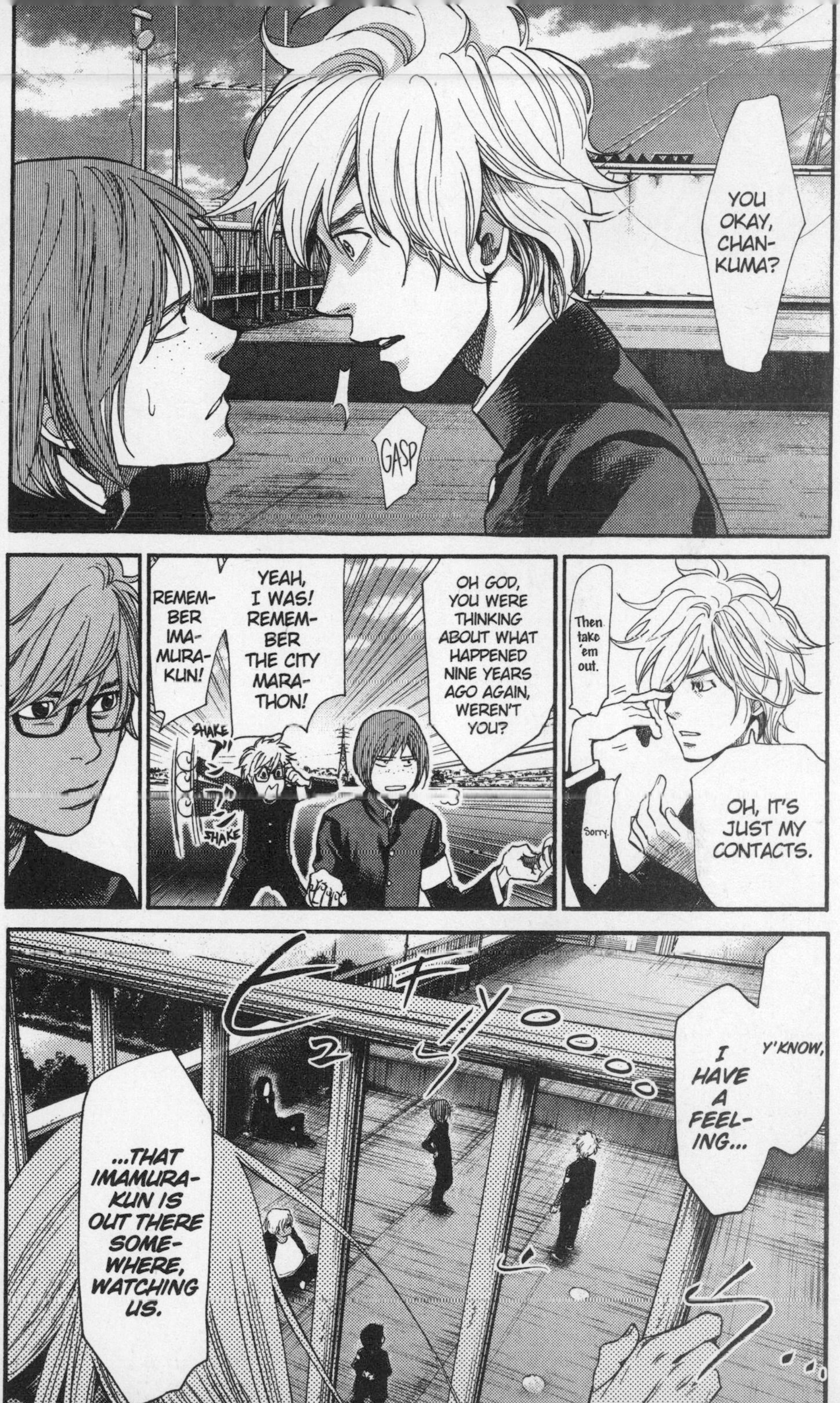
YOU OKAY, CHAN-KUMA?
GASP
OH, IT'S JUST MY CONTACTS.
Then take 'em out.
Sorry.
OH GOD, YOU WERE THINKING ABOUT WHAT HAPPENED NINE YEARS AGO AGAIN, WEREN'T YOU?
YEAH, I WAS! REMEMBER THE CITY MARATHON!
REMEMBER IMAMURA-KUN!
SHAKE
SHAKE
Y'KNOW,
I HAVE A FEELING...
...THAT IMAMURA-KUN IS OUT THERE SOMEWHERE, WATCHING US.

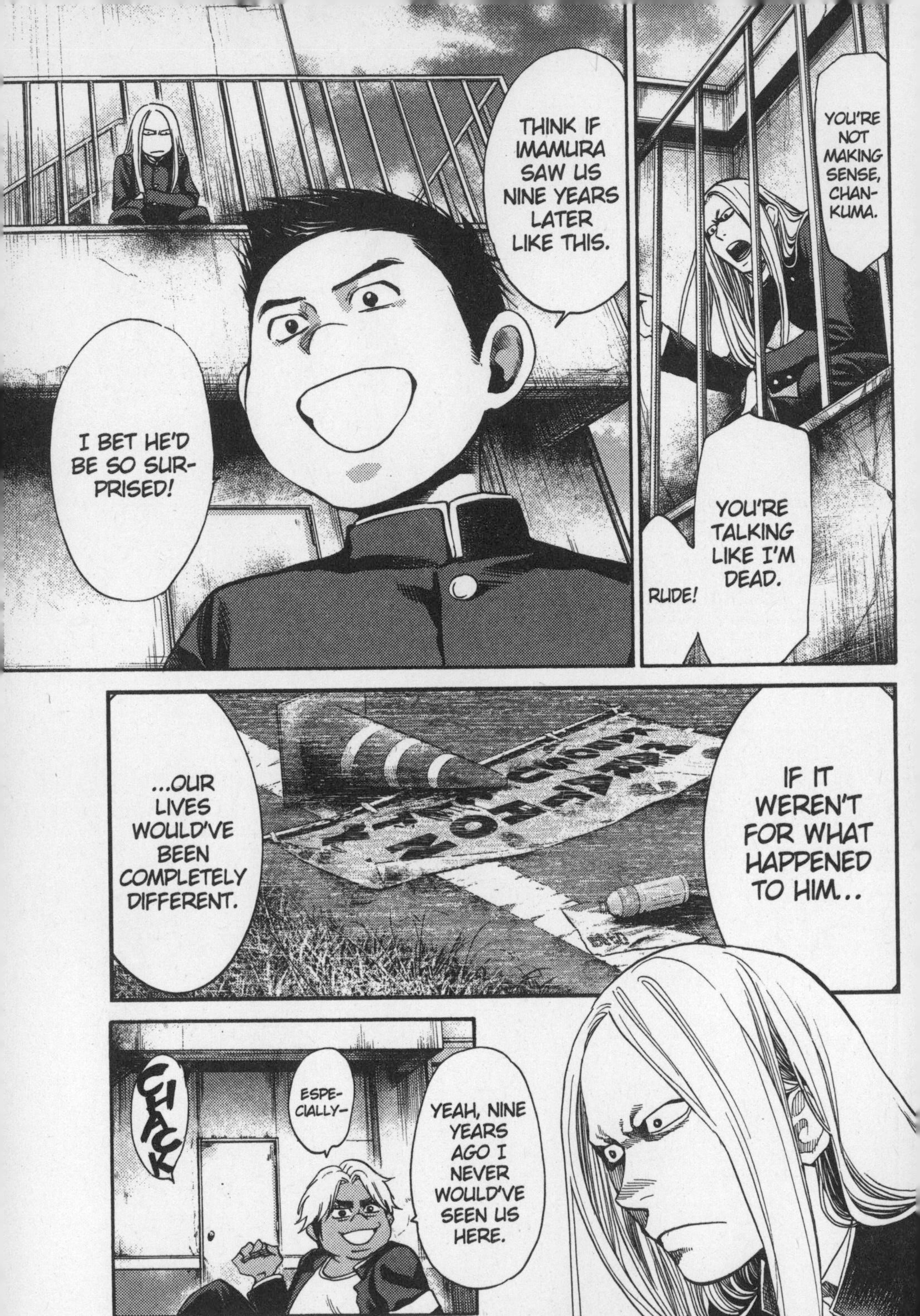
YOU'RE NOT MAKING SENSE, CHAN-KUMA.
YOU'RE TALKING LIKE I'M DEAD.
RUDE!
THINK IF IMAMURA SAW US NINE YEARS LATER LIKE THIS.
I BET HE'D BE SO SUR-PRISED!
IF IT WEREN'T FOR WHAT HAPPENED TO HIM...
...OUR LIVES WOULD'VE BEEN COMPLETELY DIFFERENT.
YEAH, NINE YEARS AGO I NEVER WOULD'VE SEEN US HERE.
ESPE-CIALLY-
CHACK

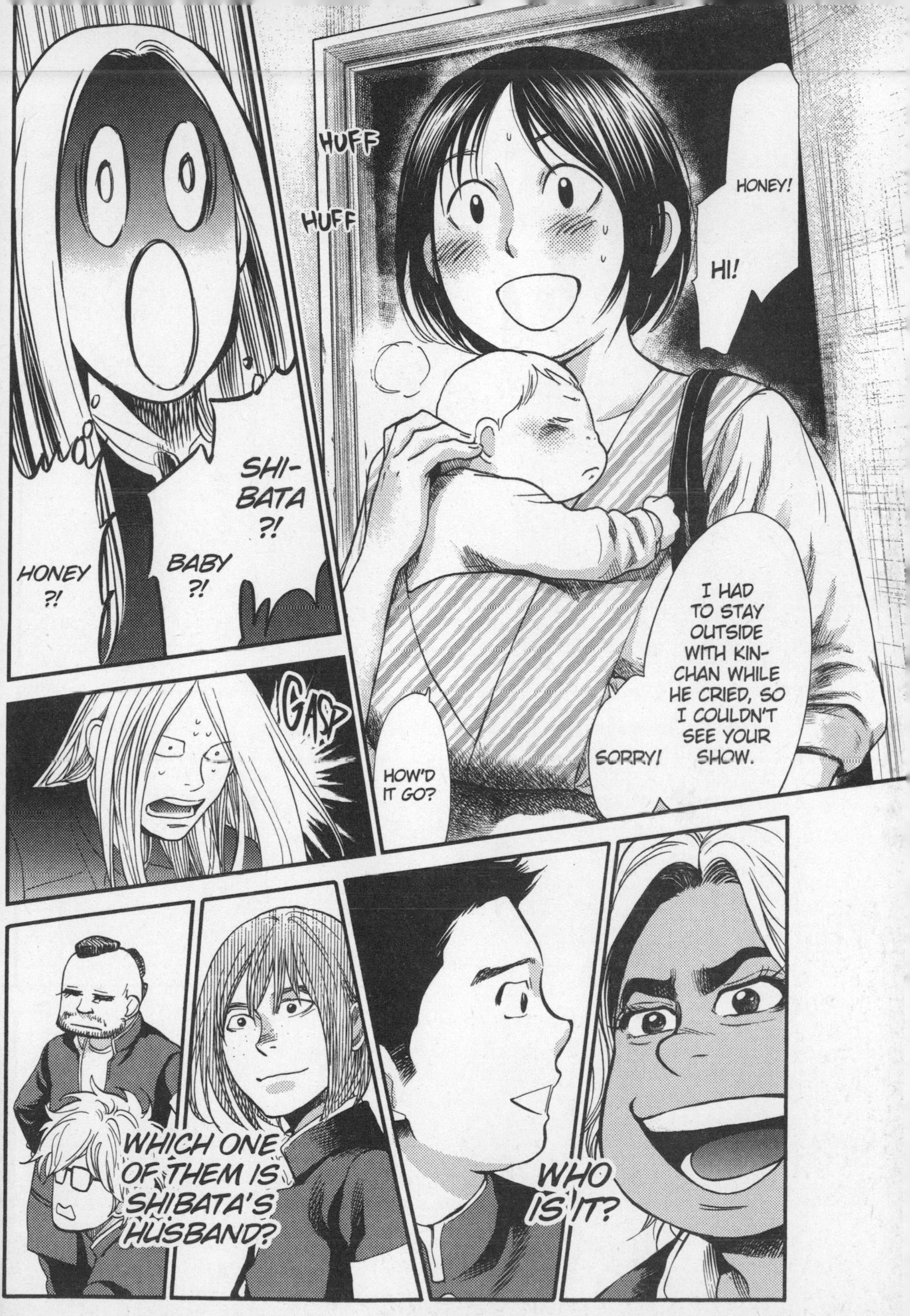
HONEY!
HI!
HUFF
HUFF
I HAD TO STAY OUTSIDE WITH KIN-CHAN WHILE HE CRIED, SO I COULDN'T SEE YOUR SHOW.
SORRY!
HOW'D IT GO?
SHI-BATA ?!
BABY ?!
HONEY ?!
GASP
WHO IS IT?
WHICH ONE OF THEM IS SHIBATA'S HUSBAND?

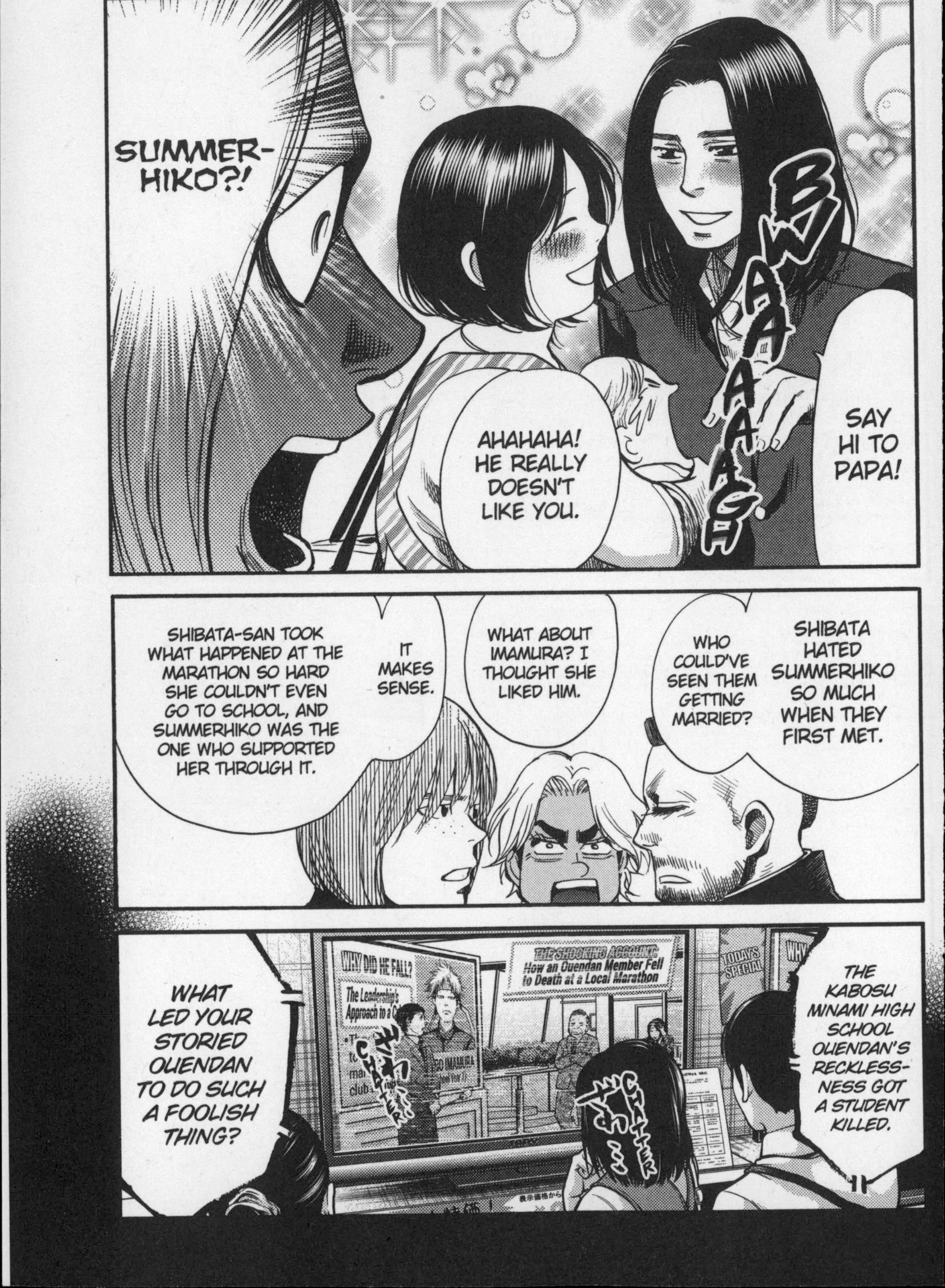
SAY HI TO PAPA!
BWAAAAAGH
AHAHAHA! HE REALLY DOESN'T LIKE YOU.
SUMMER-HIKO?!
SHIBATA HATED SUMMERHIKO SO MUCH WHEN THEY FIRST MET.
WHO COULD'VE SEEN THEM GETTING MARRIED?
WHAT ABOUT IMAMURA? I THOUGHT SHE LIKED HIM.
IT MAKES SENSE.
SHIBATA-SAN TOOK WHAT HAPPENED AT THE MARATHON SO HARD SHE COULDN'T EVEN GO TO SCHOOL, AND SUMMERHIKO WAS THE ONE WHO SUPPORTED HER THROUGH IT.
THE KABOSU MINAMI HIGH SCHOOL OUENDAN'S RECKLESS-NESS GOT A STUDENT KILLED.
TODAY'S SPECIAL
THE SHOCKING ACCOUNT: How an Ouendan Member Fell to Death at a Local Marathon
WHY DID HE FALL?
CHATTER
CHATTER
WHAT LED YOUR STORIED OUENDAN TO DO SUCH A FOOLISH THING?

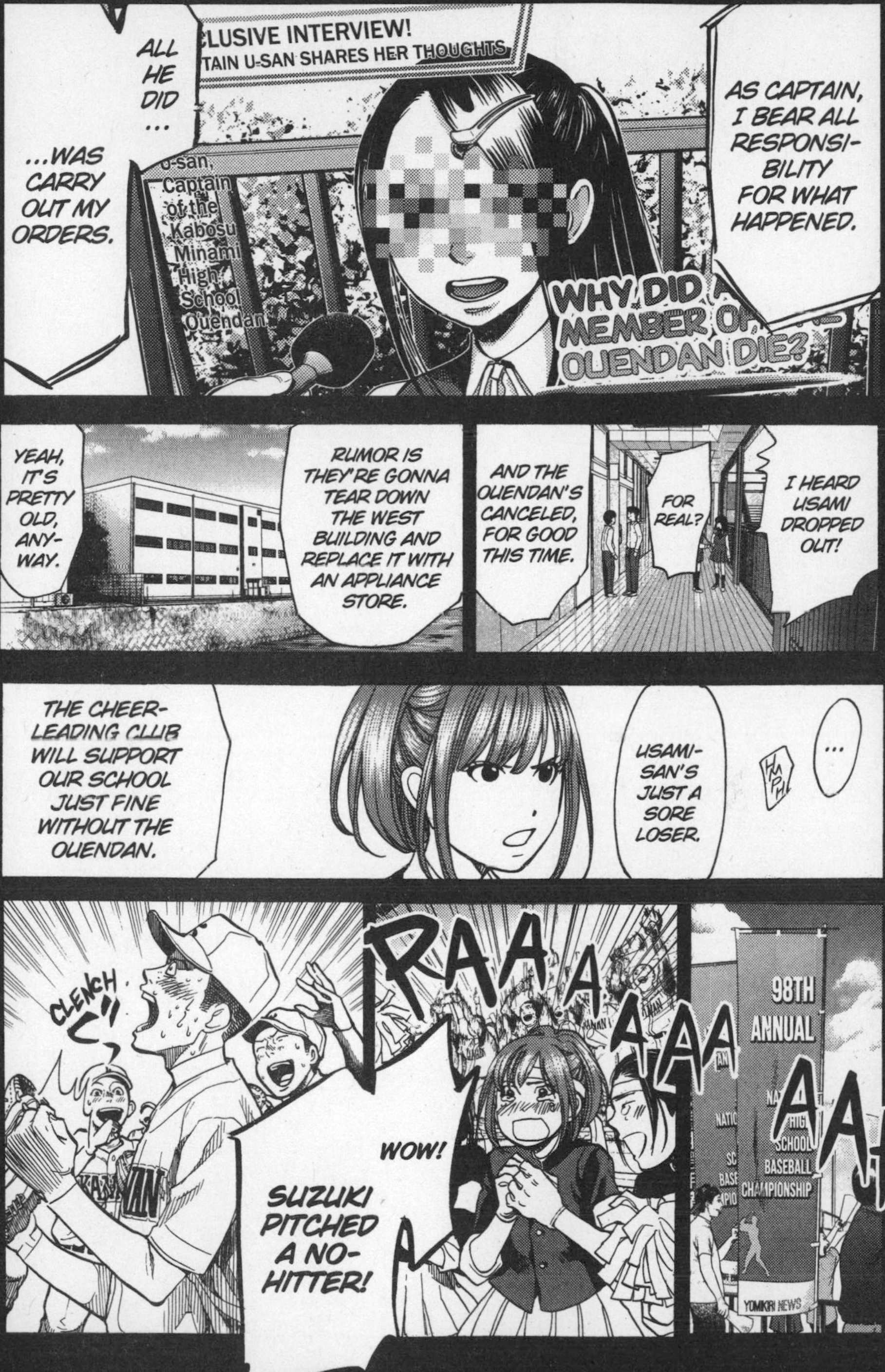
CLUSIVE INTERVIEW!
TAIN U-SAN SHARES HER THOUGHTS
AS CAPTAIN, I BEAR ALL RESPONSIBILITY FOR WHAT HAPPENED.
ALL HE DID...
...WAS CARRY OUT MY ORDERS.
U-san, Captain of the Kabosu Minami High School Ouendan
WHY DID A
MEMBER OF
OUENDAN DIE?
I HEARD USAMI DROPPED OUT!
FOR REAL?
AND THE OUENDAN'S CANCELED, FOR GOOD THIS TIME.
RUMOR IS THEY'RE GONNA TEAR DOWN THE WEST BUILDING AND REPLACE IT WITH AN APPLIANCE STORE.
YEAH, IT'S PRETTY OLD, ANYWAY.
...
HMPH
USAMI-SAN'S JUST A SORE LOSER.
THE CHEERLEADING CLUB WILL SUPPORT OUR SCHOOL JUST FINE WITHOUT THE OUENDAN.
98TH ANNUAL
HIGH SCHOOL BASEBALL CHAMPIONSHIP
RAAAAAAAAAH
WOW!
SUZUKI PITCHED A NO-HITTER!
CLENCH

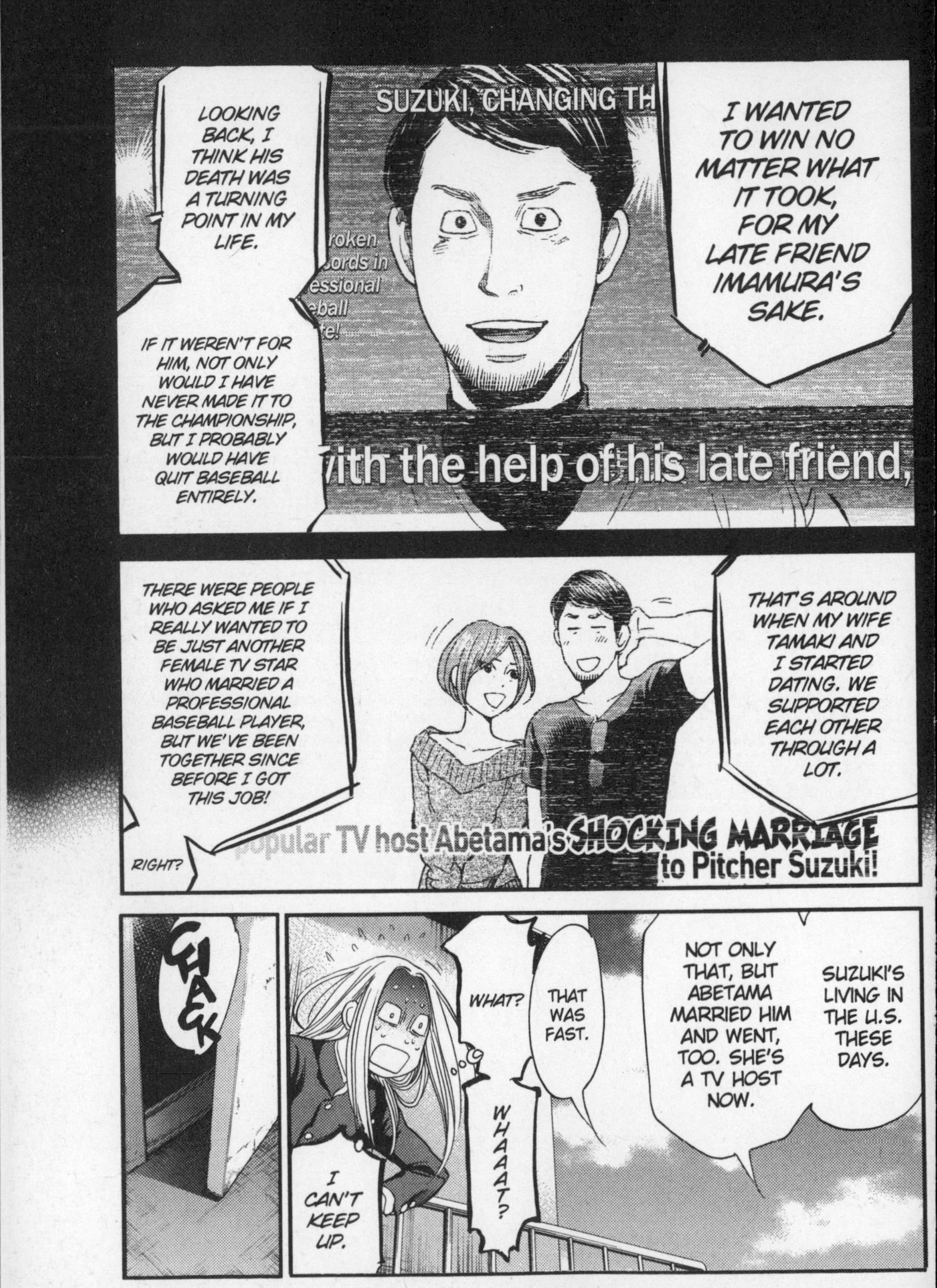
I WANTED TO WIN NO MATTER WHAT IT TOOK, FOR MY LATE FRIEND IMAMURA'S SAKE.
SUZUKI, CHANGING TH
LOOKING BACK, I THINK HIS DEATH WAS A TURNING POINT IN MY LIFE.
IF IT WEREN'T FOR HIM, NOT ONLY WOULD I HAVE NEVER MADE IT TO THE CHAMPIONSHIP, BUT I PROBABLY WOULD HAVE QUIT BASEBALL ENTIRELY.
vith the help of his late friend,
THAT'S AROUND WHEN MY WIFE TAMAKI AND I STARTED DATING. WE SUPPORTED EACH OTHER THROUGH A LOT.
THERE WERE PEOPLE WHO ASKED ME IF I REALLY WANTED TO BE JUST ANOTHER FEMALE TV STAR WHO MARRIED A PROFESSIONAL BASEBALL PLAYER, BUT WE'VE BEEN TOGETHER SINCE BEFORE I GOT THIS JOB!
RIGHT?
popular TV host Abetama's SHOCKING MARRIAGE to Pitcher Suzuki!
SUZUKI'S LIVING IN THE U.S. THESE DAYS.
NOT ONLY THAT, BUT ABETAMA MARRIED HIM AND WENT, TOO. SHE'S A TV HOST NOW.
THAT WAS FAST.
WHAT?
WHAAAAT?
I CAN'T KEEP UP.
CHACK

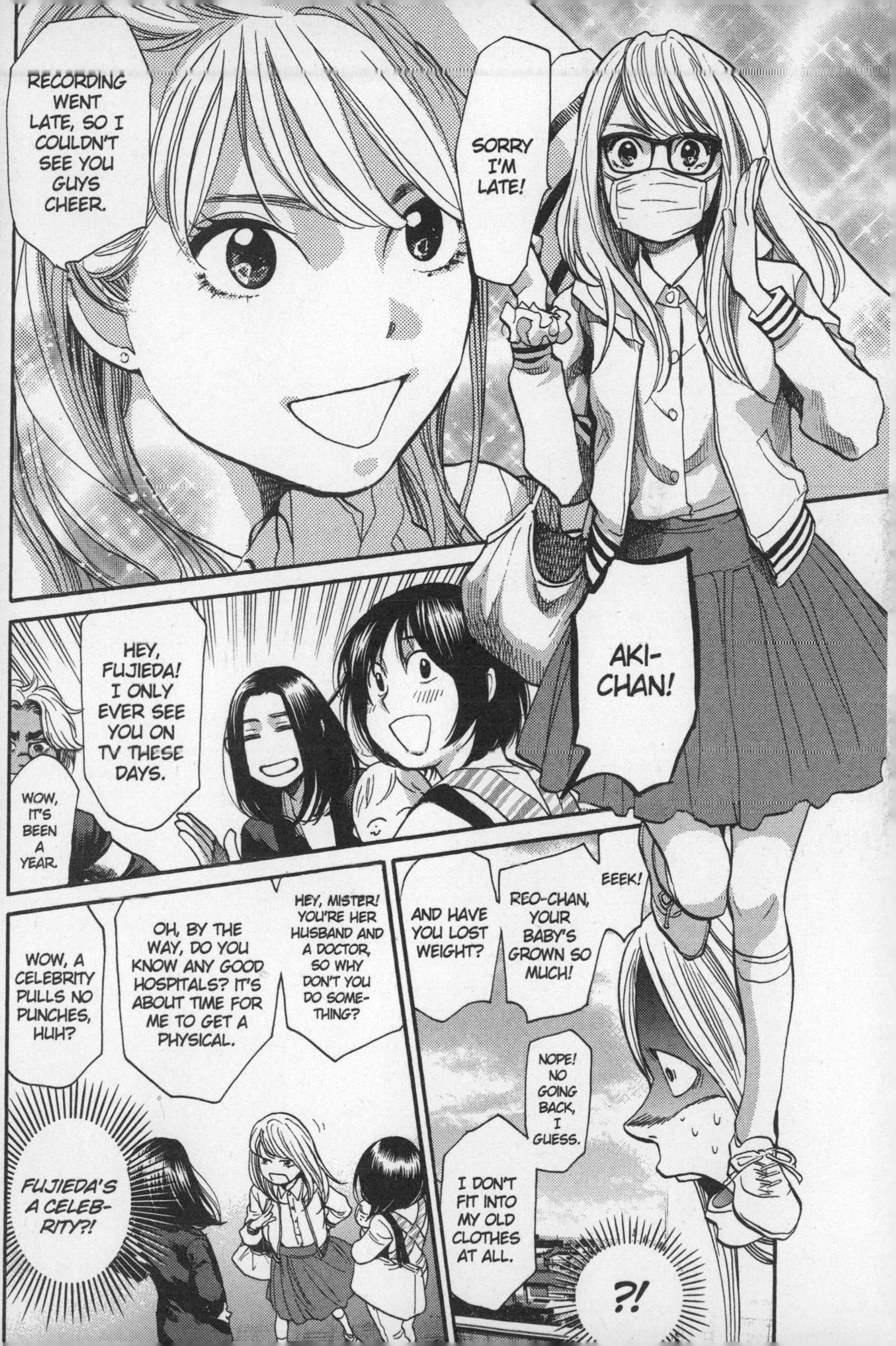
SORRY I'M LATE!
RECORDING WENT LATE, SO I COULDN'T SEE YOU GUYS CHEER.
AKI-CHAN!
HEY, FUJIEDA! I ONLY EVER SEE YOU ON TV THESE DAYS.
WOW, IT'S BEEN A YEAR.
REO-CHAN, YOUR BABY'S GROWN SO MUCH!
EEEK!
AND HAVE YOU LOST WEIGHT?
NOPE! NO GOING BACK, I GUESS.
I DON'T FIT INTO MY OLD CLOTHES AT ALL.
HEY, MISTER! YOU'RE HER HUSBAND AND A DOCTOR, SO WHY DON'T YOU DO SOME-THING?
OH, BY THE WAY, DO YOU KNOW ANY GOOD HOSPITALS? IT'S ABOUT TIME FOR ME TO GET A PHYSICAL.
WOW, A CELEBRITY PULLS NO PUNCHES, HUH?
?!
FUJIEDA'S A CELEB-RITY?!

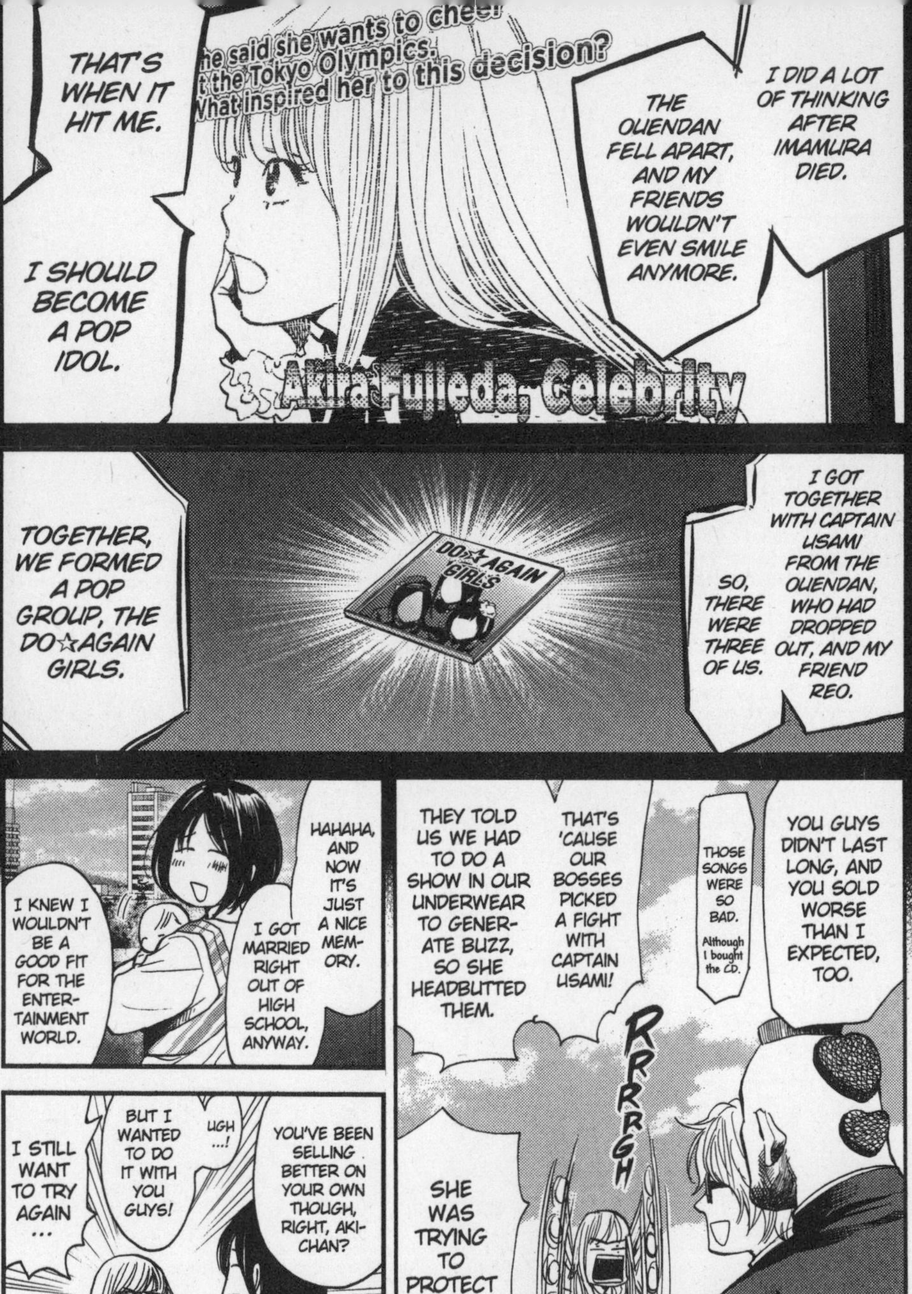
I DID A LOT OF THINKING AFTER IMAMURA DIED.
THE OUENDAN FELL APART, AND MY FRIENDS WOULDN'T EVEN SMILE ANYMORE.
he said she wants to cheer
t the Tokyo Olympics.
hat inspired her to this decision?
THAT'S WHEN IT HIT ME.
I SHOULD BECOME A POP IDOL.
Akira Fujieda, Celebrity
I GOT TOGETHER WITH CAPTAIN USAMI FROM THE OUENDAN, WHO HAD DROPPED OUT, AND MY FRIEND REO.
SO, THERE WERE THREE OF US.
DO☆AGAIN GIRLS
TOGETHER, WE FORMED A POP GROUP, THE DO☆AGAIN GIRLS.
YOU GUYS DIDN'T LAST LONG, AND YOU SOLD WORSE THAN I EXPECTED, TOO.
THOSE SONGS WERE SO BAD.
Although I bought the CD.
THAT'S 'CAUSE OUR BOSSES PICKED A FIGHT WITH CAPTAIN USAMI!
THEY TOLD US WE HAD TO DO A SHOW IN OUR UNDERWEAR TO GENER-ATE BUZZ, SO SHE HEADBUTTED THEM.
RRRRGH
SHE WAS TRYING TO PROTECT US!
HAHAHA, AND NOW IT'S JUST A NICE MEM-ORY.
I GOT MARRIED RIGHT OUT OF HIGH SCHOOL, ANYWAY.
I KNEW I WOULDN'T BE A GOOD FIT FOR THE ENTER-TAINMENT WORLD.
YOU'VE BEEN SELLING BETTER ON YOUR OWN THOUGH, RIGHT, AKI-CHAN?
UGH ...!
BUT I WANTED TO DO IT WITH YOU GUYS!
I STILL WANT TO TRY AGAIN ...

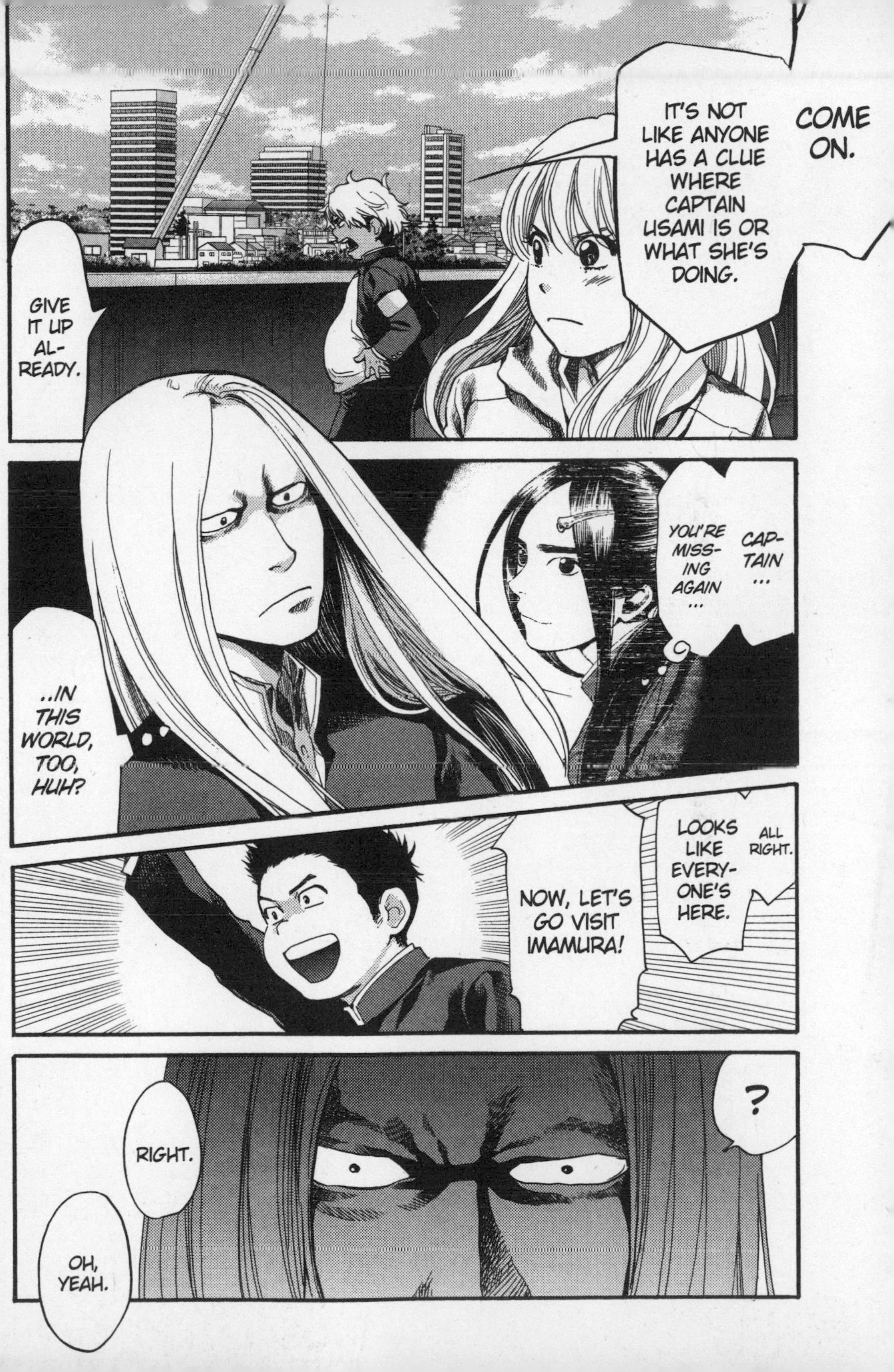
COME ON.
IT'S NOT LIKE ANYONE HAS A CLUE WHERE CAPTAIN USAMI IS OR WHAT SHE'S DOING.
GIVE IT UP AL-READY.
CAP-TAIN ...
YOU'RE MISS-ING AGAIN ...
..IN THIS WORLD, TOO, HUH?
ALL RIGHT.
LOOKS LIKE EVERY-ONE'S HERE.
NOW, LET'S GO VISIT IMAMURA!
?
RIGHT.
OH, YEAH.

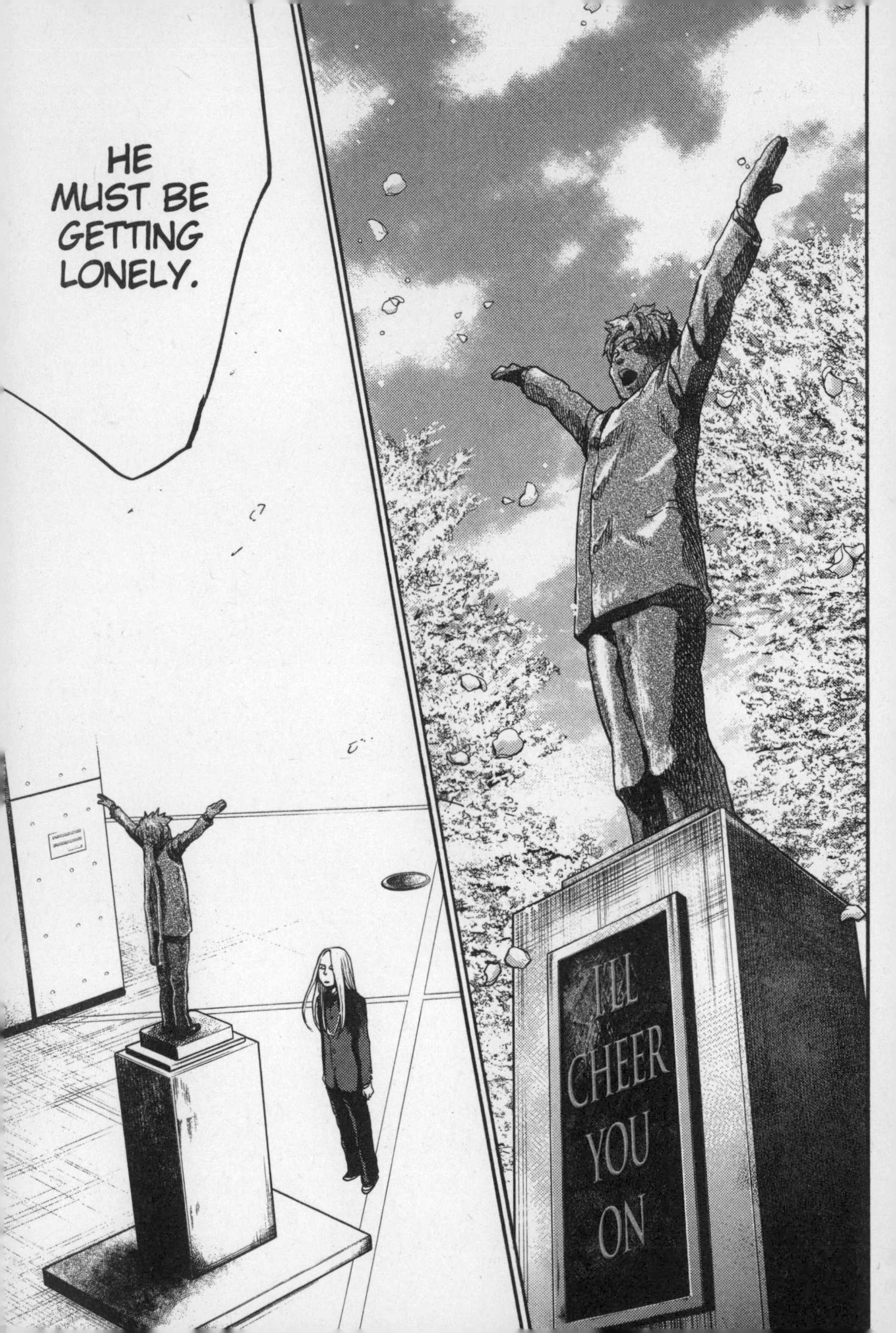
I'LL CHEER YOU ON
HE MUST BE GETTING LONELY.

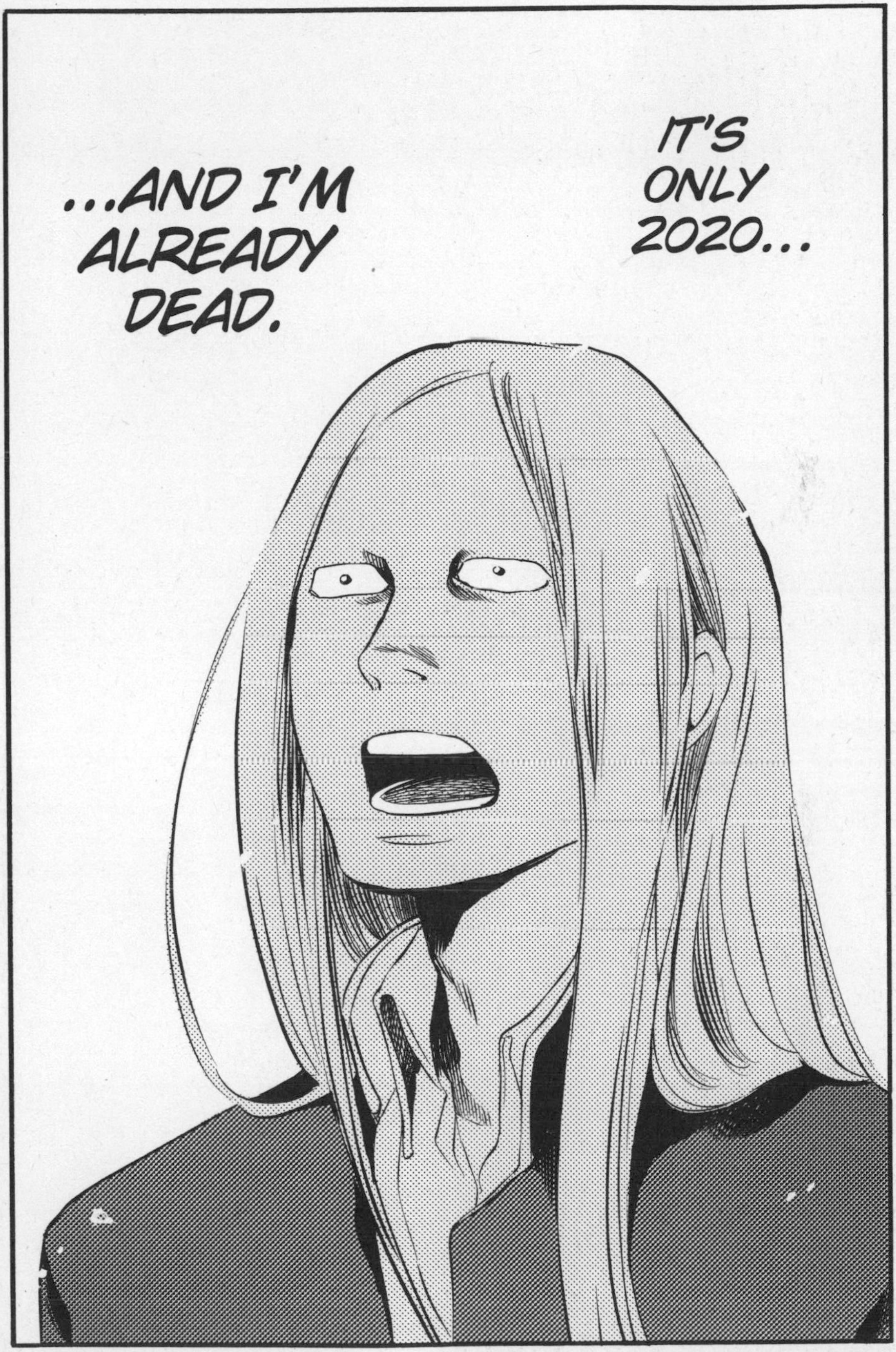
IT'S ONLY 2020...
...AND I'M ALREADY DEAD.

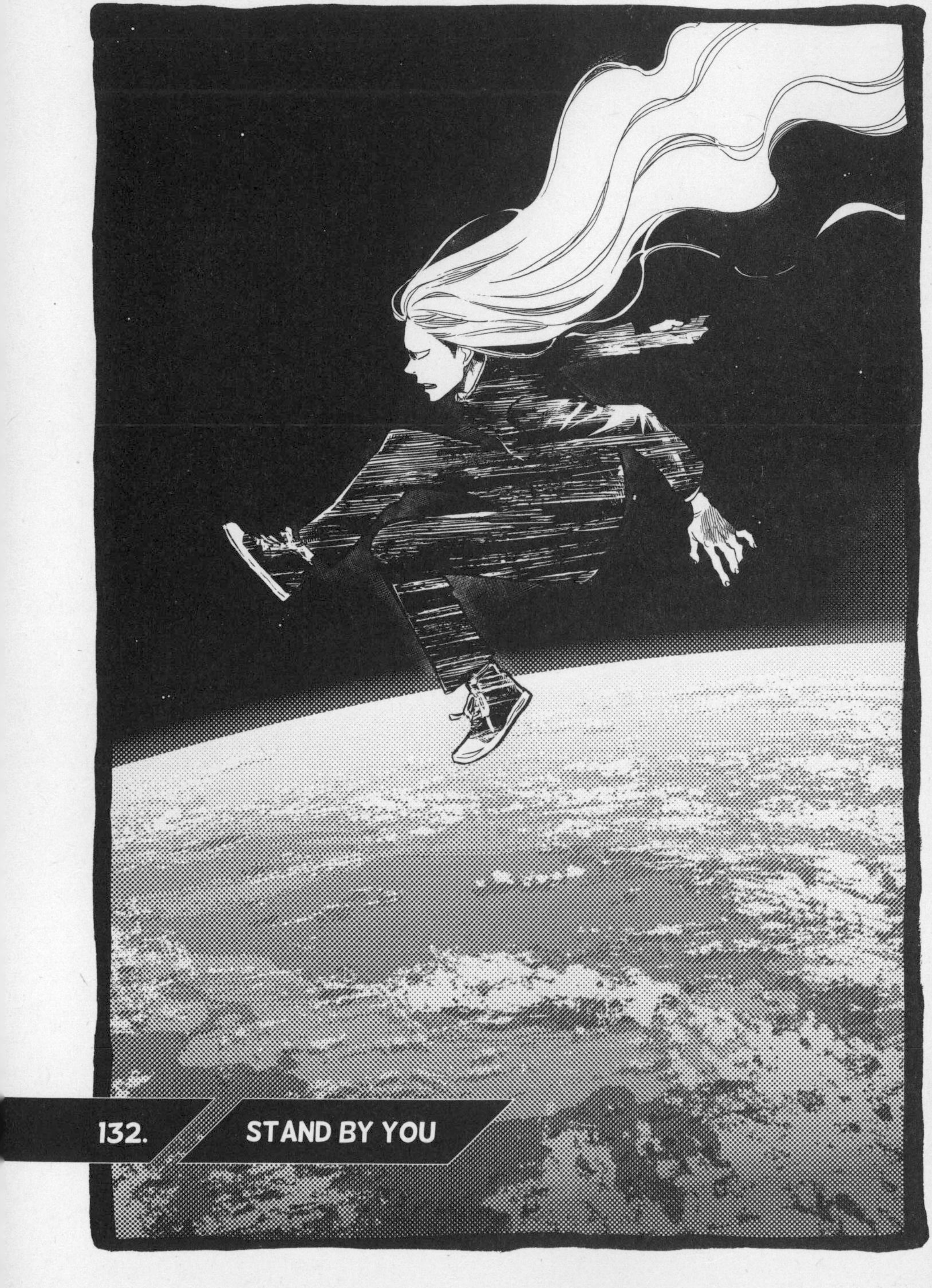
132.
STAND BY YOU

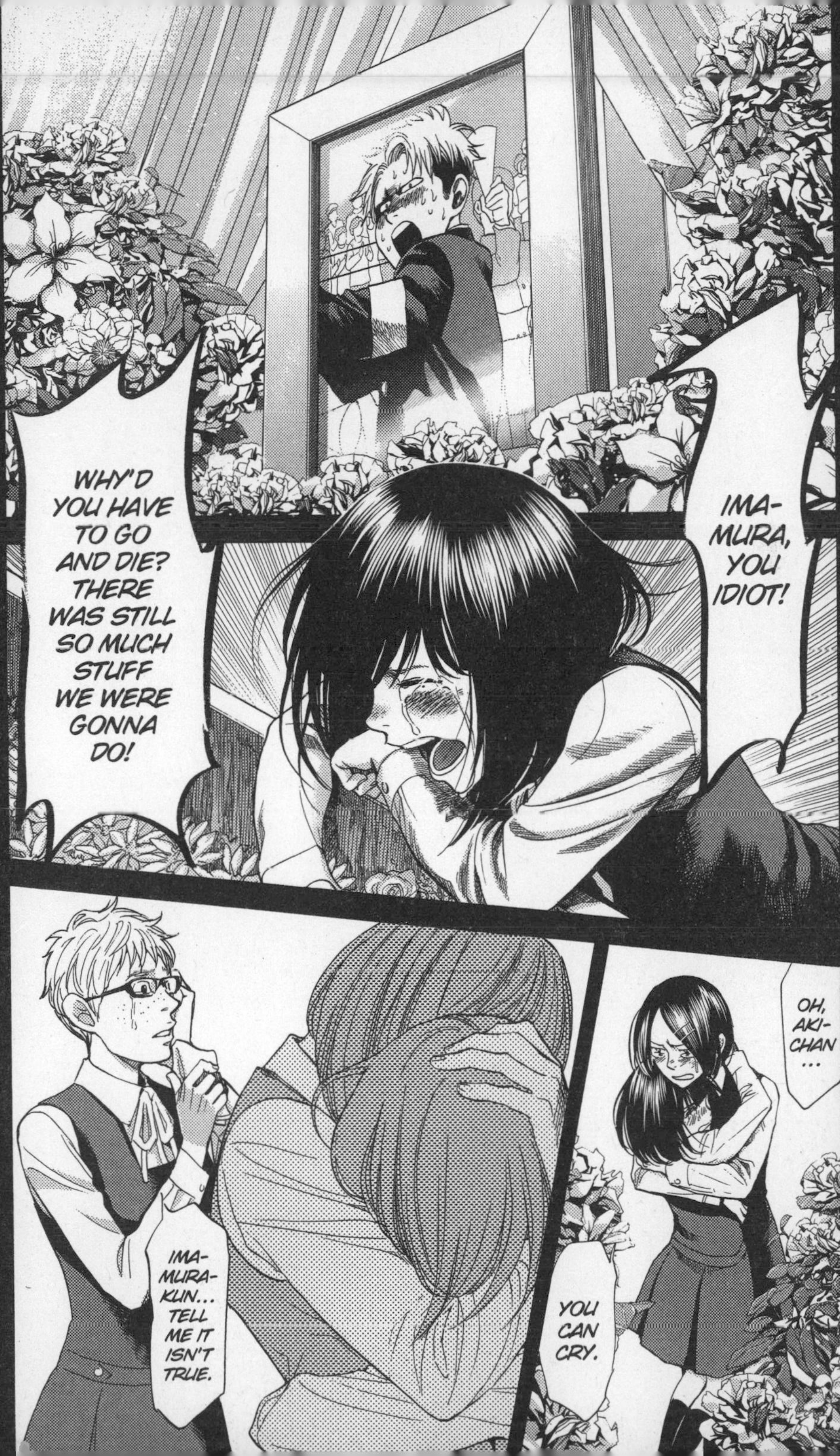
IMA-MURA, YOU IDIOT!
WHY'D YOU HAVE TO GO AND DIE? THERE WAS STILL SO MUCH STUFF WE WERE GONNA DO!
OH, AKI-CHAN...
YOU CAN CRY.
IMA-MURA-KUN... TELL ME IT ISN'T TRUE.

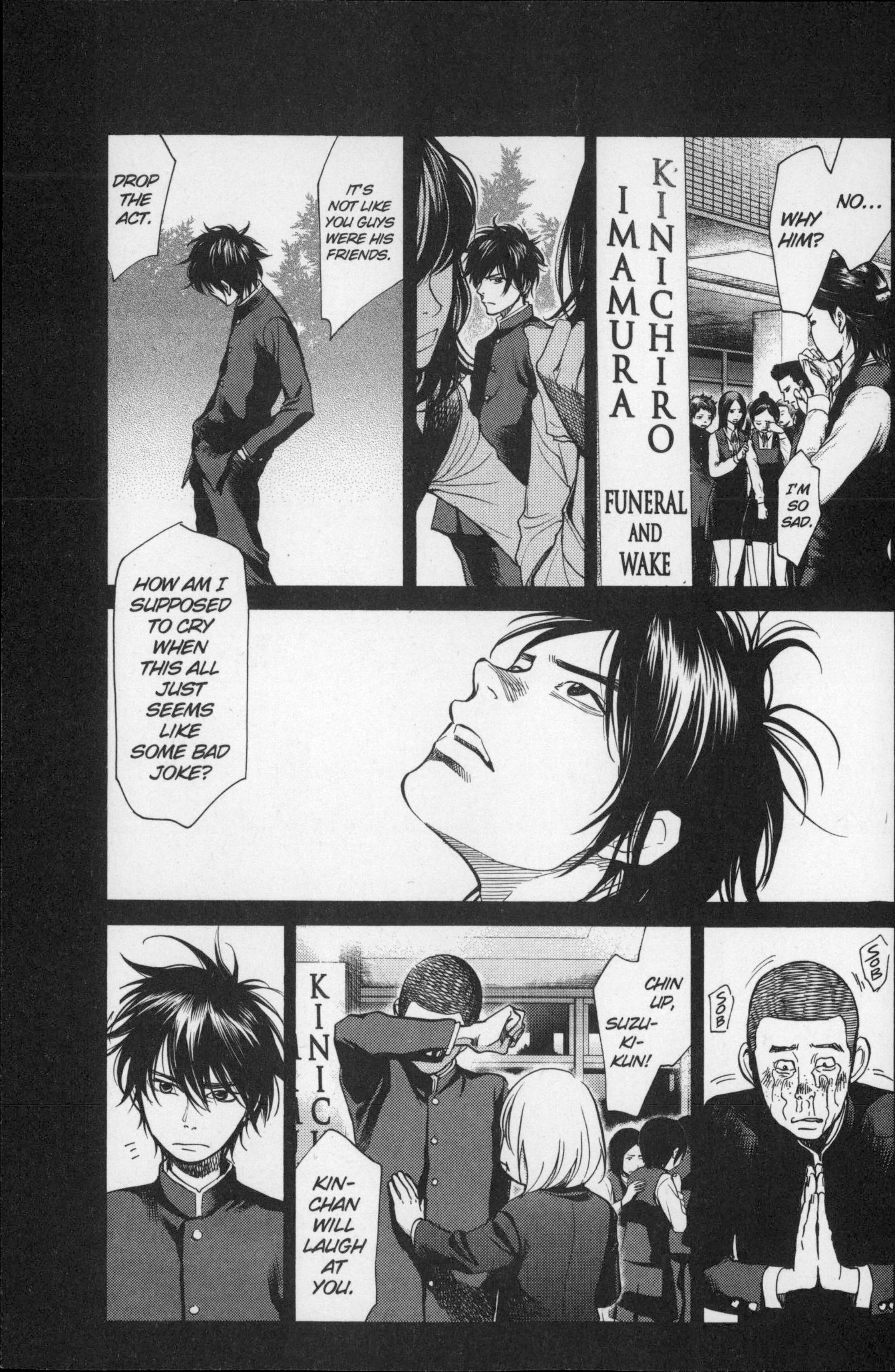
NO... WHY HIM?
I'M SO SAD.
KINICHIRO IMAMURA
FUNERAL AND WAKE
IT'S NOT LIKE YOU GUYS WERE HIS FRIENDS.
DROP THE ACT.
HOW AM I SUPPOSED TO CRY WHEN THIS ALL JUST SEEMS LIKE SOME BAD JOKE?
SOB
SOB
CHIN UP, SUZUKI-KUN!
KIN-CHAN WILL LAUGH AT YOU.

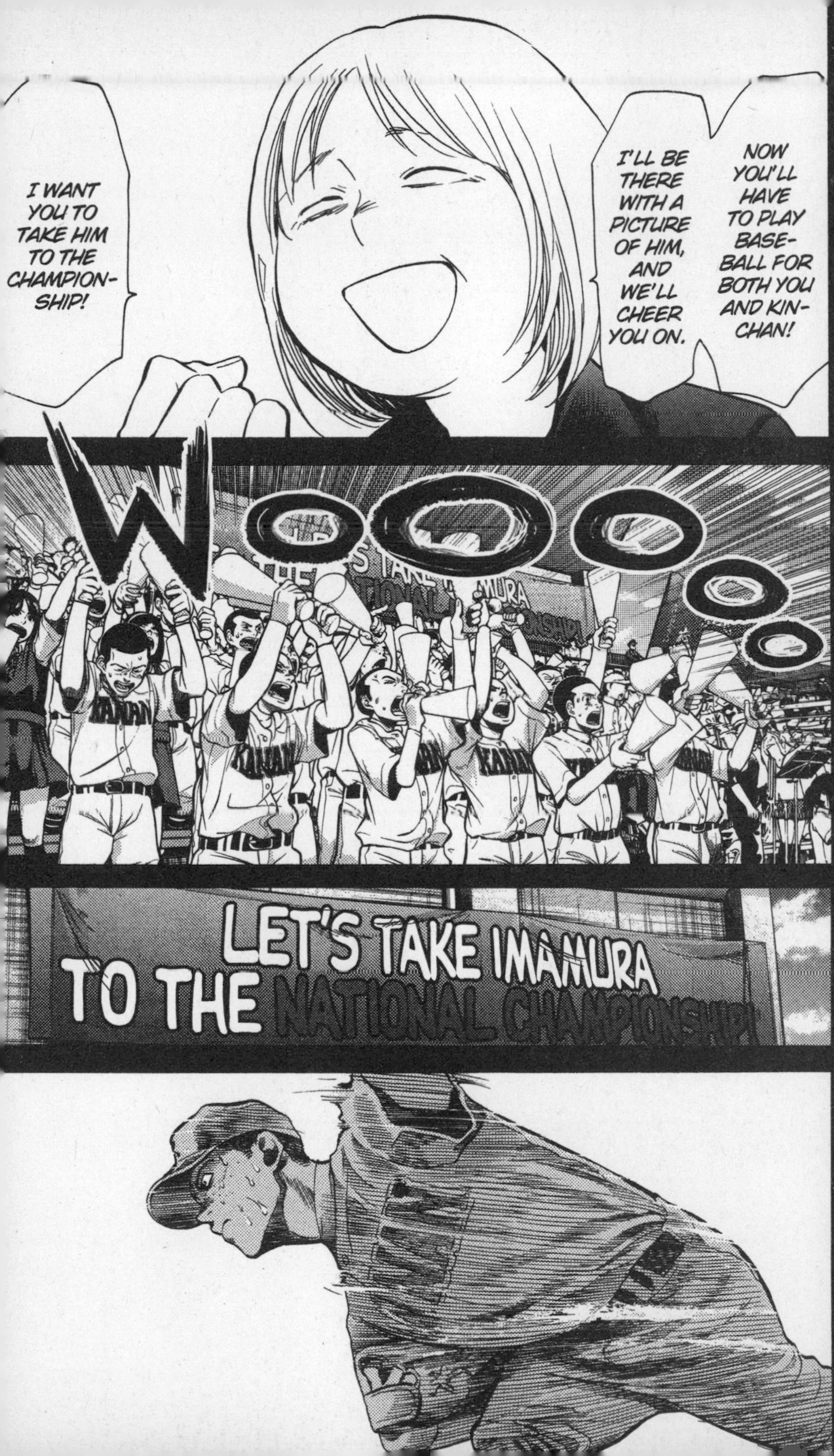
I'LL BE THERE WITH A PICTURE OF HIM, AND WE'LL CHEER YOU ON.
NOW YOU'LL HAVE TO PLAY BASE-BALL FOR BOTH YOU AND KIN-CHAN!
I WANT YOU TO TAKE HIM TO THE CHAMPION-SHIP!
WOOOOO
KANAN
LET'S TAKE IMAMURA TO THE NATIONAL CHAMPIONSHIP!

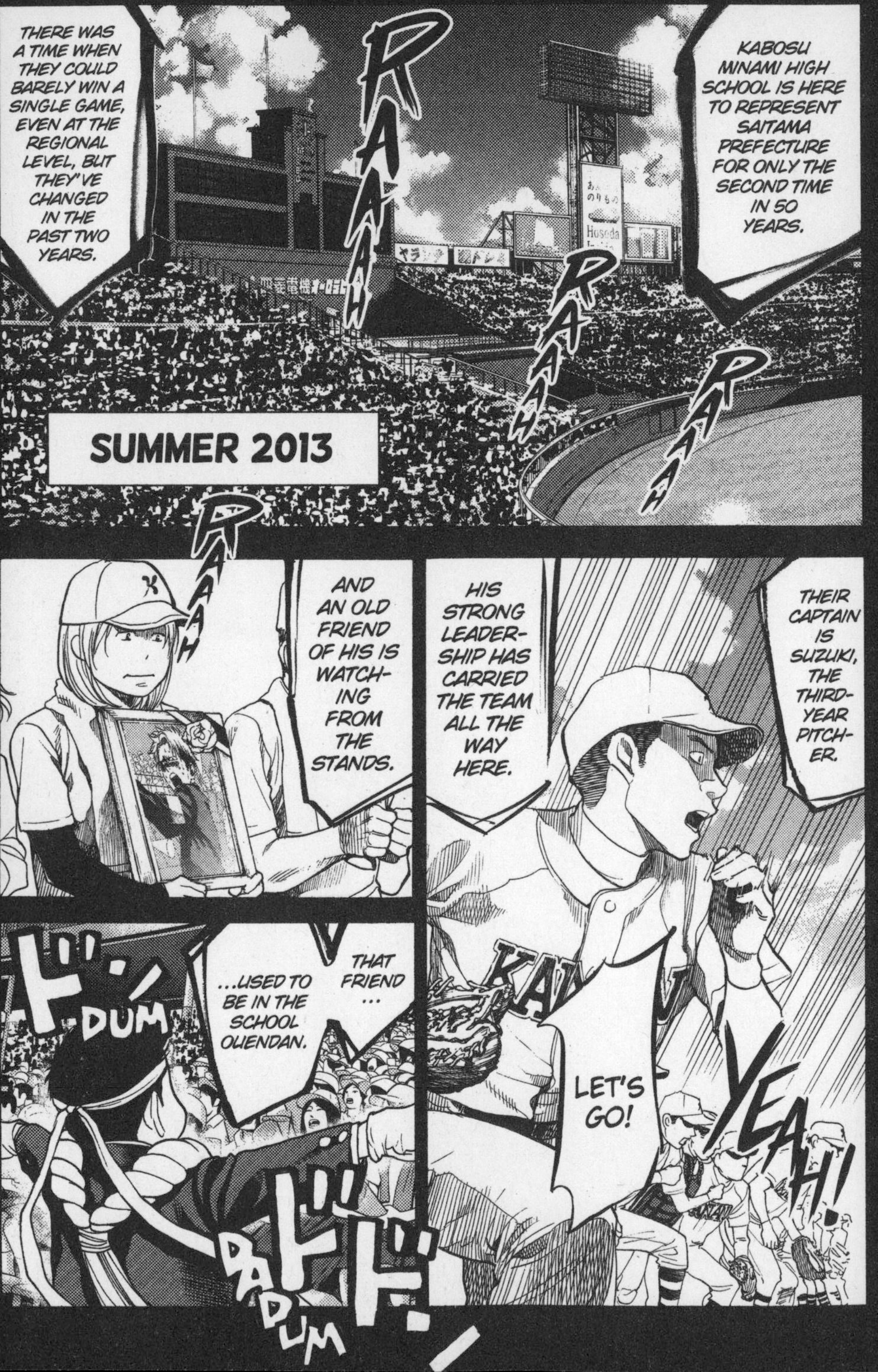
KABOSU MINAMI HIGH SCHOOL IS HERE TO REPRESENT SAITAMA PREFECTURE FOR ONLY THE SECOND TIME IN 50 YEARS.
RAAAAH
RAAAAH
RAAAAH
THERE WAS A TIME WHEN THEY COULD BARELY WIN A SINGLE GAME, EVEN AT THE REGIONAL LEVEL, BUT THEY'VE CHANGED IN THE PAST TWO YEARS.
SUMMER 2013
RAAAAH
THEIR CAPTAIN IS SUZUKI, THE THIRD-YEAR PITCHER.
HIS STRONG LEADERSHIP HAS CARRIED THE TEAM ALL THE WAY HERE.
YEAH!
LET'S GO!
AND AN OLD FRIEND OF HIS IS WATCHING FROM THE STANDS.
THAT FRIEND...
...USED TO BE IN THE SCHOOL OUENDAN.
DUM
DADUM

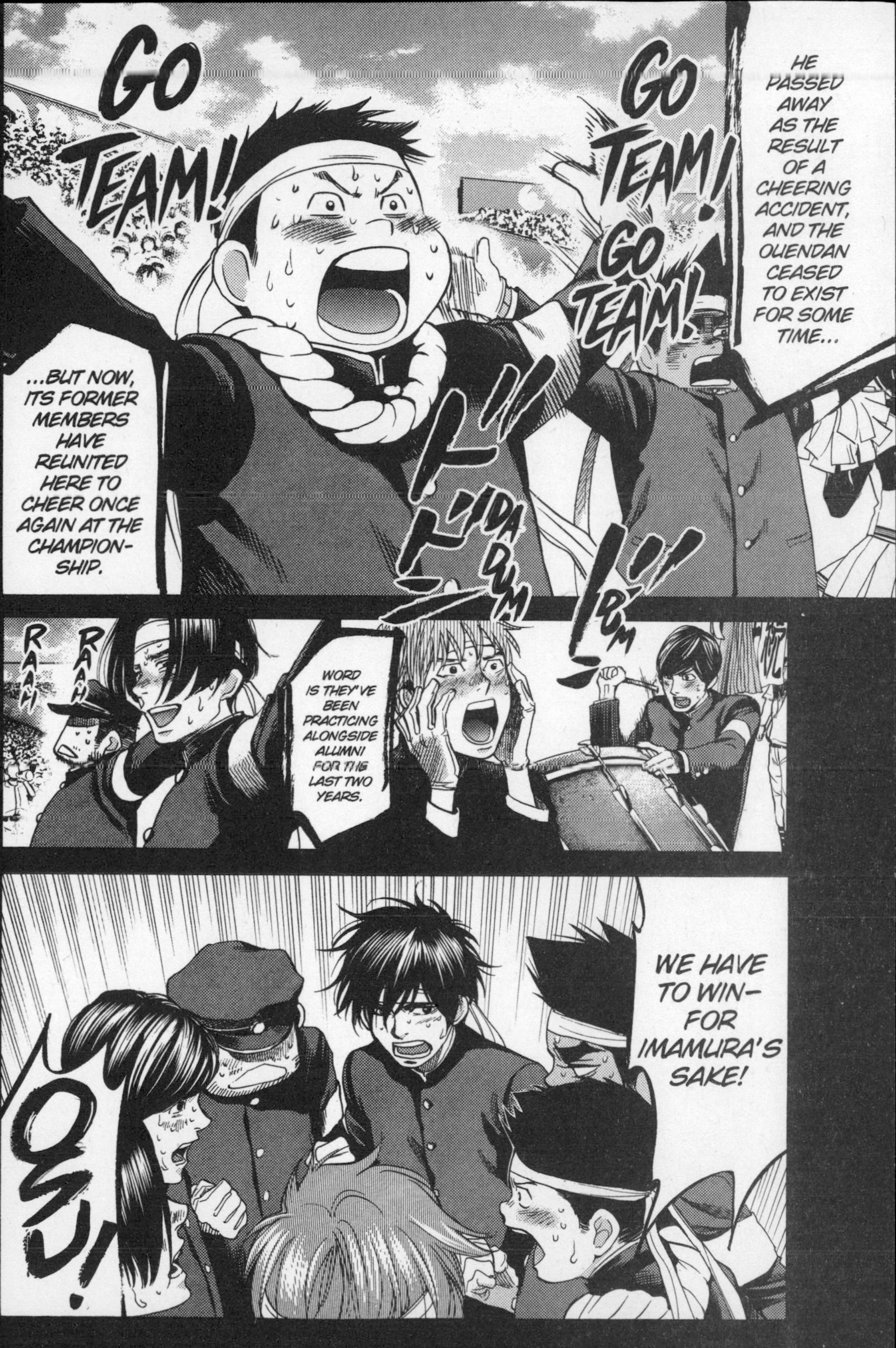
HE PASSED AWAY AS THE RESULT OF A CHEERING ACCIDENT, AND THE OUENDAN CEASED TO EXIST FOR SOME TIME...
GO TEAM!
GO TEAM!
GO TEAM!!
...BUT NOW, ITS FORMER MEMBERS HAVE REUNITED HERE TO CHEER ONCE AGAIN AT THE CHAMPIONSHIP.
DA DUM
DUM
WORD IS THEY'VE BEEN PRACTICING ALONGSIDE ALUMNI FOR THE LAST TWO YEARS.
RAAH
RAAH
WE HAVE TO WIN-FOR IMAMURA'S SAKE!
OSU!

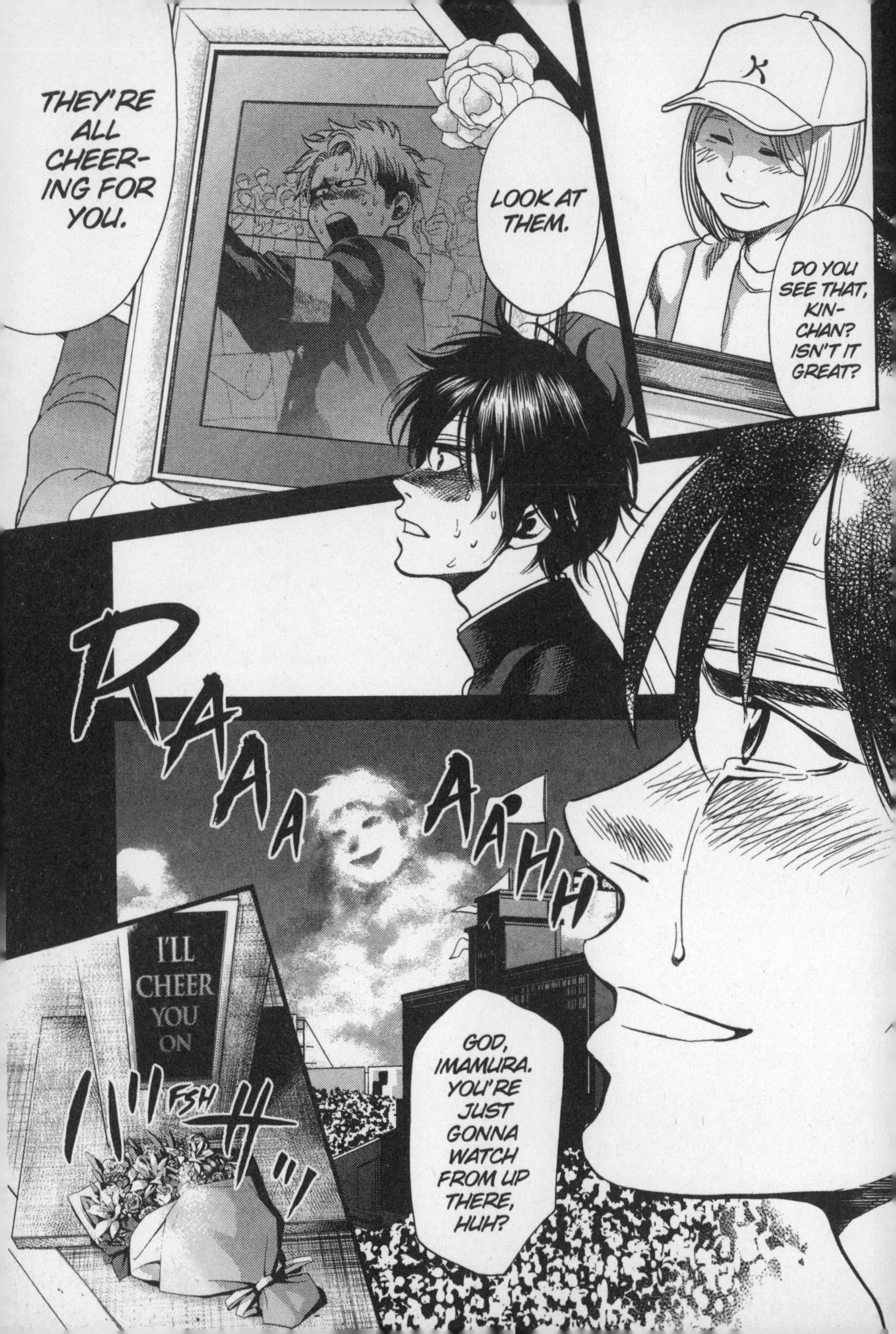
DO YOU SEE THAT, KIN-CHAN? ISN'T IT GREAT?
LOOK AT THEM.
THEY'RE ALL CHEERING FOR YOU.
RAAAAAHH
GOD, IMAMURA. YOU'RE JUST GONNA WATCH FROM UP THERE, HUH?
I'LL CHEER YOU ON
FSH

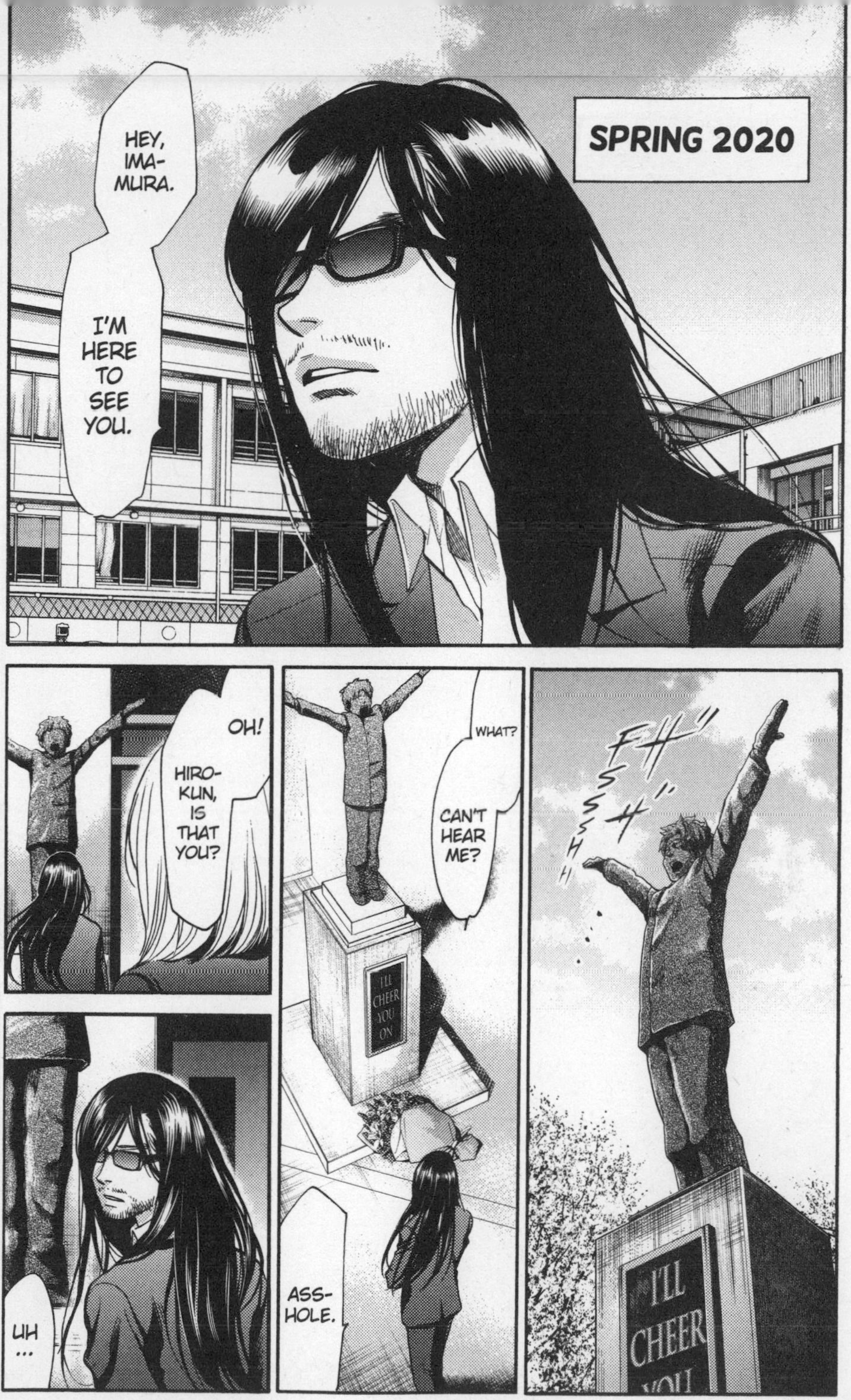
SPRING 2020
HEY, IMAMURA.
I'M HERE TO SEE YOU.
WHAT?
CAN'T HEAR ME?
ASSHOLE.
OH! HIRO-KUN, IS THAT YOU?
I'LL CHEER YOU ON
UH ...

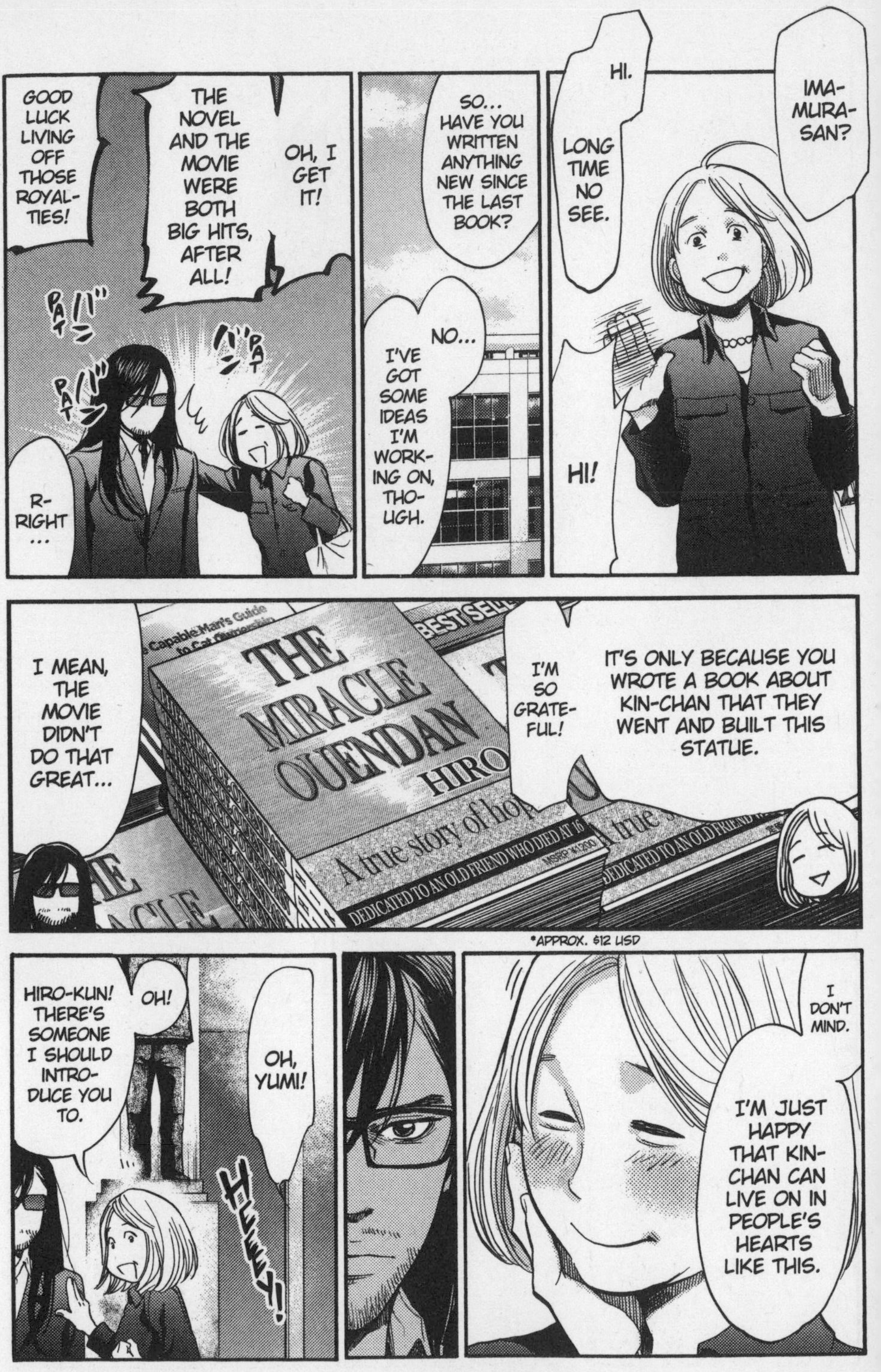
IMA-MURA-SAN?
HI.
LONG TIME NO SEE.
HI!
SO... HAVE YOU WRITTEN ANYTHING NEW SINCE THE LAST BOOK?
NO...
I'VE GOT SOME IDEAS I'M WORKING ON, THOUGH.
OH, I GET IT!
THE NOVEL AND THE MOVIE WERE BOTH BIG HITS, AFTER ALL!
GOOD LUCK LIVING OFF THOSE ROYALTIES!
PAT
PAT
PAT
R-RIGHT...
IT'S ONLY BECAUSE YOU WROTE A BOOK ABOUT KIN-CHAN THAT THEY WENT AND BUILT THIS STATUE.
I'M SO GRATEFUL!
I MEAN, THE MOVIE DIDN'T DO THAT GREAT...
BEST SELL
Capable Man's Guide to Cat Ownership
THE MIRACLE OUENDAN
HIRO
A true story of hop
DEDICATED TO AN OLD FRIEND WHO DIED AT 16
MSRP ¥1200
*APPROX. $12 USD
I DON'T MIND.
I'M JUST HAPPY THAT KIN-CHAN CAN LIVE ON IN PEOPLE'S HEARTS LIKE THIS.
OH!
HIRO-KUN! THERE'S SOMEONE I SHOULD INTRODUCE YOU TO.
OH, YUMI!
HEEEY!

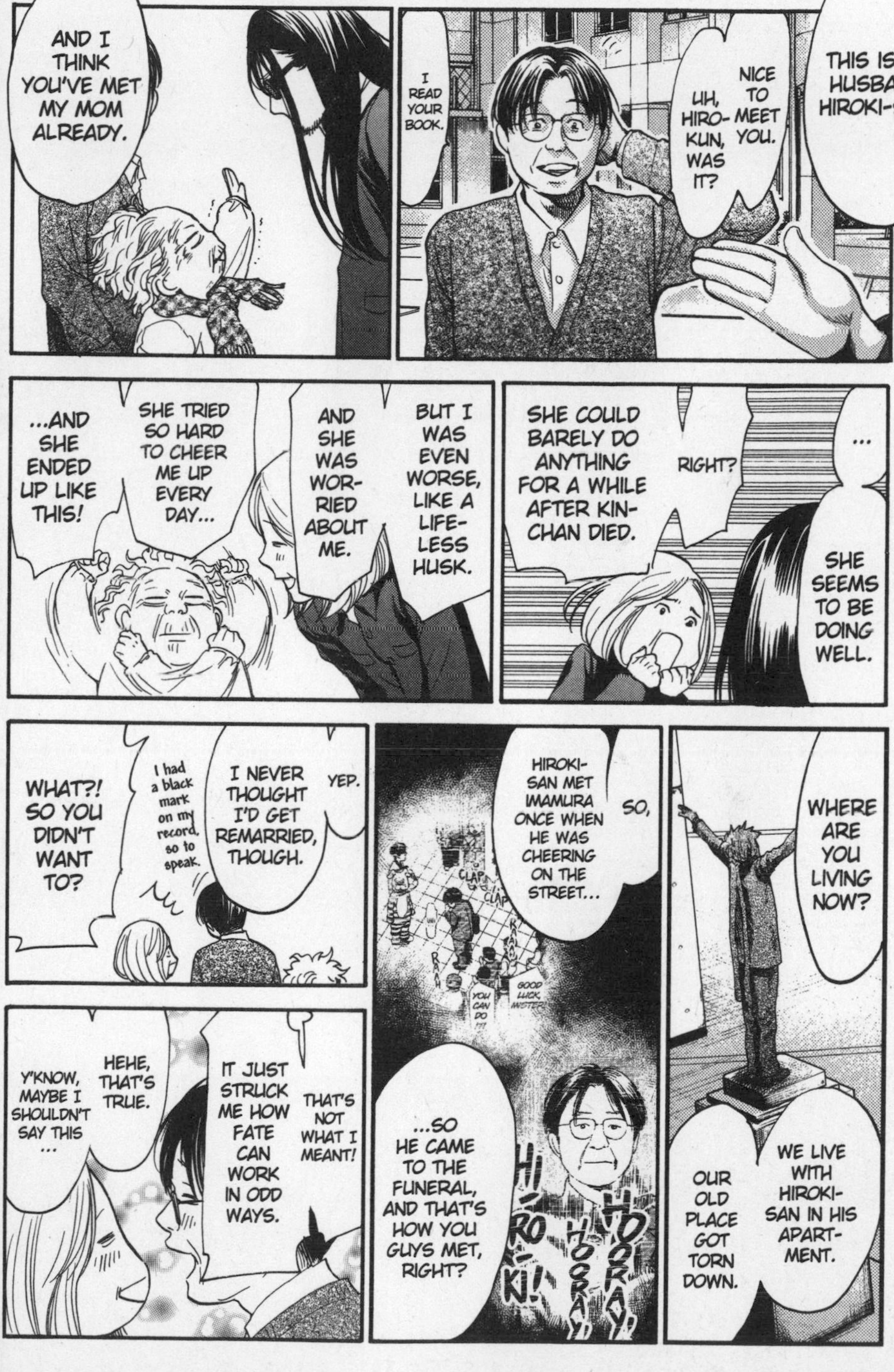
THIS IS MY HUSBAND, HIROKI-SAN.
NICE TO MEET YOU.
UH, HIRO-KUN, WAS IT?
I READ YOUR BOOK.
AND I THINK YOU'VE MET MY MOM ALREADY.
...
SHE SEEMS TO BE DOING WELL.
RIGHT?
SHE COULD BARELY DO ANYTHING FOR A WHILE AFTER KIN-CHAN DIED.
BUT I WAS EVEN WORSE, LIKE A LIFELESS HUSK.
AND SHE WAS WORRIED ABOUT ME.
SHE TRIED SO HARD TO CHEER ME UP EVERY DAY...
...AND SHE ENDED UP LIKE THIS!
WHERE ARE YOU LIVING NOW?
WE LIVE WITH HIROKI-SAN IN HIS APARTMENT.
OUR OLD PLACE GOT TORN DOWN.
SO,
HIROKI-SAN MET IMAMURA ONCE WHEN HE WAS CHEERING ON THE STREET...
CLAP
CLAP
GOOD LUCK, MISTER
HIROKI!
HOORAY!
HOORAY!
...SO HE CAME TO THE FUNERAL, AND THAT'S HOW YOU GUYS MET, RIGHT?
YEP.
I NEVER THOUGHT I'D GET REMARRIED, THOUGH.
I had a black mark on my record, so to speak.
WHAT?! SO YOU DIDN'T WANT TO?
THAT'S NOT WHAT I MEANT!
IT JUST STRUCK ME HOW FATE CAN WORK IN ODD WAYS.
HEHE, THAT'S TRUE.
Y'KNOW, MAYBE I SHOULDN'T SAY THIS ...

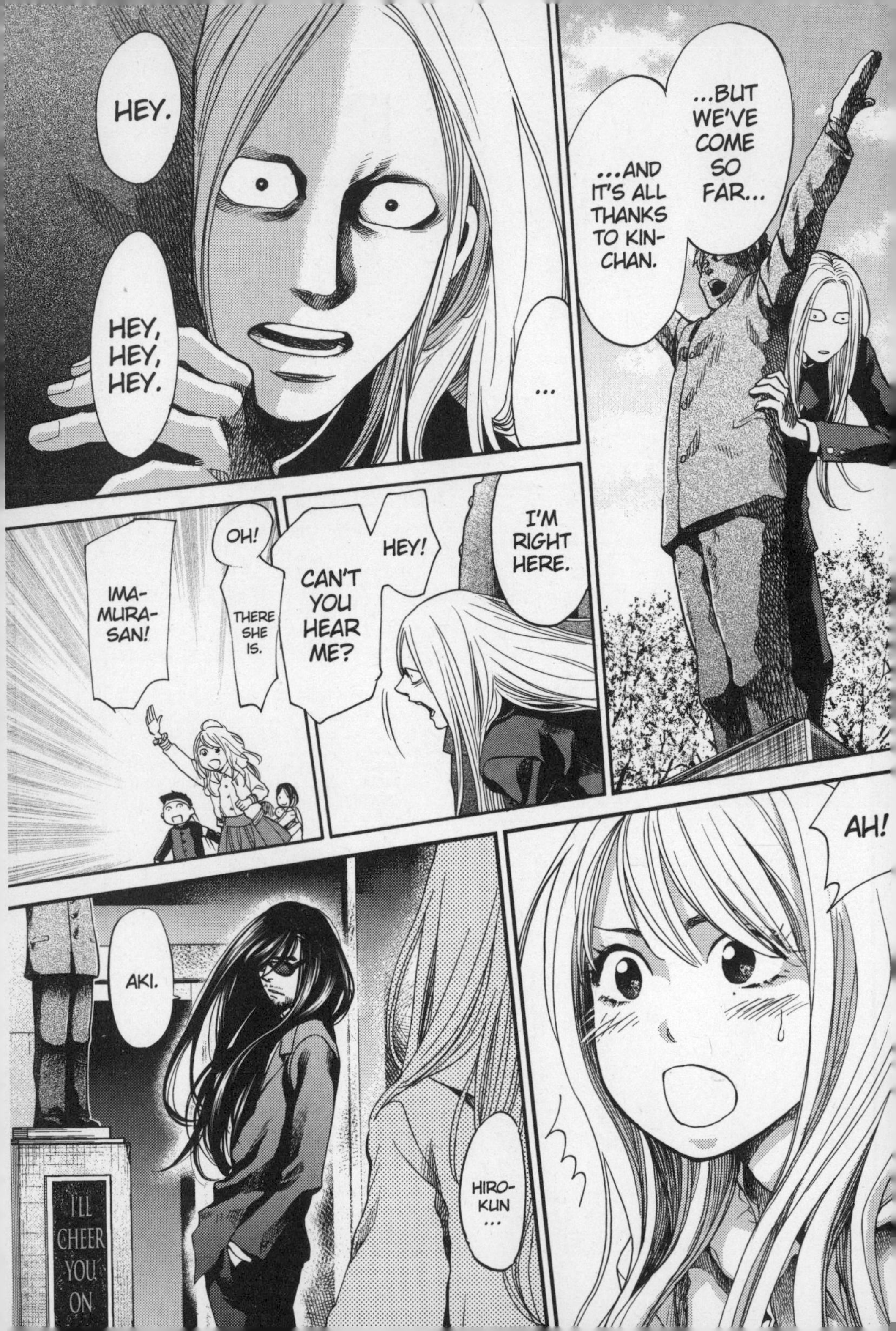
...BUT WE'VE COME SO FAR...
...AND IT'S ALL THANKS TO KIN-CHAN.
HEY.
HEY, HEY, HEY.
...
I'M RIGHT HERE.
HEY!
CAN'T YOU HEAR ME?
OH!
THERE SHE IS.
IMA-MURA-SAN!
AH!
HIRO-KUN...
AKI.
I'LL CHEER YOU ON

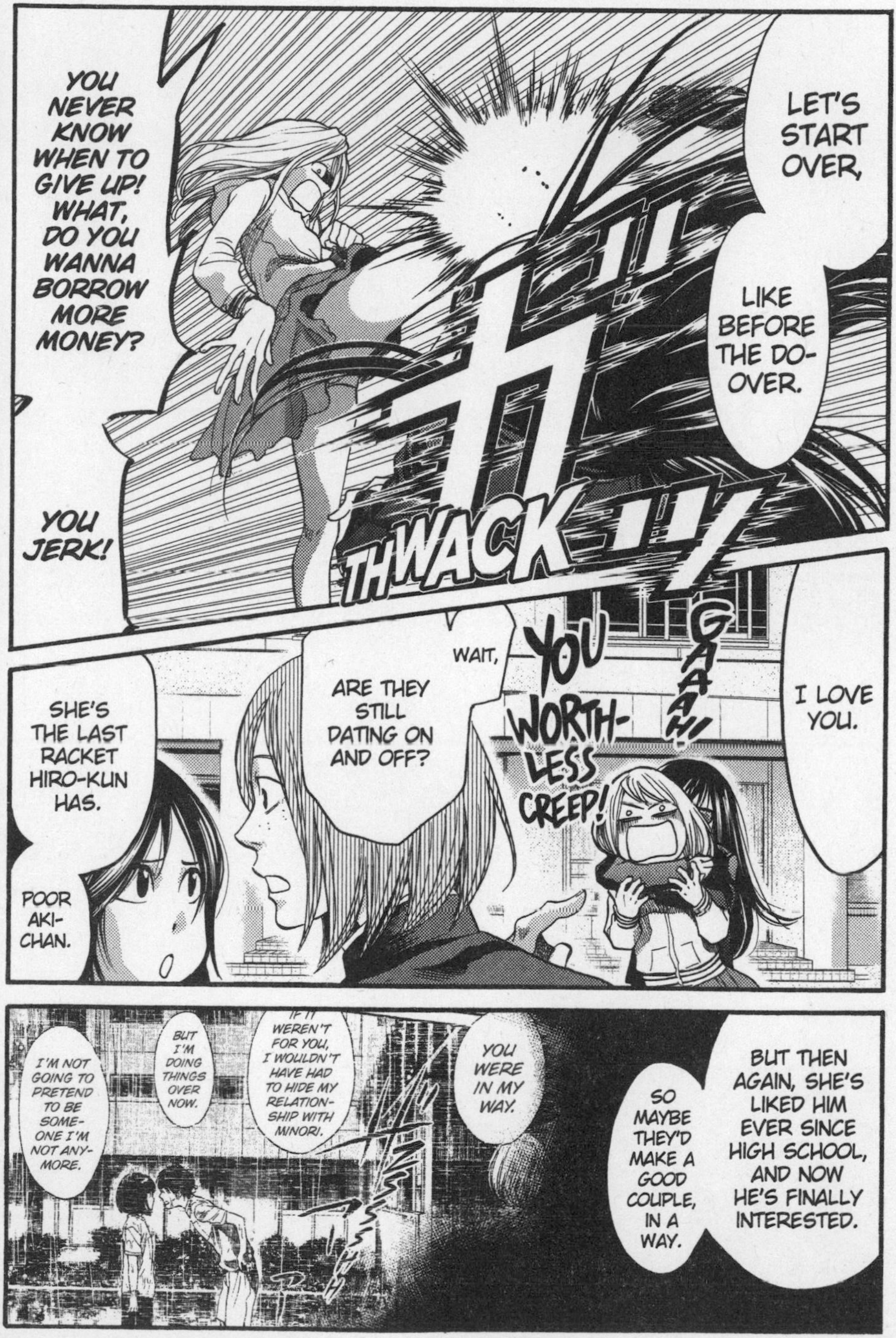
LET'S START OVER,
LIKE BEFORE THE DO-OVER.
YOU NEVER KNOW WHEN TO GIVE UP! WHAT, DO YOU WANNA BORROW MORE MONEY?
YOU JERK!
THWACK!!
I LOVE YOU.
GAAAH!
YOU WORTHLESS CREEP!
WAIT,
ARE THEY STILL DATING ON AND OFF?
SHE'S THE LAST RACKET HIRO-KUN HAS.
POOR AKI-CHAN.
BUT THEN AGAIN, SHE'S LIKED HIM EVER SINCE HIGH SCHOOL, AND NOW HE'S FINALLY INTERESTED.
SO MAYBE THEY'D MAKE A GOOD COUPLE, IN A WAY.
YOU WERE IN MY WAY.
IF IT WEREN'T FOR YOU, I WOULDN'T HAVE HAD TO HIDE MY RELATIONSHIP WITH MINORI.
BUT I'M DOING THINGS OVER NOW.
I'M NOT GOING TO PRETEND TO BE SOMEONE I'M NOT ANYMORE.

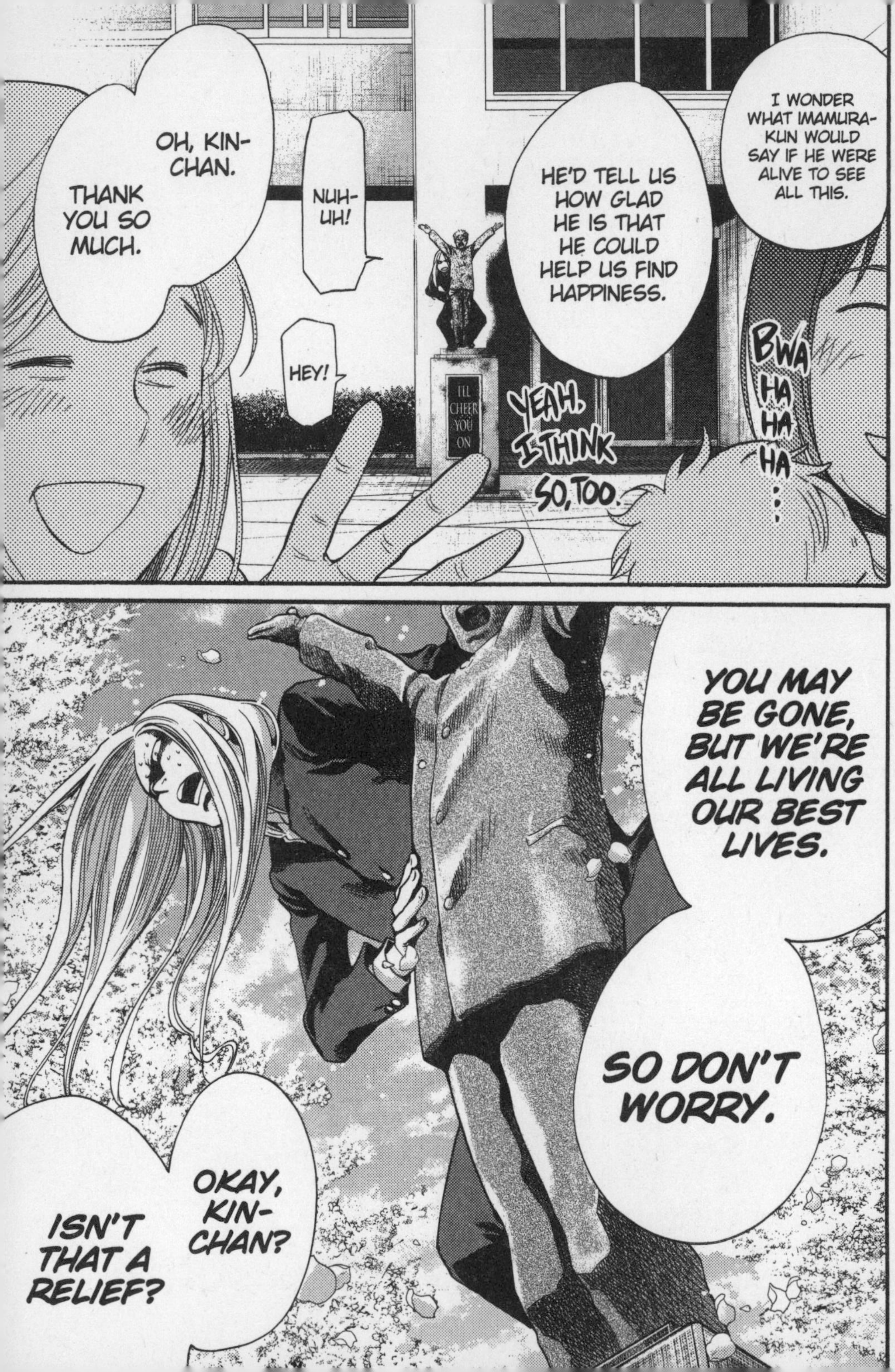
I WONDER WHAT IMAMURA-KUN WOULD SAY IF HE WERE ALIVE TO SEE ALL THIS.
BWA HA HA HA...
HE'D TELL US HOW GLAD HE IS THAT HE COULD HELP US FIND HAPPINESS.
YEAH. I THINK SO, TOO.
I'LL CHEER YOU ON
NUH-UH!
HEY!
OH, KIN-CHAN.
THANK YOU SO MUCH.
YOU MAY BE GONE, BUT WE'RE ALL LIVING OUR BEST LIVES.
SO DON'T WORRY.
OKAY, KIN-CHAN?
ISN'T THAT A RELIEF?

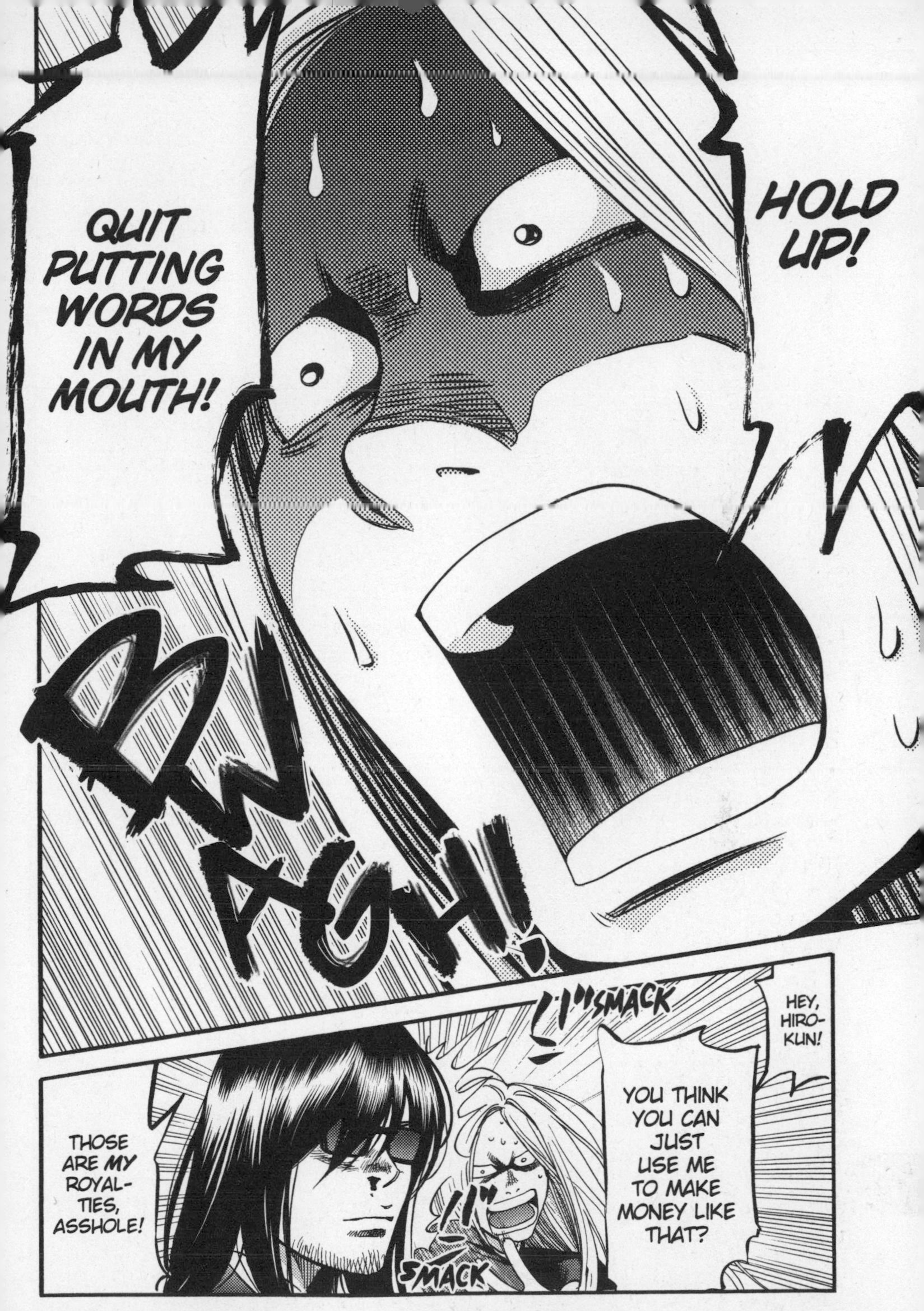

HOLD UP!
QUIT PUTTING WORDS IN MY MOUTH!
BWAGH!!
SMACK
HEY, HIRO-KUN!
YOU THINK YOU CAN JUST USE ME TO MAKE MONEY LIKE THAT?
SMACK
THOSE ARE MY ROYAL-TIES, ASSHOLE!

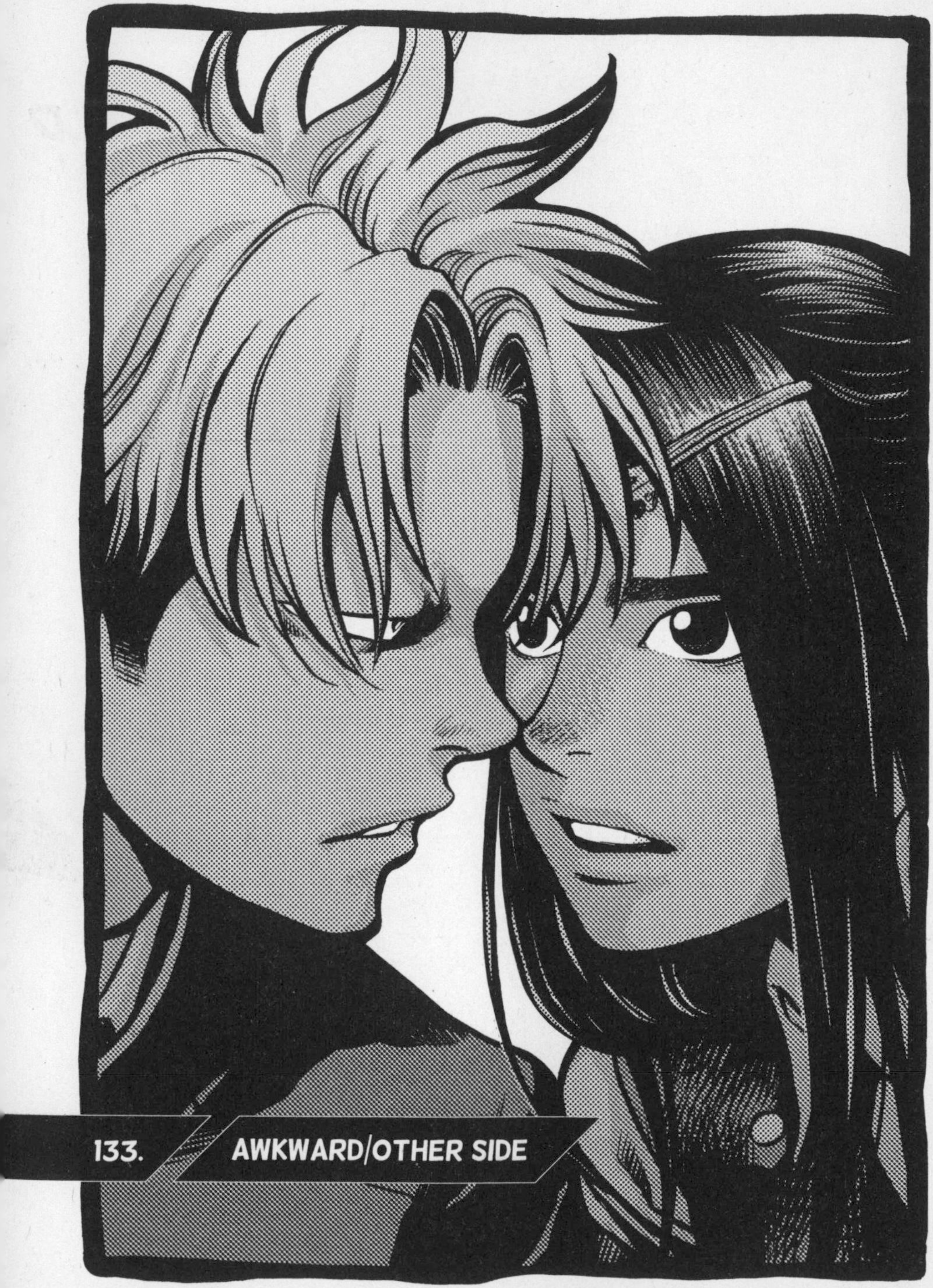
133.
AWKWARD/OTHER SIDE

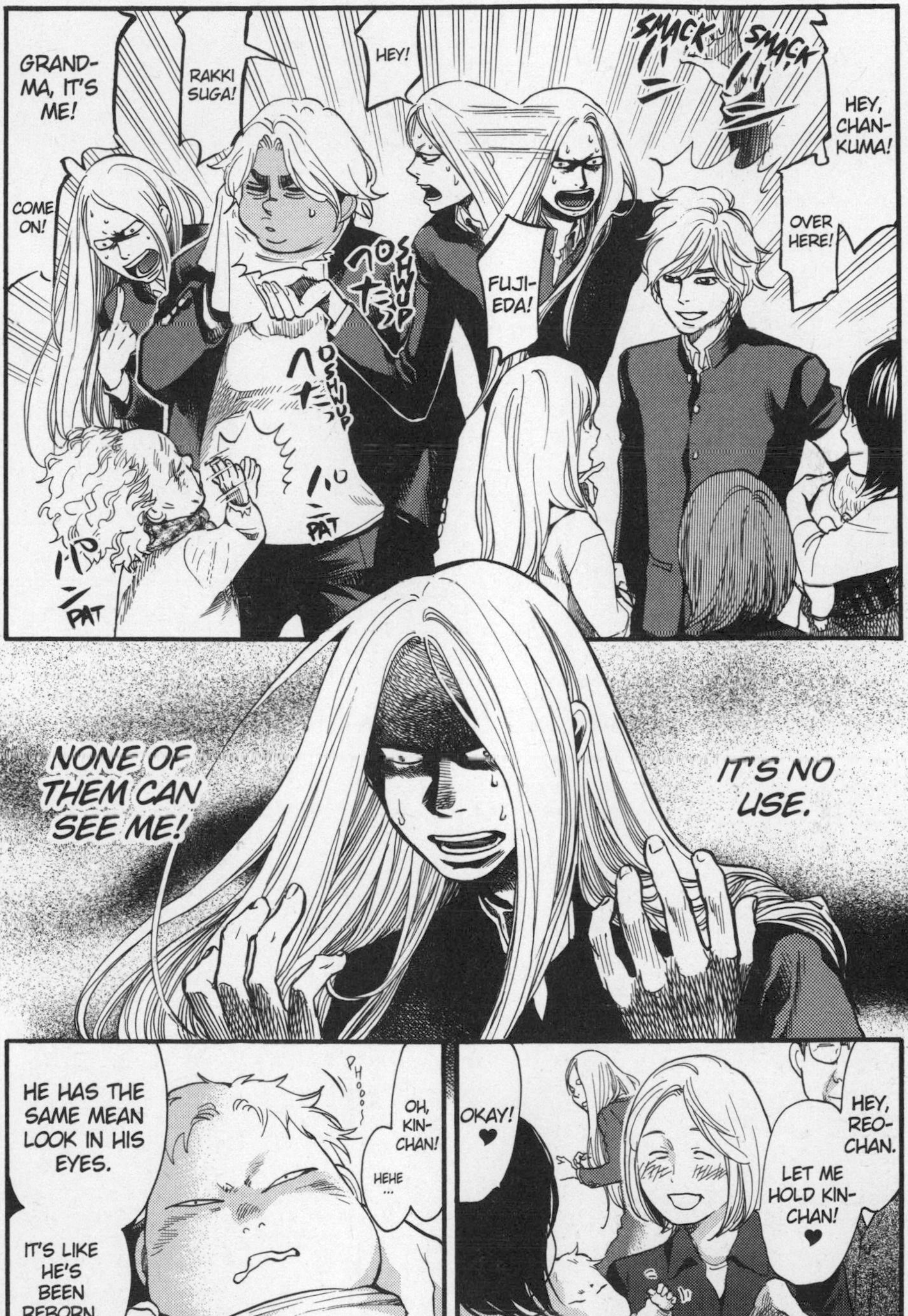
SMACK
SMACK
HEY, CHAN-KUMA!
OVER HERE!
FUJI-EDA!
HEY!
RAKKI SUGA!
GRAND-MA, IT'S ME!
COME ON!
SHWUP
SHWUP
PAT
PAT
IT'S NO USE.
NONE OF THEM CAN SEE ME!
HEY, REO-CHAN.
LET ME HOLD KIN-CHAN! ♥
OKAY! ♥
PHOOO
OH, KIN-CHAN!
HEHE ...
HE HAS THE SAME MEAN LOOK IN HIS EYES.
IT'S LIKE HE'S BEEN REBORN. ♥

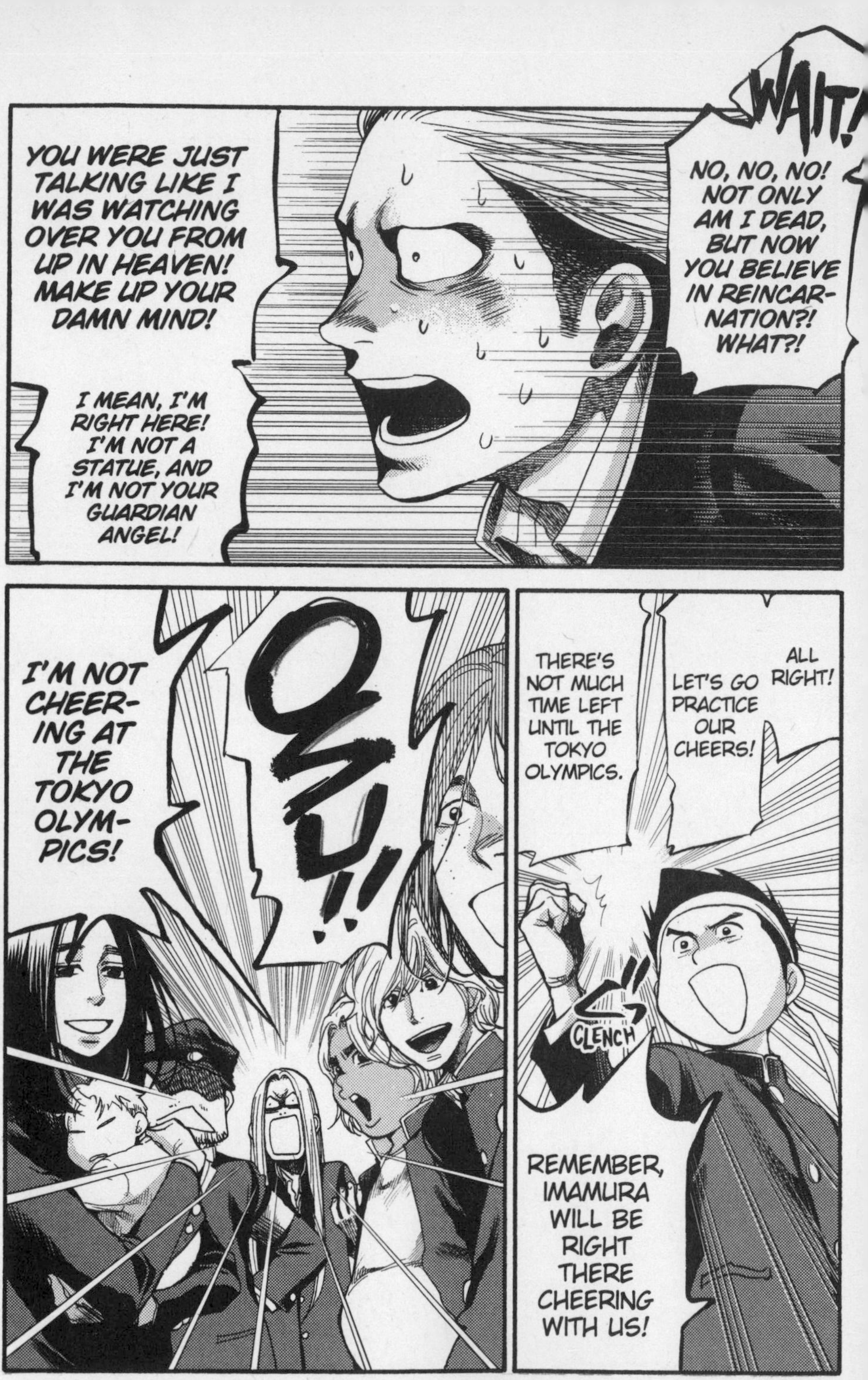
WAIT!
NO, NO, NO! NOT ONLY AM I DEAD, BUT NOW YOU BELIEVE IN REINCARNATION?! WHAT?!
YOU WERE JUST TALKING LIKE I WAS WATCHING OVER YOU FROM UP IN HEAVEN! MAKE UP YOUR DAMN MIND!
I MEAN, I'M RIGHT HERE! I'M NOT A STATUE, AND I'M NOT YOUR GUARDIAN ANGEL!
ALL RIGHT!
LET'S GO PRACTICE OUR CHEERS!
THERE'S NOT MUCH TIME LEFT UNTIL THE TOKYO OLYMPICS.
CLENCH
REMEMBER, IMAMURA WILL BE RIGHT THERE CHEERING WITH US!
I'M NOT CHEER-ING AT THE TOKYO OLYM-PICS!

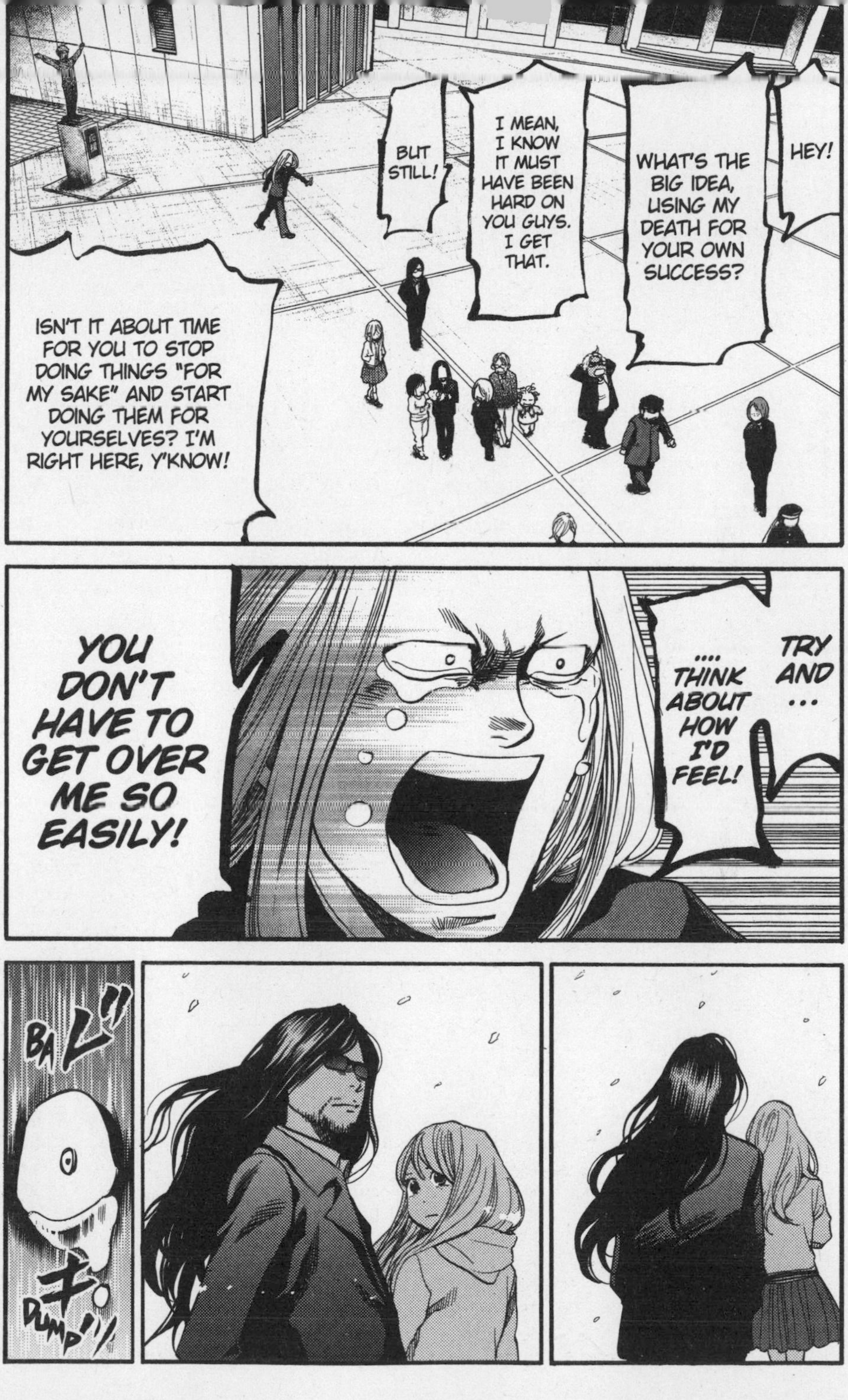
HEY!
WHAT'S THE BIG IDEA, USING MY DEATH FOR YOUR OWN SUCCESS?
I MEAN, I KNOW IT MUST HAVE BEEN HARD ON YOU GUYS. I GET THAT.
BUT STILL!
ISN'T IT ABOUT TIME FOR YOU TO STOP DOING THINGS "FOR MY SAKE" AND START DOING THEM FOR YOURSELVES? I'M RIGHT HERE, Y'KNOW!
TRY AND...
....THINK ABOUT HOW I'D FEEL!
YOU DON'T HAVE TO GET OVER ME SO EASILY!
BA
DUMP!!

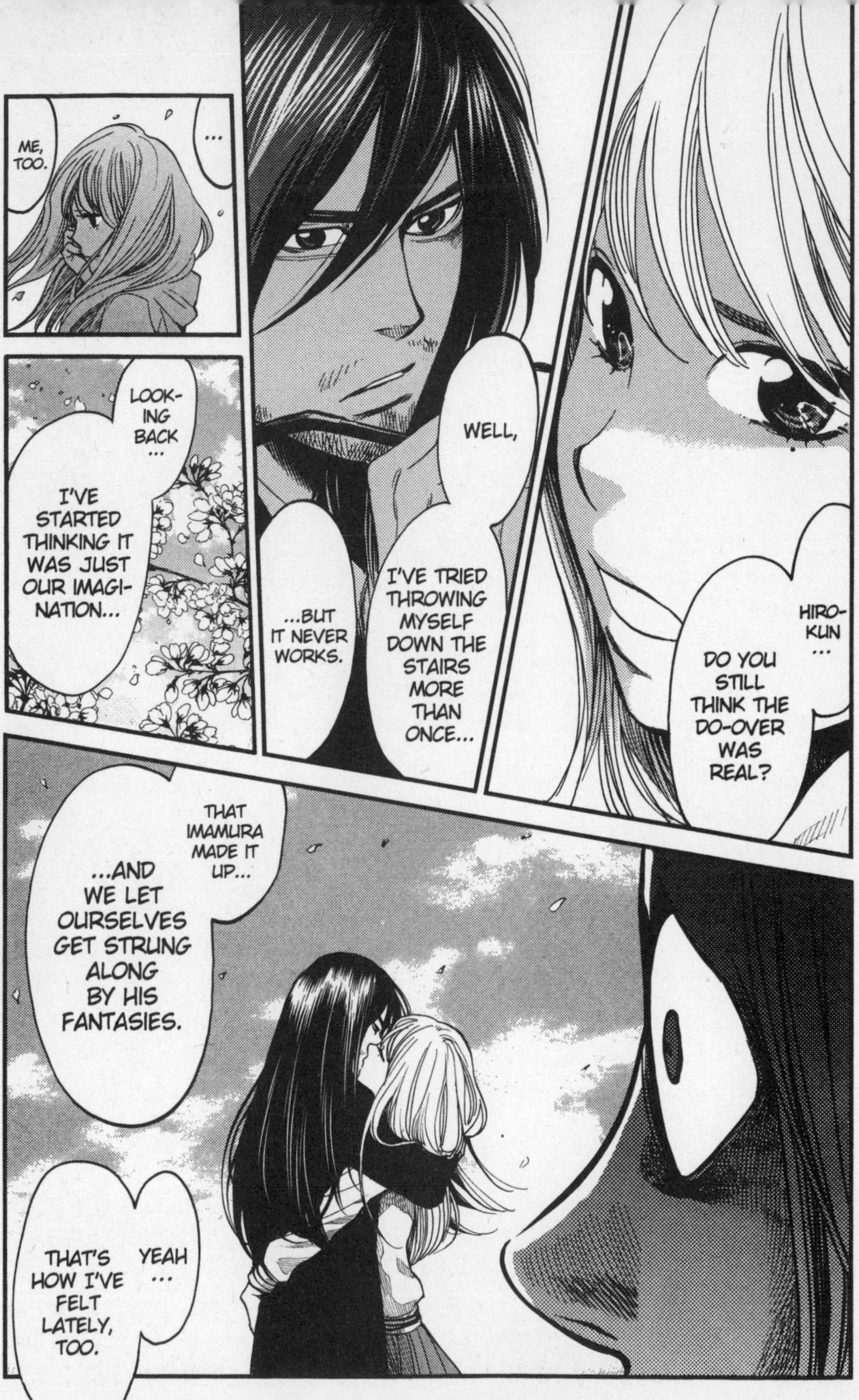
HIRO-KUN...
DO YOU STILL THINK THE DO-OVER WAS REAL?
WELL,
I'VE TRIED THROWING MYSELF DOWN THE STAIRS MORE THAN ONCE...
...BUT IT NEVER WORKS.
...
ME, TOO.
LOOKING BACK...
I'VE STARTED THINKING IT WAS JUST OUR IMAGINATION...
THAT IMAMURA MADE IT UP...
...AND WE LET OURSELVES GET STRUNG ALONG BY HIS FANTASIES.
YEAH...
THAT'S HOW I'VE FELT LATELY, TOO.

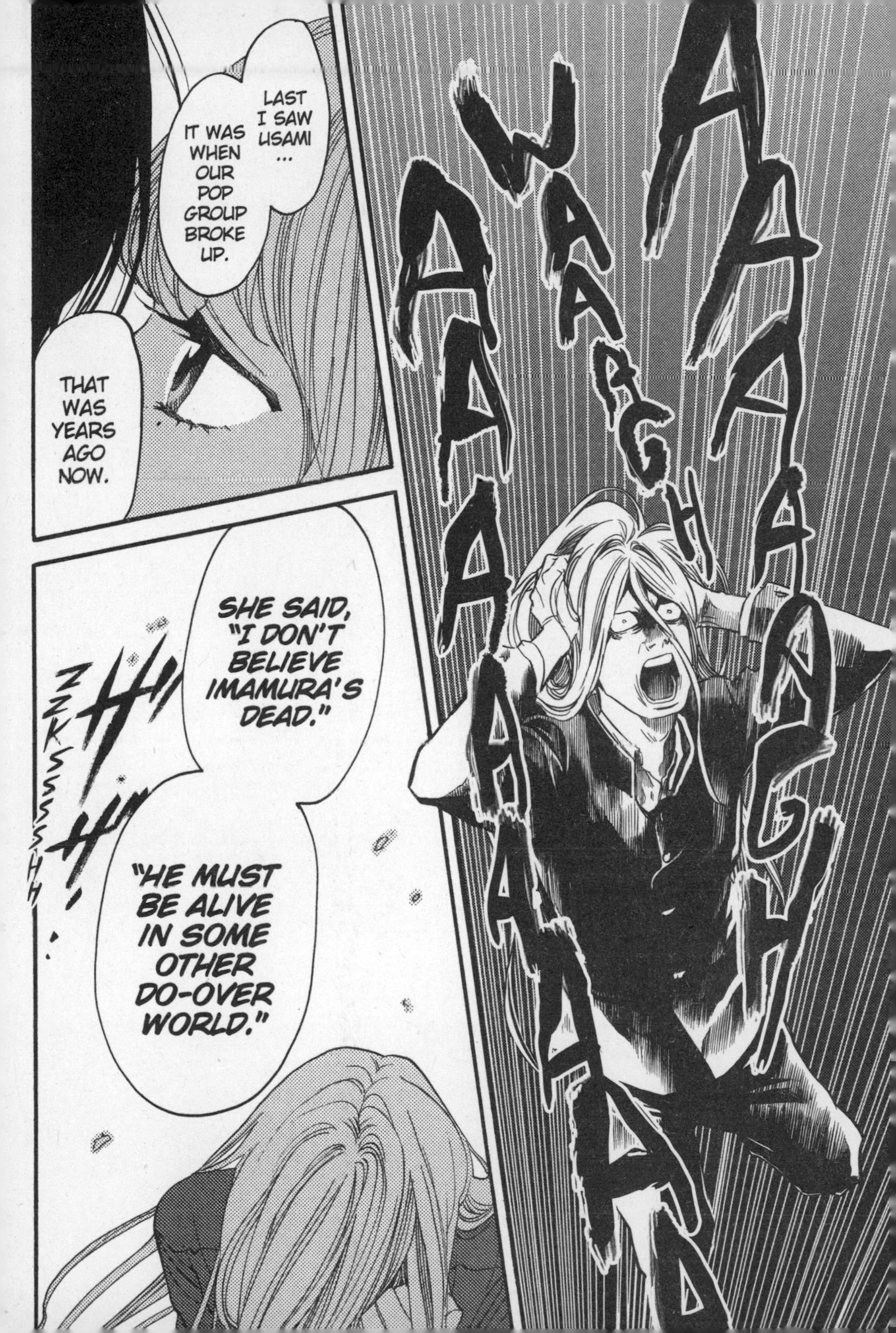
LAST I SAW USAMI ...
IT WAS WHEN OUR POP GROUP BROKE UP.
THAT WAS YEARS AGO NOW.
SHE SAID, "I DON'T BELIEVE IMAMURA'S DEAD."
"HE MUST BE ALIVE IN SOME OTHER DO-OVER WORLD."
ZZKSSSSHH

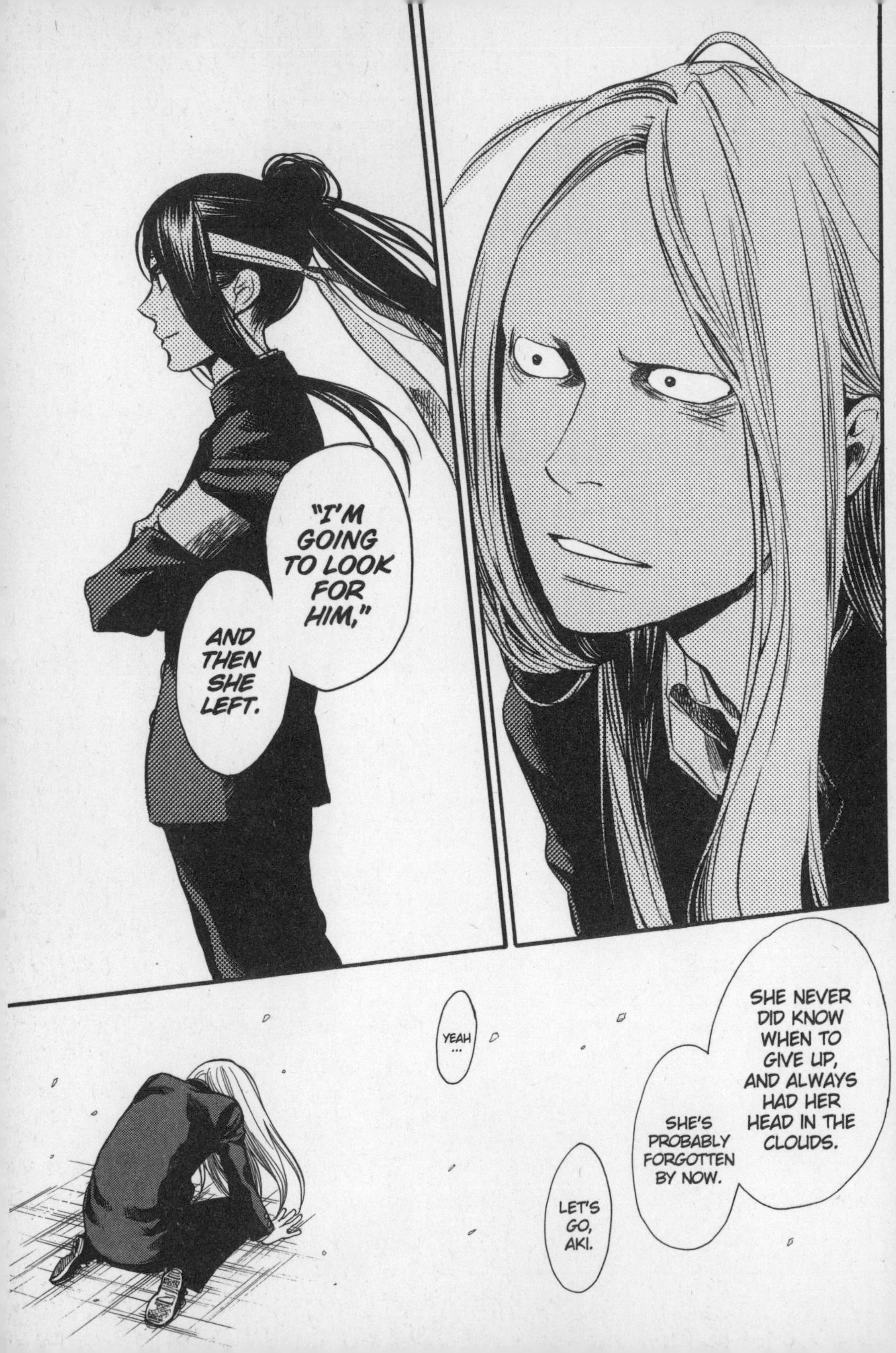
"I'M GOING TO LOOK FOR HIM,"
AND THEN SHE LEFT.
SHE NEVER DID KNOW WHEN TO GIVE UP, AND ALWAYS HAD HER HEAD IN THE CLOUDS.
SHE'S PROBABLY FORGOTTEN BY NOW.
LET'S GO, AKI.
YEAH...

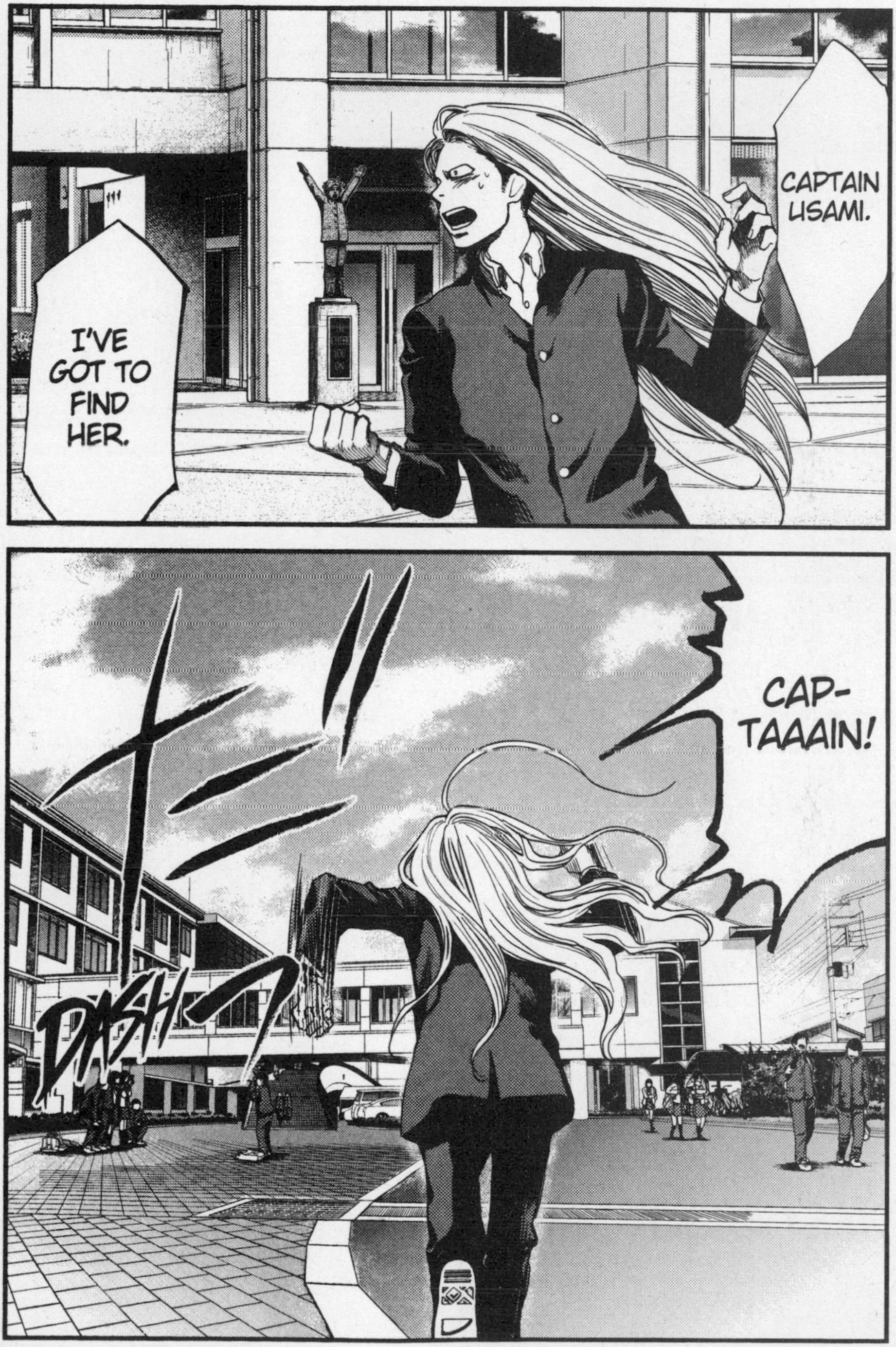
CAPTAIN USAMI.
I'VE GOT TO FIND HER.
CAP-TAAAIN!
DASH

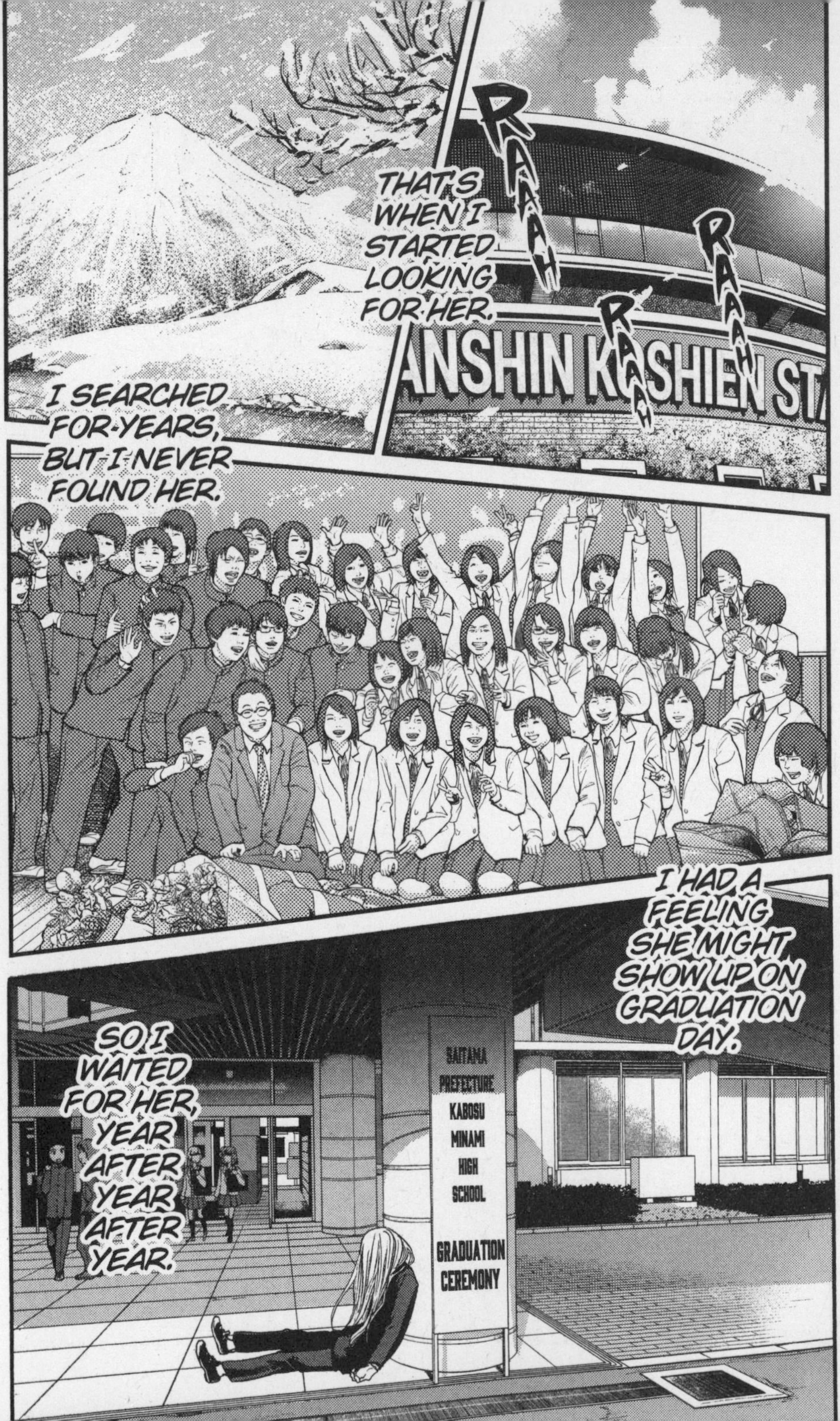
THAT'S WHEN I STARTED LOOKING FOR HER.
RAAAAH
RAAAAH
RAAAH
ANSHIN K SHIEN ST
I SEARCHED FOR YEARS, BUT I NEVER FOUND HER.
I HAD A FEELING SHE MIGHT SHOW UP ON GRADUATION DAY.
SAITAMA PREFECTURE KABOSU MINAMI HIGH SCHOOL
GRADUATION CEREMONY
SO I WAITED FOR HER, YEAR AFTER YEAR AFTER YEAR.

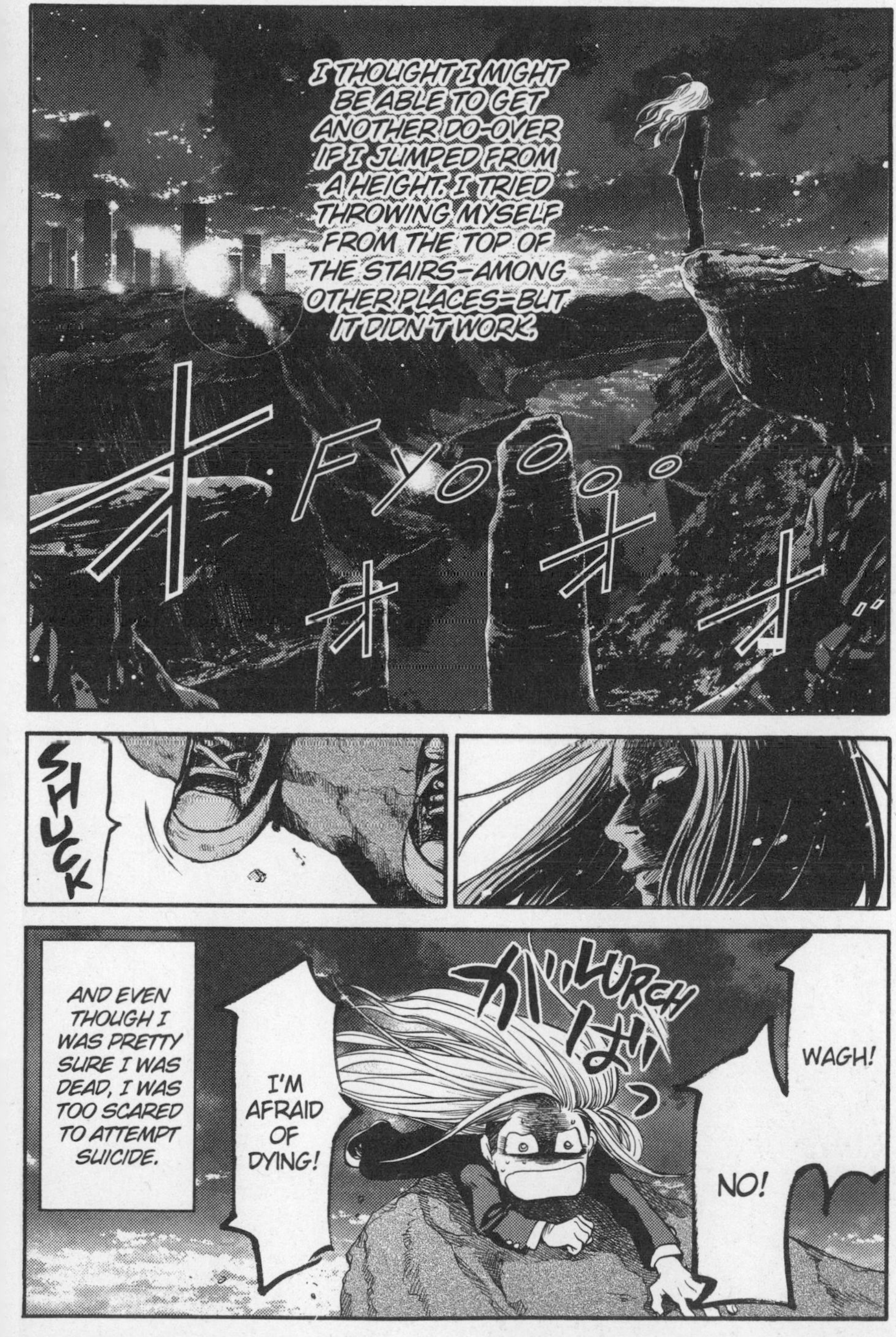
I THOUGHT I MIGHT BE ABLE TO GET ANOTHER DO-OVER IF I JUMPED FROM A HEIGHT. I TRIED THROWING MYSELF FROM THE TOP OF THE STAIRS—AMONG OTHER PLACES—BUT IT DIDN'T WORK.
FYOOOO
SHUCK
WAGH!
NO!
LURCH
I'M AFRAID OF DYING!
AND EVEN THOUGH I WAS PRETTY SURE I WAS DEAD, I WAS TOO SCARED TO ATTEMPT SUICIDE.

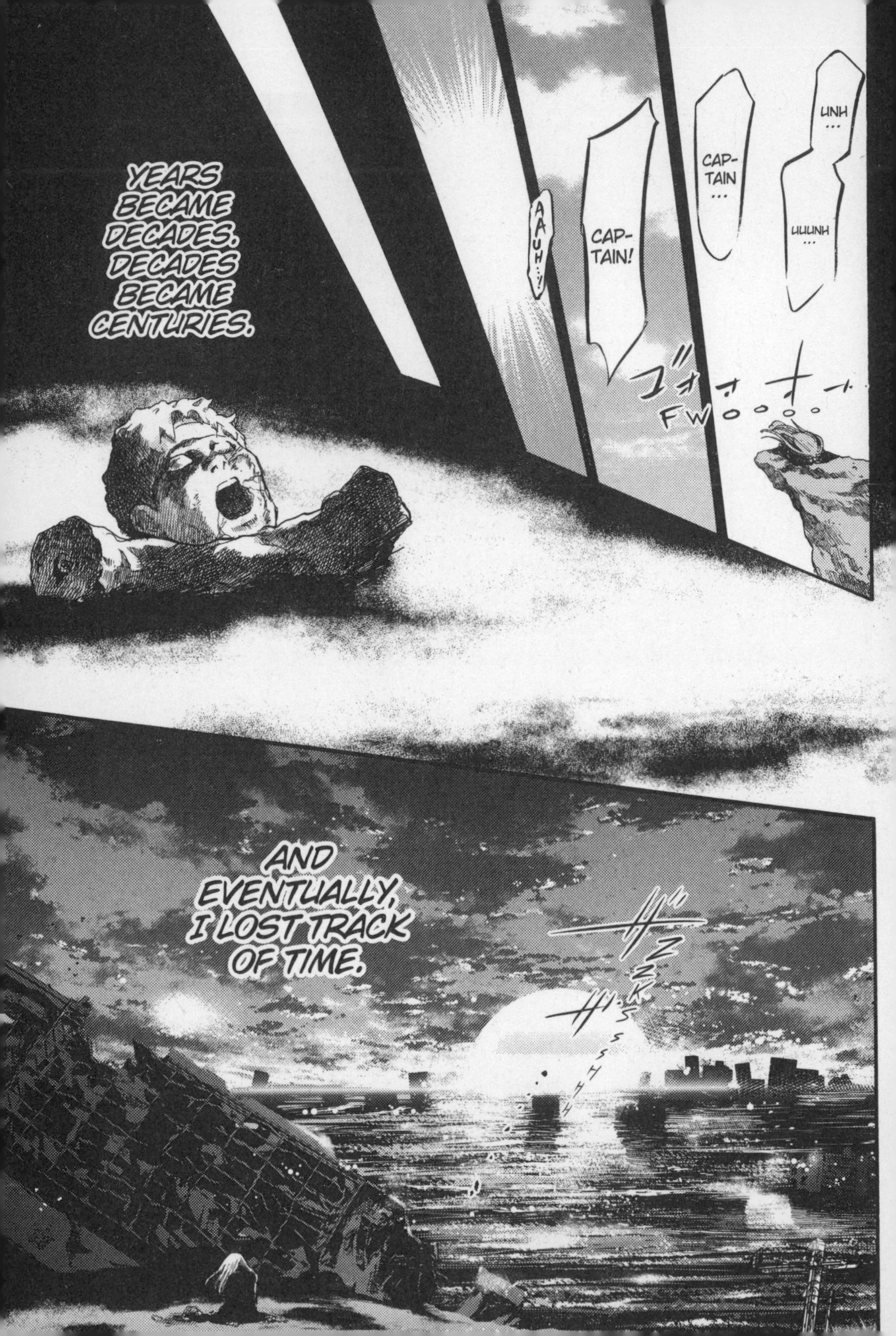
UNH...
UUUNH...
FWOOOOO
CAP-TAIN...
CAP-TAIN!
AAUH...!?
YEARS BECAME DECADES. DECADES BECAME CENTURIES.
AND EVENTUALLY, I LOST TRACK OF TIME.
ZZKSSSHHH

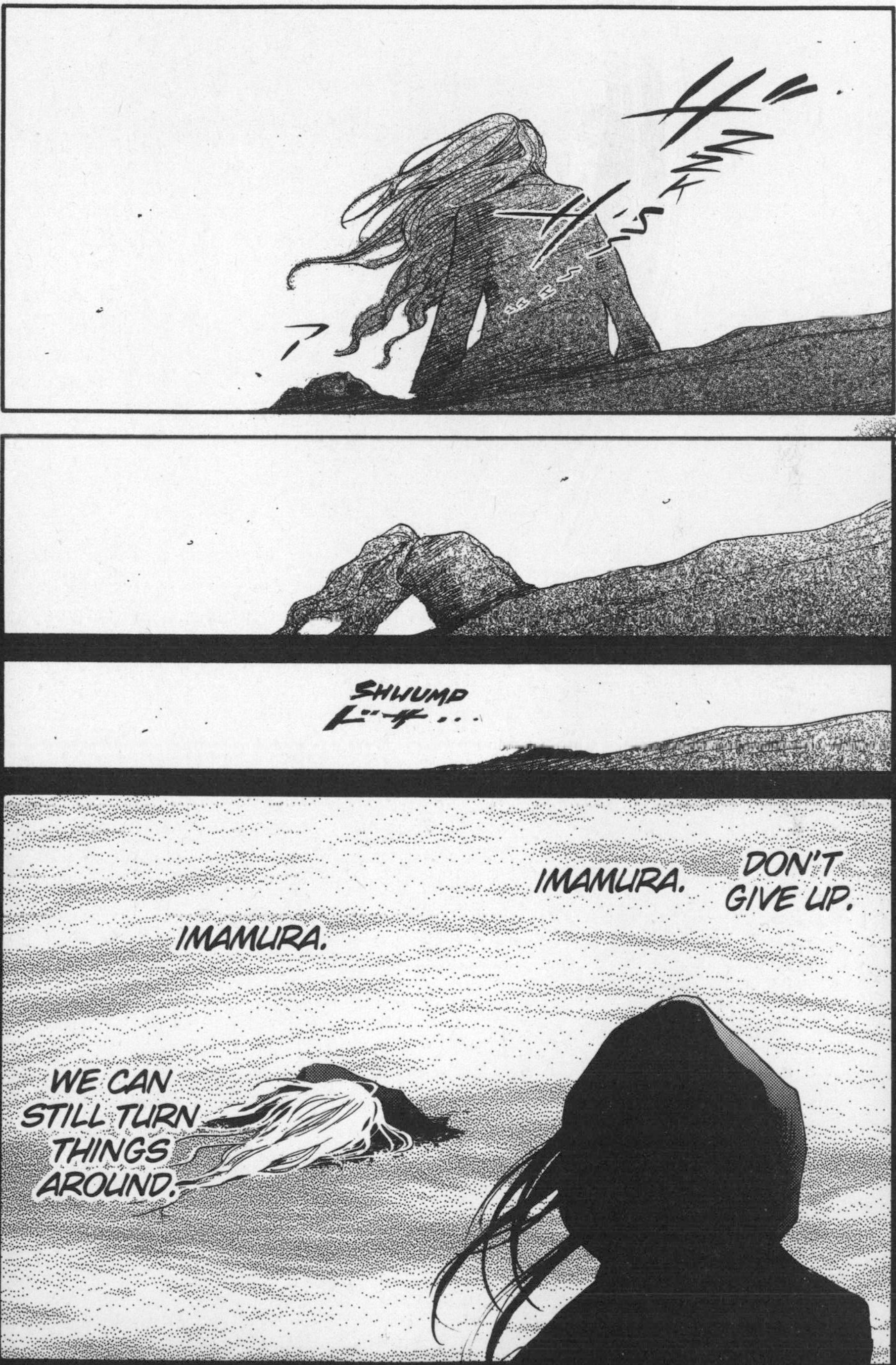
ZZZK
SHWUMP
IMAMURA.
DON'T GIVE UP.
IMAMURA.
WE CAN STILL TURN THINGS AROUND.

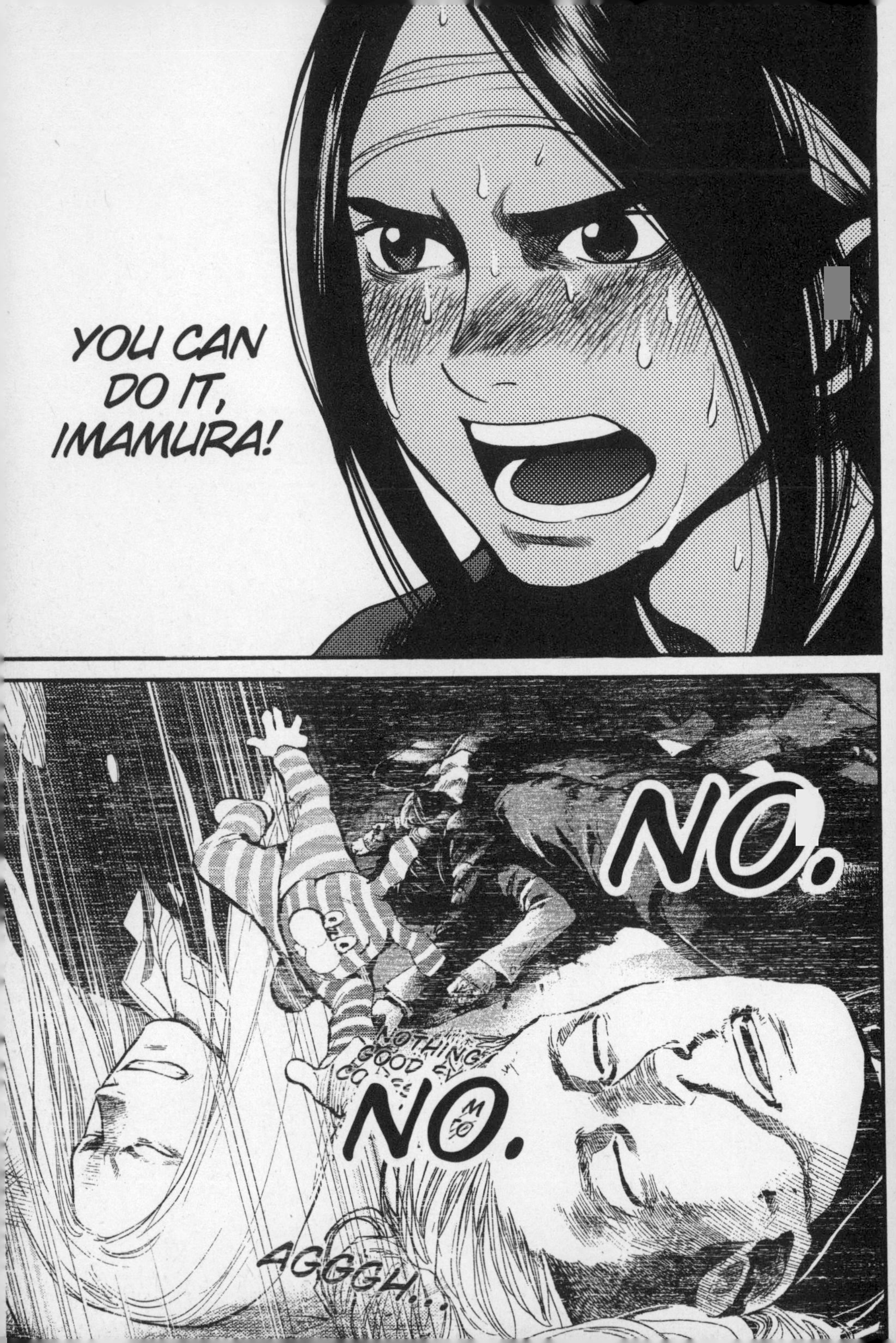
YOU CAN DO IT, IMAMURA!
NO.
NOTHING GOOD CO
NO.
AGGGH...

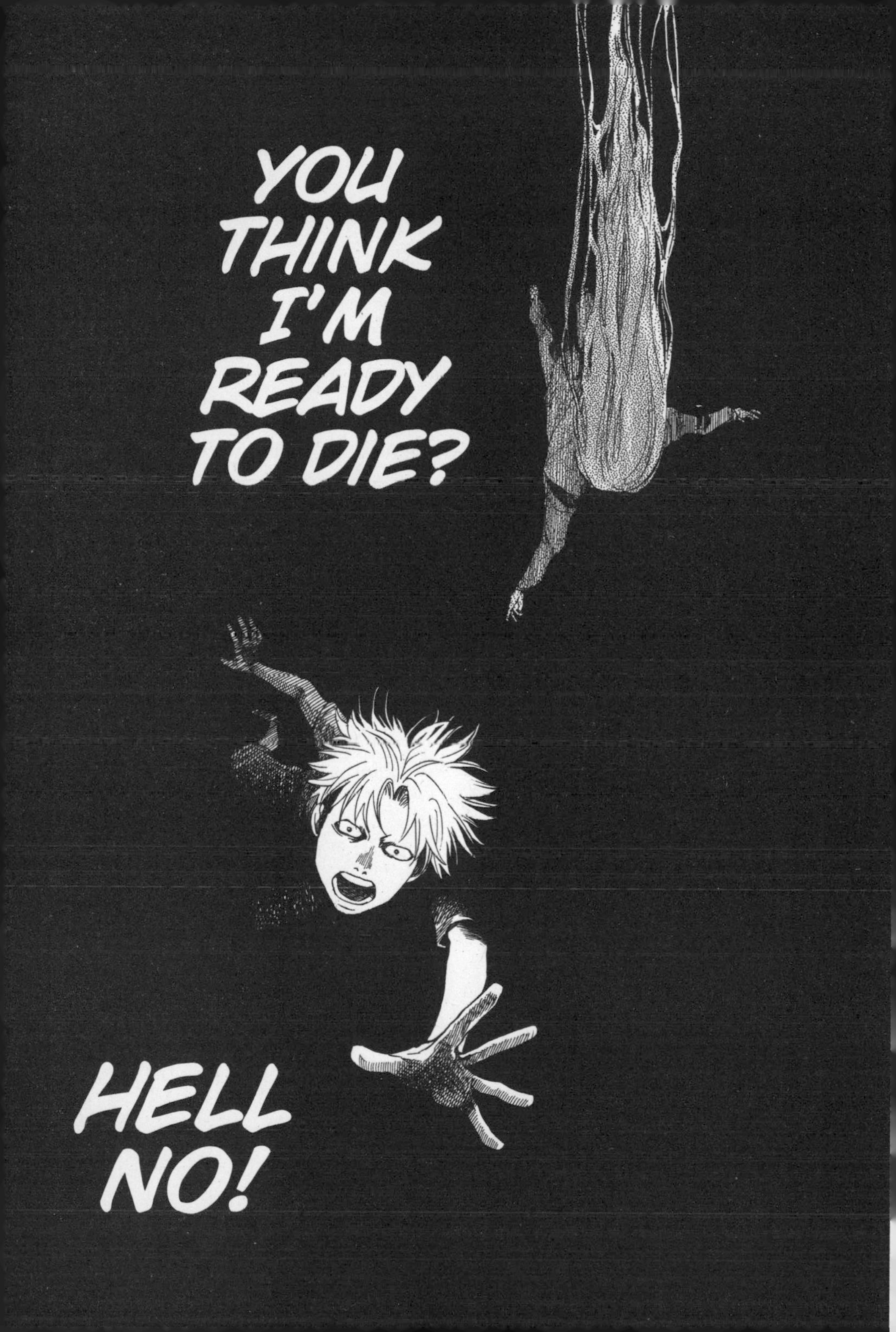
YOU THINK I'M READY TO DIE?
HELL NO!

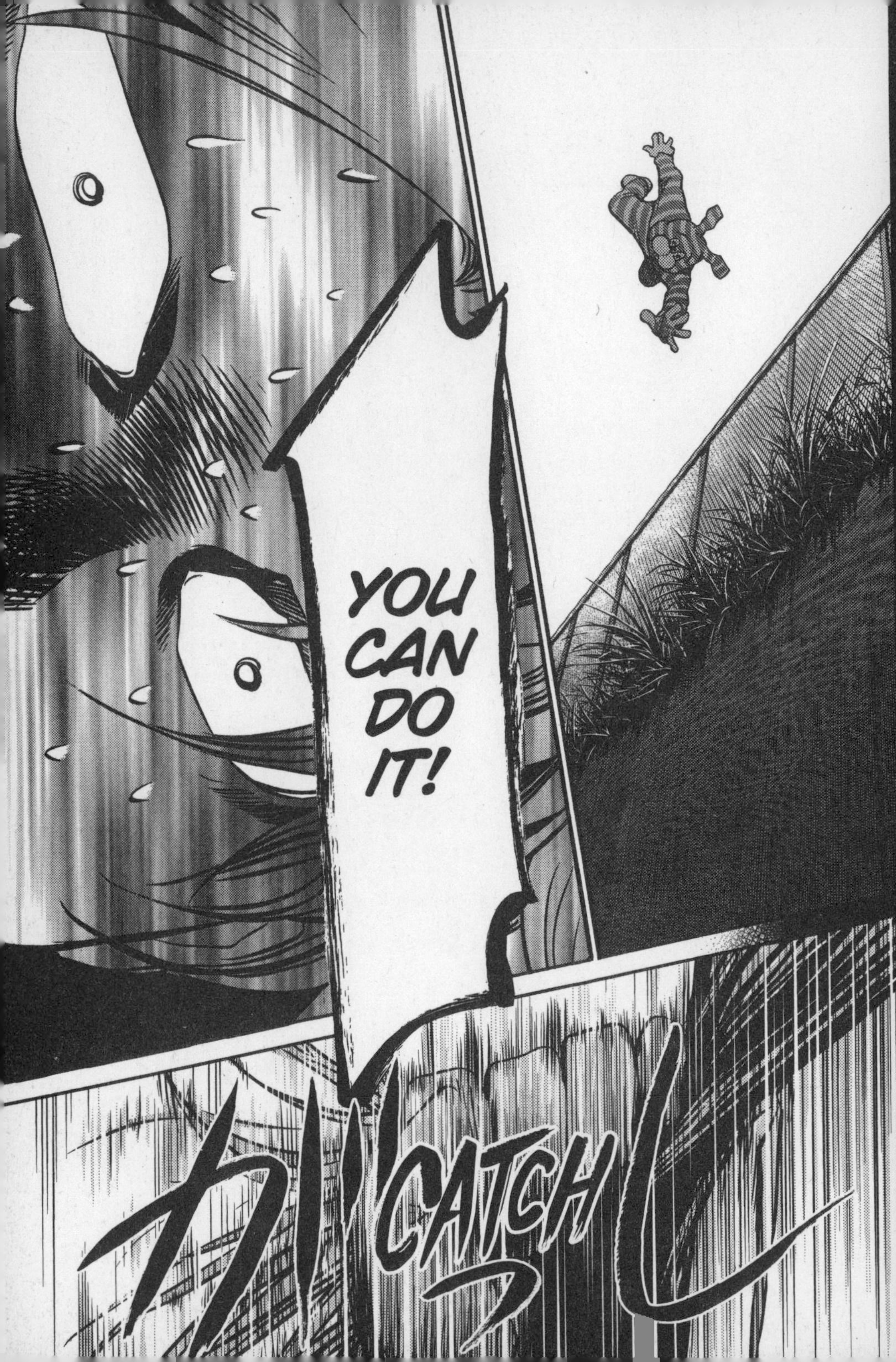
YOU CAN DO IT!
CATCH

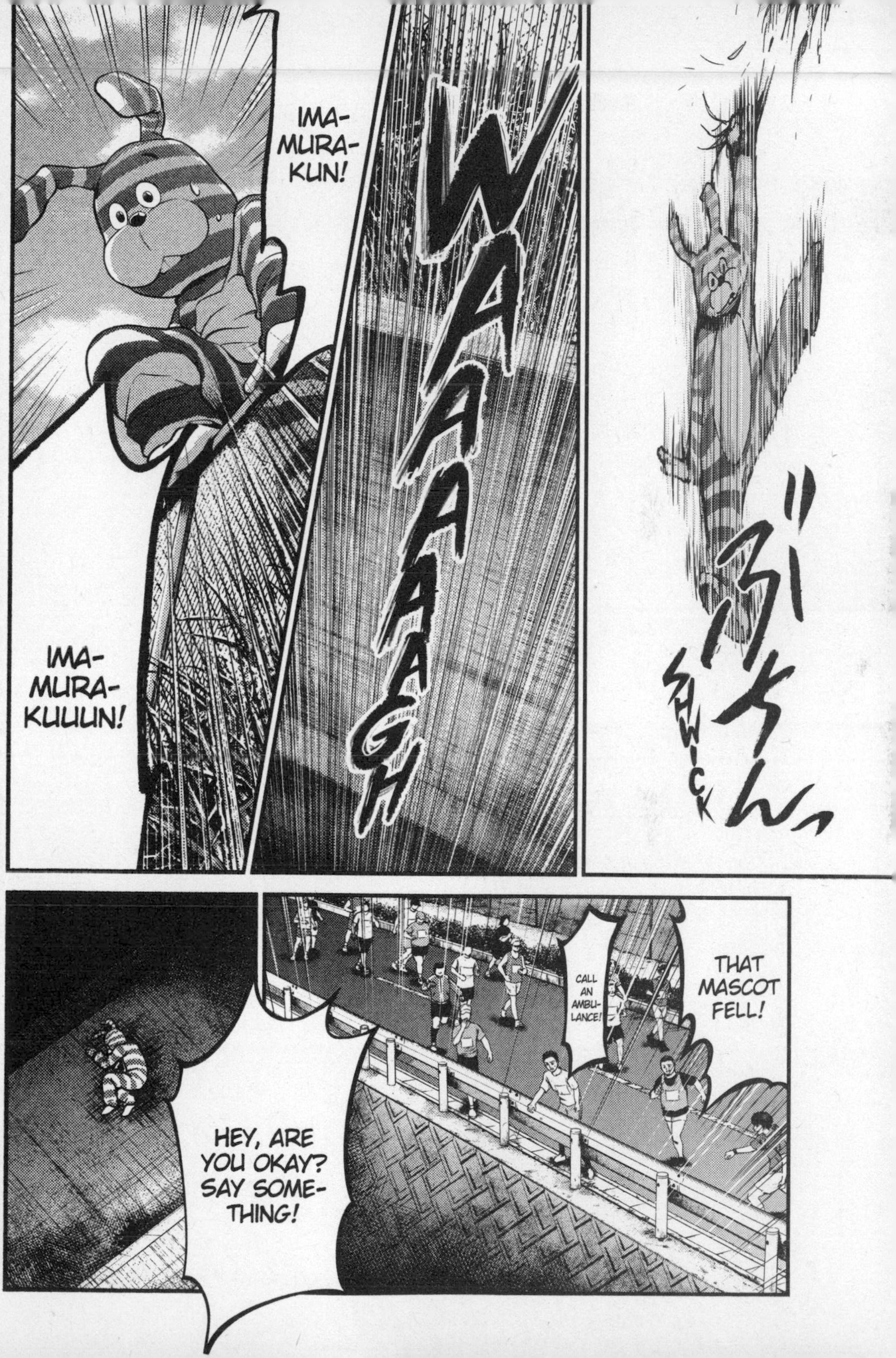
SHWICK
WAAAAAAGH
IMA-MURA-KUN!
IMA-MURA-KUUUN!
THAT MASCOT FELL!
CALL AN AMBULANCE!
HEY, ARE YOU OKAY? SAY SOME-THING!

134. A SIMPLE CHEER

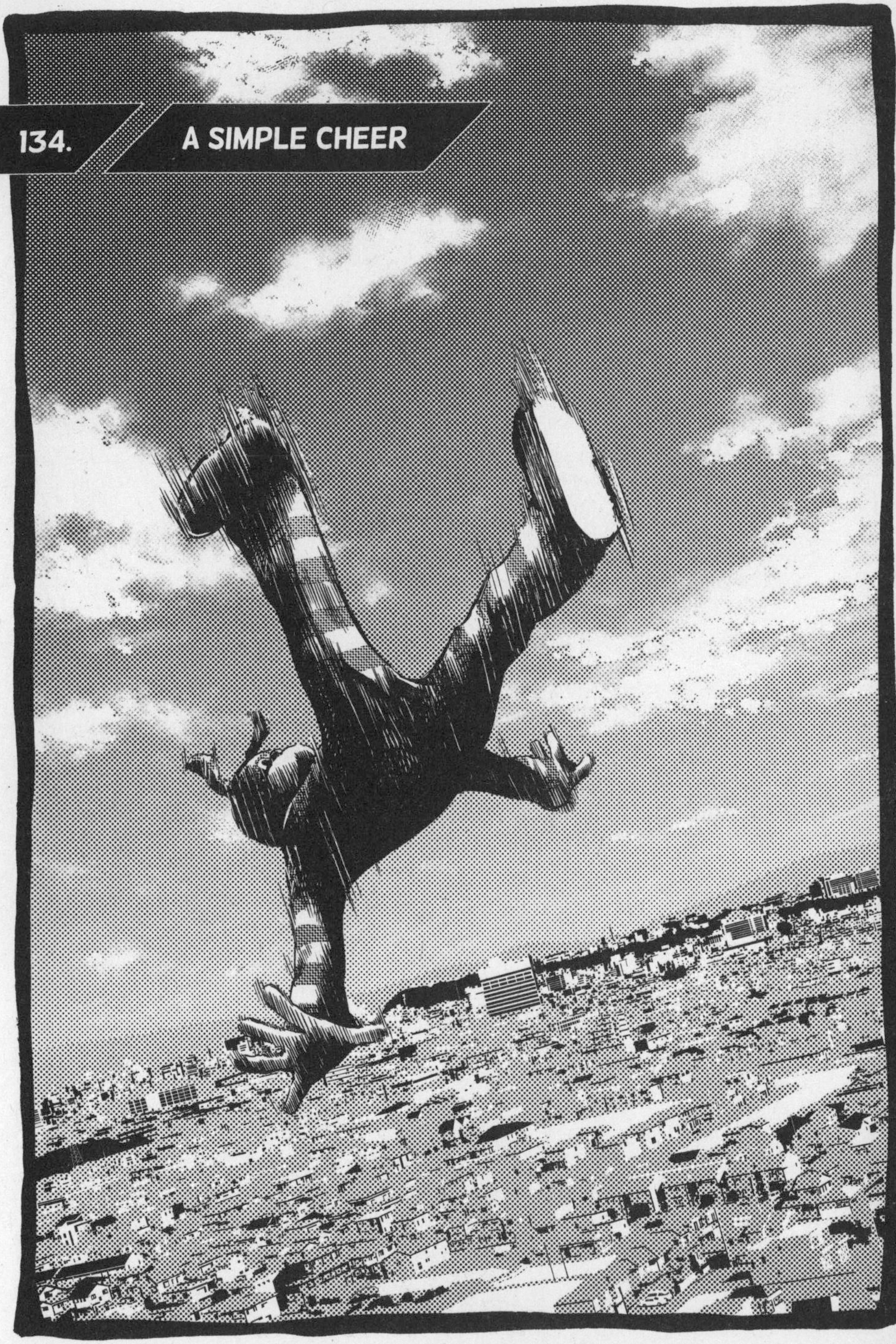

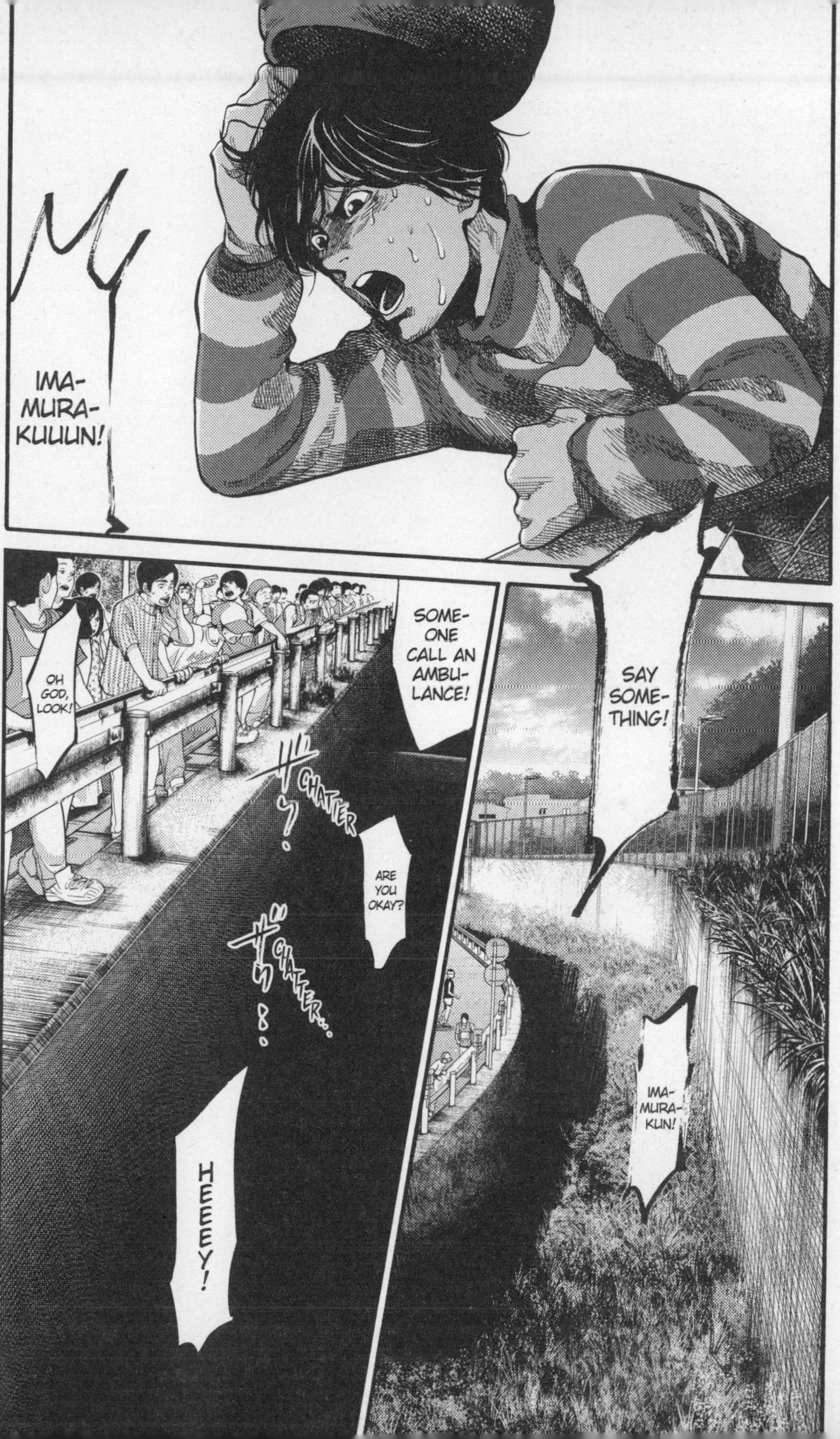
IMA-MURA-KUUUN!
SAY SOME-THING!
IMA-MURA-KUN!
SOME-ONE CALL AN AMBU-LANCE!
OH GOD, LOOK!
CHATTER
ARE YOU OKAY?
CHATTER...
HEEEY!

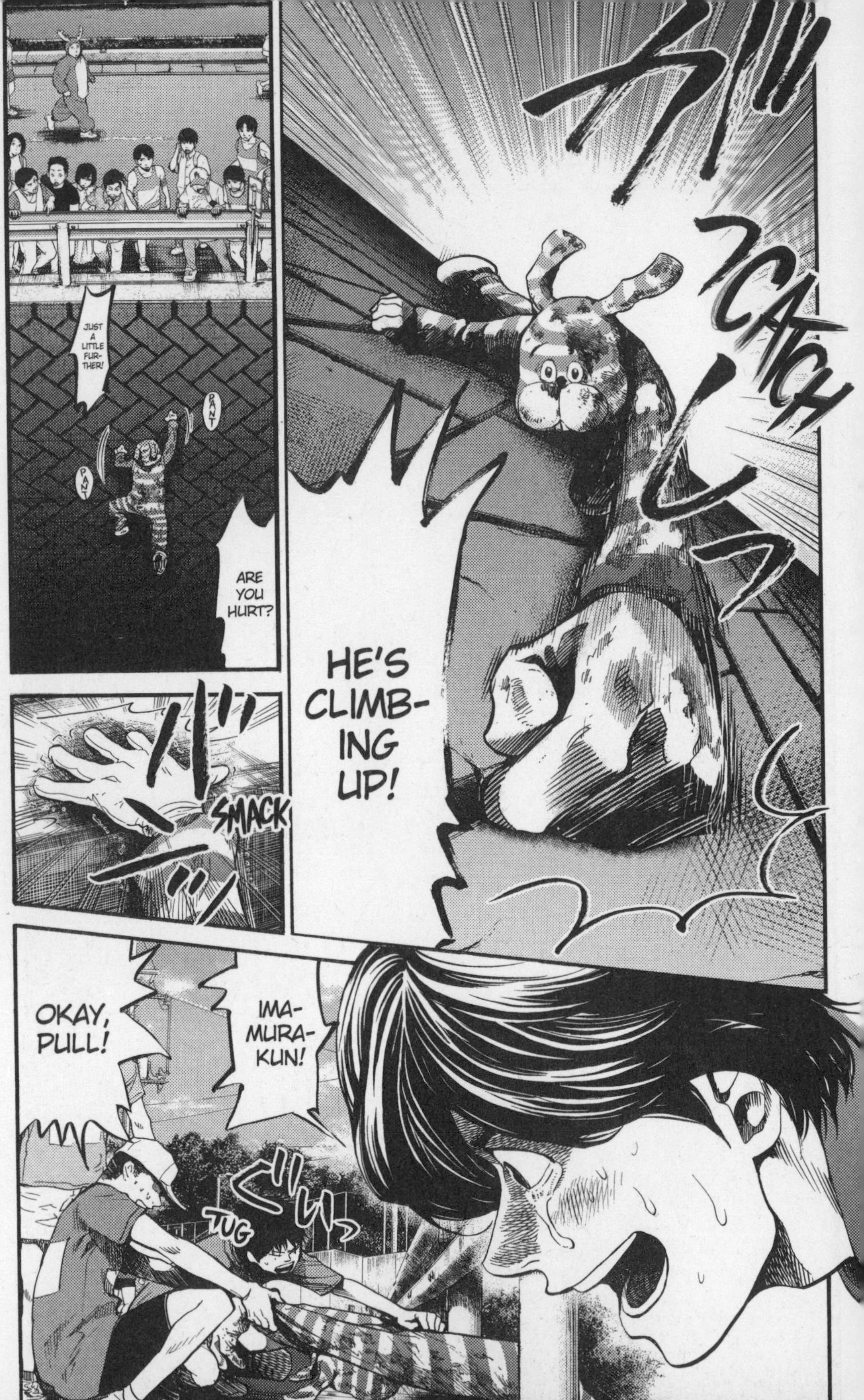

CATCH
HE'S CLIMBING-ING UP!
JUST A LITTLE FUR-THER!
PANT
PANT
ARE YOU HURT?
SMACK
IMA-MURA-KUN!
OKAY, PULL!
TUG

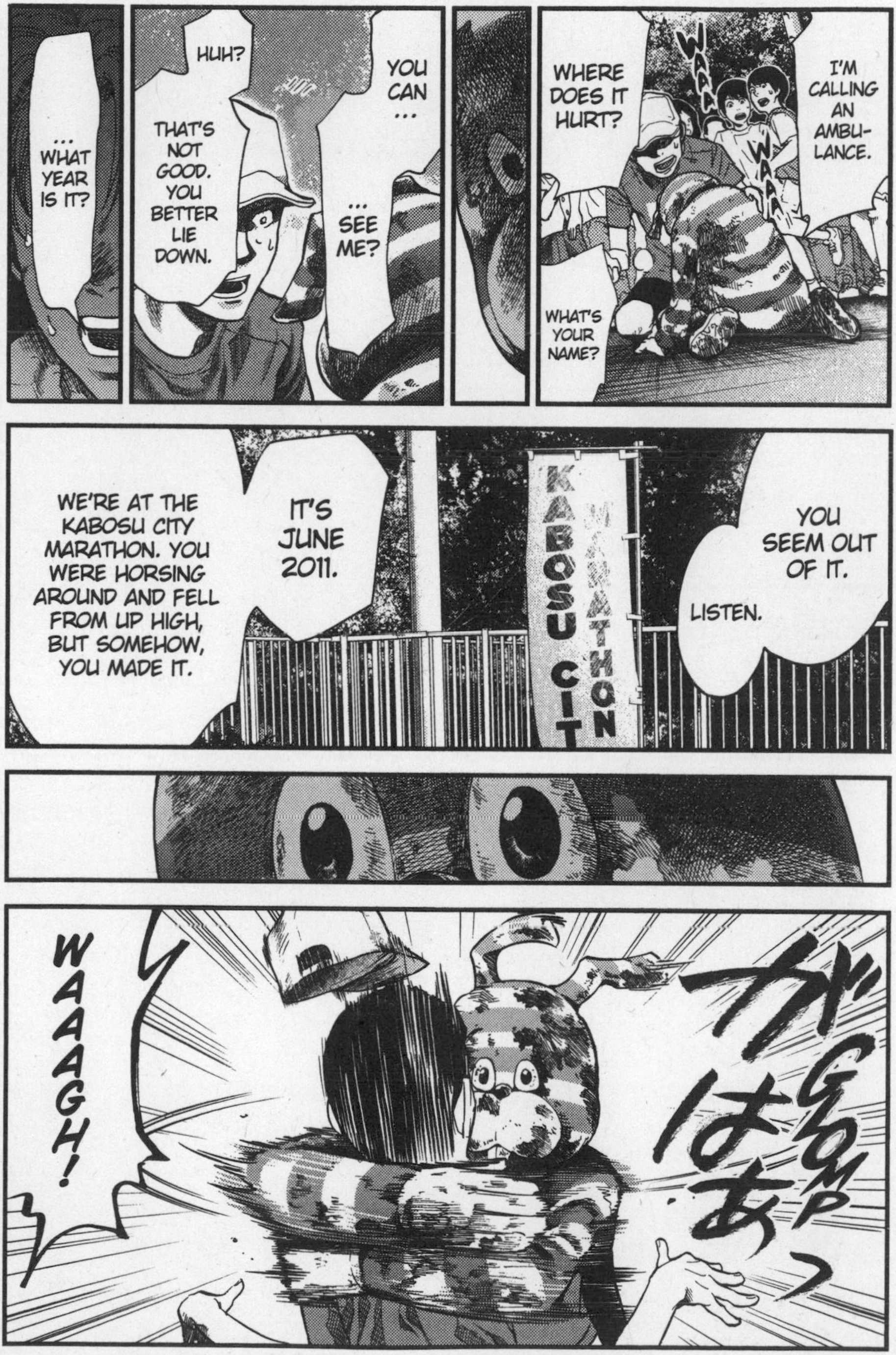
I'M CALLING AN AMBULANCE.
WAAA
WAAA
WHERE DOES IT HURT?
WHAT'S YOUR NAME?
YOU CAN ...
... SEE ME?
HUH?
THAT'S NOT GOOD. YOU BETTER LIE DOWN.
... WHAT YEAR IS IT?
YOU SEEM OUT OF IT.
LISTEN.
KABOSU CITY MARATHON
IT'S JUNE 2011.
WE'RE AT THE KABOSU CITY MARATHON. YOU WERE HORSING AROUND AND FELL FROM UP HIGH, BUT SOMEHOW, YOU MADE IT.
GOMP
WAAAGH!

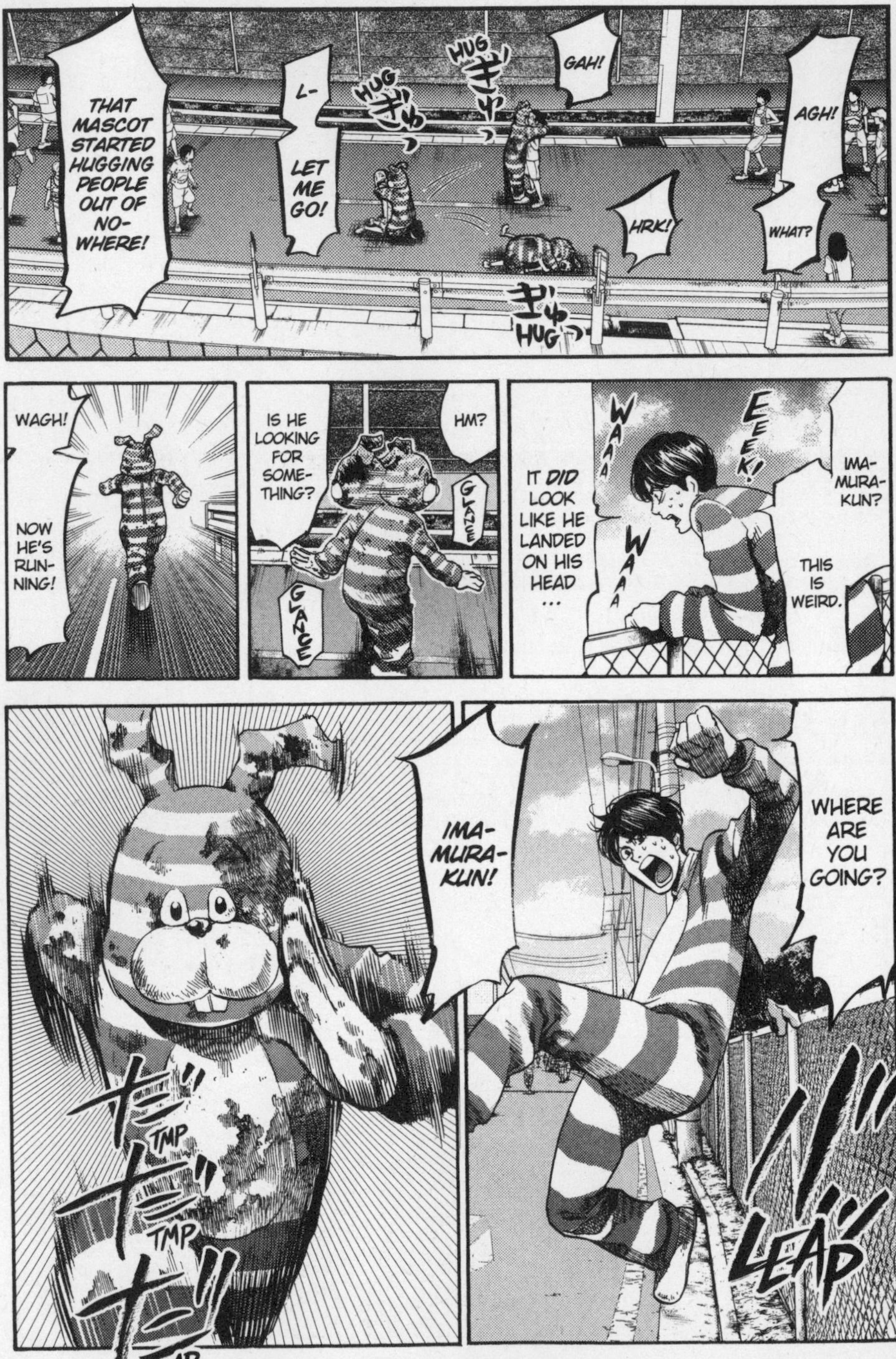
AGH!
WHAT?
GAH!
HUG
HRK!
HUG
L-
LET ME GO!
THAT MASCOT STARTED HUGGING PEOPLE OUT OF NO-WHERE!
HUG
IMA-MURA-KUN?
THIS IS WEIRD.
EEEK!
WAAA
WAAA
IT DID LOOK LIKE HE LANDED ON HIS HEAD...
HM?
GLANCE
IS HE LOOKING FOR SOME-THING?
GLANCE
WAGH!
NOW HE'S RUN-NING!
WHERE ARE YOU GOING?
IMA-MURA-KUN!
LEAP
TMP
TMP
TMP

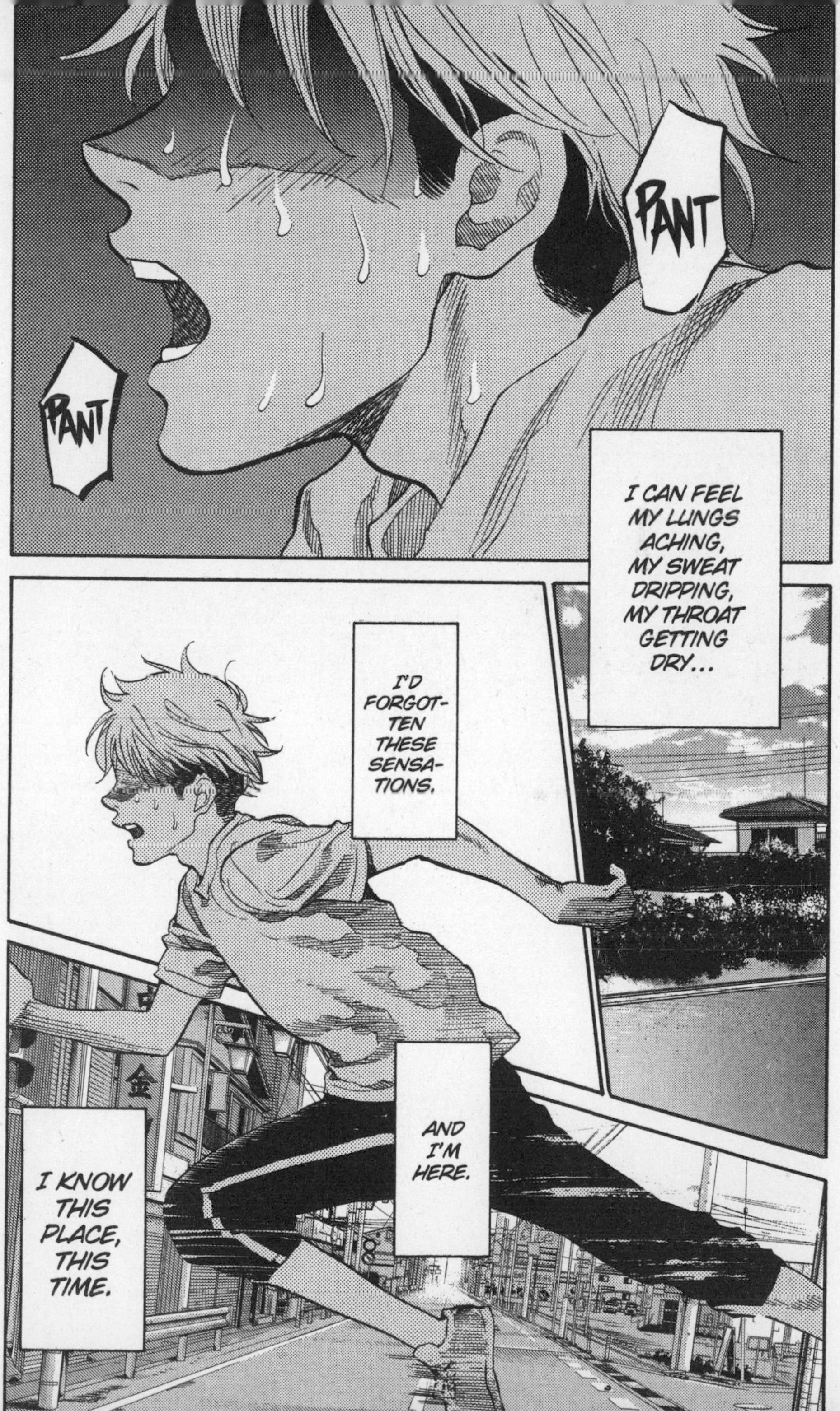
PANT
PANT
I CAN FEEL MY LUNGS ACHING, MY SWEAT DRIPPING, MY THROAT GETTING DRY...
I'D FORGOT-TEN THESE SENSA-TIONS.
AND I'M HERE.
I KNOW THIS PLACE, THIS TIME.

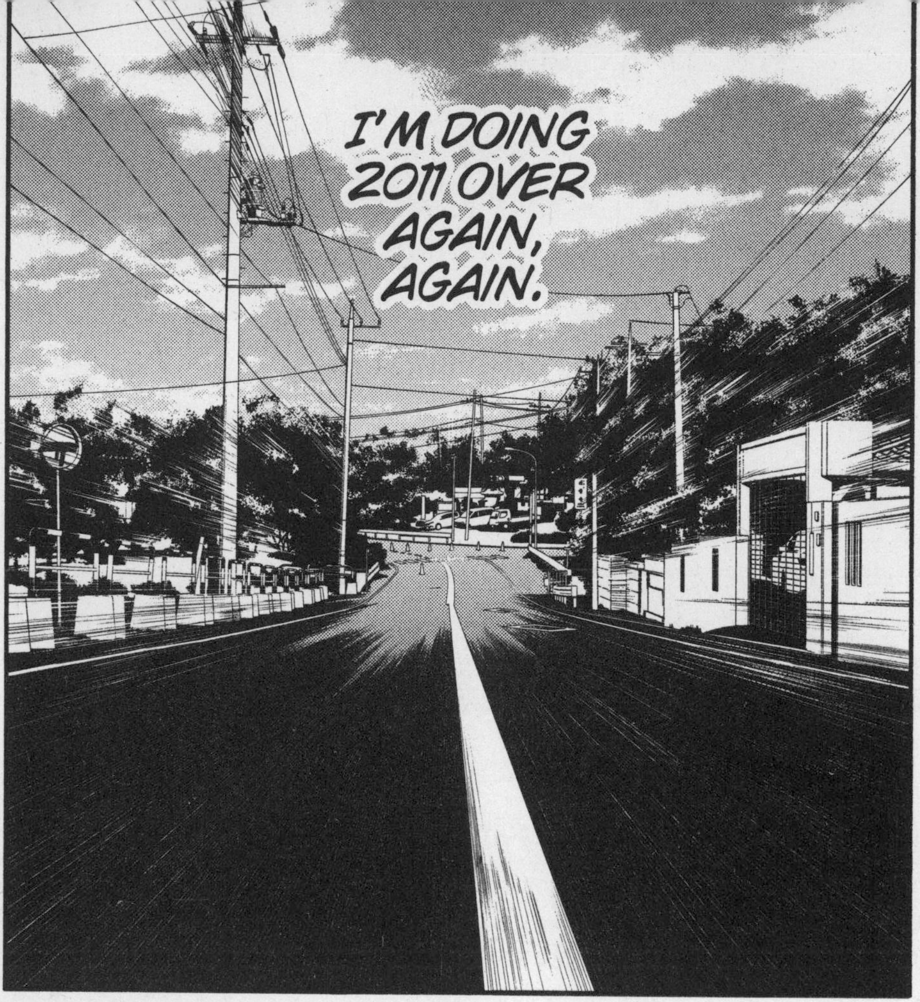
I'M DOING 2011 OVER AGAIN, AGAIN.

I NEED TO SEE HER.

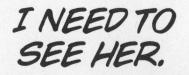

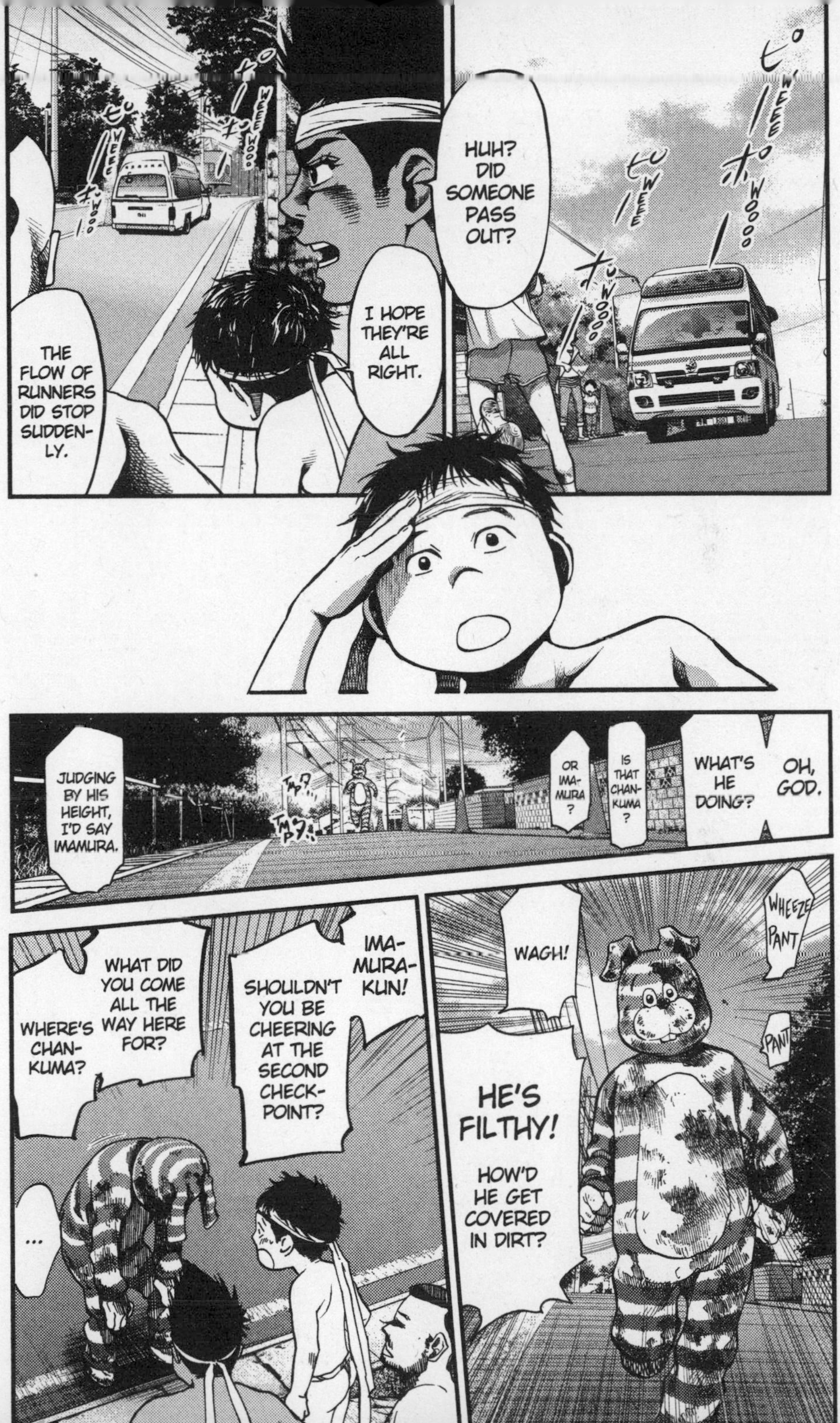

WEEE WOOOO
WEEE WOOOO
HUH? DID SOMEONE PASS OUT?
WEEE WOOO
WEEE WOOO
I HOPE THEY'RE ALL RIGHT.
THE FLOW OF RUNNERS DID STOP SUDDEN-LY.
OH, GOD.
WHAT'S HE DOING?
IS THAT CHAN-KUMA?
OR IMA-MURA?
TMP TMP
JUDGING BY HIS HEIGHT, I'D SAY IMAMURA.
WHEEZE PANT
WAGH!
PANT
HE'S FILTHY!
HOW'D HE GET COVERED IN DIRT?
IMA-MURA-KUN!
SHOULDN'T YOU BE CHEERING AT THE SECOND CHECK-POINT?
WHAT DID YOU COME ALL THE WAY HERE FOR?
WHERE'S CHAN-KUMA?
...

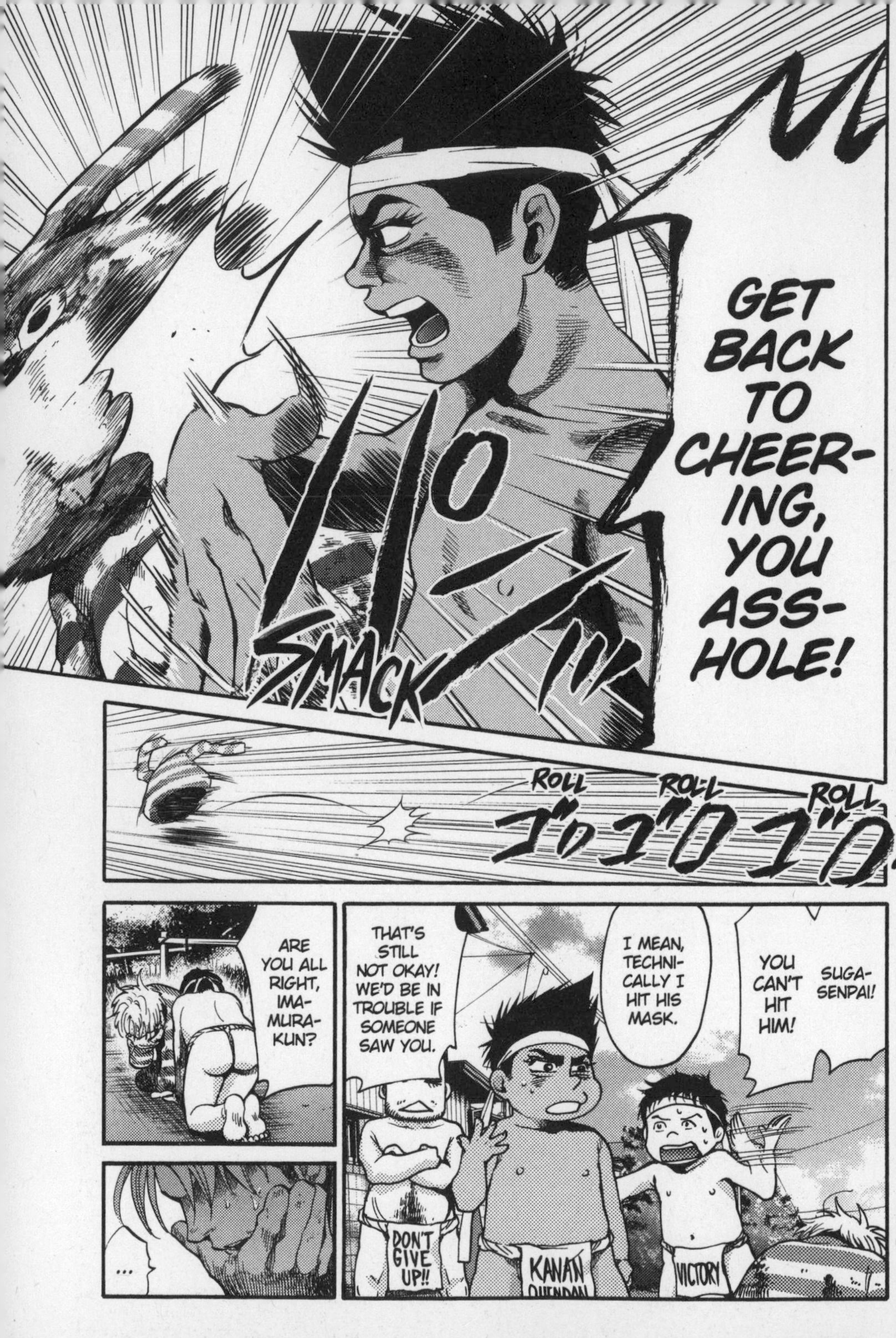
GET BACK TO CHEERING, YOU ASSHOLE!
SMACK
ROLL ROLL ROLL
ゴロゴロゴロ
SUGA-SENPAI!
YOU CAN'T HIT HIM!
I MEAN, TECHNICALLY I HIT HIS MASK.
THAT'S STILL NOT OKAY! WE'D BE IN TROUBLE IF SOMEONE SAW YOU.
VICTORY
KANAN
DON'T GIVE UP!!
ARE YOU ALL RIGHT, IMAMURA-KUN?
...

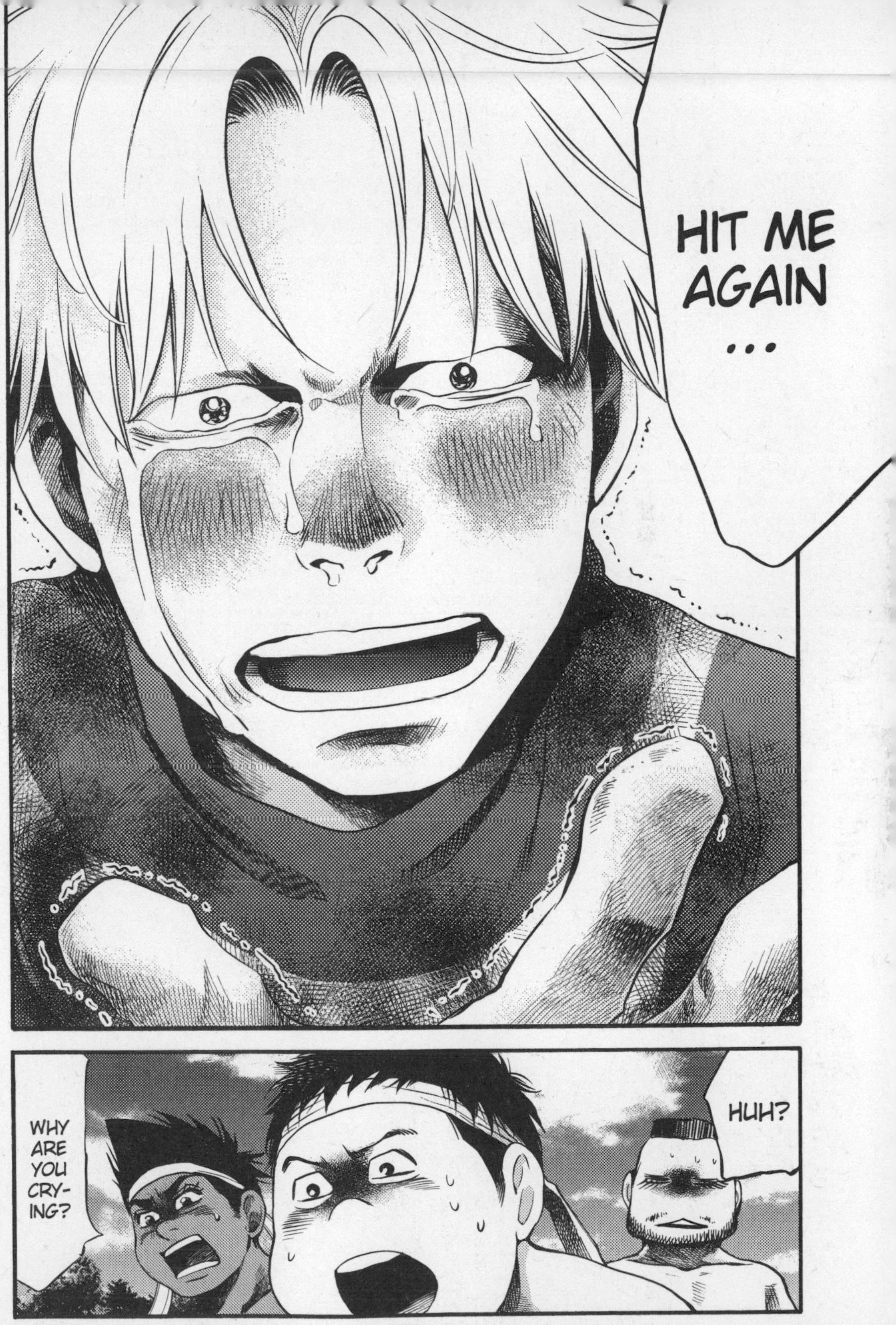
HIT ME AGAIN ...
HUH?
WHY ARE YOU CRY-ING?

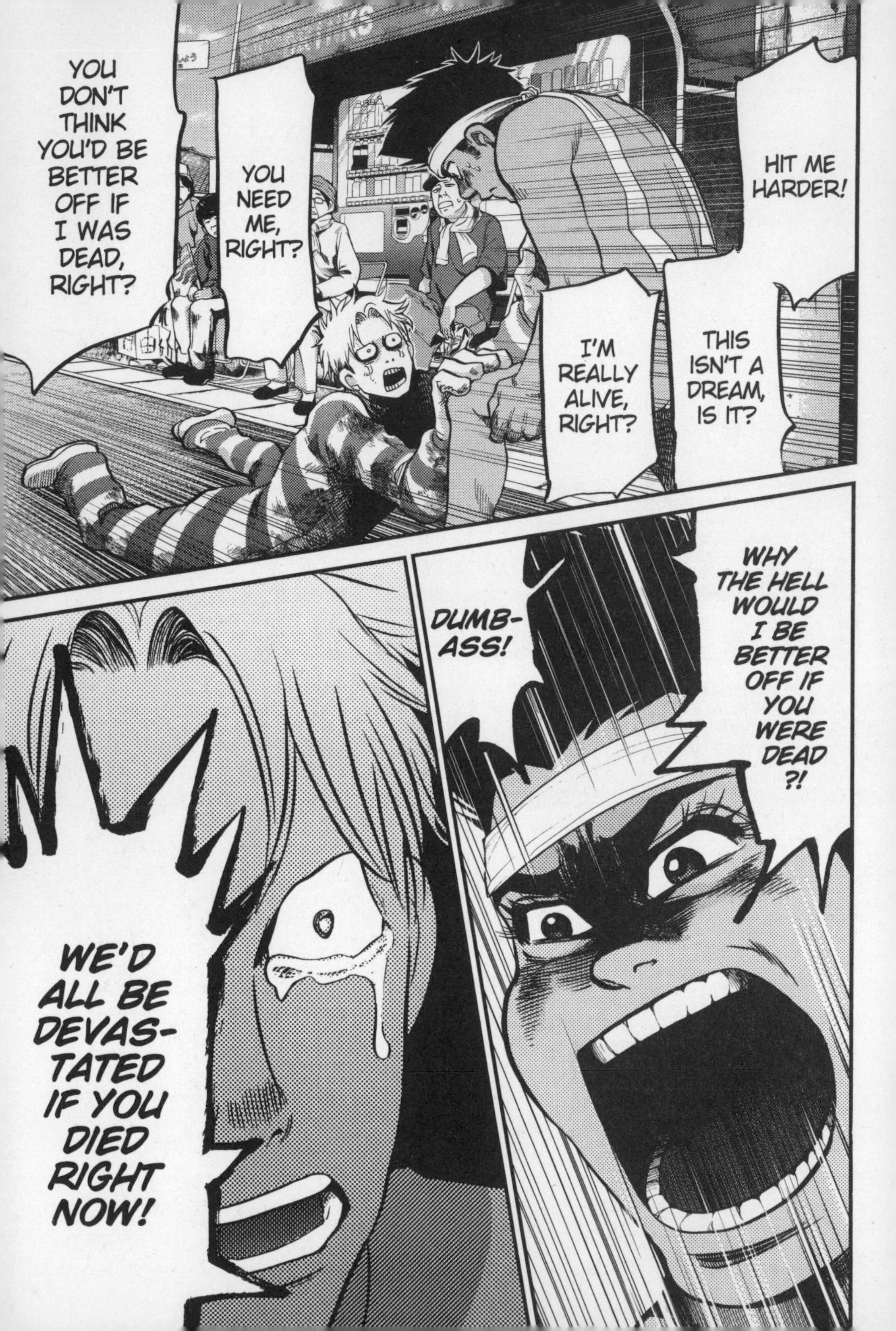
HIT ME HARDER!
THIS ISN'T A DREAM, IS IT?
I'M REALLY ALIVE, RIGHT?
YOU NEED ME, RIGHT?
YOU DON'T THINK YOU'D BE BETTER OFF IF I WAS DEAD, RIGHT?
WHY THE HELL WOULD I BE BETTER OFF IF YOU WERE DEAD?!
DUMB-ASS!
WE'D ALL BE DEVAS-TATED IF YOU DIED RIGHT NOW!

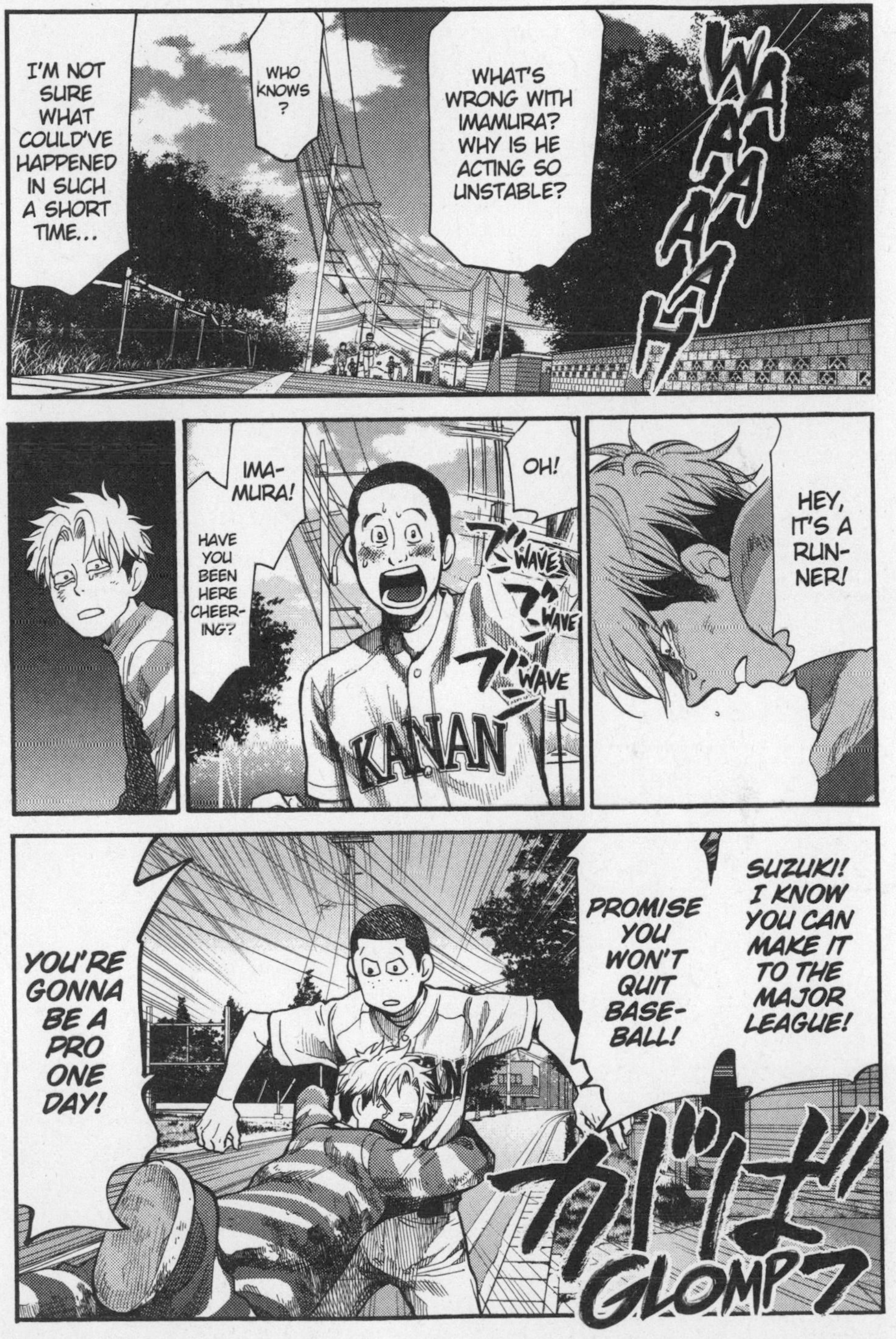
WAAAAAH
WHAT'S WRONG WITH IMAMURA? WHY IS HE ACTING SO UNSTABLE?
WHO KNOWS?
I'M NOT SURE WHAT COULD'VE HAPPENED IN SUCH A SHORT TIME...
HEY, IT'S A RUN-NER!
OH!
IMA-MURA!
HAVE YOU BEEN HERE CHEERING?
WAVE
WAVE
WAVE
KANAN
SUZUKI! I KNOW YOU CAN MAKE IT TO THE MAJOR LEAGUE!
PROMISE YOU WON'T QUIT BASE-BALL!
YOU'RE GONNA BE A PRO ONE DAY!
GLOMP

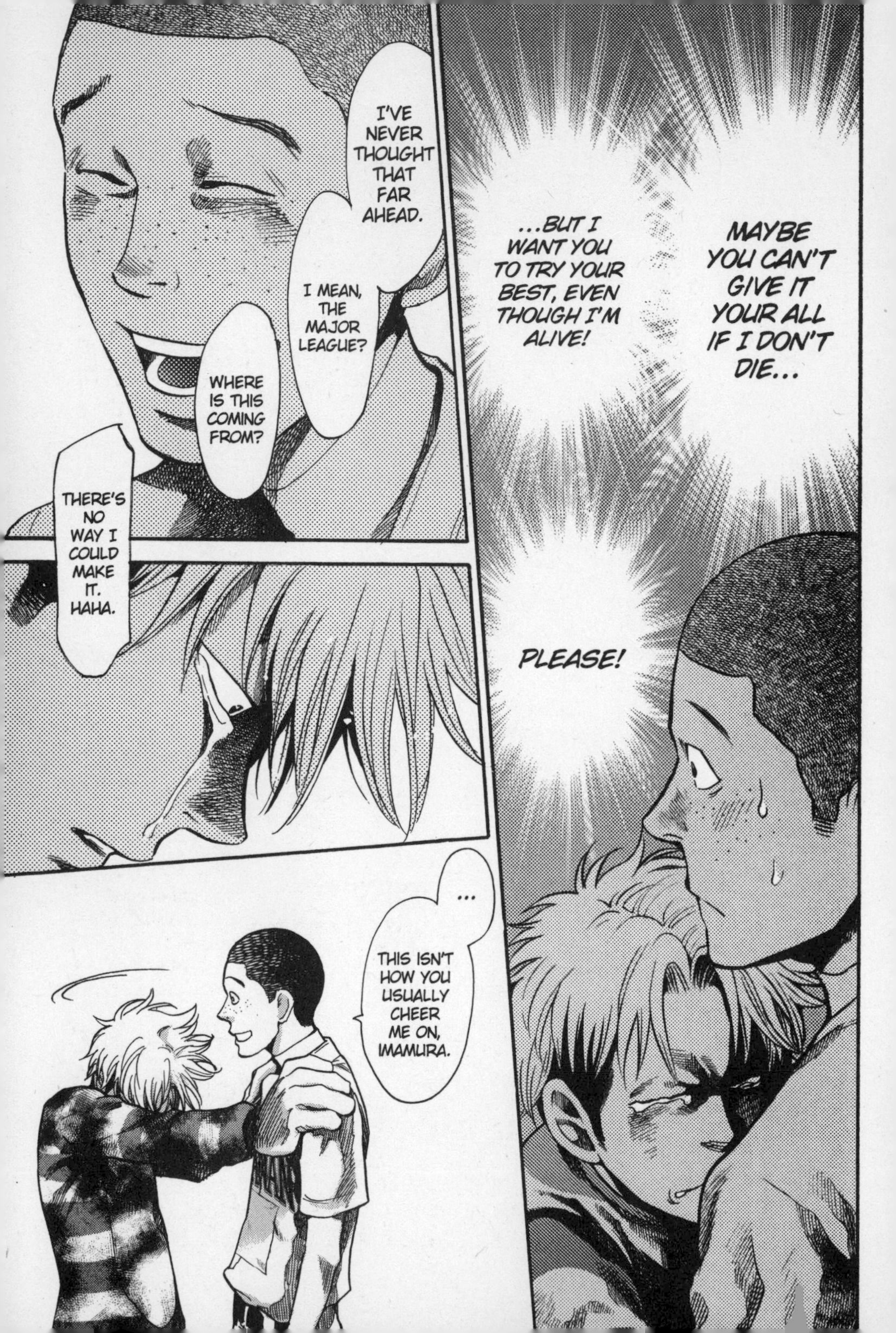
MAYBE YOU CAN'T GIVE IT YOUR ALL IF I DON'T DIE...
...BUT I WANT YOU TO TRY YOUR BEST, EVEN THOUGH I'M ALIVE!
PLEASE!
I'VE NEVER THOUGHT THAT FAR AHEAD.
I MEAN, THE MAJOR LEAGUE?
WHERE IS THIS COMING FROM?
THERE'S NO WAY I COULD MAKE IT. HAHA.
...
THIS ISN'T HOW YOU USUALLY CHEER ME ON, IMAMURA.

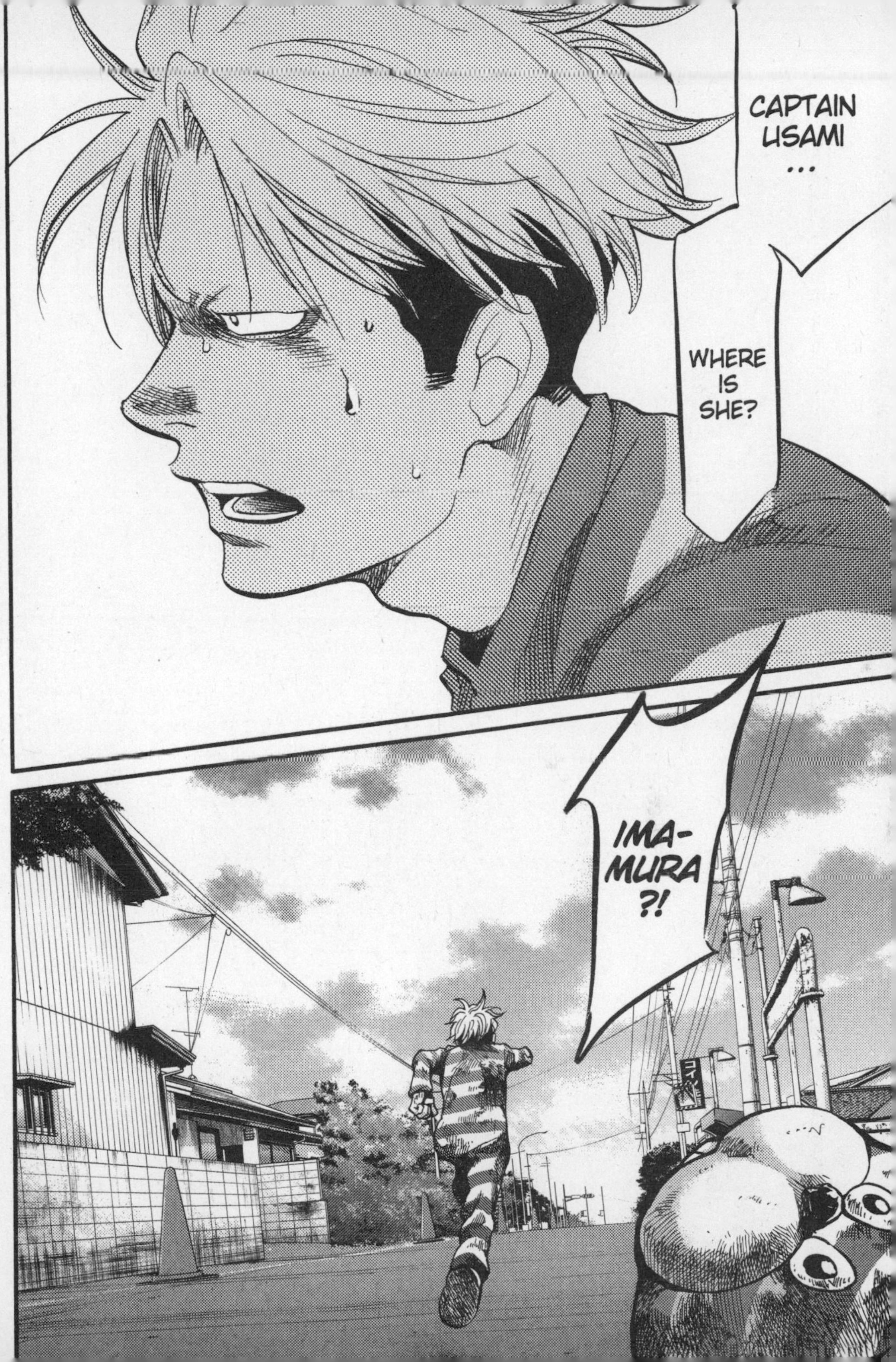
CAPTAIN USAMI ...
WHERE IS SHE?
IMA-MURA ?!

135. RESURRECTION OF THE BLOND WOLF

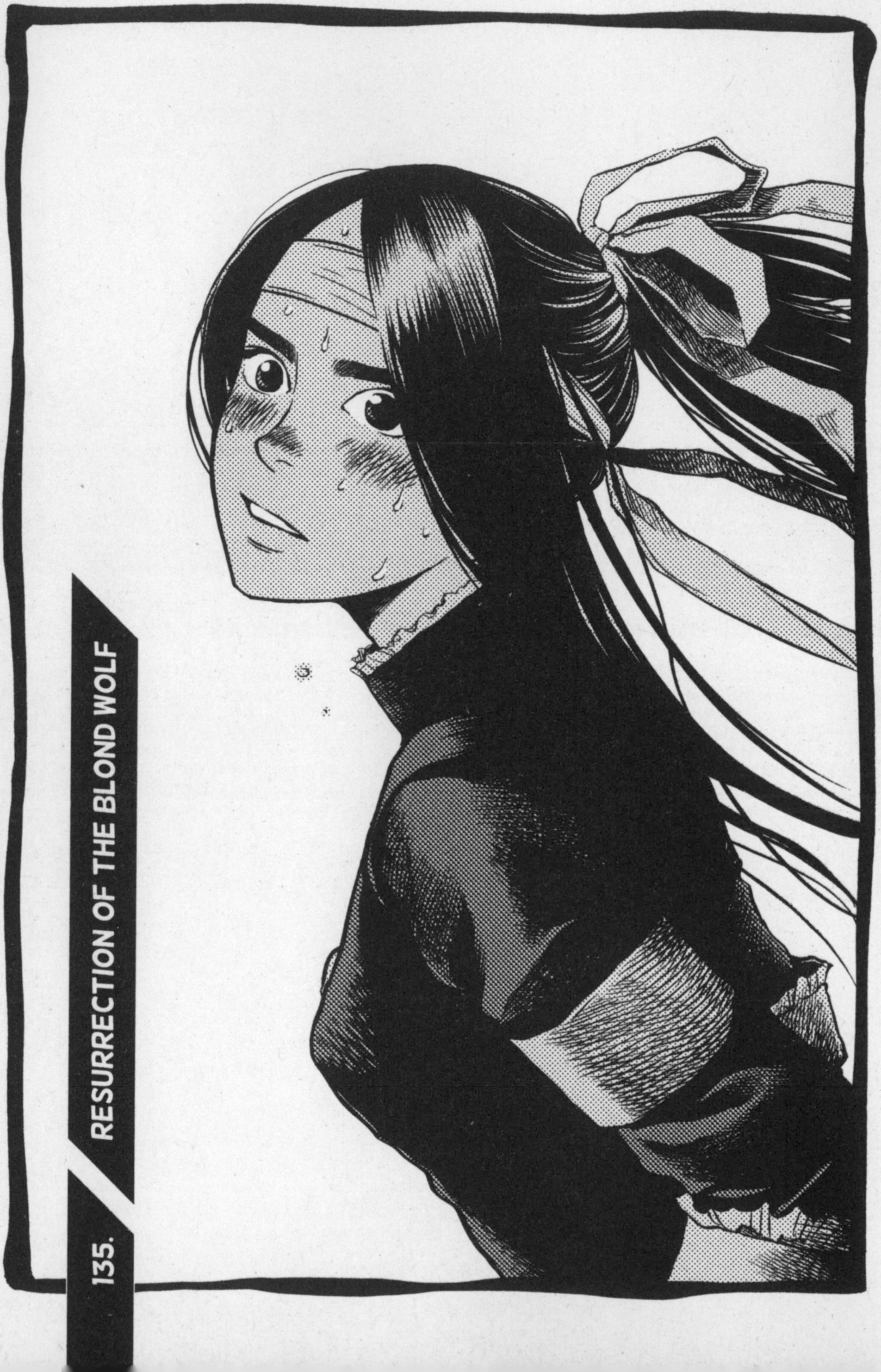

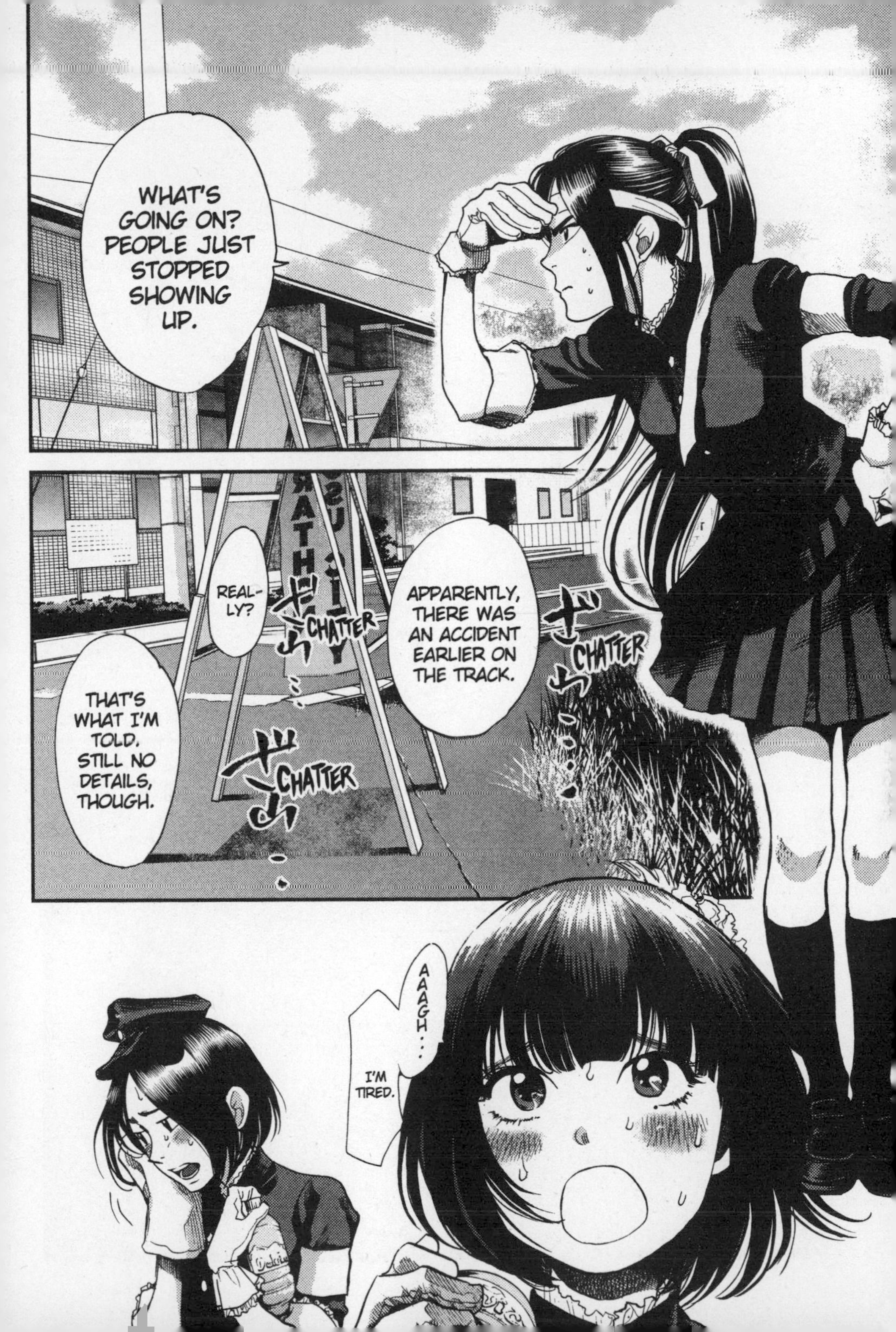
WHAT'S GOING ON? PEOPLE JUST STOPPED SHOWING UP.
APPARENTLY, THERE WAS AN ACCIDENT EARLIER ON THE TRACK.
CHATTER
REAL-LY?
CHATTER
THAT'S WHAT I'M TOLD. STILL NO DETAILS, THOUGH.
CHATTER
AAAGH...
I'M TIRED.

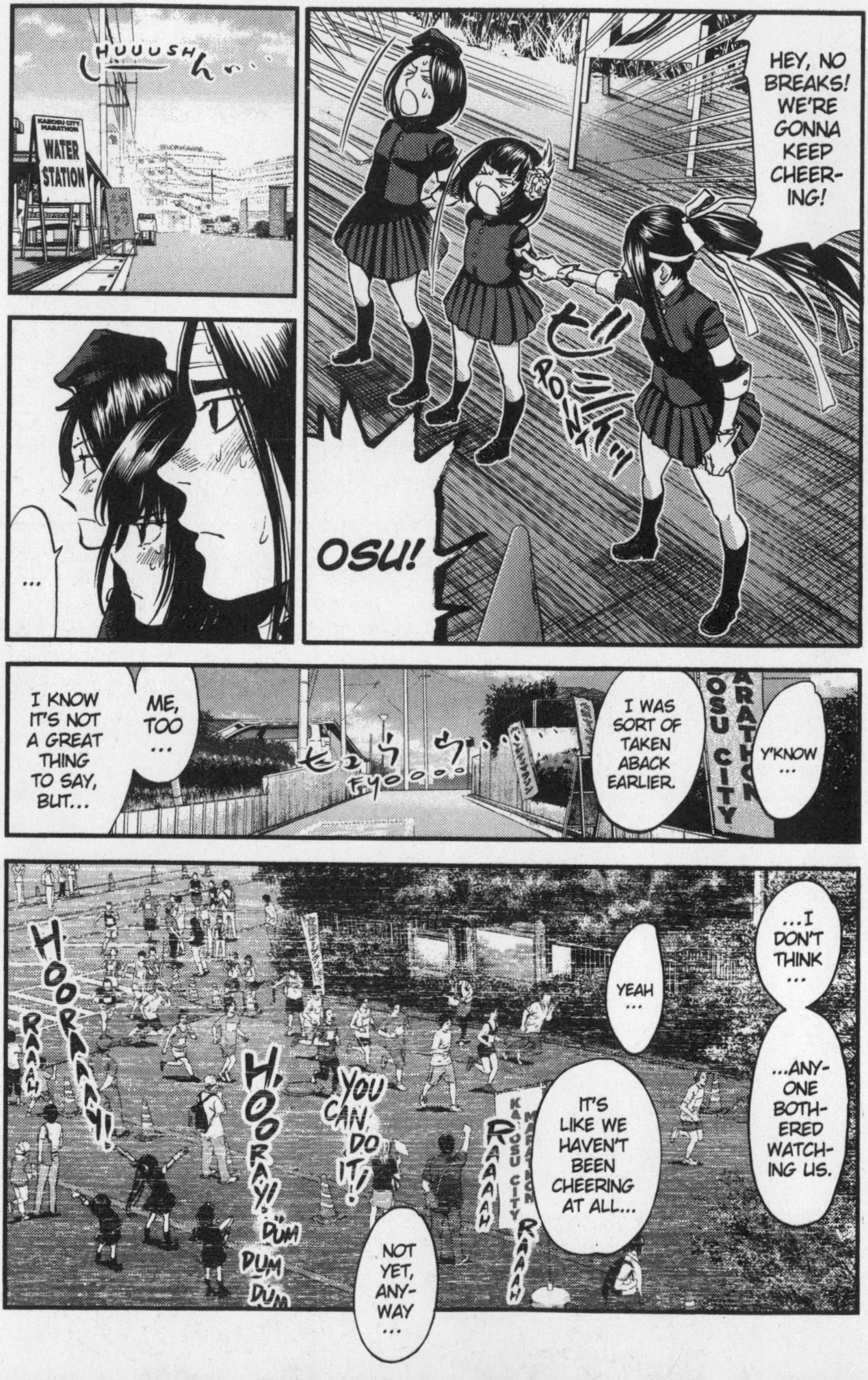
HEY, NO BREAKS! WE'RE GONNA KEEP CHEER-ING!
POINT
OSU!
HUUUSH...
KAROSU CITY MARATHON
WATER STATION
...
Y'KNOW ...
I WAS SORT OF TAKEN ABACK EARLIER.
FYOOOO...
ME, TOO ...
I KNOW IT'S NOT A GREAT THING TO SAY, BUT...
...I DON'T THINK ...
...ANY-ONE BOTH-ERED WATCH-ING US.
YEAH ...
IT'S LIKE WE HAVEN'T BEEN CHEERING AT ALL...
NOT YET, ANY-WAY ...
RAAAAH
KAROSU CITY MARATHON
RAAAAH
YOU CAN DO IT!
HOORAY!
DUM DUM DUM
HOORAAAY!
RAAAAH

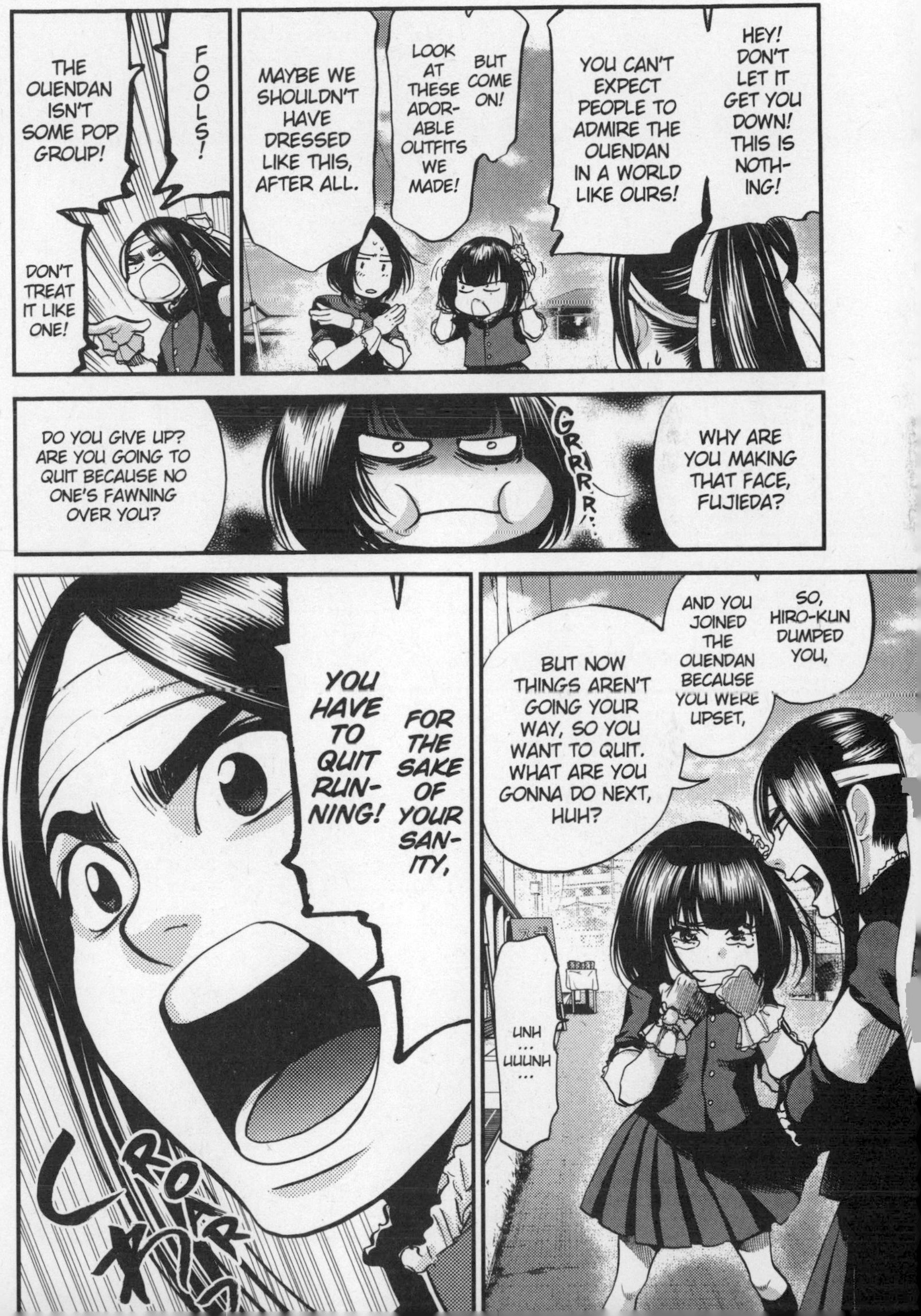
HEY! DON'T LET IT GET YOU DOWN! THIS IS NOTHING!
YOU CAN'T EXPECT PEOPLE TO ADMIRE THE OUENDAN IN A WORLD LIKE OURS!
BUT COME ON!
LOOK AT THESE ADORABLE OUTFITS WE MADE!
MAYBE WE SHOULDN'T HAVE DRESSED LIKE THIS, AFTER ALL.
FOOLS!
THE OUENDAN ISN'T SOME POP GROUP!
DON'T TREAT IT LIKE ONE!
WHY ARE YOU MAKING THAT FACE, FUJIEDA?
GRRRR...
DO YOU GIVE UP? ARE YOU GOING TO QUIT BECAUSE NO ONE'S FAWNING OVER YOU?
SO, HIRO-KUN DUMPED YOU,
AND YOU JOINED THE OUENDAN BECAUSE YOU WERE UPSET,
BUT NOW THINGS AREN'T GOING YOUR WAY, SO YOU WANT TO QUIT. WHAT ARE YOU GONNA DO NEXT, HUH?
UNH ... UUUNH ...
FOR THE SAKE OF YOUR SANITY,
YOU HAVE TO QUIT RUNNING!
ROAR

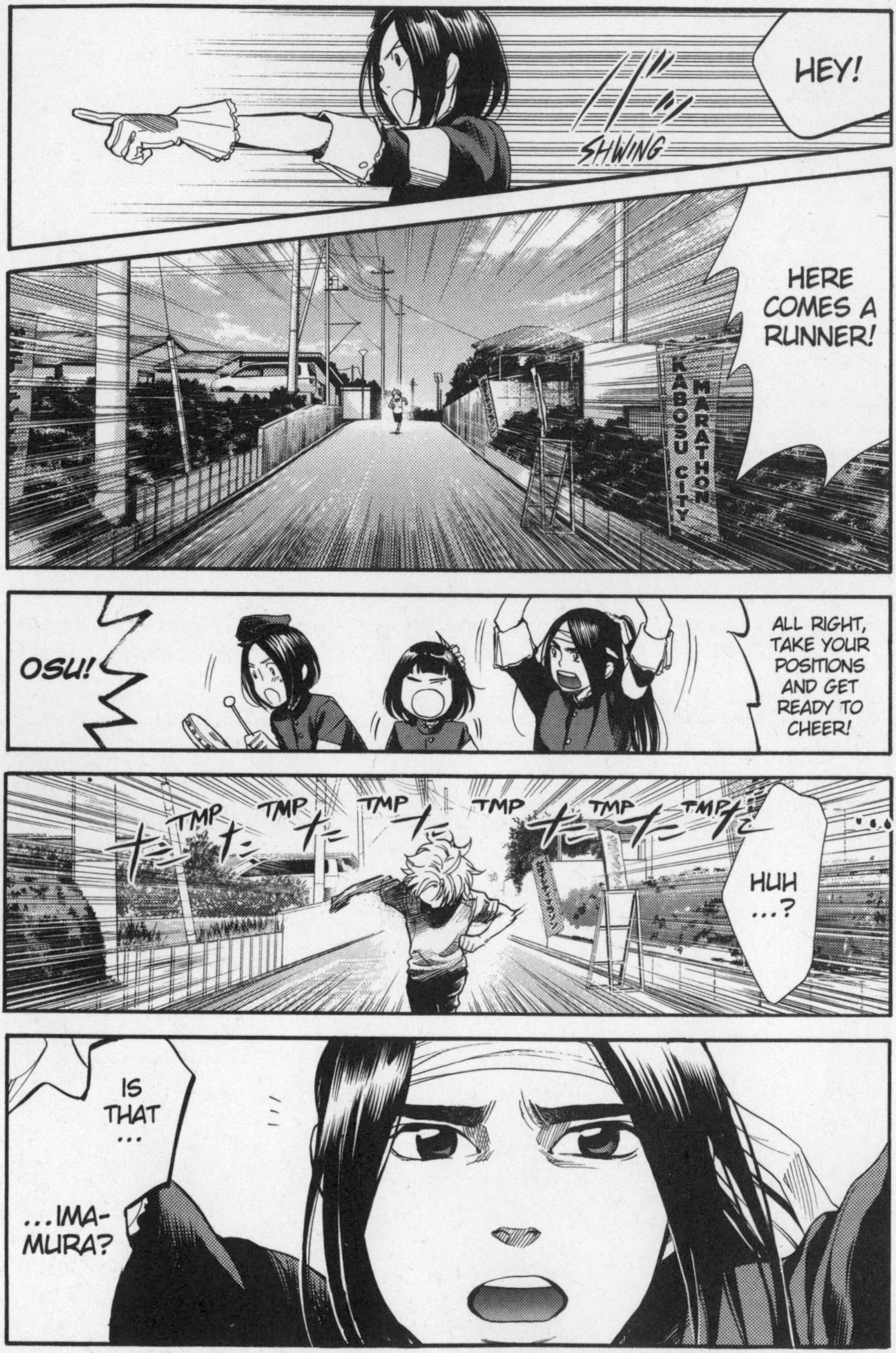
HEY!
SHWING
HERE COMES A RUNNER!
KABOSU CITY MARATHON
ALL RIGHT, TAKE YOUR POSITIONS AND GET READY TO CHEER!
OSU!
...
HUH ...?
TMP TMP TMP TMP TMP TMP
IS THAT ...
...IMA-MURA?

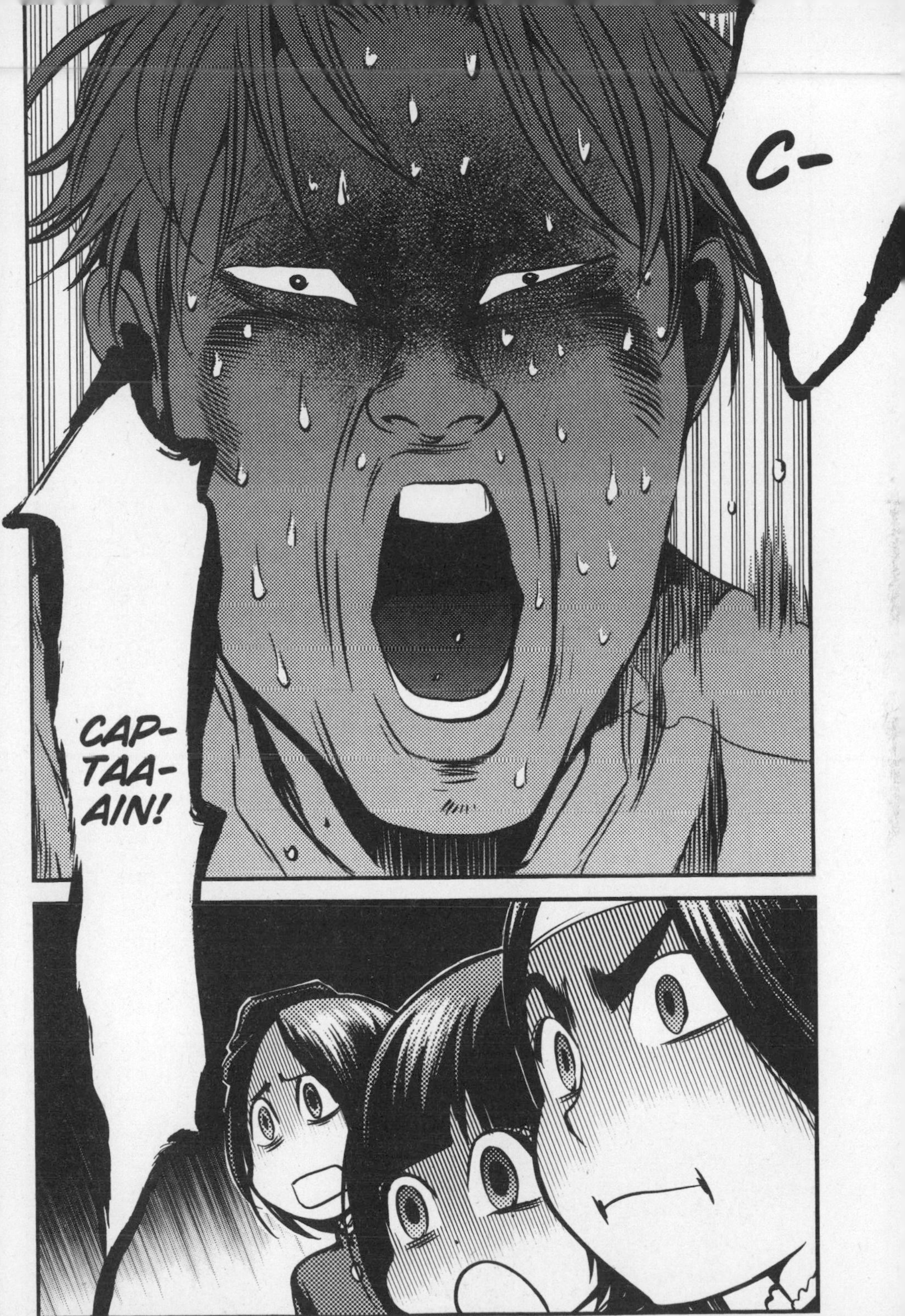
C-
CAP-TAA-AIN!

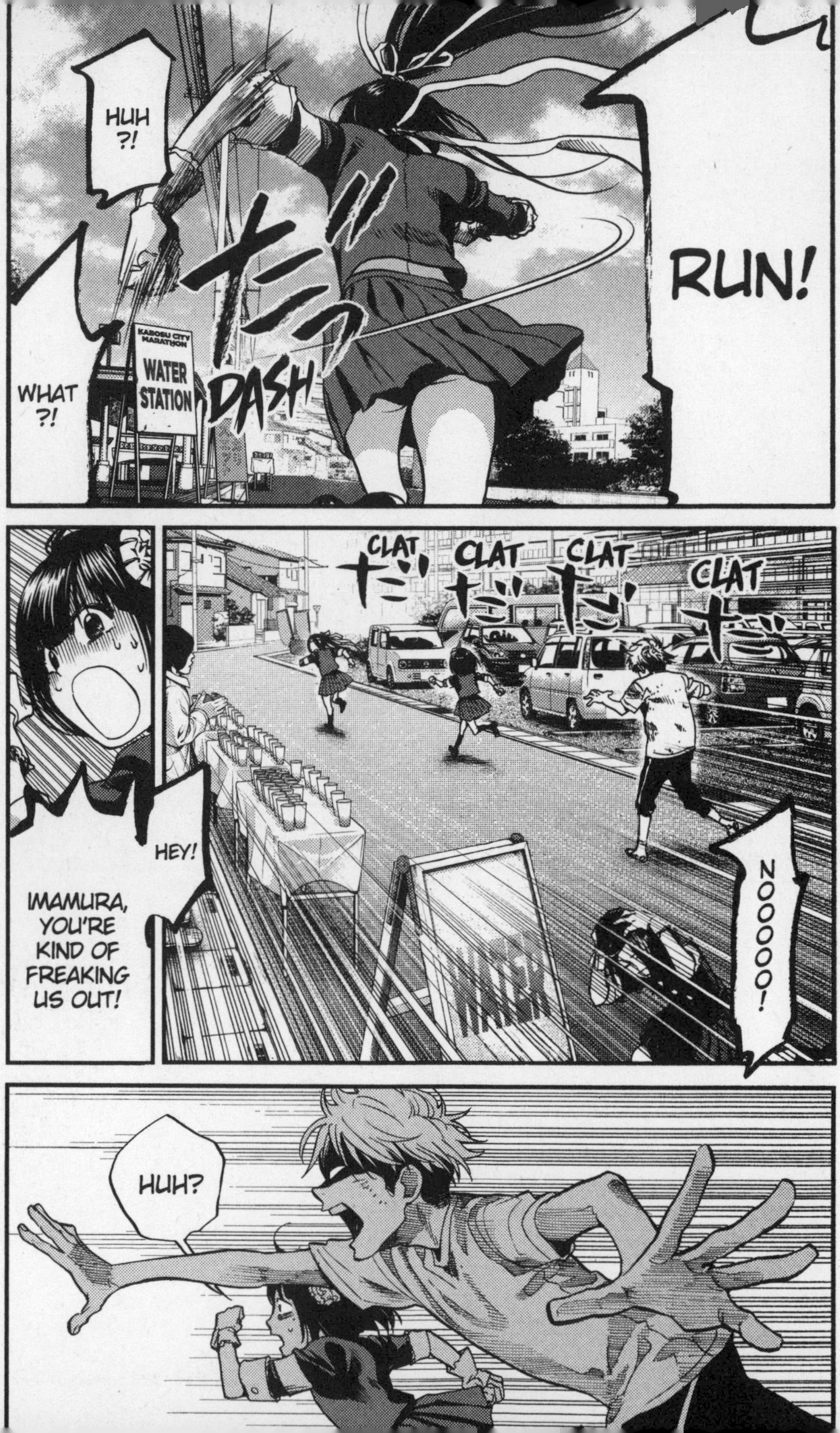
RUN!
HUH ?!
DASH
KAROSU CITY MARATHON
WATER STATION
WHAT ?!
CLAT
CLAT
CLAT
CLAT
NOOOOOO!
HEY!
IMAMURA, YOU'RE KIND OF FREAKING US OUT!
HUH?

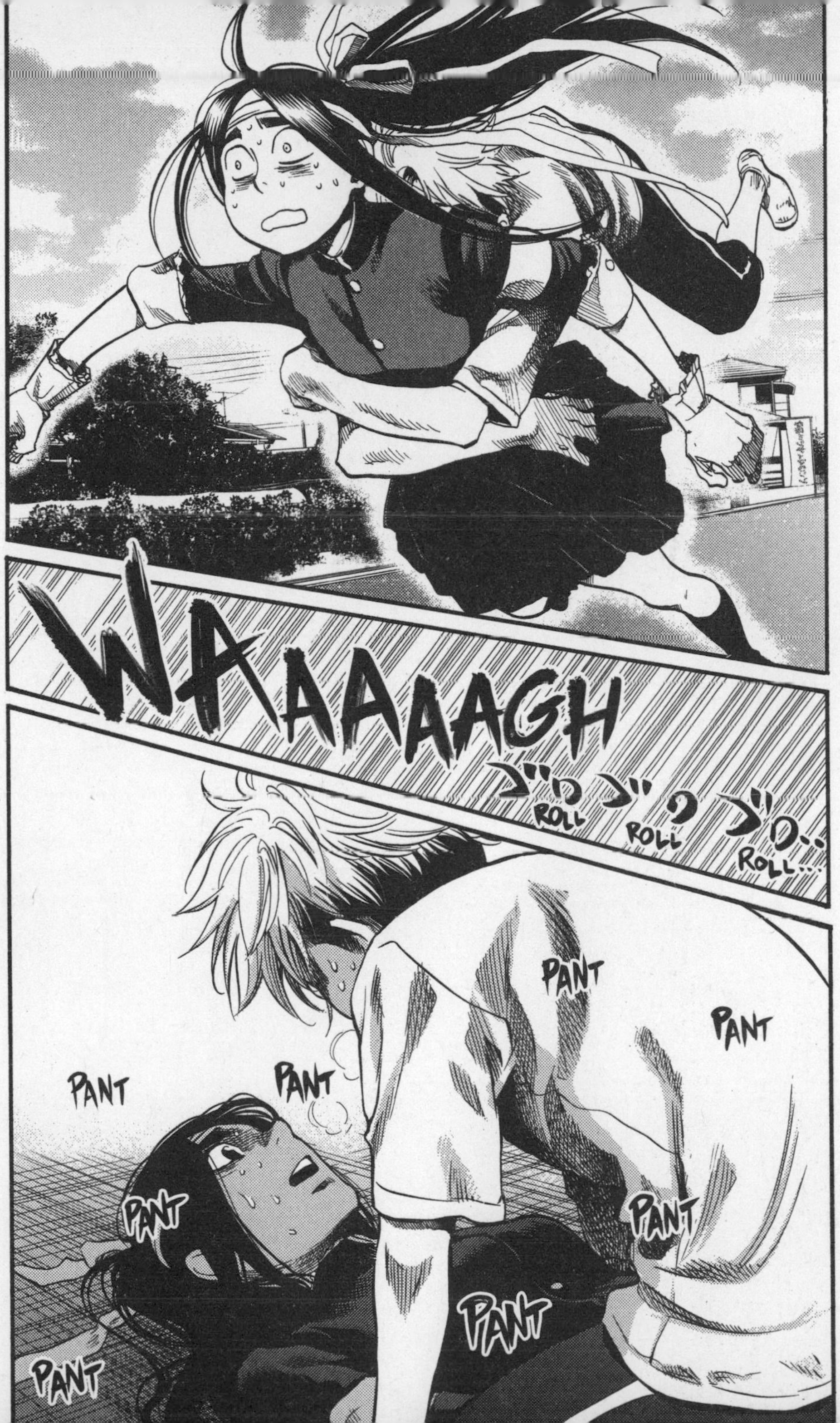
WAAAAAGH
ゴロ ROLL
ゴロ ROLL
ゴロ.. ROLL...
PANT
PANT
PANT
PANT
PANT
PANT
PANT
PANT

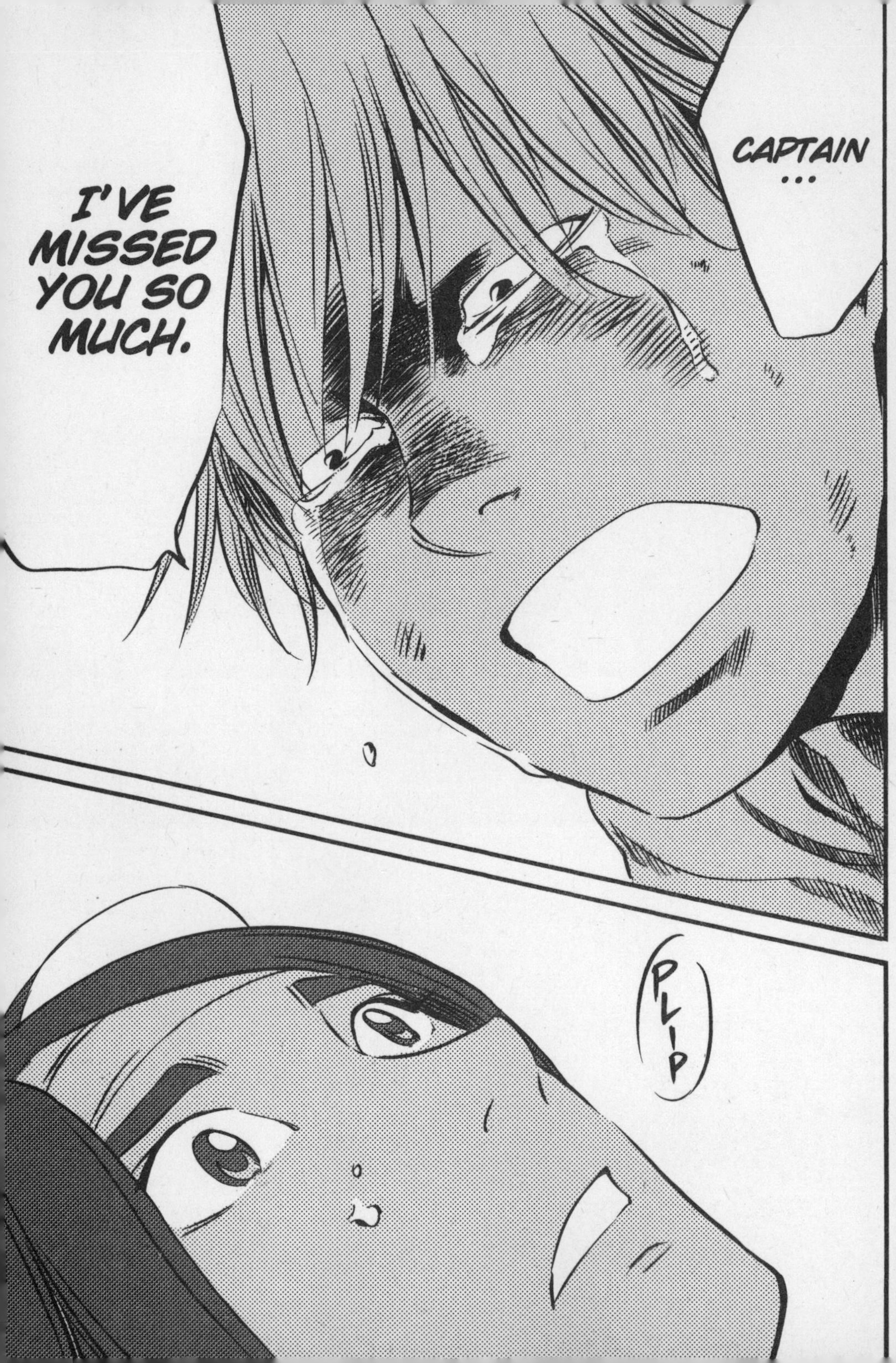
CAPTAIN ...
I'VE MISSED YOU SO MUCH.
PLIP

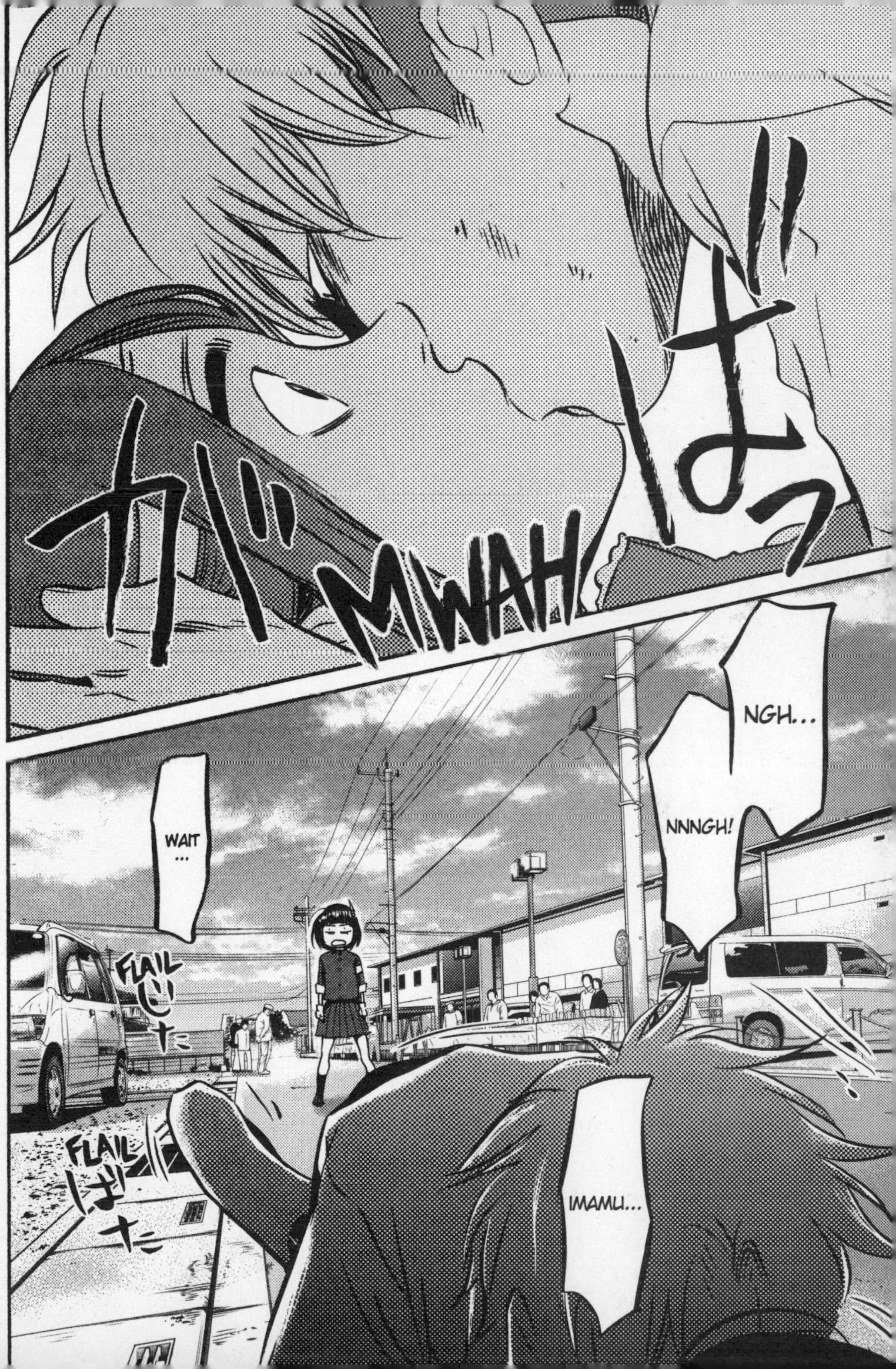
はっ
MWAH
カブ
NGH...
NNNGH!
WAIT ...
FLAIL じたっ
FLAIL ばたっ
IMAMU...

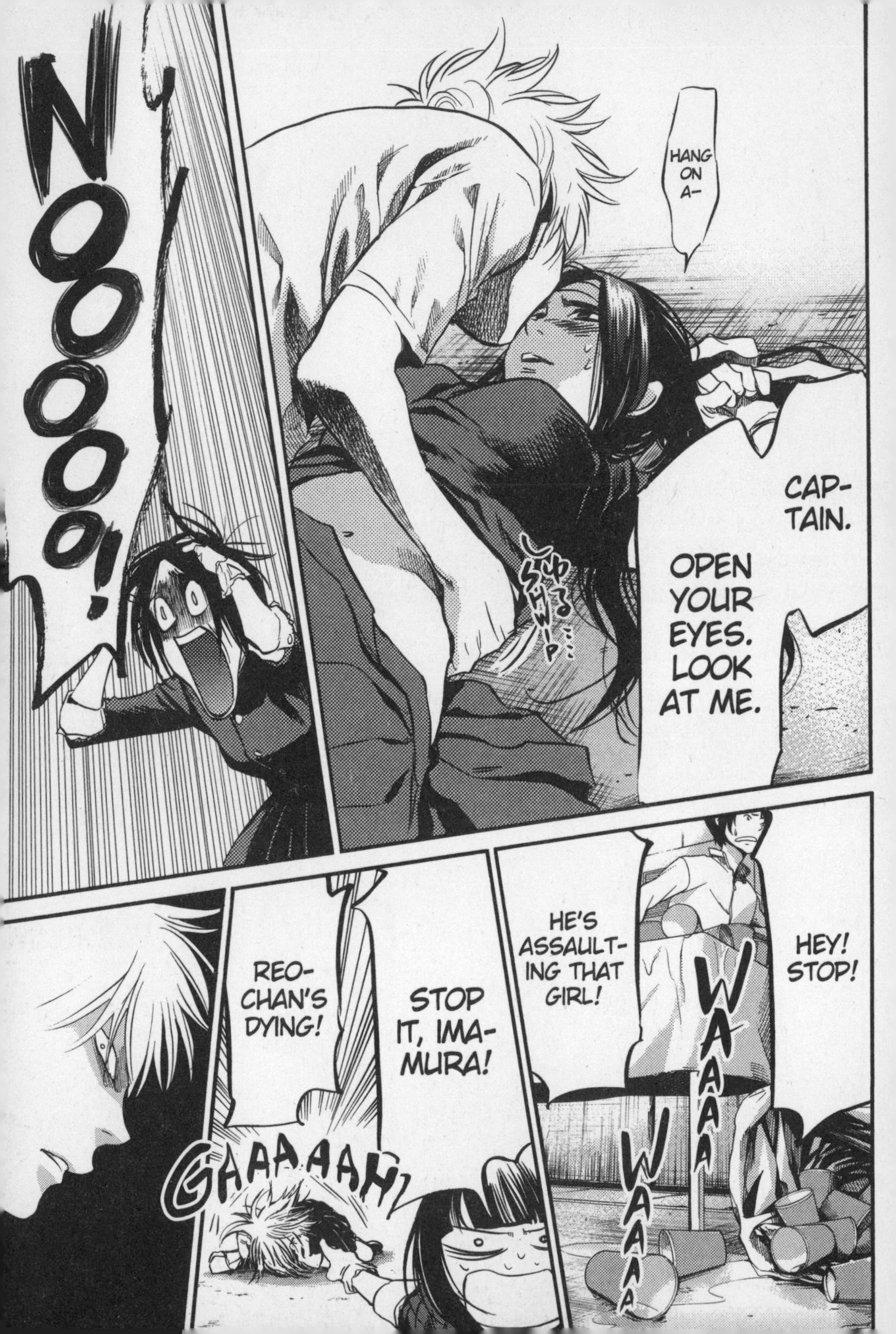
HANG ON A–
CAPTAIN.
OPEN YOUR EYES. LOOK AT ME.
しゅる…
SHWIP
NOOOOO!
HEY! STOP!
HE'S ASSAULTING THAT GIRL!
WAAAAA
WAAAA
STOP IT, IMAMURA!
REO-CHAN'S DYING!
GAAAAAH!

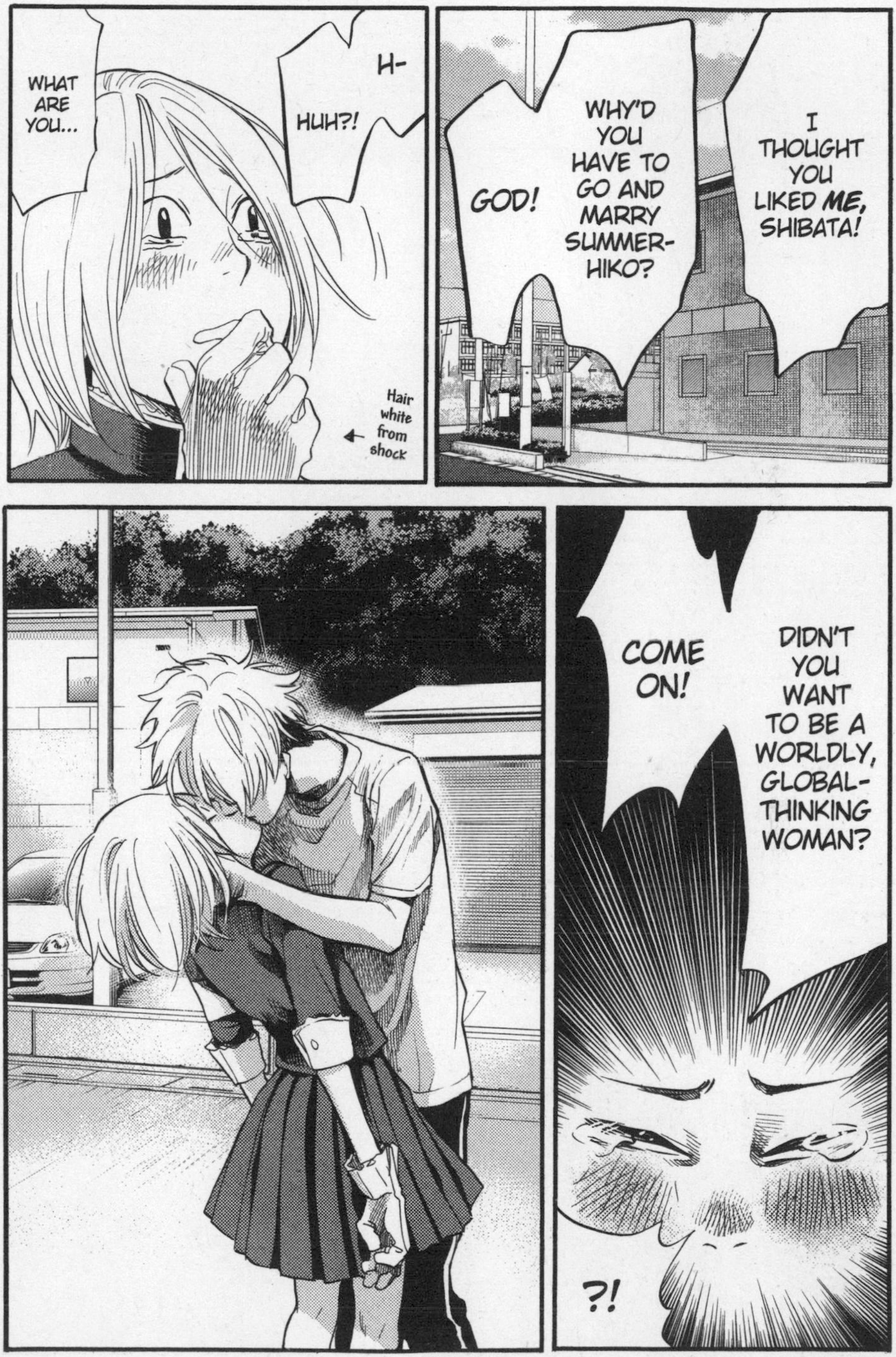
I THOUGHT YOU LIKED ME, SHIBATA!
WHY'D YOU HAVE TO GO AND MARRY SUMMER-HIKO?
GOD!
H- HUH?!
WHAT ARE YOU...
Hair white from shock
DIDN'T YOU WANT TO BE A WORLDLY, GLOBAL-THINKING WOMAN?
COME ON!
?!

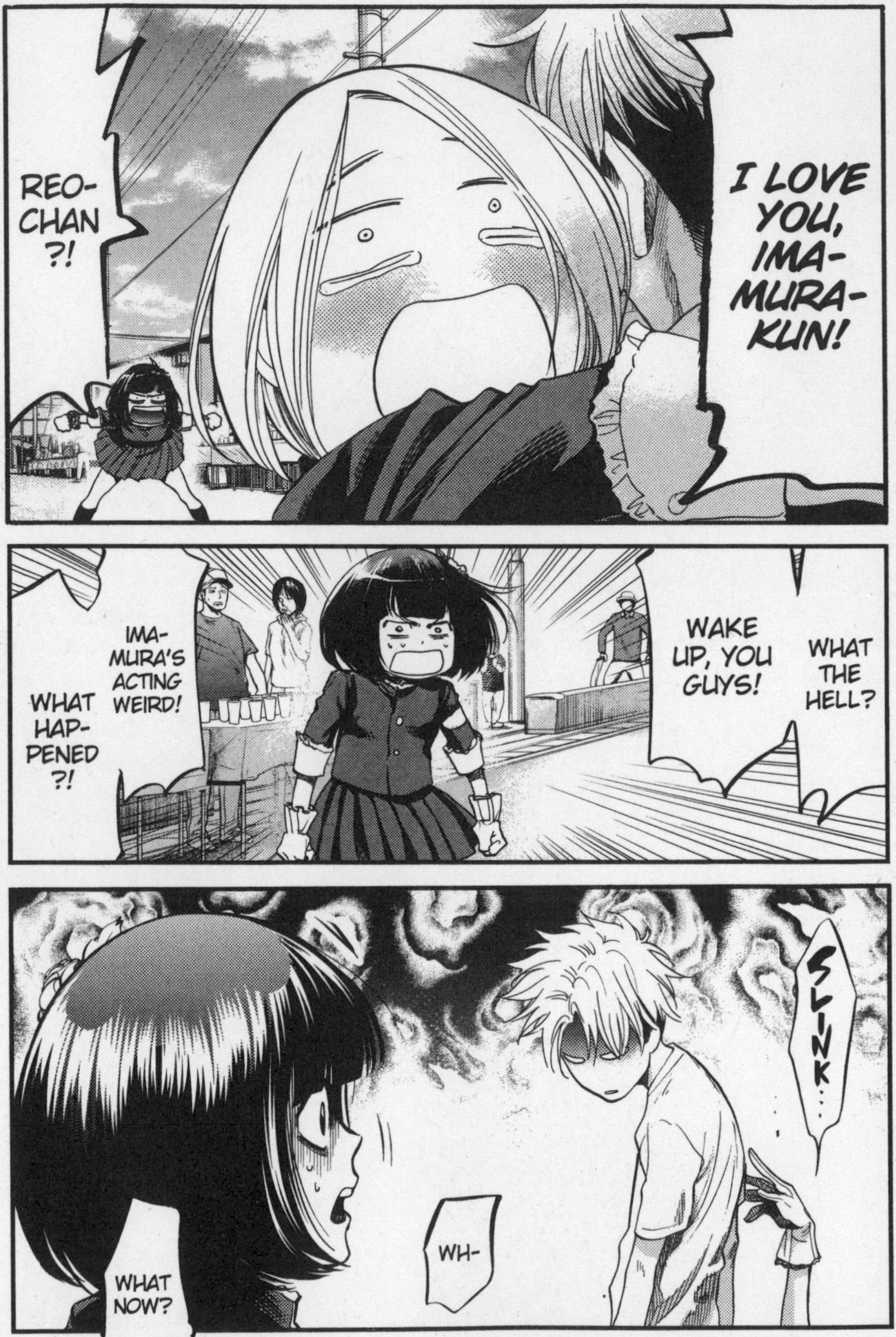

I LOVE YOU, IMAMURA-KUN!
REO-CHAN?!
WHAT THE HELL?
WAKE UP, YOU GUYS!
IMAMURA'S ACTING WEIRD!
WHAT HAPPENED?!
SLINK...
WH-
WHAT NOW?

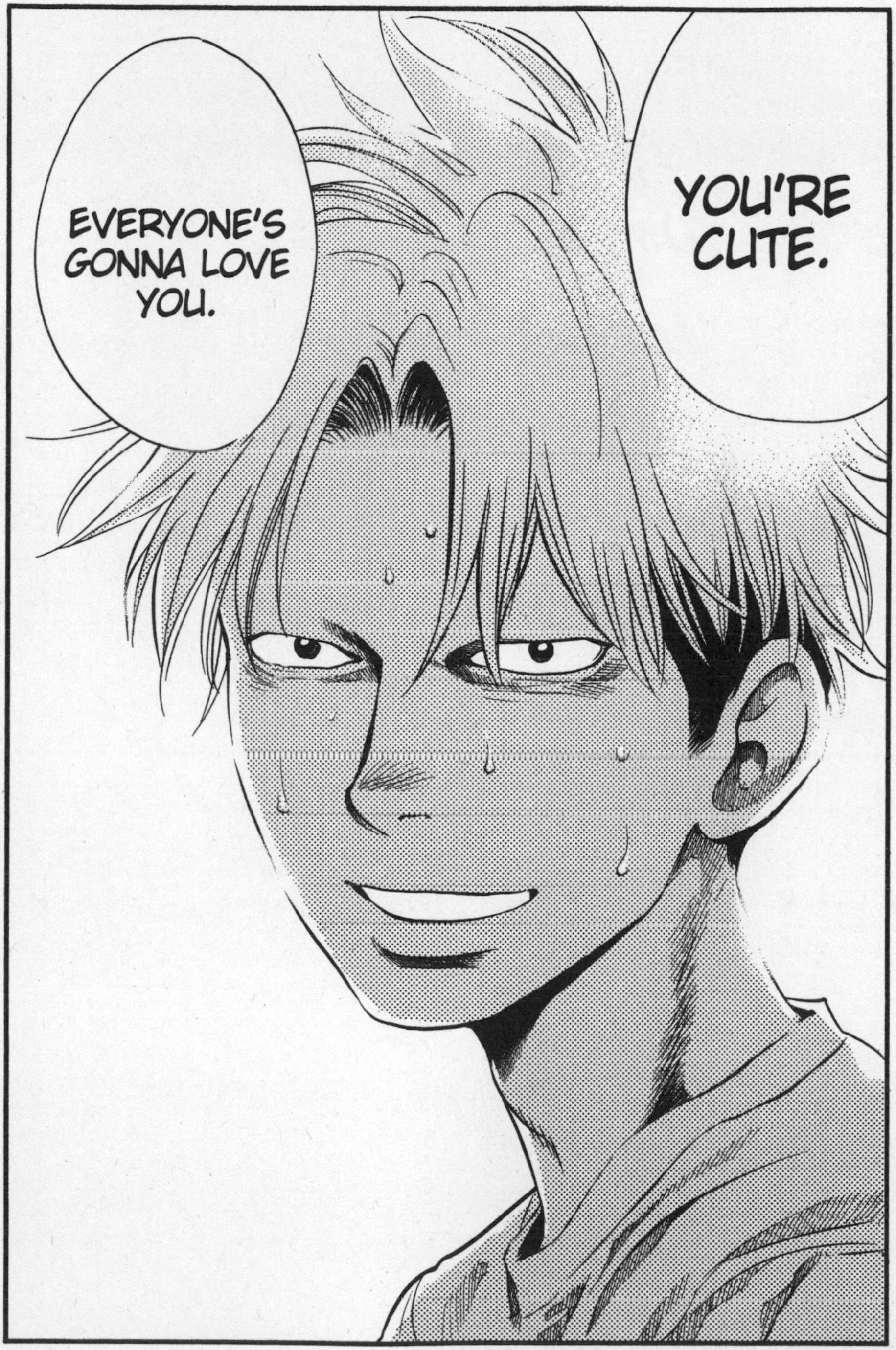
YOU'RE CUTE.
EVERYONE'S GONNA LOVE YOU.

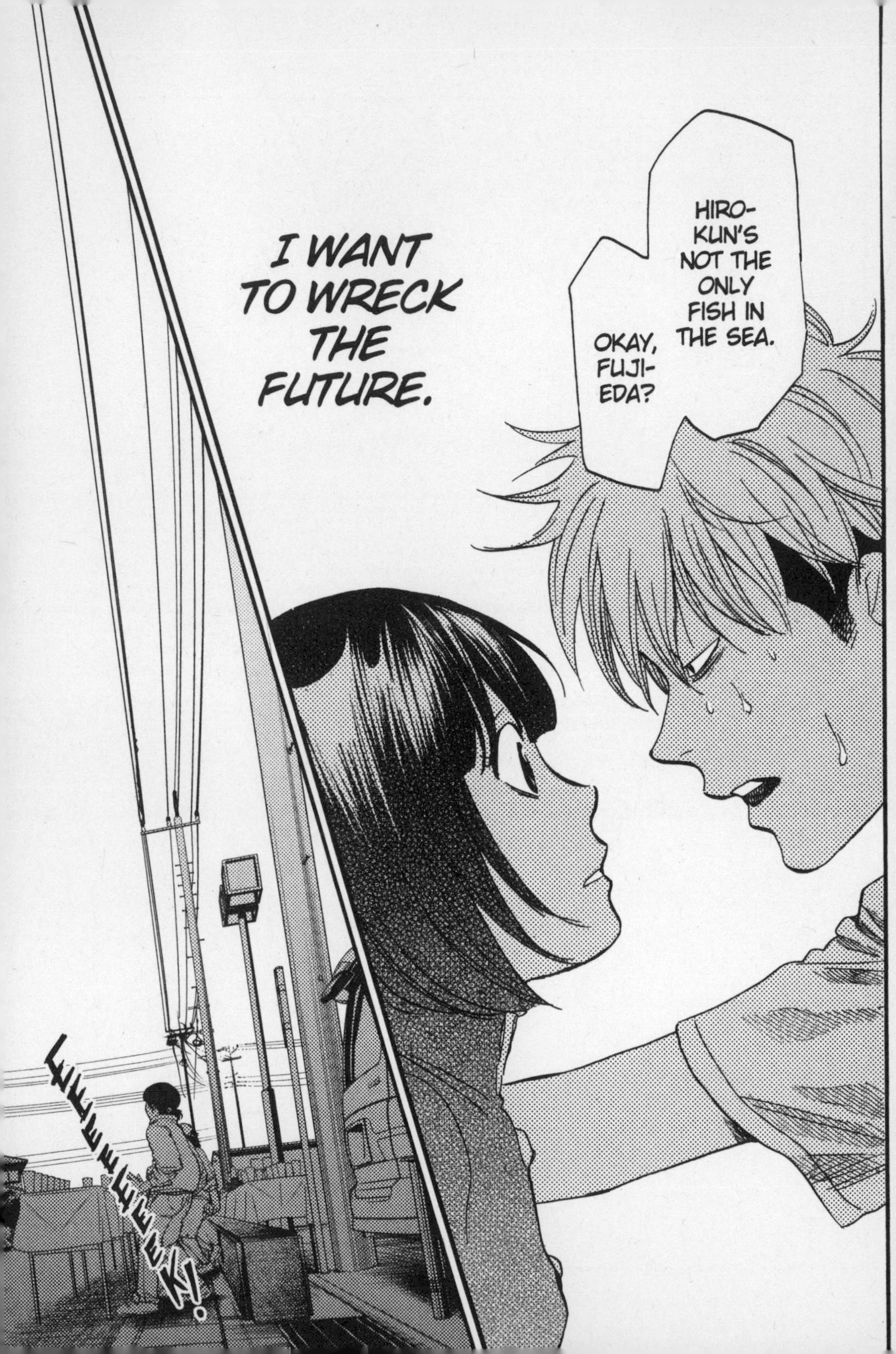
HIRO-KUN'S NOT THE ONLY FISH IN THE SEA.
OKAY, FUJI-EDA?
I WANT TO WRECK THE FUTURE.
EEEEEEEEEK!

THANK YOU FOR CHEERING ME ON SO MUCH!

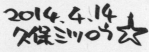

Mitsurou Kubo ☆
April 14, 2014

☆ My Editors: Suzuki-san,
Takigawa-san, Zenzai-san, Ebitani-san
☆ Research Partners: Saitama
Prefectural Fudooka High School
Nagasaki Prefectural Sasebo
Minami High School
☆ My Agent: Hiromi Sakitani
Kuboken Staff: Ema Yamanouchi
☆ My Assistants: Shunsuke Ono,
Youko Mikuni, Hiromu Kitano
Koushi Tezuka, Kouhei Mihara
Rana Satou

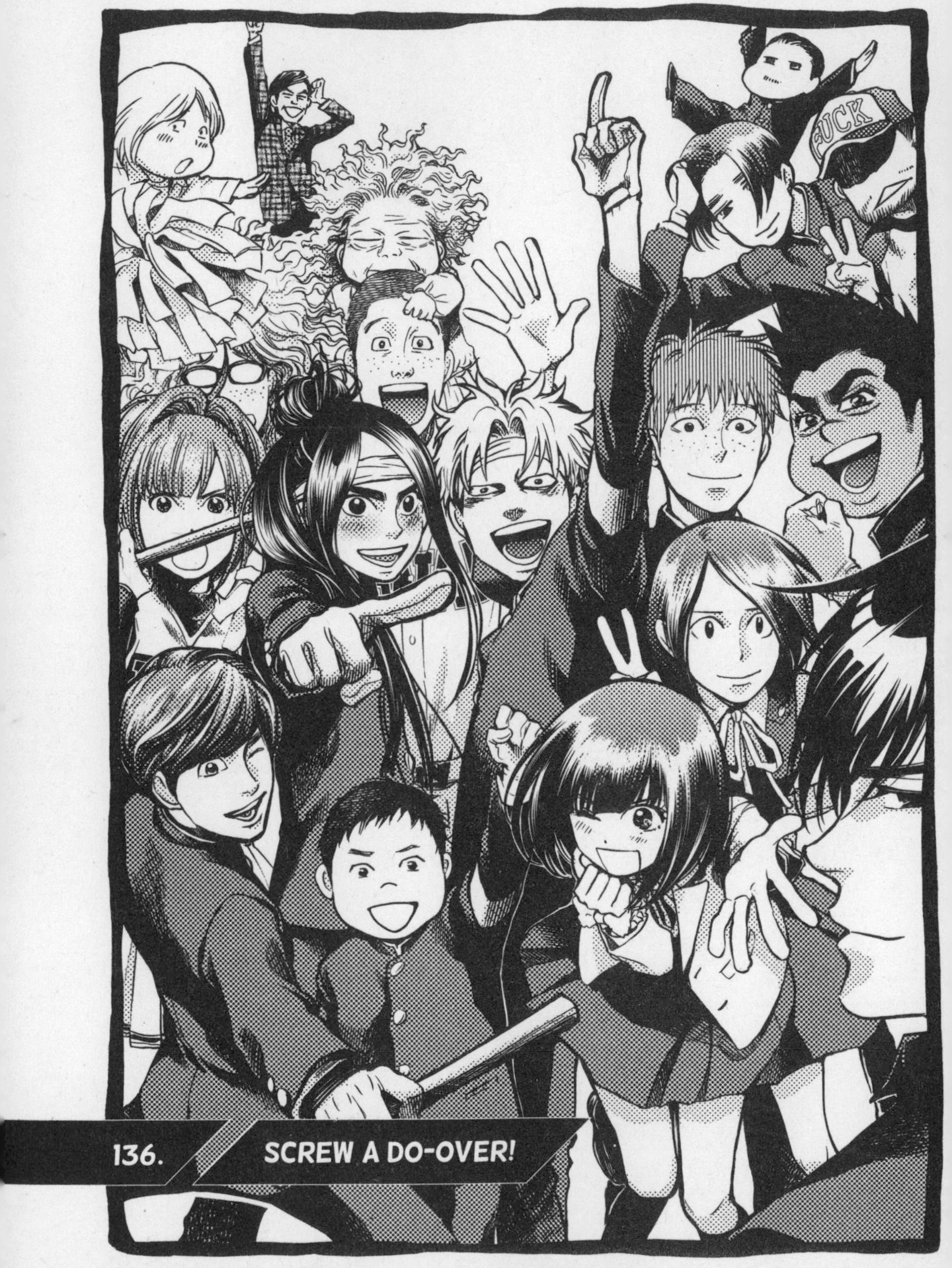
FUCK

136. SCREW A DO-OVER!

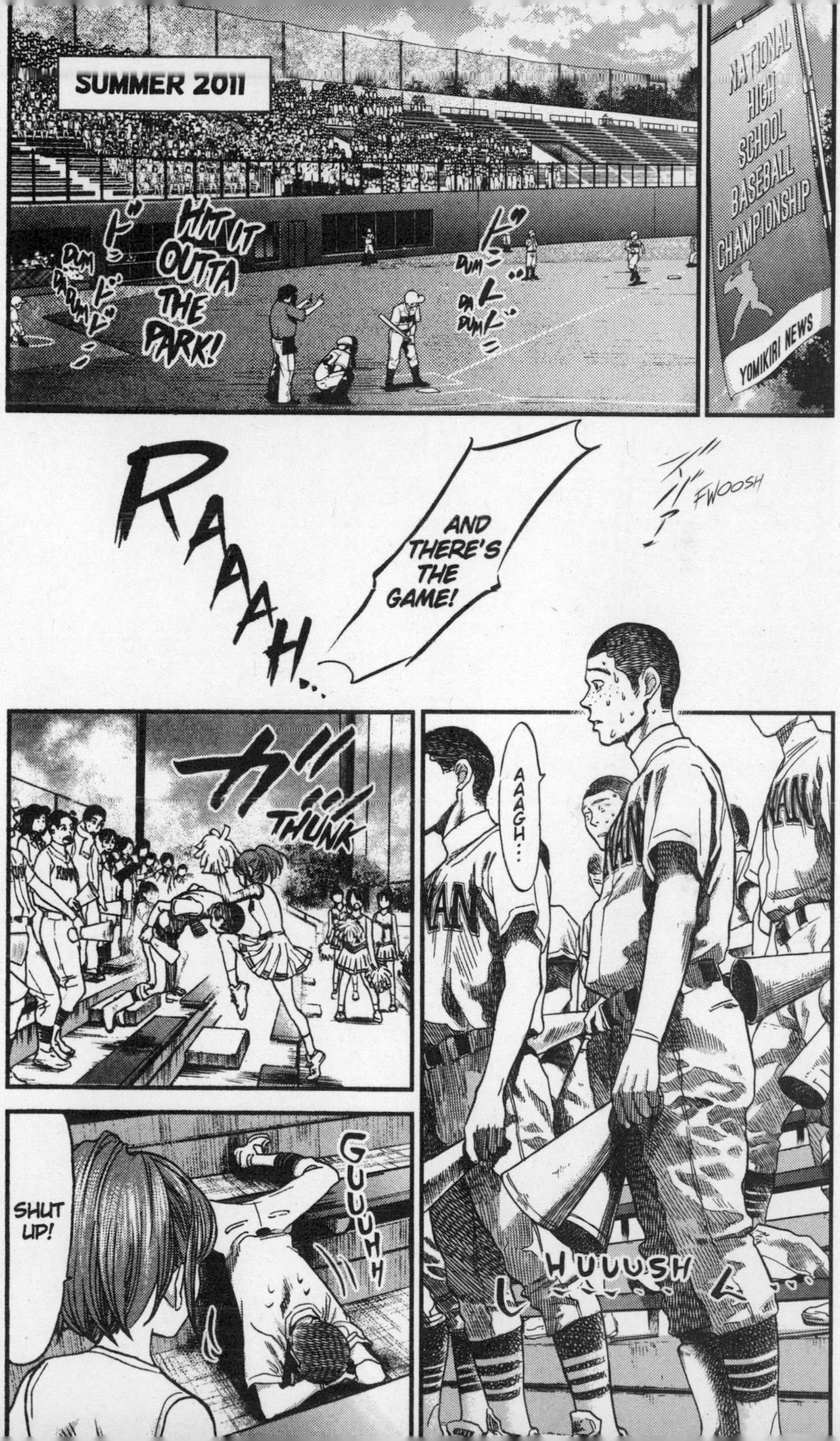
NATIONAL HIGH SCHOOL BASEBALL CHAMPIONSHIP
YOMIKIRI NEWS
SUMMER 2011
DUM DADUM
HIT IT OUTTA THE PARK!
DUM DADUM
FWOOSH
AND THERE'S THE GAME!
RAAAAH...
AAAGH...
HUUUSH
THUNK
GUUUHH
SHUT UP!

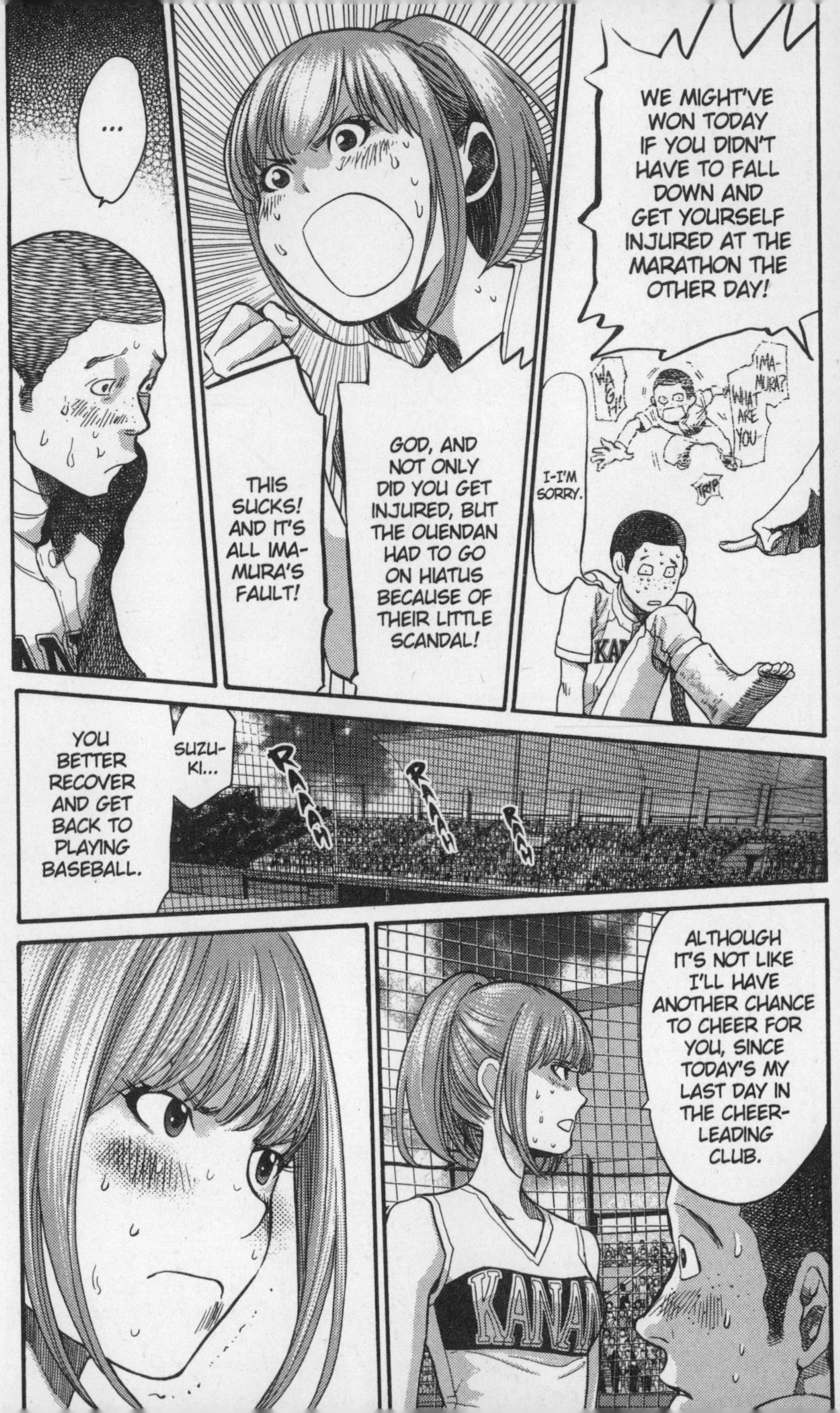
WE MIGHT'VE WON TODAY IF YOU DIDN'T HAVE TO FALL DOWN AND GET YOURSELF INJURED AT THE MARATHON THE OTHER DAY!
IMA-MURA? WHAT ARE YOU
WAGH!
TRIP
I-I'M SORRY.
GOD, AND NOT ONLY DID YOU GET INJURED, BUT THE OUENDAN HAD TO GO ON HIATUS BECAUSE OF THEIR LITTLE SCANDAL!
THIS SUCKS! AND IT'S ALL IMA-MURA'S FAULT!
...
SUZU-KI...
YOU BETTER RECOVER AND GET BACK TO PLAYING BASEBALL.
ALTHOUGH IT'S NOT LIKE I'LL HAVE ANOTHER CHANCE TO CHEER FOR YOU, SINCE TODAY'S MY LAST DAY IN THE CHEER-LEADING CLUB.

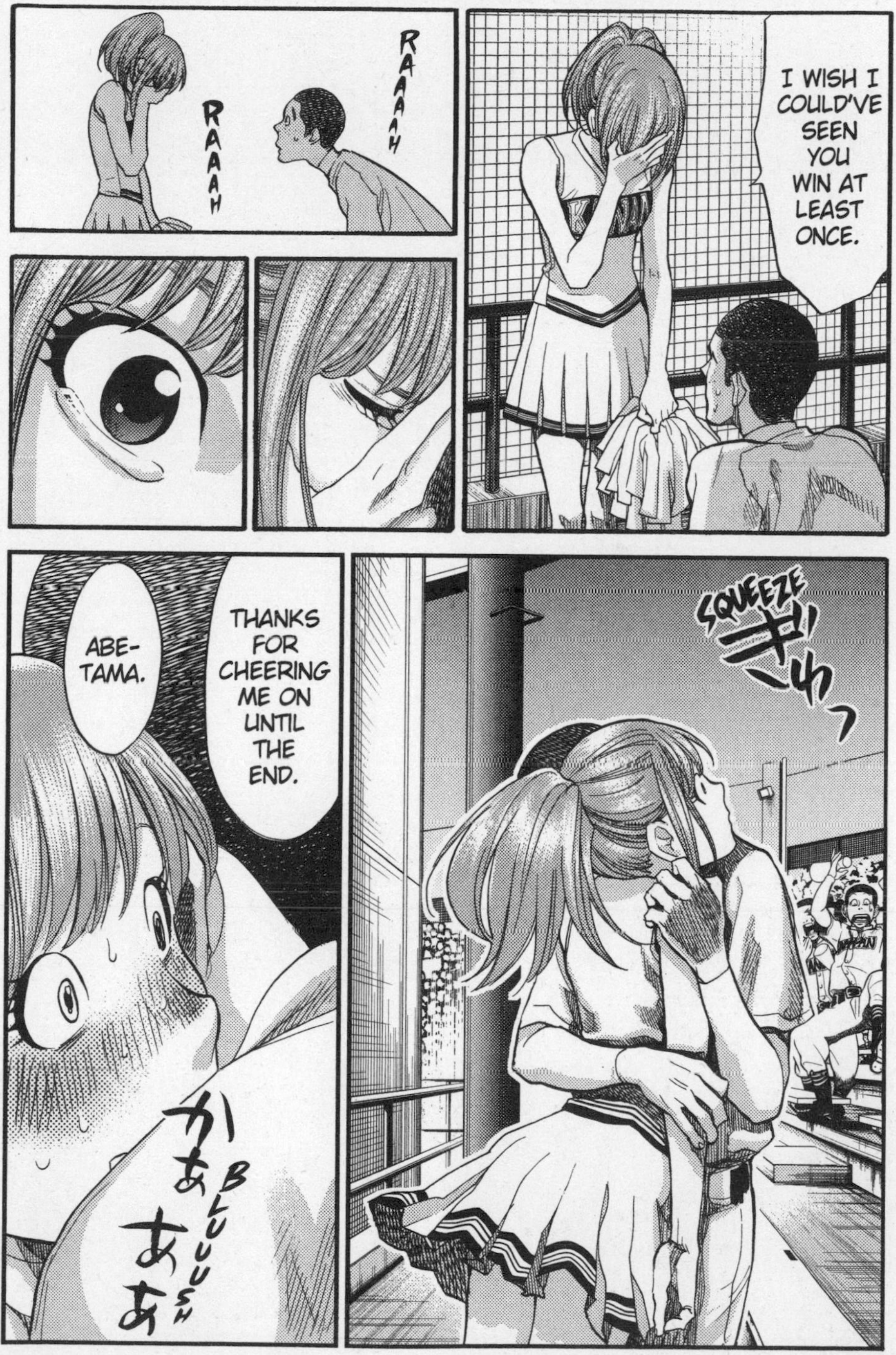
I WISH I COULD'VE SEEN YOU WIN AT LEAST ONCE.
RAAAAH
RAAAH
SQUEEZE
ぎゅっ
THANKS FOR CHEERING ME ON UNTIL THE END.
ABE-TAMA.
かあああ
BLUUUSH

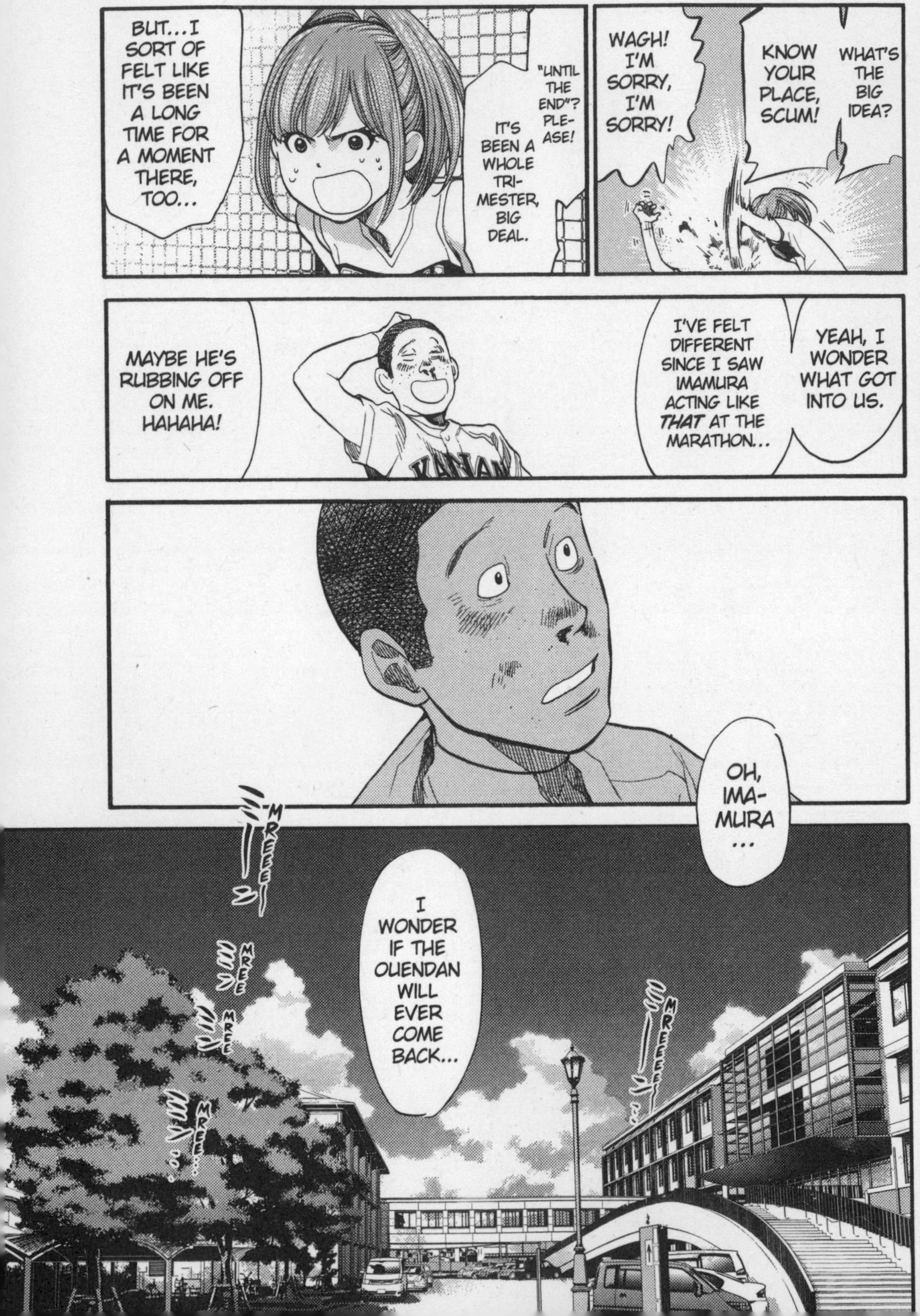
WHAT'S THE BIG IDEA?
KNOW YOUR PLACE, SCUM!
WAGH! I'M SORRY, I'M SORRY!
"UNTIL THE END"? PLE-ASE!
IT'S BEEN A WHOLE TRI-MESTER, BIG DEAL.
BUT...I SORT OF FELT LIKE IT'S BEEN A LONG TIME FOR A MOMENT THERE, TOO...
YEAH, I WONDER WHAT GOT INTO US.
I'VE FELT DIFFERENT SINCE I SAW IMAMURA ACTING LIKE *THAT* AT THE MARATHON...
MAYBE HE'S RUBBING OFF ON ME. HAHAHA!
OH, IMA-MURA...
MREEEEE
MREEEEE
I WONDER IF THE OUENDAN WILL EVER COME BACK...
MREE
MREE
MREE...

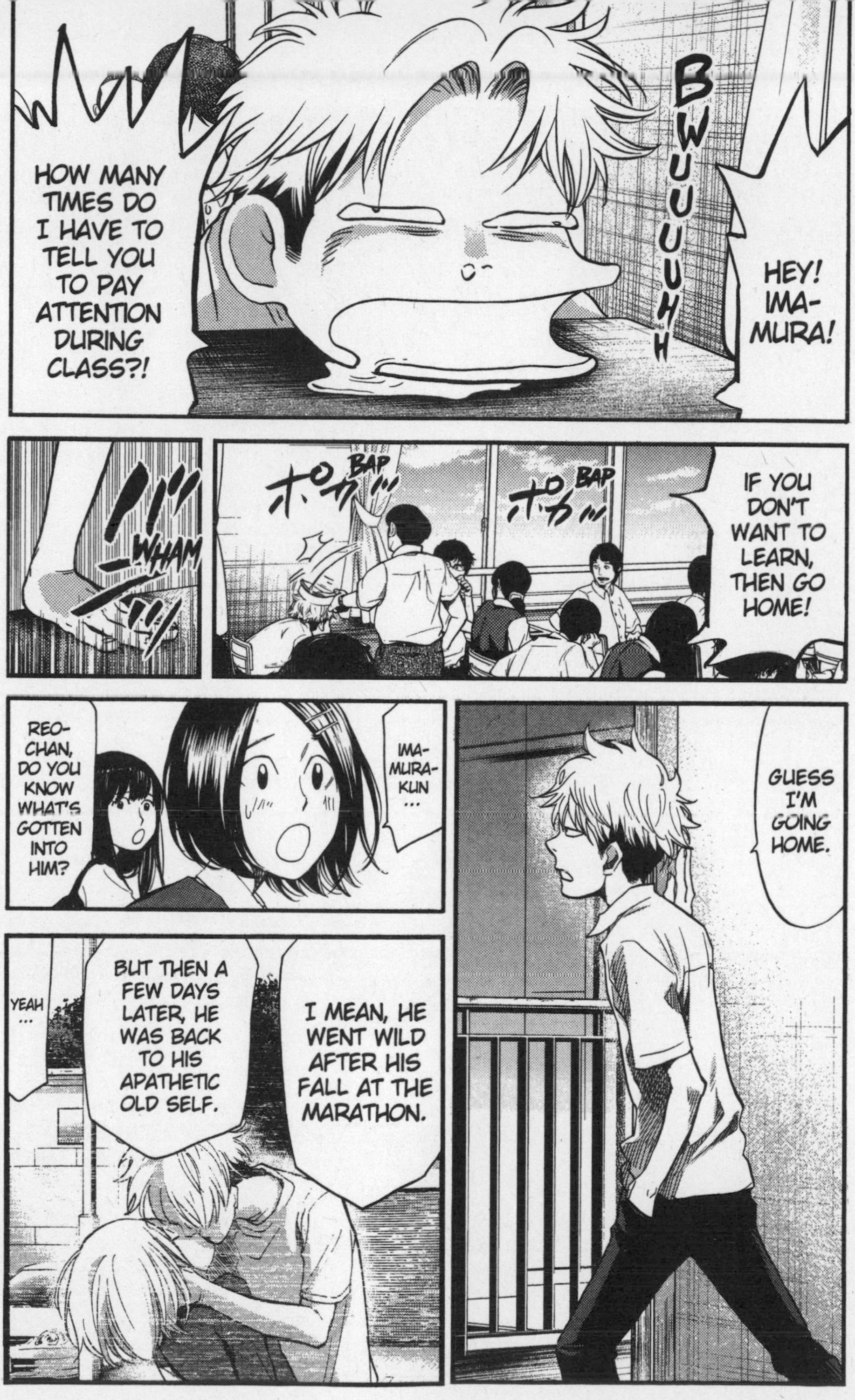
BWUUUUUHH
HEY! IMA-MURA!
HOW MANY TIMES DO I HAVE TO TELL YOU TO PAY ATTENTION DURING CLASS?!
IF YOU DON'T WANT TO LEARN, THEN GO HOME!
BAP
BAP
WHAM
GUESS I'M GOING HOME.
IMA-MURA-KUN ...
REO-CHAN, DO YOU KNOW WHAT'S GOTTEN INTO HIM?
I MEAN, HE WENT WILD AFTER HIS FALL AT THE MARATHON.
BUT THEN A FEW DAYS LATER, HE WAS BACK TO HIS APATHETIC OLD SELF.
YEAH ...

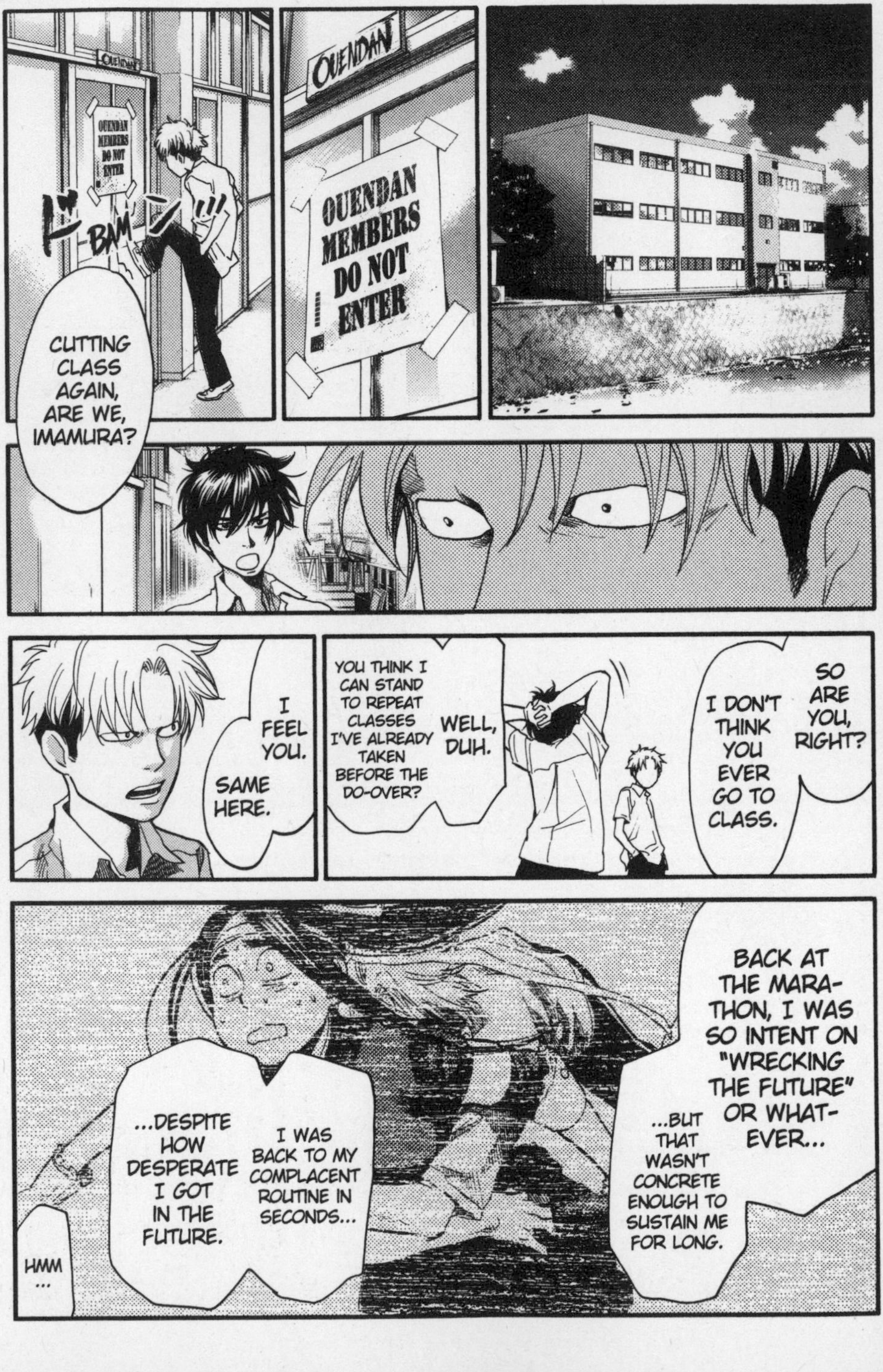
OUENDAN
OUENDAN MEMBERS DO NOT ENTER
OUENDAN
OUENDAN MEMBERS DO NOT ENTER
BAM
CUTTING CLASS AGAIN, ARE WE, IMAMURA?
SO ARE YOU, RIGHT?
I DON'T THINK YOU EVER GO TO CLASS.
WELL, DUH.
YOU THINK I CAN STAND TO REPEAT CLASSES I'VE ALREADY TAKEN BEFORE THE DO-OVER?
I FEEL YOU.
SAME HERE.
BACK AT THE MARA-THON, I WAS SO INTENT ON "WRECKING THE FUTURE" OR WHAT-EVER...
...BUT THAT WASN'T CONCRETE ENOUGH TO SUSTAIN ME FOR LONG.
I WAS BACK TO MY COMPLACENT ROUTINE IN SECONDS...
...DESPITE HOW DESPERATE I GOT IN THE FUTURE.
HMM...

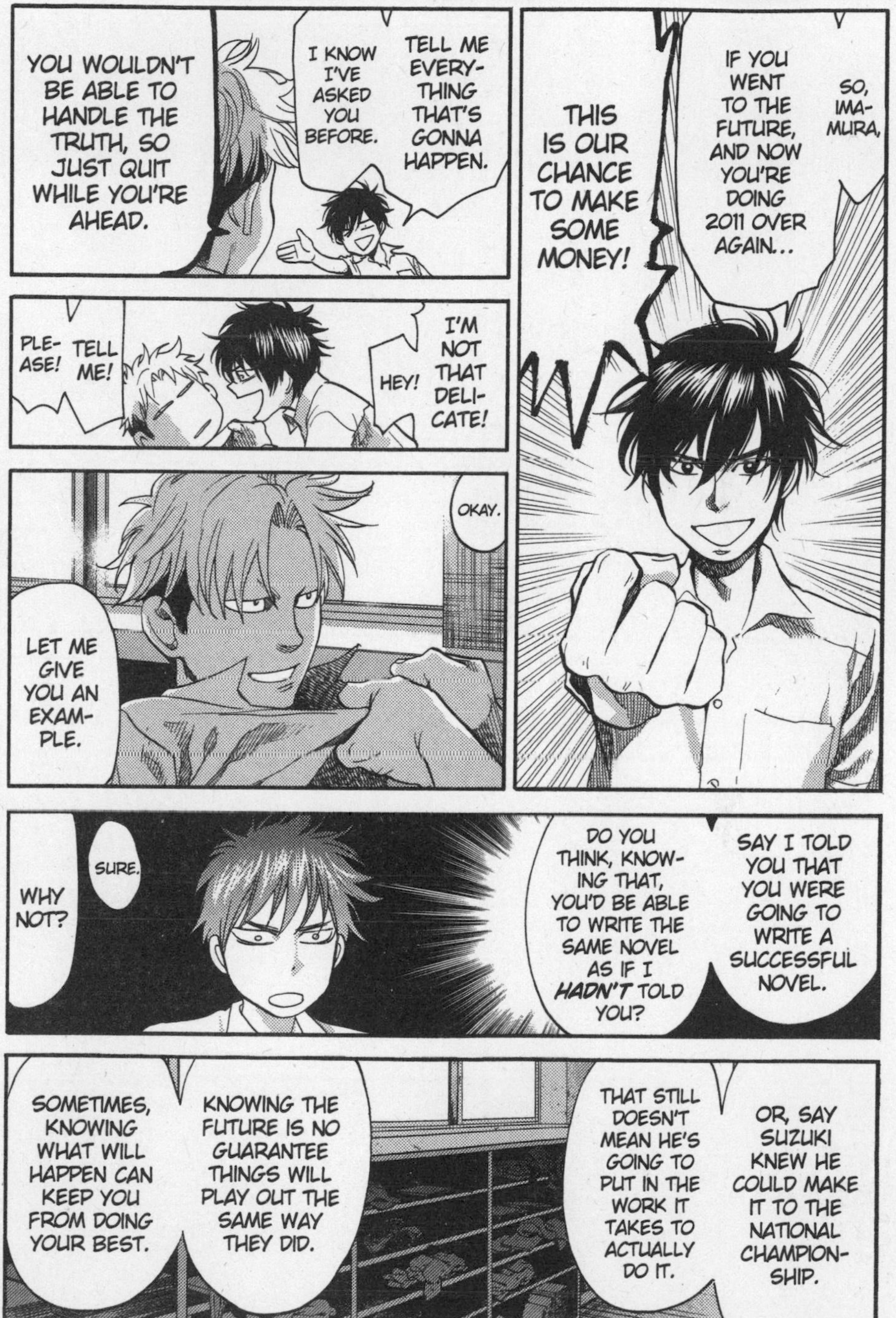
SO, IMAMURA,
IF YOU WENT TO THE FUTURE, AND NOW YOU'RE DOING 2011 OVER AGAIN...
THIS IS OUR CHANCE TO MAKE SOME MONEY!
TELL ME EVERYTHING THAT'S GONNA HAPPEN.
I KNOW I'VE ASKED YOU BEFORE.
YOU WOULDN'T BE ABLE TO HANDLE THE TRUTH, SO JUST QUIT WHILE YOU'RE AHEAD.
I'M NOT THAT DELICATE!
HEY!
TELL ME!
PLEASE!
OKAY.
LET ME GIVE YOU AN EXAMPLE.
SAY I TOLD YOU THAT YOU WERE GOING TO WRITE A SUCCESSFUL NOVEL.
DO YOU THINK, KNOWING THAT, YOU'D BE ABLE TO WRITE THE SAME NOVEL AS IF I *HADN'T* TOLD YOU?
SURE.
WHY NOT?
OR, SAY SUZUKI KNEW HE COULD MAKE IT TO THE NATIONAL CHAMPIONSHIP.
THAT STILL DOESN'T MEAN HE'S GOING TO PUT IN THE WORK IT TAKES TO ACTUALLY DO IT.
KNOWING THE FUTURE IS NO GUARANTEE THINGS WILL PLAY OUT THE SAME WAY THEY DID.
SOMETIMES, KNOWING WHAT WILL HAPPEN CAN KEEP YOU FROM DOING YOUR BEST.

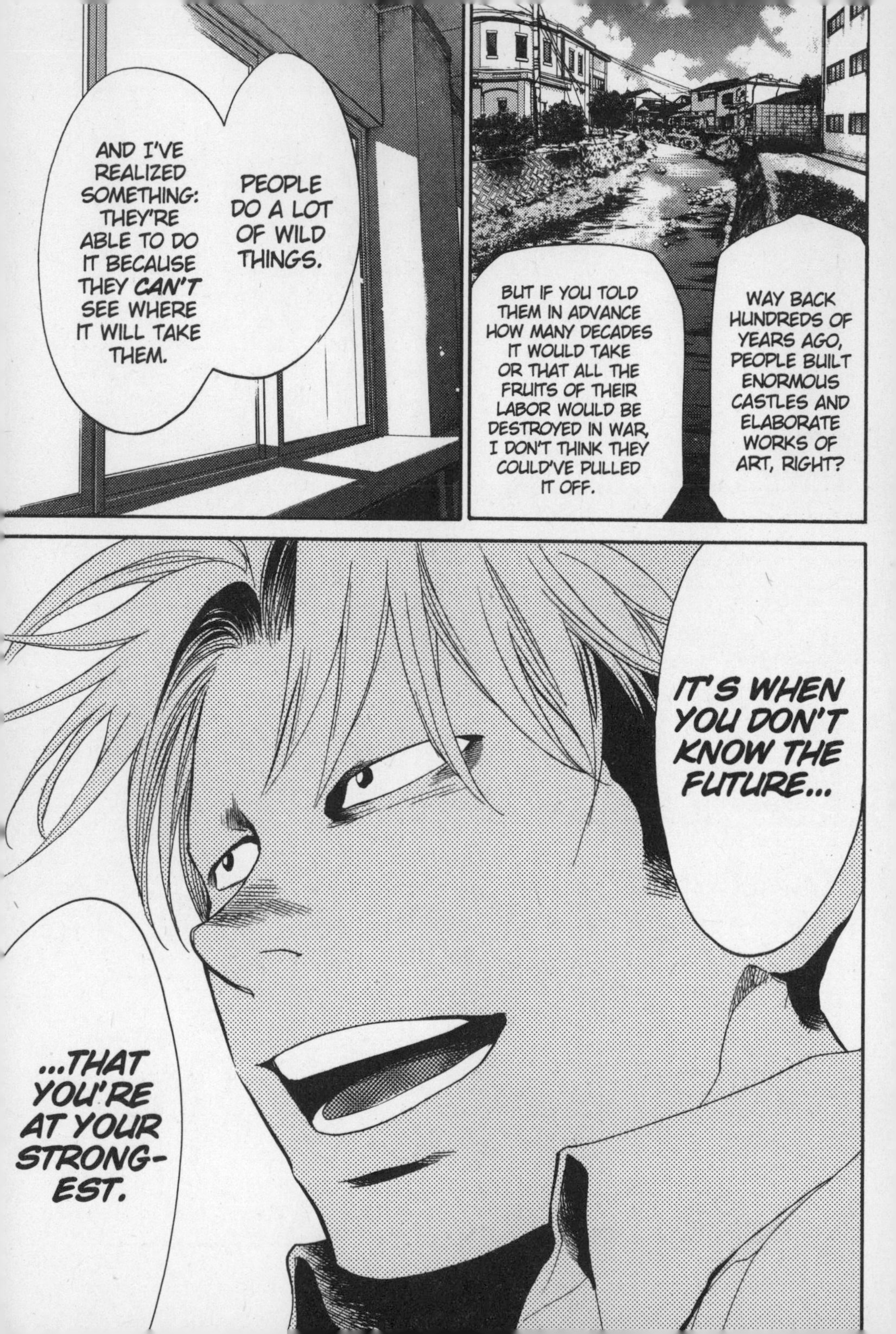
WAY BACK HUNDREDS OF YEARS AGO, PEOPLE BUILT ENORMOUS CASTLES AND ELABORATE WORKS OF ART, RIGHT?
BUT IF YOU TOLD THEM IN ADVANCE HOW MANY DECADES IT WOULD TAKE OR THAT ALL THE FRUITS OF THEIR LABOR WOULD BE DESTROYED IN WAR, I DON'T THINK THEY COULD'VE PULLED IT OFF.
PEOPLE DO A LOT OF WILD THINGS.
AND I'VE REALIZED SOMETHING: THEY'RE ABLE TO DO IT BECAUSE THEY *CAN'T* SEE WHERE IT WILL TAKE THEM.
IT'S WHEN YOU DON'T KNOW THE FUTURE...
...THAT YOU'RE AT YOUR STRONG-EST.

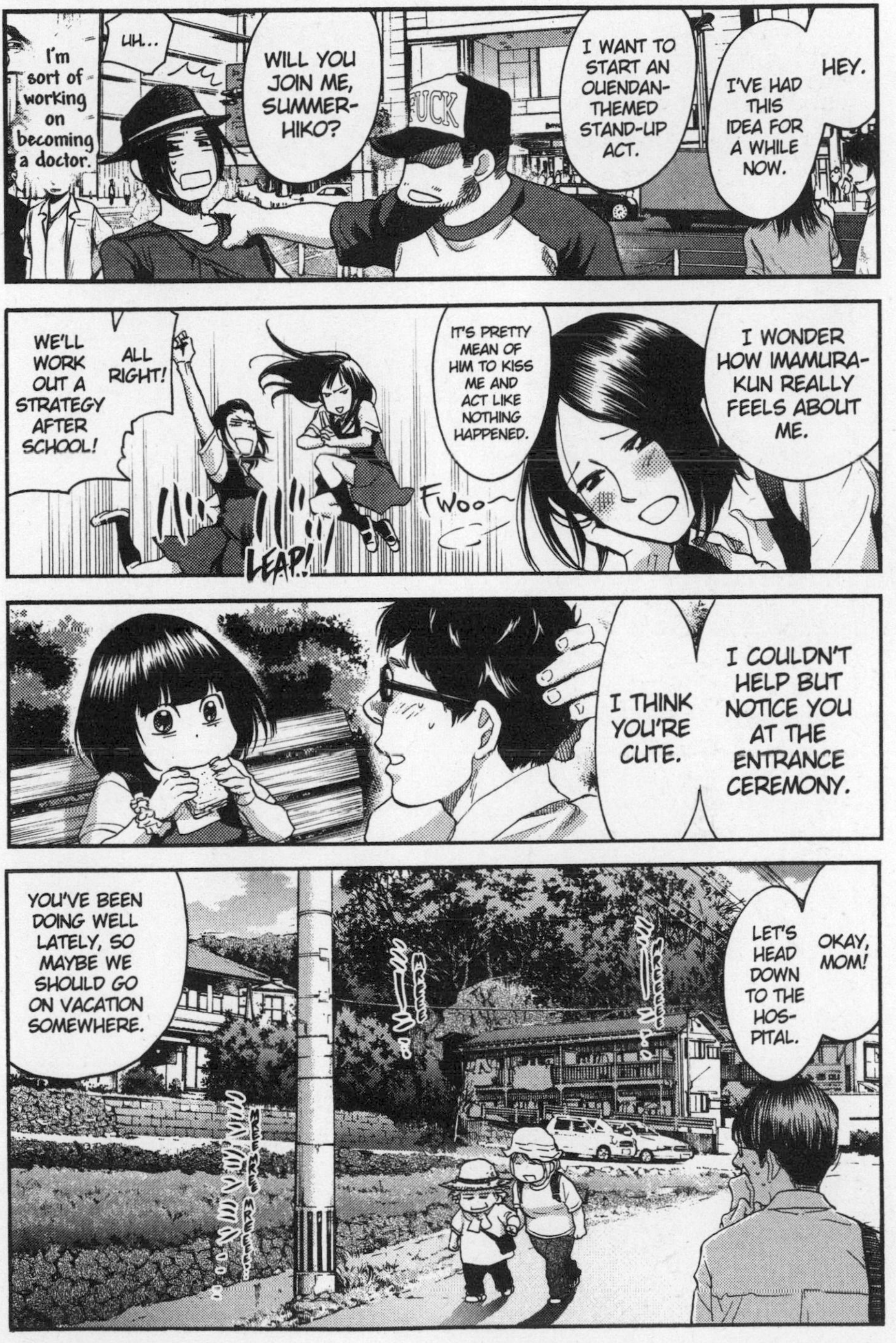
HEY.
I'VE HAD THIS IDEA FOR A WHILE NOW.
I WANT TO START AN OUENDAN-THEMED STAND-UP ACT.
WILL YOU JOIN ME, SUMMER-HIKO?
UH...
I'm sort of working on becoming a doctor.
I WONDER HOW IMAMURA-KUN REALLY FEELS ABOUT ME.
IT'S PRETTY MEAN OF HIM TO KISS ME AND ACT LIKE NOTHING HAPPENED.
FWOO~
ALL RIGHT!
WE'LL WORK OUT A STRATEGY AFTER SCHOOL!
LEAP!
I COULDN'T HELP BUT NOTICE YOU AT THE ENTRANCE CEREMONY.
I THINK YOU'RE CUTE.
OKAY, MOM!
LET'S HEAD DOWN TO THE HOS-PITAL.
YOU'VE BEEN DOING WELL LATELY, SO MAYBE WE SHOULD GO ON VACATION SOMEWHERE.

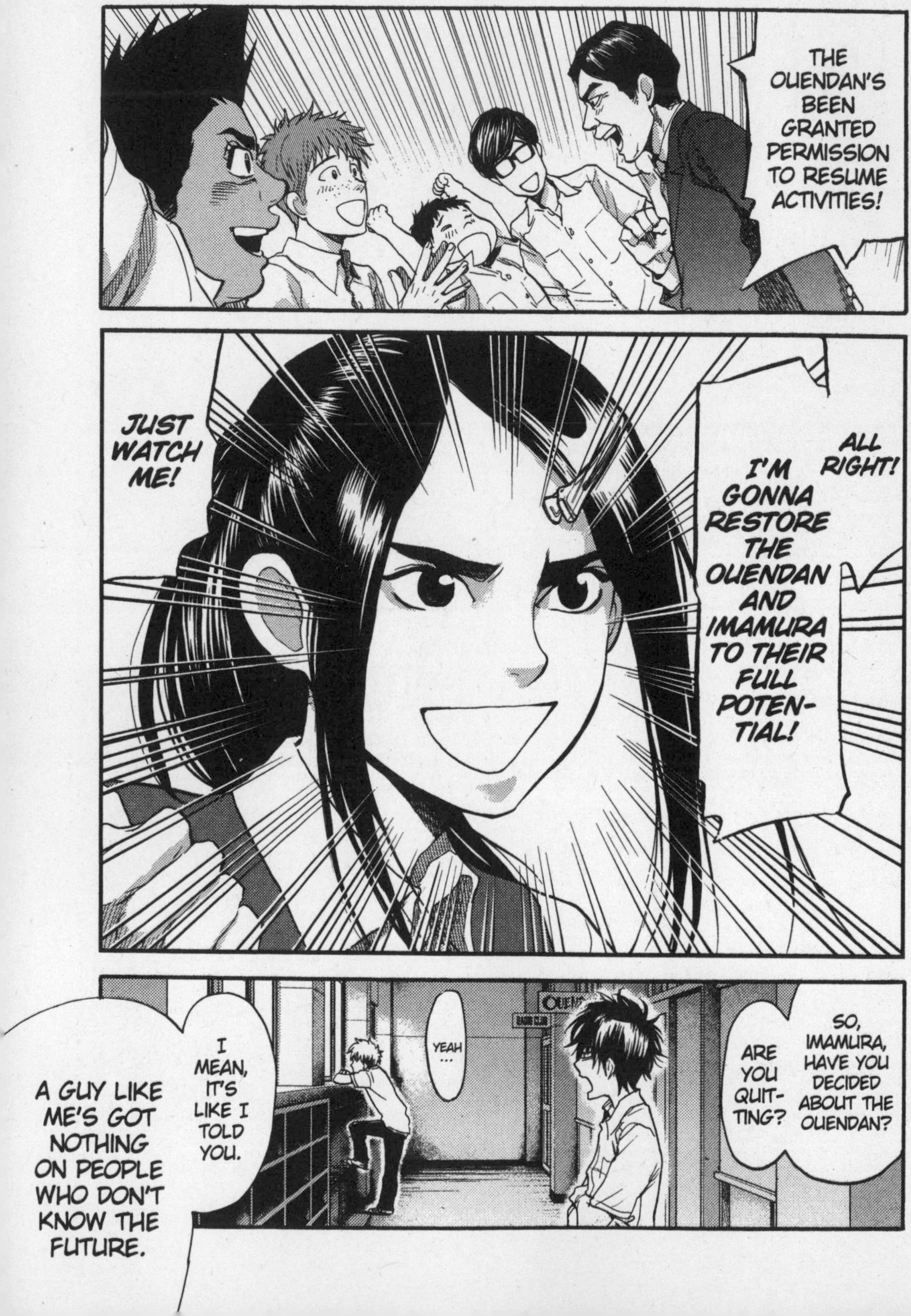
THE OUENDAN'S BEEN GRANTED PERMISSION TO RESUME ACTIVITIES!
ALL RIGHT!
I'M GONNA RESTORE THE OUENDAN AND IMAMURA TO THEIR FULL POTEN-TIAL!
JUST WATCH ME!
SO, IMAMURA, HAVE YOU DECIDED ABOUT THE OUENDAN?
ARE YOU QUIT-TING?
YEAH...
I MEAN, IT'S LIKE I TOLD YOU.
A GUY LIKE ME'S GOT NOTHING ON PEOPLE WHO DON'T KNOW THE FUTURE.

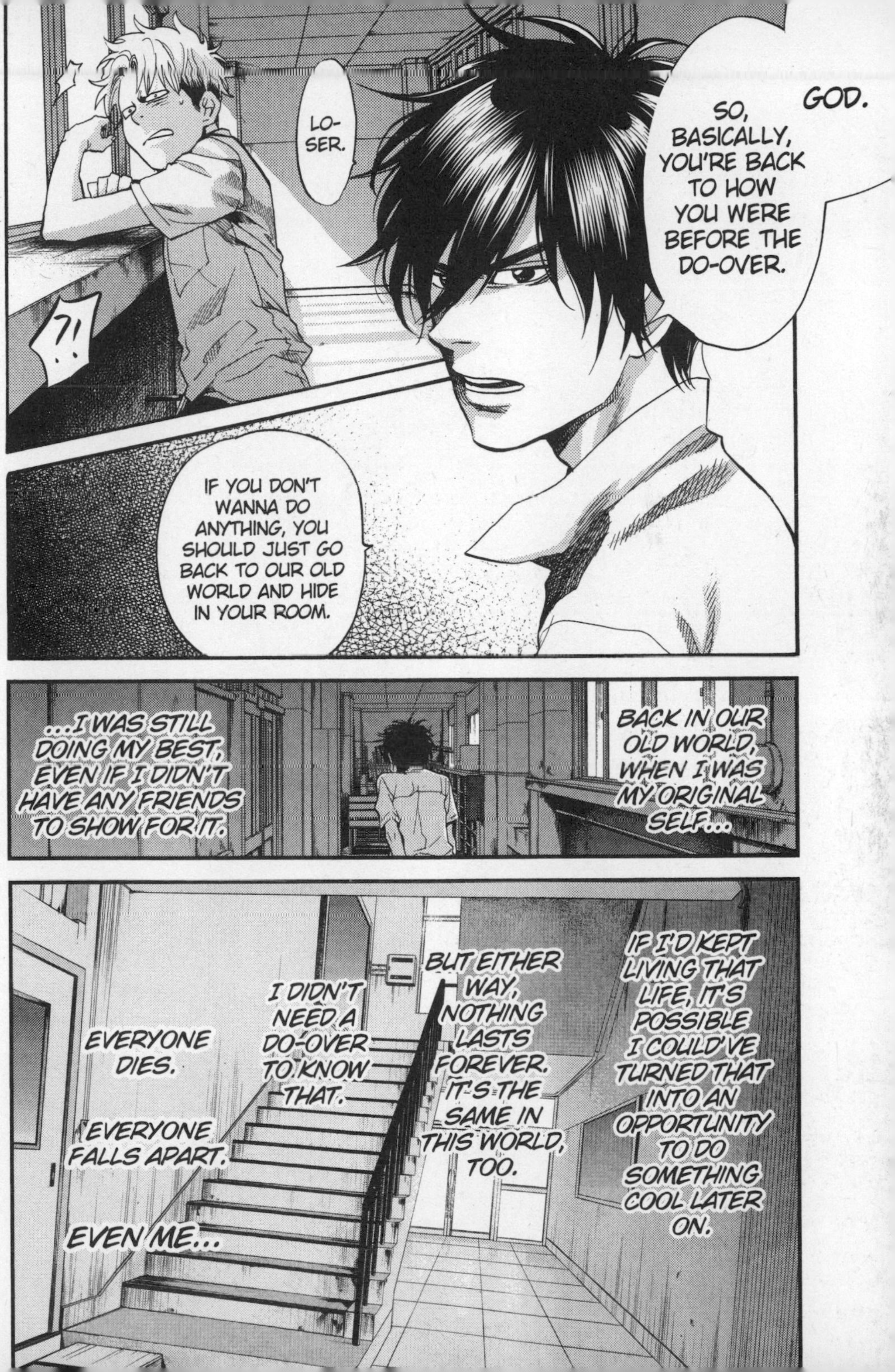
GOD.
SO, BASICALLY, YOU'RE BACK TO HOW YOU WERE BEFORE THE DO-OVER.
LO-SER.
?!
IF YOU DON'T WANNA DO ANYTHING, YOU SHOULD JUST GO BACK TO OUR OLD WORLD AND HIDE IN YOUR ROOM.
BACK IN OUR OLD WORLD, WHEN I WAS MY ORIGINAL SELF...
...I WAS STILL DOING MY BEST, EVEN IF I DIDN'T HAVE ANY FRIENDS TO SHOW FOR IT.
IF I'D KEPT LIVING THAT LIFE, IT'S POSSIBLE I COULD'VE TURNED THAT INTO AN OPPORTUNITY TO DO SOMETHING COOL LATER ON.
BUT EITHER WAY, NOTHING LASTS FOREVER. IT'S THE SAME IN THIS WORLD, TOO.
I DIDN'T NEED A DO-OVER TO KNOW THAT.
EVERYONE DIES.
EVERYONE FALLS APART.
EVEN ME...

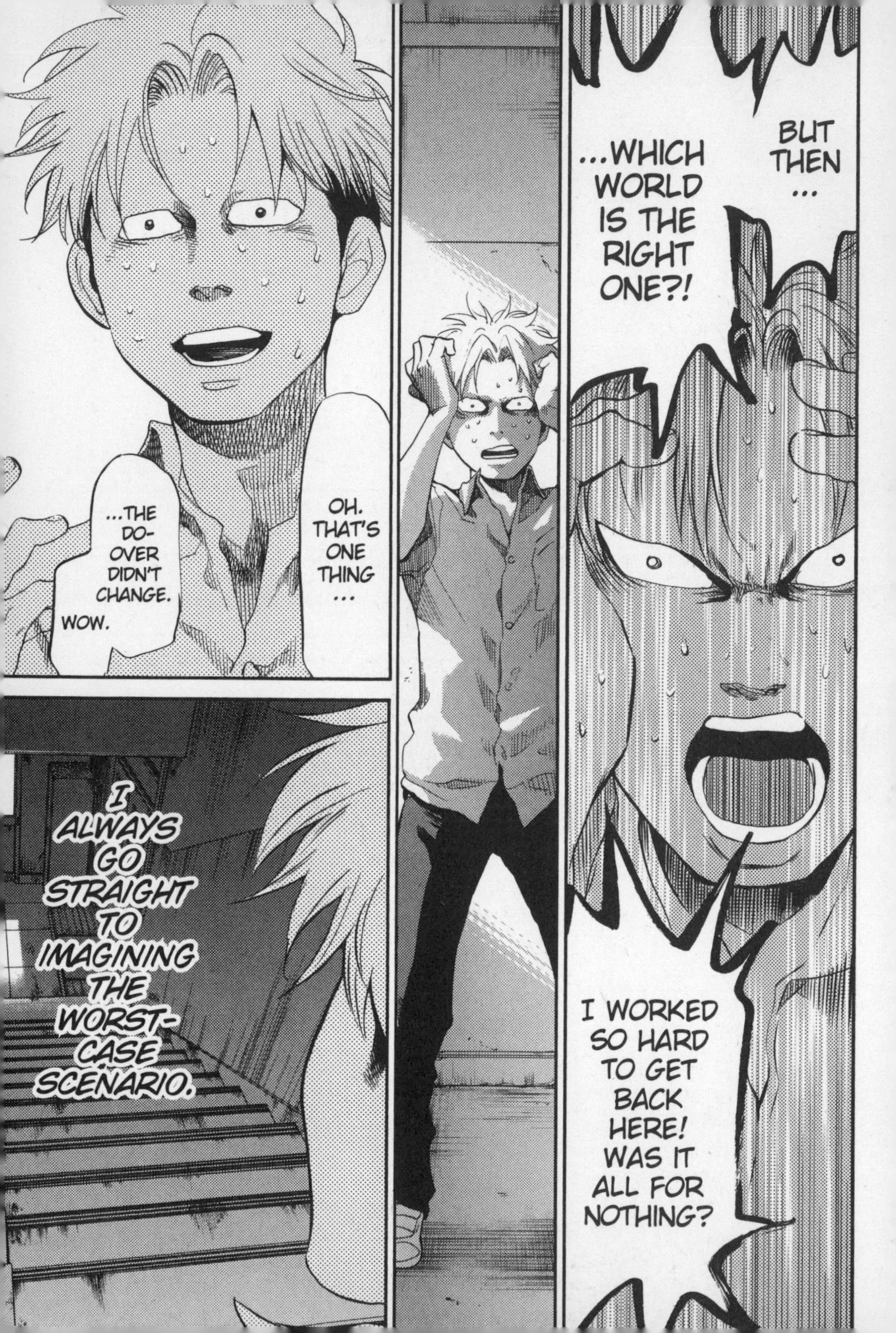
BUT THEN...
...WHICH WORLD IS THE RIGHT ONE?!
I WORKED SO HARD TO GET BACK HERE! WAS IT ALL FOR NOTHING?
OH. THAT'S ONE THING...
...THE DO-OVER DIDN'T CHANGE.
WOW.
I ALWAYS GO STRAIGHT TO IMAGINING THE WORST-CASE SCENARIO.

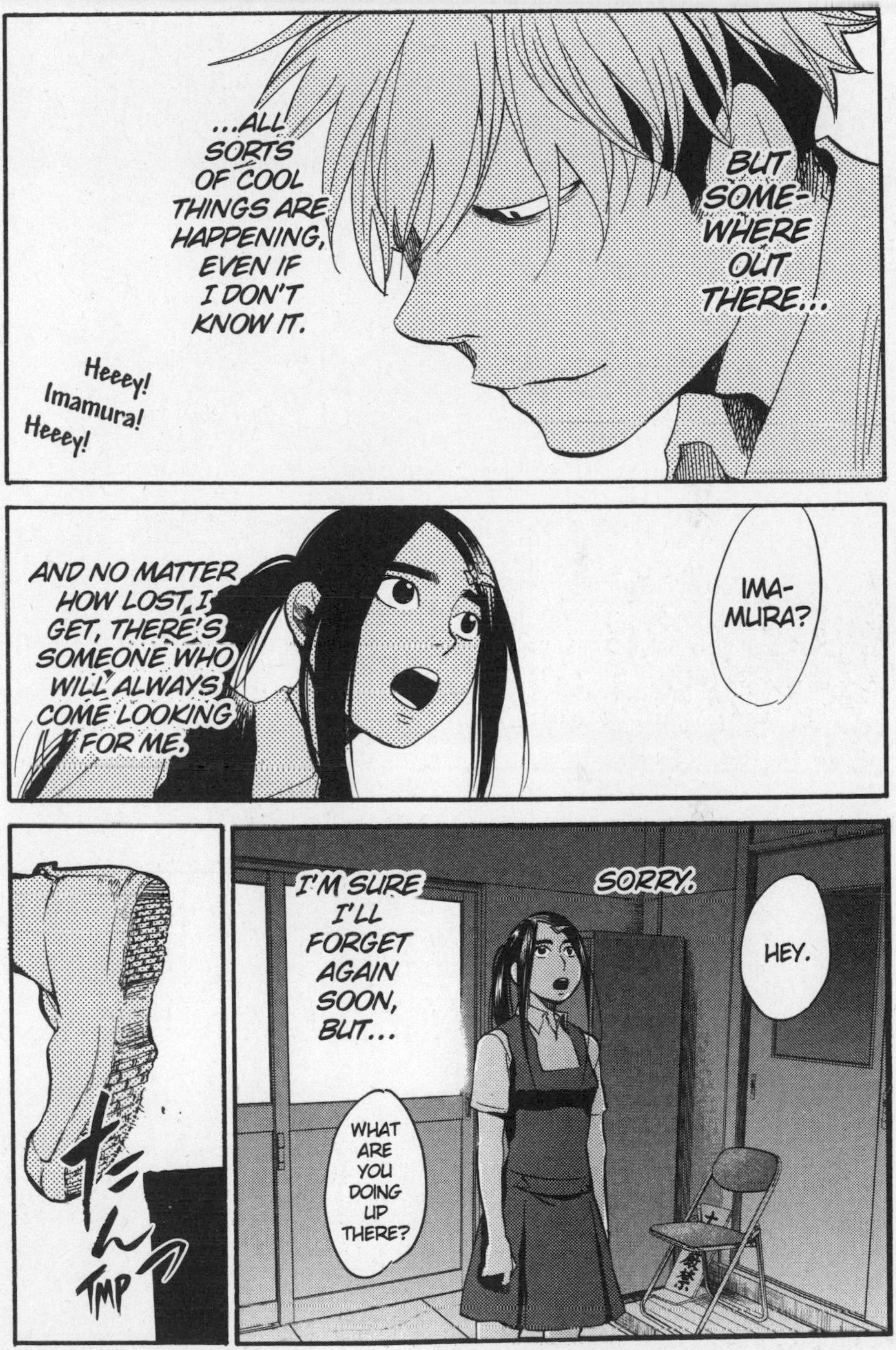
BUT SOMEWHERE OUT THERE...
...ALL SORTS OF COOL THINGS ARE HAPPENING, EVEN IF I DON'T KNOW IT.
Heeey! Imamura! Heeey!
IMAMURA?
AND NO MATTER HOW LOST I GET, THERE'S SOMEONE WHO WILL ALWAYS COME LOOKING FOR ME.
HEY.
SORRY.
I'M SURE I'LL FORGET AGAIN SOON, BUT...
WHAT ARE YOU DOING UP THERE?
TMP

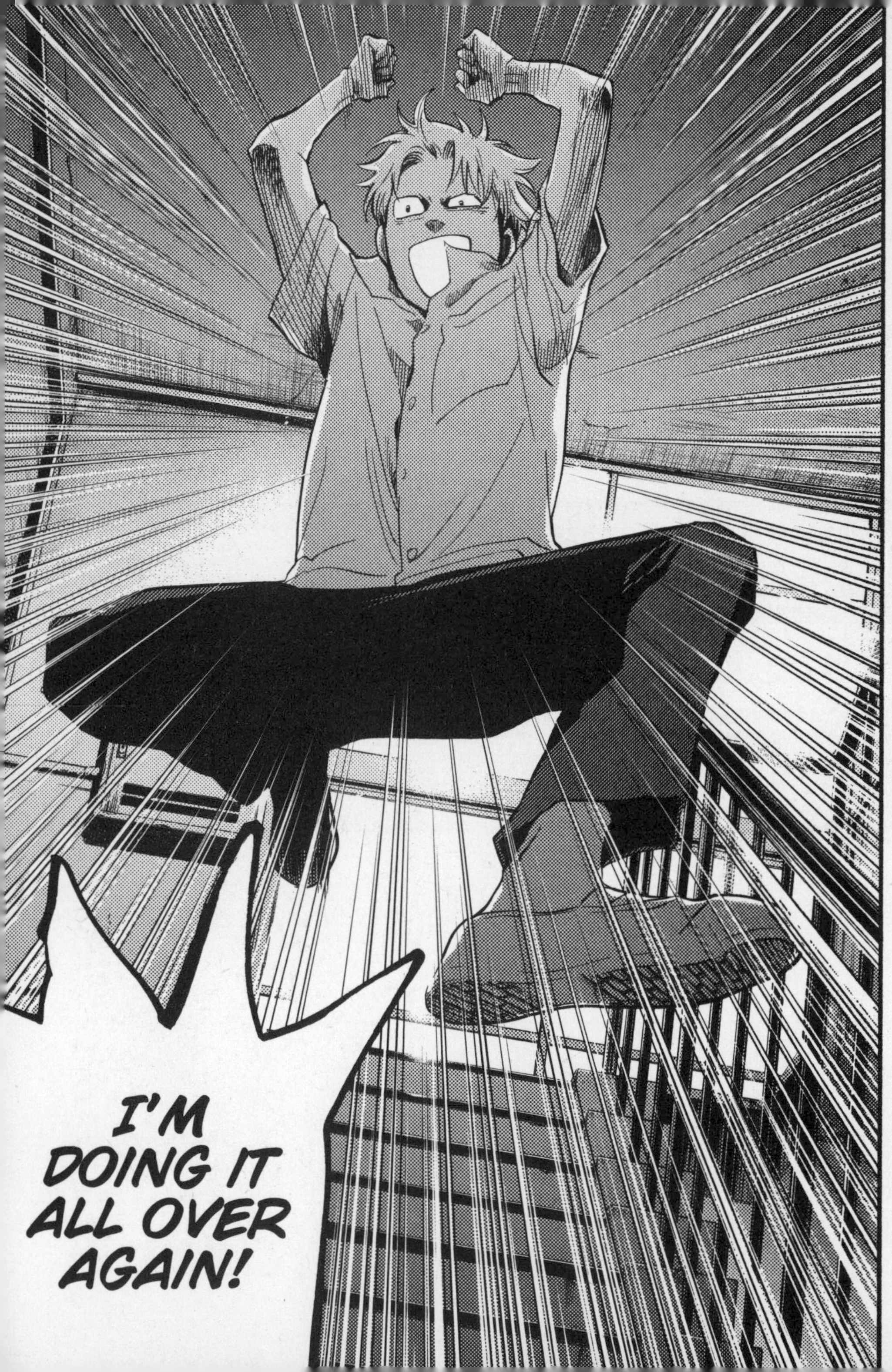
I'M DOING IT ALL OVER AGAIN!

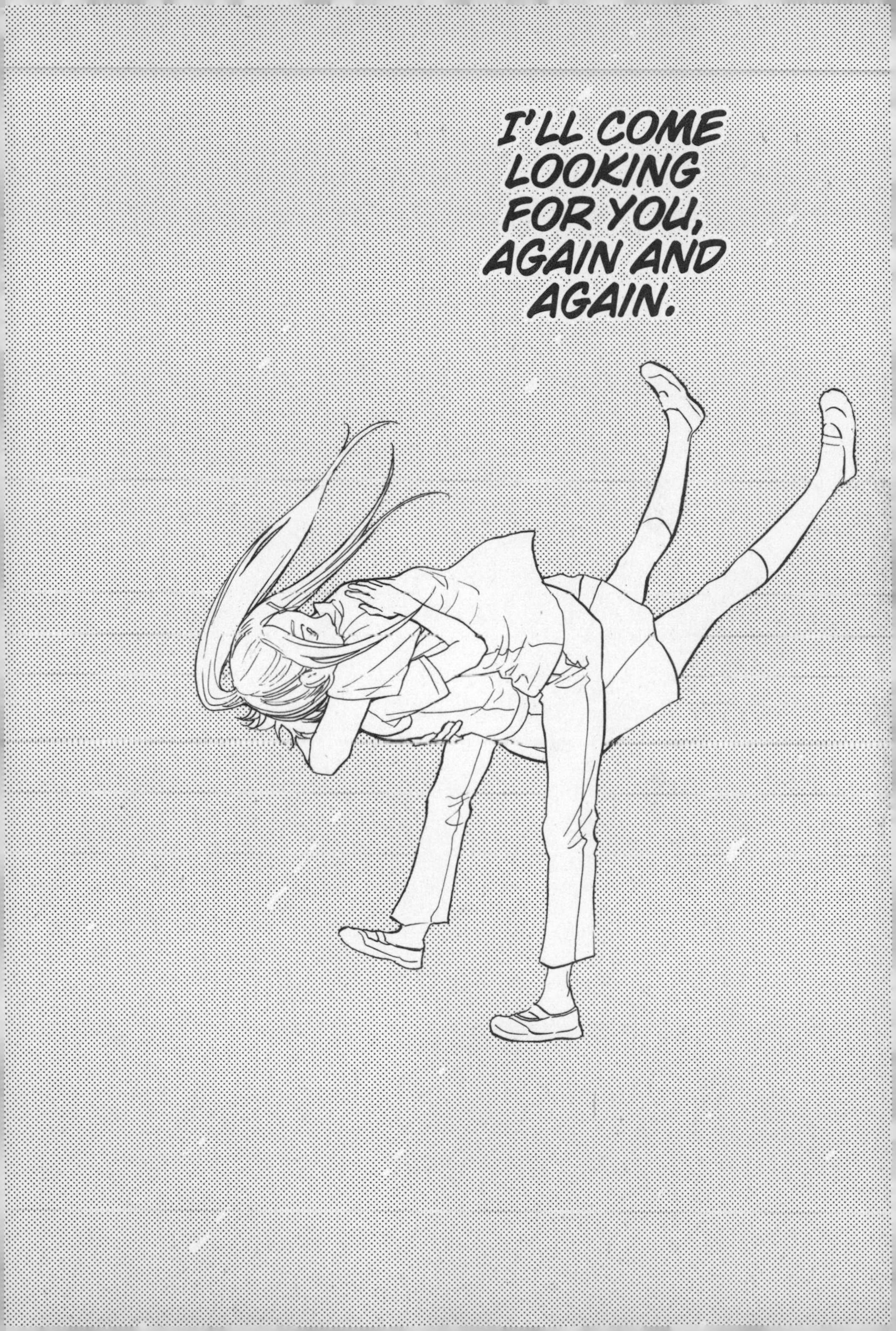
I'LL COME LOOKING FOR YOU, AGAIN AND AGAIN.

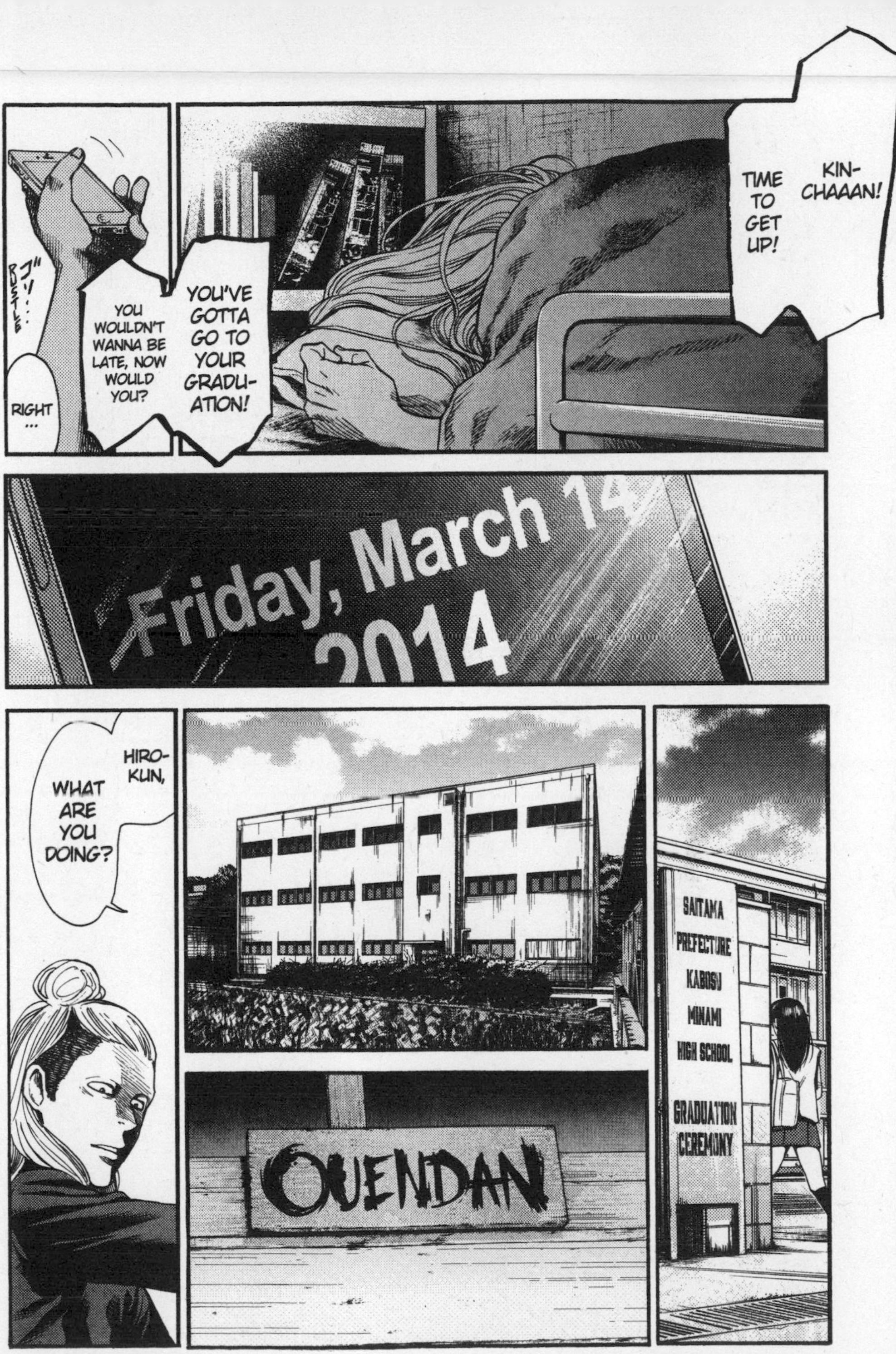
KIN-CHAAAN!
TIME TO GET UP!
YOU'VE GOTTA GO TO YOUR GRADUATION!
YOU WOULDN'T WANNA BE LATE, NOW WOULD YOU?
ゴソ…
RUSTLE
RIGHT...
Friday, March 14
2014
SAITAMA PREFECTURE KABOSU MINAMI HIGH SCHOOL
GRADUATION CEREMONY
OUENDAN
HIRO-KUN,
WHAT ARE YOU DOING?

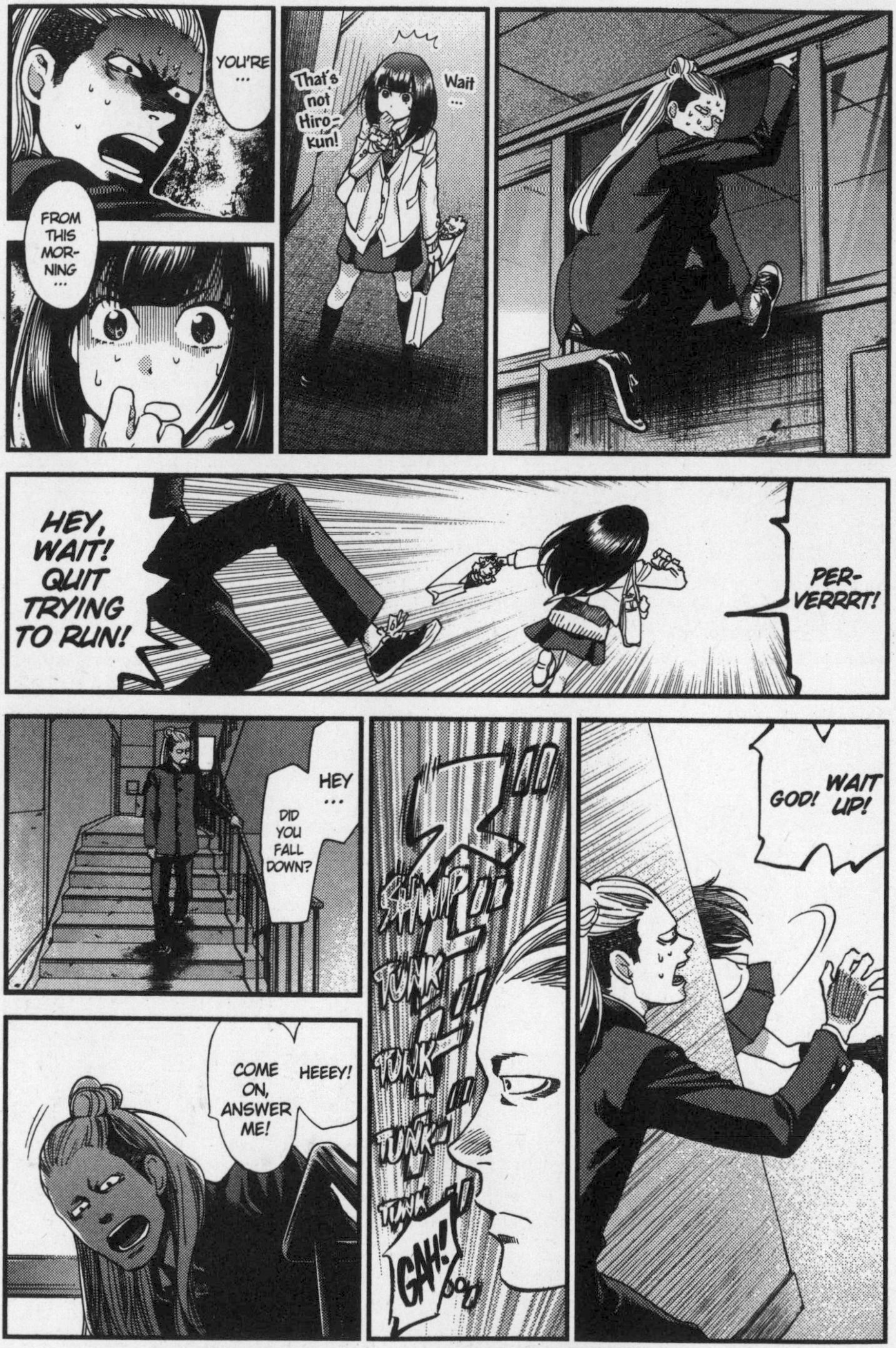
Wait ...
That's not Hiro-kun!
YOU'RE ...
FROM THIS MORNING ...
PER-VERRRT!
HEY, WAIT! QUIT TRYING TO RUN!
GOD! WAIT UP!
SHWIP
TUNK
TUNK
TUNK
TUNK
GAH!
HEY ...
DID YOU FALL DOWN?
HEEEY!
COME ON, ANSWER ME!

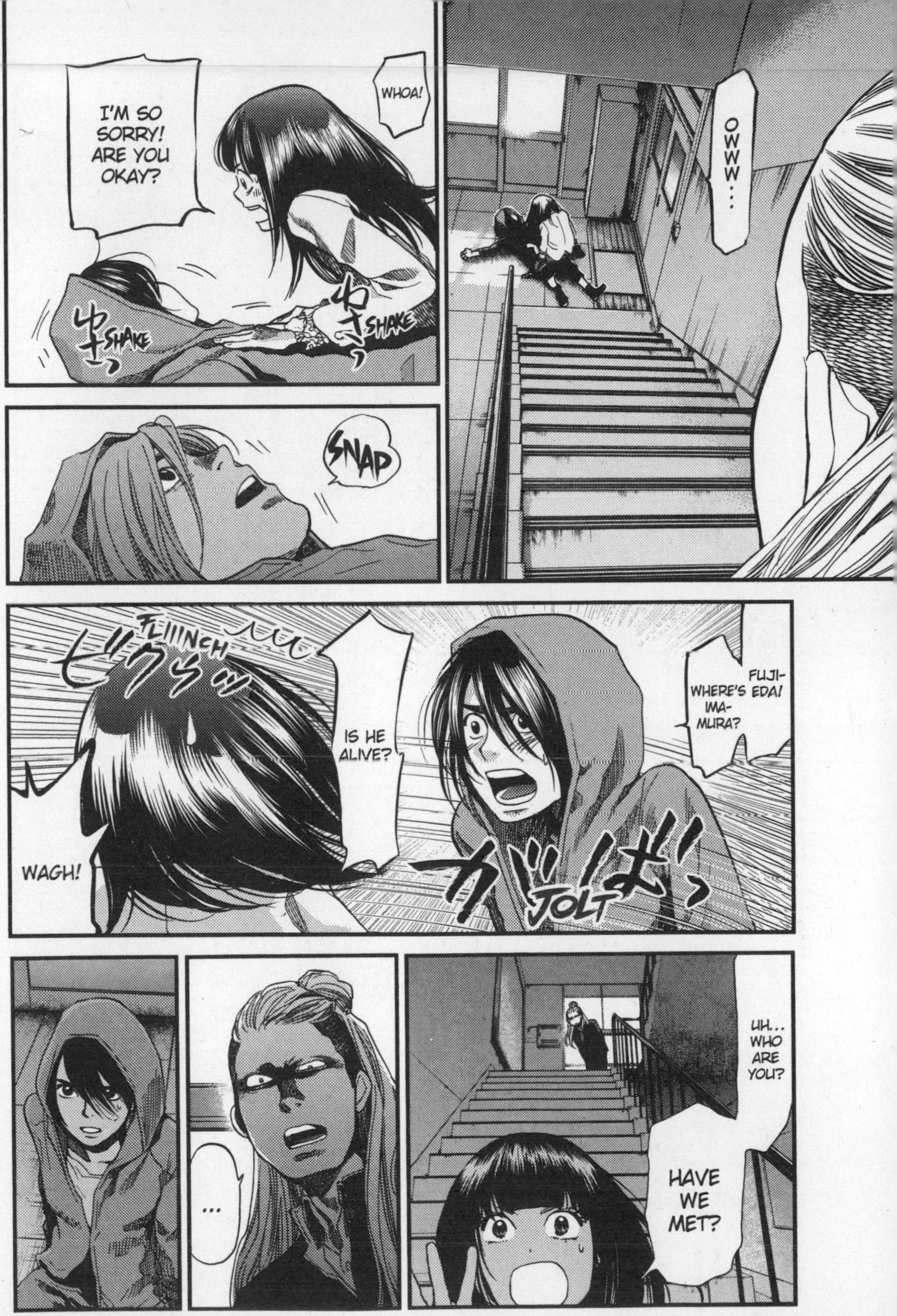
OWWW...
WHOA!
I'M SO SORRY! ARE YOU OKAY?
SHAKE
SHAKE
SNAP
FUJI-EDA! WHERE'S IMAMURA?
IS HE ALIVE?
FLIIINCH
WAGH!
JOLT
UH... WHO ARE YOU?
HAVE WE MET?
...

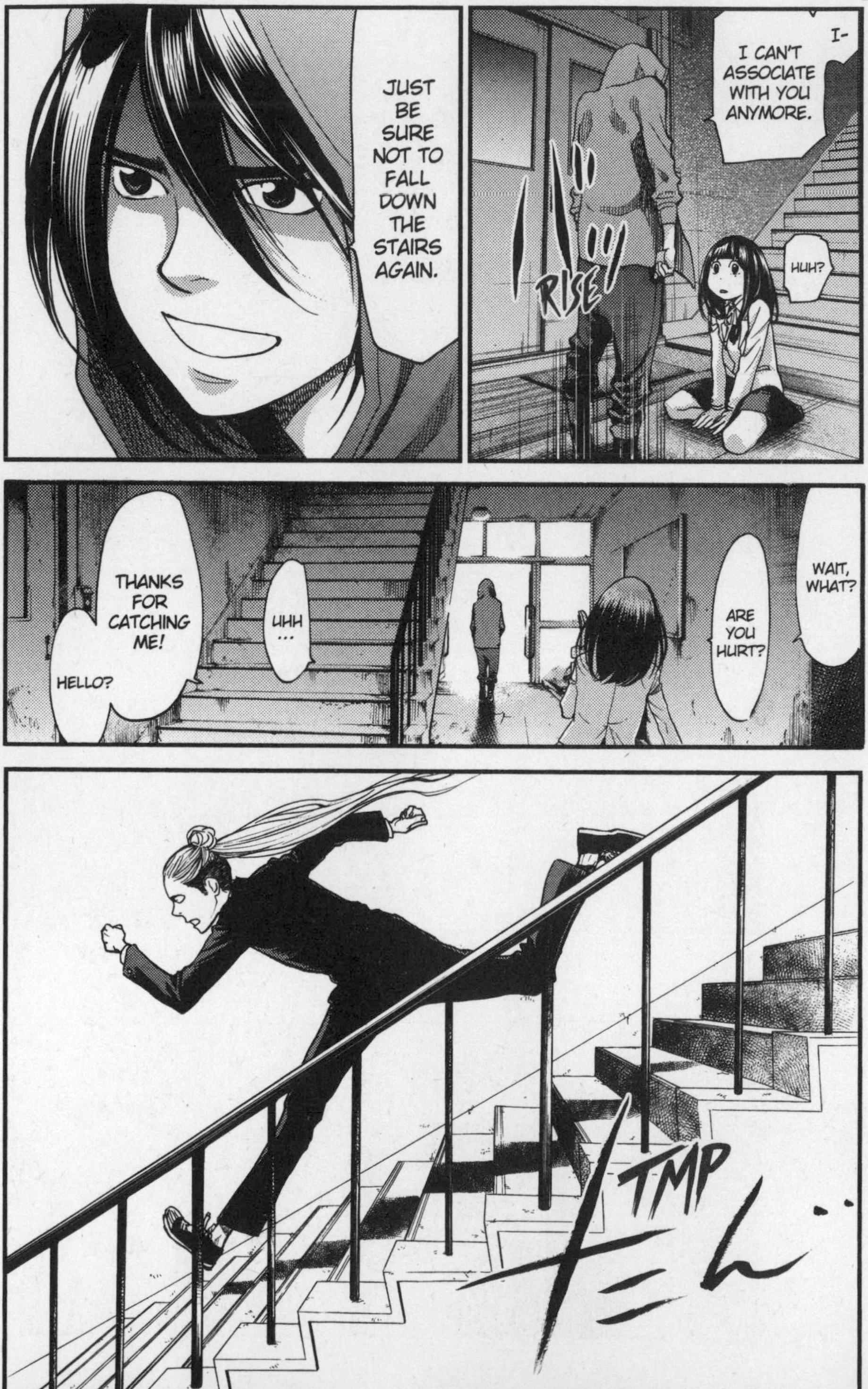
I-
I CAN'T ASSOCIATE WITH YOU ANYMORE.
HUH?
RISE
JUST BE SURE NOT TO FALL DOWN THE STAIRS AGAIN.
WAIT, WHAT?
ARE YOU HURT?
UHH...
THANKS FOR CATCHING ME!
HELLO?
TMP

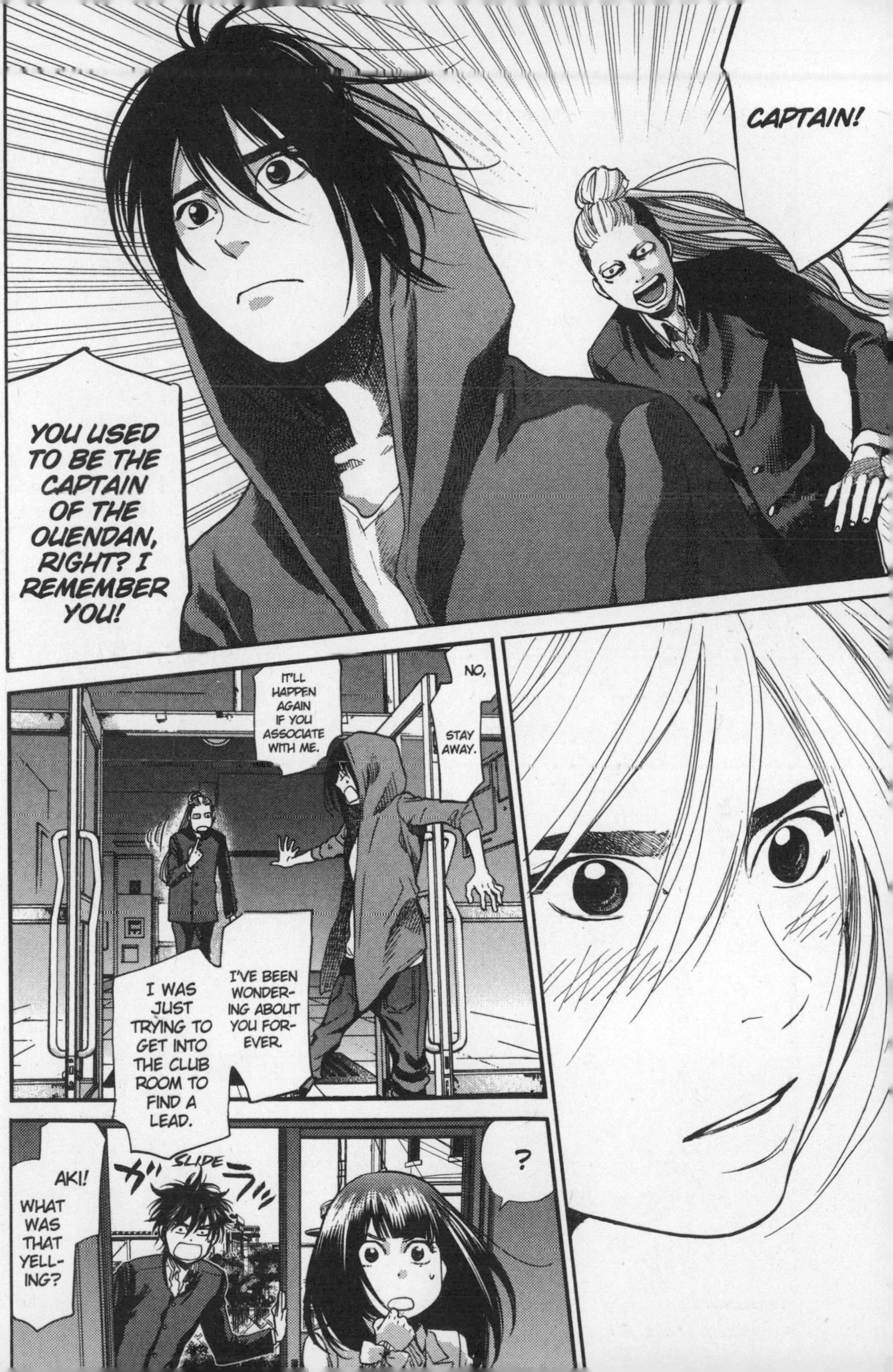

CAPTAIN!
YOU USED TO BE THE CAPTAIN OF THE OUENDAN, RIGHT? I REMEMBER YOU!
NO,
STAY AWAY.
IT'LL HAPPEN AGAIN IF YOU ASSOCIATE WITH ME.
I'VE BEEN WONDERING ABOUT YOU FOREVER.
I WAS JUST TRYING TO GET INTO THE CLUB ROOM TO FIND A LEAD.
?
SLIDE
AKI!
WHAT WAS THAT YELLING?

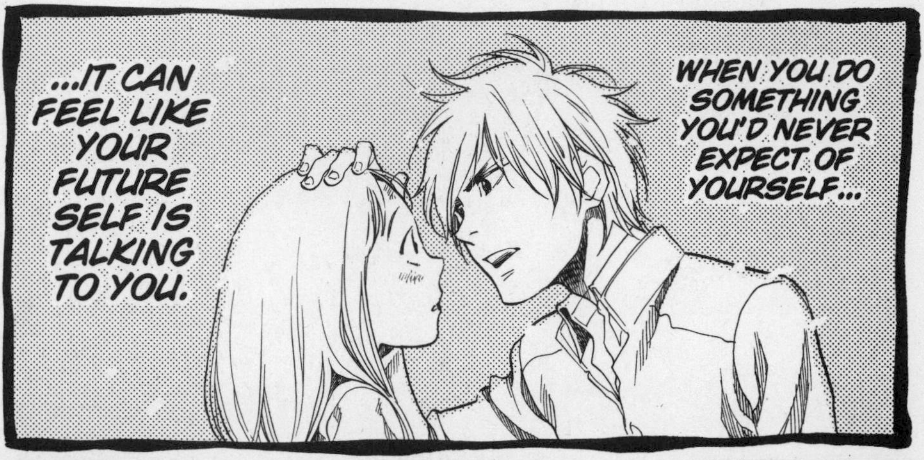
WHEN YOU DO SOMETHING YOU'D NEVER EXPECT OF YOURSELF...
...IT CAN FEEL LIKE YOUR FUTURE SELF IS TALKING TO YOU.

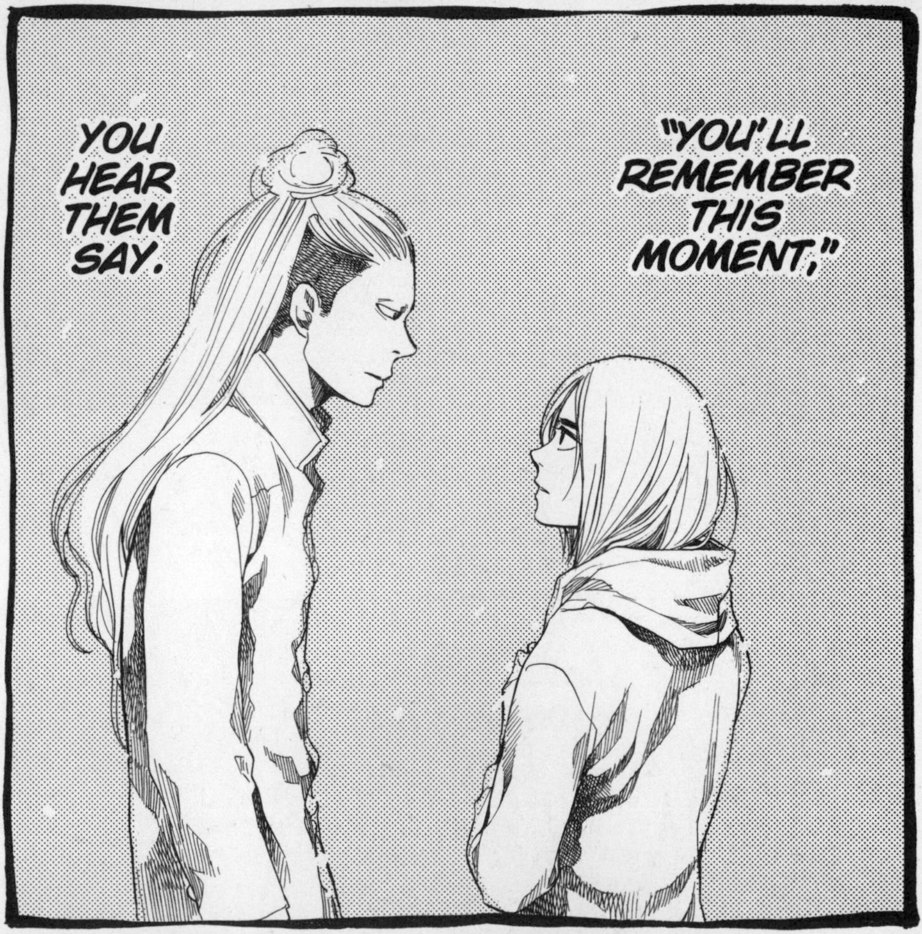
"YOU'LL REMEMBER THIS MOMENT,"
YOU HEAR THEM SAY.

AGAIN!! - THE END

A Kodansha Comics Trade Paperback Original
Again!! volume 12 copyright © 2014 Mitsurou Kubo
English translation copyright © 2019 Mitsurou Kubo

All rights reserved.

Published in the United States by Kodansha Comics, an imprint of Kodansha USA Publishing, LLC, New York.

Publication rights for this English edition arranged through Kodansha Ltd., Tokyo.

First published in Japan in 2014 by Kodansha Ltd., Tokyo as *Agein!!*, volume 12.

ISBN 978-1-63236-827-0

Printed in the United States of America.

www.kodanshacomics.com

9 8 7 6 5 4 3 2 1
Translation: Rose Padgett
Lettering: E. K. Weaver
Editing: Tiff Ferentini
Kodansha Comics edition cover design by Phil Balsman

Publisher: Kiichiro Sugawara
Managing editor: Maya Rosewood
Vice president of marketing & publicity: Naho Yamada

Director of publishing services: Ben Applegate
Associate director of operations: Stephen Pakula
Publishing services managing editor: Noelle Webster
Assistant production manager: Emi Lotto